Sexism in the City

Sexism in the City

Women Stockbrokers in Modern Britain

JAMES TAYLOR

Great Clarendon Street, Oxford, OX2 6DP,
United Kingdom

Oxford University Press is a department of the University of Oxford.
It furthers the University's objective of excellence in research, scholarship,
and education by publishing worldwide. Oxford is a registered trade mark of
Oxford University Press in the UK and in certain other countries

© James Taylor 2025

The moral rights of the author have been asserted

All rights reserved. No part of this publication may be reproduced, stored in a retrieval system, transmitted, used for text and data mining, or used for training artificial intelligence, in any form or by any means, without the prior permission in writing of Oxford University Press, or as expressly permitted by law, by licence or under terms agreed with the appropriate reprographics rights organization. Enquiries concerning reproduction outside the scope of the above should be sent to the Rights Department, Oxford University Press, at the address above.

You must not circulate this work in any other form
and you must impose this same condition on any acquirer

Published in the United States of America by Oxford University Press
198 Madison Avenue, New York, NY 10016, United States of America

British Library Cataloguing in Publication Data
Data available

Library of Congress Control Number: 2024946502

ISBN 9780198879817

DOI: 10.1093/9780191990397.001.0001

Printed and bound by
CPI Group (UK) Ltd, Croydon, CR0 4YY

Links to third party websites are provided by Oxford in good faith and
for information only. Oxford disclaims any responsibility for the materials
contained in any third party website referenced in this work.

The manufacturer's authorised representative in the EU for product safety is Oxford University Press España S.A. of El Parque Empresarial San Fernando de Henares, Avenida de Castilla, 2 – 28830 Madrid (www.oup.es/en or product.safety@oup.com). OUP España S.A. also acts as importer into Spain of products made by the manufacturer.

For Marianne, with love

Acknowledgements

This is an accidental book. When researching the 'outside stockbrokers' of late Victorian London for another project, I came across an interview with Amy Bell, a female broker. Without searching for them, I began to find references to other women—Lizzie Beech, Jane Walker, Alice Beauclerk—in this market. Fascinated, I began to think in terms of a journal article, so I started looking more systematically for female stockbrokers, extending my focus beyond the capital, and pushing into the twentieth century. As I accumulated yet more material, I realized that a short book might be possible, and eventually had to admit that a longer work was necessary to do the subject justice.

The mission of locating women stockbrokers and learning about their lives and careers would have been far harder without the digitization projects that have transformed historical research over the past couple of decades, so I am particularly obliged to the British Library, Gale, ProQuest, Ancestry, Findmypast, and others for making so many sources accessible and searchable. I'd also like to thank staff at the Bank of England Archive, Guildhall Library, the History of Advertising Trust, Liverpool Record Office, London Metropolitan Archives, Manchester Archives and Local Studies, the National Archives, Sheffield City Archives, West Yorkshire Archive Service, the Wolfson Centre for Archival Research, and the Women's Library at the London School of Economics, for helping me locate the traces women stockbrokers left behind in their collections. The original work on the outside market from which this book grew was funded by a Carnevali Small Research Grant, awarded by the Economic History Society, and a Lancaster University Faculty of Arts and Social Sciences Research Grant. I am grateful for this financial support, as well as for the two periods of research leave that I needed to see the work through to completion.

The book has benefited from input from many people. I would like to thank participants at the Women's History seminar at the Institute of Historical Research, the Entrepreneurs who Made Glasgow workshop at Strathclyde Business School, and the University of York's Centre for Contemporary Business History and Society research seminar for their helpful feedback. I have appreciated conversations with Hazel Vosper, Corinna Peniston-Bird, Michael Winstanley, and Janette Rutterford on women and money. I am particularly indebted to Nancy Henry, George Robb, Amy Edwards, Alexia Yates, Orsi Husz, Elin Åström Rudberg, David Larsson Heidenblad, and Jennifer Aston for reading and commenting on book chapters, and to Henrice Altink and OUP's readers for feedback on the original book proposal. Their comments undoubtedly made the

viii ACKNOWLEDGEMENTS

book stronger. I am grateful to Matthew Hollow for putting me in touch with Anthea Gaukroger, which led to a delightful lunch and conversation with her and Hilary Pearson, and later to an equally enjoyable meeting with Susan Shaw. Their memories have informed Chapters 6 and 7 of the book in particular. Thanks also to Kira Mourao for sharing family memories and photographs of Helen Smellie, and to Richard Day, Christopher Goddard, and William Richmond for information on Olivia Bingham, Emma Robson, and Connie Whittaker respectively. And I am obliged to Matthew Cotton and Imogene Haslam at OUP for their help and guidance, and to Chris Bessant for careful copyediting.

I would like to express my gratitude to Sylvia, Colin, Rachel, Deke, Elly, and Willem for their love, support, and encouragement over the years. Above all, thank you to Marianne for keeping me going. She has lived this project with me for years, discussing ideas, reading and commenting on drafts, making many helpful and astute suggestions, and dealing heroically with the miseries of living with a distracted academic. I could not have completed this book without her, and so I dedicate it to Marianne, with all my love.

Contents

Introduction: Feminism and Finance	1
1. Devils in Petticoats: Women and Finance in the Eighteenth and Nineteenth Centuries	12
2. Being a Female Stockbroker in Late Victorian and Edwardian Britain	35
3. Not in the House? Attitudes to Women Stockbrokers in Late Victorian and Edwardian Britain	59
4. Careers for Your Daughters: Women Stockbrokers, 1914–1939	88
5. Angels in the House: Women Stockbrokers and the Stock Exchanges, 1914–1945	117
6. Something in the City: Women Stockbrokers after 1945	144
7. Invading the Stock Exchange: The Road to 1973	172
Epilogue: Forever Other?	202
Notes	215
Bibliography	265
Index	287

Introduction

Feminism and Finance

On Monday, 26 March 1973, women were admitted to the trading floor of the London Stock Exchange as members for the first time in the institution's 200-year history. The belatedness of this milestone, coming over half a century after the country's first female Members of Parliament, barristers, and chartered accountants, had made the blocking strategies of the Stock Exchange's male membership the subject of much discussion, and increasingly vocal condemnation. As a result, press reporters from all over the country piled into the visitors' gallery to witness the long-anticipated fall of one of the country's last 'male bastions'. Yet some accounts, like the one that appeared in the *Newcastle Journal*, were tinged with a sense of anti-climax:

> It seemed a rather undramatic piece of history. Share prices moved ahead strongly, reflecting the more liberal attitude, but the smell of burning bras and the strident victory cries of women's liberationists were notably absent as Mrs. Susan Shaw of Thomas Clarke stepped on to the floor at 9.36 a.m.

The report gave little sense of how Susan and her peers actually experienced the occasion, beyond quoting her that the members 'were very kind and friendly. I got a very cordial reception.'[1] Susan Shaw's diary, however, tells us more, hinting at the close attention to physical appearance necessary in order for a woman to be accepted in this masculine environment ('Must look my best today but not too conspicuous'), and the extreme anxiety felt at the point of stepping into this space for the first time ('Feel very small, knees like jelly. Can't let the side down!').[2]

But in another respect the *Newcastle Journal*'s report was revealing. Its incongruous—and facetious—juxtaposition of share prices and burning bras signals the yawning gulf that divided finance and feminism by the 1970s.[3] Those working inside the City of London to secure women's admission to the Stock Exchange had little to do with the resurgent women's rights movement of these years. When their objective was finally won, they presented it as 'a victory for logic rather than Women's Lib'.[4] In turn, for many feminists, especially socialist feminists, the struggle of City women was a minority cause of little consequence compared to strikes for equal pay and other forms of grassroots activism. Some even saw it as counterproductive since it shifted attention away from the realities of class-based inequalities.[5] As one put it, 'the right of women to be managing directors, or to enter the stock exchange, has no part in our campaign'.[6]

This rupture between finance and feminism had major implications for how history was subsequently written. The 1970s saw the emergence of a new generation of feminist scholars determined to address the invisibility of women in most historical accounts. For two leading figures, Sally Alexander and Anna Davin, feminist history meant 'bringing women into the foreground of historical enquiry'. By doing so, they argued, 'our knowledge of production, of working class politics and culture, of class struggle, of the welfare state, will be transformed'.[7] Broadly aligned with socialist and Marxist historiographies, the overarching aim was to explore the manifold ways in which 'women in the past had been affected by the development of a capitalist mode of production'.[8] In particular, historians focused on women's roles before and during the industrial revolution, revisiting and building on pioneering early twentieth-century work by scholars including Alice Clark and Ivy Pinchbeck.[9] Though this work did much to identify women as important players in narratives of industrialization, and establish the sexual division of labour as a central object of study, it did leave important areas unexplored.[10] As Wendy Gamber argues, it was an interpretative stance that included 'downtrodden women wage-workers', but excluded many other ways in which women, especially women outside the working classes, may have engaged with the market.[11] As a result, growing numbers of scholars since the 1990s have been re-evaluating women's roles in the historical development of capitalism. In Amy Froide's words, rather than imagining capitalism only 'as something that acted on or affected women', historians also need to understand how women 'participated in and were agents of capitalist enterprises'.[12]

An early step was taken in this direction by Amy Erickson in an influential article of 2005. Rather than focusing on capitalism's effects on gender relations, Erickson recommended reversing the question, 'to look at the role of gender in the *creation* of a widespread capitalist economy in the first place'. She argued that in contrast to the rest of Europe, English legal practices facilitated women's economic participation. The ostensibly draconian law of coverture, which dictated that a married woman's property belonged to her husband, could be circumvented by legal manoeuvres and did not prevent married women from investing.[13] Indeed, around this time scholars were beginning to unearth the evidence to demonstrate that—long before the London Stock Exchange even existed— women were significant players on the financial markets. Though earlier work, most notably Leonore Davidoff and Catherine Hall's influential monograph *Family Fortunes*, first published in 1987, had acknowledged the 'hidden investment' made by middle-class women in the financial wellbeing of the family, their emphasis had been on the limits of this involvement, especially 'the strict familial contours of female involvement'.[14] But now, case studies of individual wealthy female investors were complemented by broader studies corroborating women's early, extensive, and confident engagement with the market for stocks and shares. Though outnumbered by men, they were very much part of the investing population, pursuing a range of investment strategies, often successfully.[15] Moreover, by purchasing shares in joint-stock trading ventures, and by holding government debt, women were significant participants in the grand project of empire.[16] Though typically understood as an age of 'gentlemanly capitalism', defined by the landed class's embrace of the market economy, so high were the numbers of female fundholders by the early nineteenth century that David Green and Alastair Owens have subversively dubbed this the era of 'gentlewomanly capitalism'.[17]

Indeed, women's capital became integral to commercial development in the Victorian age, despite the rise of the ideology of 'separate spheres' which supposedly confined women to a limited range of largely domestic roles.[18] 'Expanding investment opportunities', writes Nancy Henry, allowed women 'to increase their wealth and participate in enterprises from which they were otherwise excluded'. The stock market, she argues, thus became one of the most important areas of female agency in the nineteenth century, alongside philanthropy and authorship.[19] Indeed, quantitative studies of share ownership showed women to be a significant and growing presence on the capital market.[20] The range of their economic involvement was impressive, as they became significant investors in, among other areas, joint-stock banking, railways, and shipping.[21] Women's investment continued to grow, so much so that by the early twentieth century, women were actually in the majority among the proprietorships of many leading companies: a 'feminization of capital' whose implications were profound.[22]

Though this scholarship has challenged many assumptions about women's economic capacities and behaviours, it has tended to overlook the possibility that women may have acted as financial intermediaries—such as stockbrokers—before the late twentieth century. Some historians of the early modern market, however, have found evidence, albeit fragmentary, of women doing more than providing capital for others. Sometimes inheriting a business from a deceased husband, in other cases managing and transacting investments on behalf of family members, friends, and eventually wider networks of clients, women were acting as stockbrokers in the unregulated and informal markets of the early eighteenth century.[23] Amy Froide, in particular, has painted a vivid picture of such women confidently navigating London's networks of coffee shops and other financial sites, both for themselves and for others. However, this became more difficult with the formalization and enclosure of the market ushered in by the establishment of a Stock Exchange in 1773 and its reinvention as a members-only—and male-only—club in 1801.[24] As a result, Froide conjectures that despite women's early involvement as intermediaries, 'it may not have been until the late twentieth century that women were once again so prominent in London's City and City business'.[25]

4 SEXISM IN THE CITY

Indeed, what happened between women's exclusion from the Stock Exchange in the late eighteenth century and their readmittance two centuries later has until now only been lightly sketched. Institutional histories contain brief references to attempts by individual women to join the London Stock Exchange in the twentieth century, while the situation outside the capital is even less studied.[26] But women's institutional exclusion did not in fact prevent women from acting as stockbrokers. A boom in brokerages operating outside the control of the London Stock Exchange from the 1870s, combined with the nationwide spread of small, family-run stockbroking firms, often doing business with minimal institutional oversight, created opportunities for entrepreneurial women to act as stockbrokers long before their official recognition in 1973. *Sexism in the City* uncovers the lives and careers of these forgotten women.

Entrepreneurs and Professionals

Exploring this history brings scholarship on women and finance into dialogue with a separate—though very much related—body of work on female entrepreneurship. Around the same time that business history was awakening to the importance of women as investors, it was also beginning to recognize women's entrepreneurial activities. In the 1990s, Wendy Gamber observed that the history of business as then written was 'a chronicle of masculine activity', unduly dominated by the study of the large corporation.[27] The discipline was not simply reflecting the gender bias present in the world of business, so critics began to argue, but actively ignoring women's varied and extensive activities as entrepreneurs, inventors, contractors, and owners.[28] 'Business history, even more than business itself, is man-made', as Katrina Honeyman put it in 2001.[29] By this point, some American academics had begun to embrace a more gendered approach to business history.[30] Not long afterwards, work rethinking women's role in the urban economy of eighteenth- and nineteenth-century Britain started to appear, with key monographs by Nicola Phillips, Hannah Barker, Alison Kay, and Jennifer Aston, as well as a parallel literature exploring businesswomen in Canada, Australasia, and continental Europe.[31]

In these works, traditional models which saw industrialization and urbanization triggering a decline in women's business activities were called into question. Rather than positing a feminine retreat from the public sphere, this research instead emphasized the agency of women, finding them running businesses, acquiring clients, keeping accounts, and bearing risks without loss of respectability.[32] Such activities were not restricted to widows, those 'temporary incumbents of an enterprise' as Davidoff and Hall describe them, who might have control thrust upon them until a son came of age.[33] Business, Kay argues, was also seen as a viable option 'for the insufficiently supported, not-yet-married or never-married woman'.[34] Though women's participation skewed towards 'feminine' trades which could be seen as an extension of their domestic role—millinery, food and drink retailing, running a lodging house—women were not restricted to these areas of activity, also appearing as, among others, wholesale confectioners, brewers, and silk dyers.[35] Rather than acting as peripheral presences, trading on the margins or solely from their homes, women established businesses on the main streets, advertising, donating to public causes, using the courts to protect their interests, and operating within, rather than apart from, wider business networks.[36] After reading this work, as one historian notes, it seems undeniable that 'business-women were everywhere'.[37]

Despite this, our understanding of women's business activity remains patchy. Studies have tended to focus on the eighteenth and earlier nineteenth centuries: the era when women were once thought to have been driven into the domestic sphere. Though some work, notably Aston's, pushes into the later nineteenth century, very little ventures far into the twentieth.[38] This is particularly significant given uncertainty in the literature over whether the new century heralded growing opportunities for women in the urban market or whether, by contrast, women's businesses were beginning to decline in these years.[39] Moreover, existing studies tend to be rooted in specific towns or cities, and while this strategy provides vivid pictures of the range of women's entrepreneurial activities, it comes at the cost of exploring women's experiences of one particular type of work in detail. Where historians have provided such studies, they have, naturally enough, tended to focus on occupations which saw the highest levels of women's involvement.[40] And while quantitative studies have found women's entrepreneurial participation in finance and commerce to be 'consistently low', this makes it all the more important to explore the reasons for this, and when—and why—this may have changed.[41] A better understanding of the strategies used by the smaller numbers of women attempting to carve out careers in hostile environments such as finance is surely critical for a fuller historical understanding of women in business.

Marginally more attention has been paid to financial women in the United States, partly due to the fame of Victoria Woodhull who, with her sister, established a brokerage in New York in 1870, went on to be the first woman to run for president, and has been the subject of several biographies.[42] Besides Sheri J. Caplan's popular history *Petticoats and Pinstripes* which also takes a biographical approach, telling the stories of several other ground-breaking women in finance, including Hetty Green, nicknamed the 'Queen of Wall Street', and Muriel Siebert, the first woman to buy a seat on the New York Stock Exchange, other academic studies have emerged, focusing particularly on the late nineteenth and early twentieth centuries.[43] Maggie Walker, the first African American woman to charter a bank, in an attempt to use finance to benefit black communities in a segregated society, is the focus of Shennette Garrett-Scott's *Banking on Freedom*.[44] George Robb's broader-based *Ladies of the Ticker* highlights the prominence of

6 SEXISM IN THE CITY

women both as investors and as stockbrokers between the 1870s and 1920s.[45] Nevertheless, work on financial women, particularly women in stockbroking, is in its infancy.

These careers also need to be understood in the context of histories of the professions. Though stockbroking did not have the same legal recognition or structures of formal accreditation as law, medicine, and accountancy, members of stock exchanges developed similar strategies to lawyers, doctors, and accountants for regulating entry to their ranks. Such tactics were the focus of neo-Weberian sociological work in the 1970s and 1980s which theorized professionalization as a form of occupational closure designed to limit social mobility by monopolizing the market for certain skills or services.[46] In time, feminist sociologists extended the concept of occupational closure to include gender, arguing that these 'professional projects' had gender at their core.[47] Such projects only partly involved imposing rules and regulations formally excluding women; they were also about the values that were embedded into professions. Supposedly 'masculine' qualities—objectivity, rationality, individualism—were embraced, while 'feminine' ones were repressed.[48] By these means, 'professions actively justified the exclusion of women based on the apparent mismatch between professional attributes and womanly ones'.[49] When women were included, this followed a 'demarcationary strategy', a gendered division of labour between dominant male roles and subordinate, supporting female ones, such as doctors and nurses, and accountants and bookkeepers.[50] Such distinctions conceptually distanced 'male' professions from notions of 'what women are like' or 'what women do'.[51]

Since the 1990s, historical research on women in the professions has flourished, exploring women's experiences across an ever-widening spectrum of activity, from teaching and journalism to diplomacy and science.[52] Though recognizing the impact of men's exclusionary and subordinating strategies, this scholarship has increasingly insisted that the 'boundaries and hierarchies of professional society' were permeable, exploring the agency that women could exercise, even if on the margins of professions.[53] This work has broadened the focus beyond male exclusionary strategies and women's struggle for admittance, to include the development of women's professional identities, and their attitudes to their work and their careers over time.[54] How women navigated man-made professional cultures, how they sought an equal footing within these cultures, and the impact of wider representations of women in the professions have been topics of an impressive body of work.[55]

But as with the scholarship on entrepreneurship, stockbroking is conspicuous by its absence in historical research on the professions, despite gender being integral to the occupational closure of stockbroking in the eighteenth and nineteenth centuries.[56] Women's participation in the stock market was stigmatized in the wake of the South Sea Bubble of 1720, as cultural histories of finance have emphasized. The language of 'frenzy' typical in accounts of the episode, argues Catherine

Ingrassia, linked speculation with 'hysteria, disorder and enthusiasm, distinctly transgressive impulses typically associated with females'.[57] Women disrupted the market, men stabilized it. Such views deepened in the nineteenth century. Unlike women, male financiers could control their emotions, take the broad view, and make sound judgements. They 'combined the qualities of a medical doctor and a scientific observer', as Urs Stäheli puts it.[58] Such arguments helped to justify excluding female intermediaries from the market, a form of occupational closure that coded stockbroking, along with other professions, as intrinsically masculine.

How gendered ideas about finance shaped employment patterns within the profession as it developed in the later nineteenth and twentieth centuries is one of the key themes of *Sexism in the City*. Though it charts growing opportunities for women over this period, the story it tells is not straightforward. Female employment increased alongside the persistence or intensification of gendered beliefs about finance. The admission of women to the London Stock Exchange in 1973 did little to challenge these beliefs. Indeed, the association of finance with a particular kind of performative hypermasculinity became an ever more striking feature of cultural representations of finance in the 1980s and 1990s, whose stance alternated between 'satirical and admiring'.[59] This in turn attracted sociologists and cultural anthropologists to the City of London—and to Wall Street—to interview traders and analysts to understand gendered cultures of work in modern finance.[60] Anatomizing the gendering of finance, both in discourse and in practice, became a major multidisciplinary endeavour in the wake of the global financial crisis of 2008.[61] Not for the first time, popular understanding of the crash was shaped by gender, but now, men were the focus of criticism. If women had been in charge, pundits speculated, would testosterone-fuelled recklessness have been tempered by a healthy dose of feminine caution and prudence? Though superficially marking the moment that 'feminism finally...caught up with misogyny' in the financial world, such interpretations were problematic not only for their reductionism, but also for their perpetuation of questionable stereotypes of masculine risk-taking and feminine risk-aversion.[62] Despite their marginality to scholarship on gender in the modern City, historians clearly have much to contribute to our understanding of the long-run development of professional cultures and identities in finance.

Exceptional Women?

Despite the wealth of scholarship over the past couple of decades on women as investors, as entrepreneurs, and as professionals, some are frustrated at how little this work has influenced broader historical understanding. Heidi Egginton and Zoë Thomas point to the fact that a major history of twentieth-century Britain published in 2018 could claim that whereas 'men operated in the public

8   SEXISM IN THE CITY

sphere…most women were confined to a separate private world'. They see this as 'a sobering reminder that there is still an urgent need to repeatedly evidence and assert women's historic—and contemporary—professional contributions to society in the face of scholarship which continues to efface them'.[63] Likewise, it is telling that in 2019, over twenty years after *Business History Review* first attempted to catalyse research on the history of gender and business, another leading journal in the field issued a call for papers to counter still-common 'narratives of great men…building large organizations', with a view to 'bringing both gender and feminism from the periphery of business history to its centre'.[64] It is even more revealing that the call did not produce 'a rush of submissions', leading the editors to surmise that 'the centre of business history was not a centre that many gender scholars wished to move to, nor where the debates their work contributed to were likely to be engaged with'.[65]

Clearly, efforts still need to be made to integrate different fields of study and to reassess relations between 'margins' and 'centres' of scholarship. And historians need to be attuned to how their methods and conceptual approaches might inadvertently entrench rather than challenge traditional ideas. Some time ago, Wendy Gamber suggested that it was problematic for business historians simply to present 'portraits of "exceptional women" that unintentionally reinforce the notion that business is a masculine concern'.[66] Yet when women's activities in so many fields have been ignored, it is easy for research to become preoccupied with the task of recovery at the expense, perhaps, of fully exploring the broader implications of women's presence. Recently, feminist business scholars have suggested that much work in the field could be accused of following what could be described as an 'add women and stir' approach, leaving the gendered assumptions shaping both business and business history largely intact.[67] This charge draws on foundational feminist critiques of 'compensatory' and 'contribution' histories of 'worthy women' which, though successfully 'placing women in history', fail to question frameworks, categories, and value systems created by and for men.[68] As Jill Matthews puts it, this approach can be criticized 'for using traditional conceptual frameworks, for slotting women into the empty spaces of male-defined historical scholarship, and for thus keeping women marginal to the standard canon of masculinist writing'. For Matthews, feminist scholarship should aim 'not just to add women' to the standard canon, but 'to do over the whole enterprise, to recast the discipline of history so that women's lives and experiences were as integral to it as men's'.[69]

This book unapologetically seeks to 'add women' to the history of stockbroking. When these women feature so very fleetingly in existing work, whether histories of finance, of entrepreneurship, or of professions, and when so few of them currently have entries in the *Oxford Dictionary of National Biography*, there is clearly an intrinsic value in identifying them and writing them into these histories.[70] But at the same time, the book acknowledges the limits of historical 'rescue work', and so has aims beyond this. It explores *how* women did business, their strategies and priorities, the limits placed upon them, and the development of their professional identities. Rather than generalizing about women, and regarding the category of 'woman' in finance as simple and fixed, it draws out the considerable diversity of women's approaches to and experiences of stockbroking. Instead of investigating women in isolation, it foregrounds interactions and relations between the sexes in finance. Men were employers, partners, colleagues, competitors, employees, agents, and clients of women stockbrokers. The fluctuating balance of power in these relationships demands close analysis, as do interactions between women brokers and the male-run institutions of finance.

Highlighting gender relations in this way serves to undercut notions of business and finance as somehow genderless. As Joan Scott has argued, gendering business history makes 'not only women visible, but men as well': in other words, we see how practices and institutions often imagined as gender-neutral are in fact heavily gendered.[71] The focus is thus broadened from the activities of women to encompass how gender difference is constructed. We can then begin 'to historicize and complicate the meaning of masculinity, rather than leave it an unexamined norm'.[72] Exploring the careers of women who have worked as financial intermediaries therefore becomes a means of spotlighting how institutions and identities were predicated on the intentional exclusion of women and how ideas about gendered difference in financial capacity and conduct—ideas still influential today—depended on writing women out of the picture. The book is thus as much a work of gender history as it is women's history.

The lives and careers of women stockbrokers are, in some respects at least, surprisingly recoverable, at least if we are willing to search across a wide variety of sources. Techniques of record linkage, combining published sources like newspapers, periodicals, and trade directories with genealogical sources such as census returns, birth, death, and marriage records, and probate data, make it possible to build a picture of women's activities in finance.[73] Other sources can be used to explore the cultural and institutional forces shaping and limiting stockbroking women's careers. Novels, short stories, and cartoons are used alongside press articles to analyse representations of financial women, while the archives of the London Stock Exchange and several provincial stock exchanges are mined in order to understand the attitudes of male brokers, and their strategies for excluding women. The book deploys these alongside governmental records, parliamentary papers, and debates, as well the periodicals and archives of women's organizations, chiefly the Women's Freedom League, to understand how the policies of the stock exchanges became increasingly contested.

As with any research, there are many lacunae in the archival record. Small businesses in general, and stockbroking firms in particular, rarely leave archival traces. Stock exchange records make up for this in some respects, though the minutes of the London Stock Exchange are only publicly available up to the early 1950s.[74]

10 SEXISM IN THE CITY

Yet the institution's refusal to admit women made it the subject of much public commentary in the 1960s and early 1970s, which allows its policies and the attitudes of its members to be traced in detail. Another institution, the Provincial Brokers' Stock Exchange, was more progressive when it came to women, but its records do not survive at all. It is nevertheless possible to explore its role thanks to references in other archives, and copious press coverage. More generally, the level of documentation available for individual stockbrokers varies significantly, and some remain frustratingly elusive, leaving only the faintest traces in the archive. Where careers can be documented, details are often sketchy, and the textures and nuances of individual lives can be impossible to reconstruct. But in some instances, specifics are available, whether provided in the form of interviews or, in one case, a published autobiography, that go some way towards compensating for the absences.[75]

By working with a mix of sources and methods deployed across the disciplines of business, gender, social, and cultural history, the book aims to present a rich picture of the lives and careers of women in finance. When these are made the focus of study, the historical development of modern finance is reframed in several ways. We begin to perceive the extent to which the institutions and practices of finance were based on gendered ideologies and exclusions. We also see that focusing on institutions only reveals part of the financial ecosystem, ignoring what was happening outside the formal market. And we can challenge London-centric interpretations of financial history, asking questions of the financial cultures that may have existed outside the metropolis. If we choose to look outside the official exchanges—and outside London—a more diverse financial environment comes into view. While this is chiefly a British history, Ireland is included because the Dublin Stock Exchange was in the vanguard of debates about gender in the early twentieth century, and because even after partition and independence, it remained closely linked to the broader UK securities market.[76] There are also some references to other countries, particularly the United States and France, both to suggest differences in national stockbroking cultures and also to highlight some overarching institutional similarities. Though the book focuses on stockbrokers, women working in related fields such as banking, accountancy, and financial journalism also feature to illustrate the gendering of financial occupations more broadly.

The book explores several distinct periods of stockbroking history. Chapter 1 surveys women's involvement as intermediaries in early financial markets, and the increasing gendering of the market in the later eighteenth and nineteenth centuries which made it very difficult for women to operate as brokers. The next six chapters focus on the century between 1870 and 1973. Chapters 2 and 3 document the emergence of women stockbrokers from the late nineteenth century to the First World War. Chapters 4 and 5 chart the growth of stockbroking opportunities between 1914 and 1945. Chapters 6 and 7 examine the path to the eventual admission of women to the London Stock Exchange in 1973. Chapters 2, 4, and 6 each introduce a cohort of around ten women stockbrokers (their names in bold type) who were active in that period. They are selected as the best documented cases which allow insights into women's experiences as finance professionals, though they are not the only female stockbrokers working in each era. These chapters map out the backgrounds, careers, working practices, and professional identities of the cohort. Chapters 3, 5, and 7 explore how the broader cultural context shaped women's careers and, in turn, how women's stockbroking activities increasingly influenced wider attitudes to women and finance. They also investigate how growing numbers of women aspired to join stock exchanges, and the strategies adopted by the exchanges to keep them out. The Epilogue considers the legacy of this history for women in finance since the 1970s, suggesting that women's admission did remarkably little to challenge deep-seated traditions of imagining the stock market as an intrinsically masculine environment. Any attempt to combat 'Sexism in the City' today needs to engage with this long and problematic history.[77]

Sexism in the City: Women Stockbrokers in Modern Britain. James Taylor, Oxford University Press.
© James Taylor 2025. DOI: 10.1093/9780191990397.003.0001

1

Devils in Petticoats

Women and Finance in the Eighteenth and Nineteenth Centuries

In 1700 the renowned satirist Ned Ward described a madness that had taken hold in the coffee houses that lined Exchange Alley, just off the Royal Exchange. All manner of people were leaving their 'Counting-houses, Desks and Shops' and congregating in Jonathan's coffee house to 'job' in stocks and shares:

> The Coffee-man leaves Chocolate, Tea, Coffee,
> To know what price for *Bank*-stock and *East-Indie.*
> The Lady pawns her Plate and Jewels too,
> To buy some *Shares* in *Bank,* or *Old,* or *New.*[1]

Ward's entire poem was an extended condemnation of these 'enchanted foolish giddy Creatures...dull Sots, incorrigible Sinners', typical of the fears and antipathies that speculation in stocks and shares provoked in early modern Britain.[2] Though most of the figures in this 'eager hurley burley' are male, the presence of the speculating lady in their midst is a small clue that this was not exclusively masculine territory.

Indeed, even before the stock market took recognized shape, women were players. The earliest trading companies, founded in the seventeenth century to colonize and exploit overseas territories, depended upon the capital of women as well as men. Established as joint-stock ventures with easily transferable shares, these companies quickly became popular investment vehicles with a wide variety of rentier investors. The registers of businesses such as the East India Company, the Virginia Company, and the Hudson's Bay Company feature the names of women, sometimes holding shares in more than one project.[3] As Misha Ewen has argued, early modern propertied women 'managed diverse, global investment portfolios' and were 'not averse to risk-taking.'[4] Nor were they slow to benefit from new financial opportunities, especially those created when the seventeenth-century state began to turn to its subjects for capital to meet its growing financial needs. Before the Civil War (1642–51), the City of London Corporation started borrowing from wealthy individual lenders, partly to fund its own projects, but also to lend out in turn to companies and, increasingly, the Crown. During the interregnum, goldsmith bankers emerged as significant intermediaries, accepting deposits and lending them to the government. After the Restoration, these bankers became significant conduits funnelling cash to the Crown.[5] Women were prominent minority providers of this capital: they represented close to 15 per cent of depositors with the goldsmith bankers between 1677 and 1683, and made up 23 per cent of lenders to the Corporation in the years 1638–83.[6]

Opportunities for investment—and speculation—grew with the so-called 'Financial Revolution' that followed the Glorious Revolution of 1688. A set of innovations, including the establishment of the Bank of England in 1694 tasked with managing a national debt, encouraged the development of a thriving secondary market for government bonds and other securities. Whereas such securities had previously been traded in the Royal Exchange on Cornhill, alongside commodities like silk and sugar, the market had now grown so large that it broke these bounds and migrated to Exchange Alley and its coffee shops, especially Jonathan's and Garraway's, in the late 1690s.[7] This relocation—as we can tell from Ward's poem—made women's market involvement much more visible. Over the coming years, more commentators were attracted to these locales, and Daniel Defoe was one of the first to capture the sense of the stock market as a distinct space, a world apart. His *Anatomy of Exchange Alley* (1719) described a walk around this new financial 'Kingdom', a 'Stock-jobbing Globe' comprising a cluster of streets that were easily navigated on foot.[8]

The market Ward and Defoe described was not restricted to social elites. The state's seemingly never-ending demand for money for waging war with continental enemies—above all, France—drove further innovations which opened the market to larger numbers of participants. Lotteries allowed the state to tap the savings of those with smaller sums to spare. Though tickets typically cost £10, lottery 'adventurers' often formed syndicates to spread the cost, while lottery offices offered shares as small as 1/64th.[9] Although lottery offices were a common sight in the capital, tickets were easily available outside London too, and women were particularly prominent in the ranks of players, making up perhaps a third or more of the total.[10]

Women's investment was not simply a private activity: it was also a means of developing a public economic presence, even if this was sometimes controversial and contested.[11] Female shareholders could attend company meetings and—in a far cry from parliamentary politics at the time—possessed the same voting rights as men.[12] Research has shown that women's investment activities could also shade into playing an intermediary role, acting as advisers, agents, and even brokers for others. This freedom to deal in the market was perhaps partly because, 'being a new phenomenon, no one had thought to exclude them'.[13] But this situation was soon to change.

This chapter starts by sketching women's financial activities in the early financial market, then explores how their participation came under growing pressure, especially following the South Sea Bubble of 1720. Women experienced first a

14 SEXISM IN THE CITY

conceptual exclusion, as they were increasingly defined as problematic market participants, and then a literal one, with the movement of the market to a new regulated Stock Exchange. Throughout these years, women continued to invest, though their activities remained under scrutiny and subject to censure. But their opportunities to act as financial intermediaries narrowed and eventually disappeared altogether. Though its rules did not formally bar women, the Stock Exchange became a heavily gendered space, the physical and emotional dynamics of which depended upon the exclusion of women. So deep did this culture run that women's marginalization was to continue unchallenged for much of the nineteenth century.

Informal Brokers

Historians' analyses of private correspondence from the early eighteenth century has identified several instances of women who were recognized as financial authorities within noble and mercantile families. As well as being Queen Anne's most trusted adviser, Sarah Churchill, Duchess of Marlborough, managed her family's considerable finances. Her husband, the Duke of Marlborough, signed documents empowering her to act independently, despite her coverture. Sarah also directed investments on behalf of other family members, including her mother and sister, acting, as Amy Froide puts it, 'as an informal broker'.[14] Women could perform this role for male as well as female relatives. Cassandra Willoughby, stepdaughter of Josiah Child, an East India Company director, learned about stocks and shares from an early age and helped manage the financial affairs of her nephews.[15] Marriage did not necessarily curtail such activities. In 1713, Cassandra, now in her forties, married James Brydges, the future Lord Chandos. A director of the Royal African and York Buildings Companies, Brydges valued Cassandra's financial acumen and enlisted her to help with the masses of letters he received requesting advice and help. Cassandra, argues Froide, wrote letters 'that might have come from the pen of a broker or a bank clerk'.[16]

Women did not solely invest on behalf of close family members, but could act as agents for wider circles of friends and contacts. Jane Bonnell was widow of the Irish accountant-general James Bonnell. Moving from Dublin to London in 1704, she became an energetic go-between for her extensive kin network, arranging for the purchase and sale of stock and lottery tickets, usually through Hoare's Bank, as well as operating a substantial money-lending business.[17] As her social network expanded in England, possibly through her religious activities, she began to perform the same role for several English provincial ladies, including the wealthy Lady Elizabeth Hastings and her half-sisters, who lived in Yorkshire.[18]

Bonnell's extensive web of clients were female, but this was not always the case. Johanna Cock's husband Walter, a wealthy merchant, died in 1712, leaving her

£5,660 in Bank of England stock. But rather than simply holding these assets, she became an active stock trader, as uncovered in research by Ann Carlos and Larry Neal.[19] As well as increasing her own holdings, she began acting as broker to others, diversifying into East India Company stock. This was not simply a continuation of her deceased husband's activities, since the stock ledgers do not show him acting in this way. Johanna quickly became a major trader: in 1718 and 1719 she bought £20,000 in Bank of England stock from nineteen different people, and sold £19,000 to twenty-one individuals.[20] The sources are limited and do not tell us much about how she built this business, but most of her clients were male, and several were based in the Low Countries, suggesting these might be contacts she developed as a result of her husband's mercantile activities. She certainly enjoyed a degree of fame, up to and after her bankruptcy, brought about by the crash of late 1720. Travelling through Surrey for his *Tour Through the Whole Island of Great Britain* (1724), Defoe mused upon 'the overthrow, and Catastrophe of innumerable Wealthy City Families' who had 'sunk under the Misfortunes of Business' despite being thought 'past all possibility of Danger', including 'Sir Joseph Hodges, Sir Justus Beck, the Widow Cock at Camberwell, and many others'.[21]

Johanna Cock was one of a growing number of intermediaries promising, in the context of a market growing in size and complexity, to handle investments on behalf of those without the time, skills, or contacts to do so for themselves. Putting buyers in touch with sellers, such middlemen had operated in other markets for centuries. Known as 'brokers', they were often viewed with suspicion because of the opportunity they had to manipulate prices and cheat their customers, and the City of London Corporation had regulated their activities for many centuries.[22] From 1285, all brokers had to be presented to the Lord Mayor and Court of Aldermen to be sworn in, and the Corporation's authority over brokers was reasserted and augmented by legislation in 1697.[23] All the 'sworn brokers' thus licensed were men.[24] But this Act, and subsequent attempts at official oversight, did not succeed in restricting access to the occupation, with large numbers of unsworn brokers working alongside—and probably outnumbering—those who were officially licensed.[25] This meant that women could act as brokers, even if not regarded as such officially. It is telling, for example, that in the Bank of England's ledgers, men who traded as frequently as Johanna Cock were described as 'brokers', whereas she was listed as 'a widow living in Camberwell, Surrey'.[26]

Froide's research into private correspondence in the early eighteenth century has revealed several women performing broking functions, though lacking official status as brokers. Mary Bailey's activities as a broker in the 1710s are revealed in extensive correspondence with Martha Hutchins, member of a prominent Tory family. Over a number of years, Bailey traded regularly for Hutchins, giving advice, keeping detailed accounts, and receiving commission on transactions.[27] A Mrs Sarah Beake acted as paid financial agent in the 1710s to Benjamin Poole and, when he died, to his daughter Margaret.[28] Barbara Savile and her daughter

16   SEXISM IN THE CITY

Ann Cole were active investors who in 1720 clubbed together with a 'Mrs Dyett, broaker', to jointly buy £500 shares in the York Buildings Company.[29]

Details of these brokers and their businesses are scant, and it is unclear how extensive their broking activities were, and for how long they acted in this capacity.[30] Several of Mary Bailey's male relatives appear to have been brokers themselves, so a family connection to broking was likely to have provided a way into the occupation for some at least.[31] But one thing that emerges is women's ability to navigate London's financial spaces—the coffee shops of Exchange Alley, South Sea House, East India House, the Bank of England, private banking offices, and lottery offices—to gather information, make investments, and collect dividends for themselves and on behalf of others.[32] Rather than being excluded from these spaces, women were able to operate in them confidently and effectively when they needed to. However, this visibility did increasingly generate comment and criticism, coming to a head as the notorious South Sea Bubble swelled and burst in 1720.

Lady Credit

The Bubble had its roots in the exigencies of state finance in the wake of the costly War of Spanish Succession (1701–14). Keen to get rising debt levels under control, parliament agreed to a scheme proposed by the South Sea Company. The company would sell its shares to the public in exchange for the government debt, on which it would receive a reduced interest rate. The directors created mass enthusiasm for the project by hyping the scheme in the press, making sensational dividend announcements, allowing the public to buy shares with only a small amount paid up, and releasing shares onto the market in small tranches to force up demand. The price of the company's shares rocketed through the summer months, while shares in other projects, both established companies like the Bank of England and the Royal African Company, and a raft of new projects, also took off as the public's appetite for 'stockjobbing' grew.[33]

The term 'stockjobber' had emerged in the late seventeenth century to describe market insiders who made a living from speculating in shares.[34] It was a pejorative label, underlined by an early definition offered by Ned Ward in his survey of life in the capital, *The London-Spy*. 'A Stock-Jobber is a Compound of *Knave*, *Fool*, *Shop-keeper*, *Merchant* and *Gentleman*. His whole Business is Tricking.'[35] The expression quickly devolved into a general term of abuse stigmatizing anyone engaged in trading shares, particularly the crowds who thronged Exchange Alley in 1720 eager to buy South Sea stock. Though, as we have seen, women were not unknown in the market, their prominent presence among the crowds of 1720 was singled out for particular comment. 'Stock jobbing is now become so laudable, that many great Ladies forsake their Tea, Cards, and Chat, to go to

Change-Alley; where they have a Place of Rendezvouz; whilst their Jobbs are done', observed the *Weekly Journal* before the end of March.[36] A few days later it was reported that the 'Ladies from the Court End of Town' had 'hired the China Shop at the Corner of Birchin-Lane...where they meet to buy Stock and drink Tea', conducting their affairs 'like other Stock-Jobbers'.[37] By June, one male City visitor found himself 'perfectly confounded' by 'such strange Creatures as Female Stock-Jobbers'.[38]

Over the coming months, women increasingly bore the brunt of (mostly male) public criticism of the mania not just in the press, but also in pamphlets, poems, plays, and other satires. A series of ideas, often contradictory, solidified into received wisdom through constant repetition. Women were rushing to indulge a passion for speculating which involved neglecting their regular pursuits, pawning their jewels in order to buy shares, and jeopardizing family finances.[39] Women were particularly vulnerable to the schemes of market insiders. Linkages were constantly made between speculation and sexual licence. Speculation involved a loss of virtue and reputation. It involved women in improper relations with their social inferiors, criticism which often had an antisemitic aspect. Women were even tempted to sell sexual favours for South Sea stock.[40] Above all, there was the idea that female speculation threatened to invert the 'natural' gendered order of society, defeminizing women and emasculating men. The fear of female financial independence and assertiveness was patent.

Popular understanding of the speculative economy was gendered to a remarkable degree. Many were disconcerted by the vision of this new economy based not on tangible, productive land, but on paper instruments with no intrinsic worth, whose value endlessly fluctuated according to the dictates of market opinion. Critics reached for allegorical figures in order to understand this market, imagining it in terms of the ancient goddess Fortuna, capricious and untrustworthy, or the newer figure of 'Lady Credit', as popularized in the work of Defoe. Highly sexualized, Lady Credit was 'a coy Lass', at once 'virtuous virgin' and 'spoiled mistress'.[41] Chasing after her was a losing game: she was 'a vapid and vacillating woman, who was inconstant in her affections and apt to disappoint or neglect her suitors'.[42] These ideas shaped how the companies at the heart of the boom were depicted, particularly 'the Lady of the South-Sea', an imperious and unpredictable ruler 'seated on her Throne in a most magnificent manner', suitors at her feet.[43] Those who courted her lost much more than their money: they were chasing false and superficial values, indulging their impulses and passions, and sacrificing their ability to think rationally. As a result, as Catherine Ingrassia notes, playing the market put men 'in a submissive, culturally feminine position, because it forces them to depend on opinion, reputation, and the approval of others'.[44] The most explicit contemporary articulation of this idea came from popular Scottish author Thomas Gordon, who pilloried the '*stupid Kennel of Stock-Jobbers*, who cheat us out of our Money and our Sex', and urged his

'Brethren and Countrymen, either *properly* and *patiently* put on *Petticoats*; or resume our *Manhood*, and shake off this shameful Delusion, this filthy Yoke, put upon our Necks by dull Rogues from Jonathan's'.[45]

When confidence collapsed and the bubble burst in autumn, commentaries on the market became even more sexualized. The story of the rise and decline of the South Sea Company was assimilated 'into a conventional narrative of prostitution'.[46] Once a 'fine lady', the company stood exposed as a 'common Prostitute' who, despite having ruined thousands, 'runs a whoring after new Lovers every Day' with unabated lust.[47] These kinds of critiques had a dual function. As Anne Murphy explains, they were a means of 'othering' problematic aspects of the market. With all the evils of 1720—frenzy, hysteria, instability, irrationality, deceit—linked to supposedly feminine traits, it became obvious that speculative excess was the result of 'too much oestrogen in the financial markets'.[48] These critiques also suggested the solution: an honest dose of gentlemanly virtue, skill, and rationality. Rather than regaining their masculinity by shunning the market, as Gordon had recommended, men could achieve the same outcome by mastering it. In Marieke de Goede's words, when faced with the whims and devices of Lady Credit, it became 'the responsibility of financial man to make an honest woman out of her'.[49] But this was no easy feat, given the feminizing tendencies of the market. The only route to conquering the market was self-mastery, rigorously disciplining one's own emotions, ruthlessly taming any 'womanly' passions.[50]

Thus, the aftermath of the South Sea Bubble represented an opportunity for men to regain control of the financial market, in ways which had profound implications for women's future in finance. Women were closely associated with the passions that were believed to have caused the crash. Their presence on the market was therefore problematized as inherently disruptive. Indeed, the feminizing of the market necessarily coded market actors as male. As Urs Stäheli puts it, 'female speculators occupied an impossible place in the discourse of speculation'.[51] These ideas were reinforced by the emerging language of the market which framed its operators as male, whether the 'bulls' who were speculating for a rise in prices, or the 'bears' who were banking on a fall.[52] All this represented a conceptual challenge to women as market actors, and particularly as intermediaries. Who would turn to a woman to manage their investments when she would be prone to the very hysteria and irrationality it was the job of the broker to master?

These were years in which women enjoyed a great degree of access to commercial occupations, playing a significant role in the expanding urban economy. As Christine Wiskin summarizes: 'They bought, sold, negotiated contracts, arranged credit terms, met (or failed to meet) their financial obligations, held business meetings, wrote and answered letters, and kept accounts'.[53] Though women's presence in retail has long been recognized, they were also active in manufacturing and wholesale, where Amy Erickson has found that they could sometimes run 'highly capitalised concerns'.[54] Married women were active in family businesses, often taking them over on the death of a husband, and sometimes running them for decades. Women were also involved in more specifically financial roles. Women had long been sources for 'the informal capital that kept the economic wheels of the household turning', but since the seventeenth century they were becoming increasingly engaged in formal lending secured by recognized credit instruments.[55] This could lead some women into successful careers in pawnbroking, with one study suggesting that around a quarter of London's pawnbrokers at this time were female.[56] The developing insurance industry also provided opportunities for women, who could be employed as agents for insurance companies, in the process becoming 'publicly recognised financial brokers'.[57]

But when it comes to stockbroking in the mid-eighteenth century, women are harder—though not impossible—to locate. As Erickson has noted, references to women 'brokers' are more likely to be to pawnbrokers, or dealers in second-hand clothing or furniture, than to brokers in stocks and shares.[58] Nevertheless, we can catch occasional glimpses of women, usually widows, acting as stock market intermediaries. Sometimes, admittedly, when married brokers died, their widows made arrangements for others to continue the business on their behalf rather than taking on any active role themselves, as in 1743 when adverts announced that 'the Business of the late Mr. Benjamin Cole, Broker, will be carried on, for the Benefit of the Widow, &c. by Cotton and Lambert', both at their offices next to the Royal Exchange, and at Cole's office in Exchange Alley.[59] However, other widowed women proved willing and able to take over their husbands' firms, either with help or on their own. Advertising was a crucial method to inform a firm's customers of the death and to beg 'for the continuance of their favours' under the new ownership, a method commonly employed by women in other sectors, notably shopkeeping.[60] In January 1754, Joseph Watson, 'an eminent Haberdasher of Hats in Birchin-Lane and an Exchange-Alley Broker' died.[61] Later that month, an advert appeared announcing that his widow, Elizabeth Watson, was continuing the business 'in Company with Mr. George Rutt, who has many Years assisted the said Mr. Watson, in both those Branches of his Business'. The advert continued that 'any Orders they are favoured with, shall be executed with the greatest Care and Fidelity'.[62] In 1769, Jane Adams, widow of Richard Adams, a stockbroker, decided to continue her husband's business unaided. She advertised, begging 'the Favours of her late Husband's Friends, and the Public in general at her State Lottery Office', opposite the Bank Coffee House, 'where she continues to sell Tickets and Shares of Tickets'. This seemed to be a well-set-up business, Jane informing ticket-holders that 'the earliest Account of their Success [would be] sent to any Part of Great Britain or Ireland'.[63]

It is difficult to establish much about these widows' businesses and how long they survived. A marginally better-documented case was that of Clerkenwell resident Anne Craggs in the 1770s. Her husband John was a stockbroker in partnership with his uncle. The uncle died in November 1772, and in January, John followed.[64]

20   SEXISM IN THE CITY

That month, Anne, who had five young children and was pregnant with a sixth, advertised that she would be carrying on the business 'in Partnership with a Gentleman of the strictest Reputation'. While this partnership was being finalized, adverts stipulated that the established firm of Messrs Dawes and Smithson, based in Exchange Alley, would be negotiating any business on her behalf. Yet it was suggested that Anne would remain active in the business herself, adverts noting that Dawes and Smithson would be transacting 'all the Business which I can procure'. That such an arrangement was by this point coming to be considered unusual is perhaps hinted by the line added by John's executors at the end of one of the adverts that 'We take the Liberty to add our sincerest Wishes to promote the above Measure.'[65] The planned partnership seems not to have materialized, but Anne remained in business. In May 1774, she went into print again to give 'her grateful Thanks to those Ladies and Gentlemen who have favoured her with their Commissions in the Funds' since her husband's death. The business, which was still being transacted on her behalf by Dawes and Smithson, had 'exceeded her Expectations'.[66] The advert appeared several times over the following three months, but after this the trail runs cold.[67]

Institutionalizing the Market

Richard Adams and John Craggs were described in adverts as 'stockbrokers' rather than simply 'brokers', hinting at a subtle shift towards specialization. The earliest brokers had typically combined dealing in stock with other occupations.[68] Though it remained common for such agents to work across several fields—Joseph Watson choosing to deal both in hats and in stocks was not unusual—they came increasingly to define themselves by their trade in paper. In the 1760s the 'stockbroker' firmly entered the lexicon—and the popular consciousness—as a recognizable figure. Strictly speaking, stockbrokers bought and sold on behalf of clients, in contrast with 'stockjobbers' who traded on their own account. In reality, these roles were not mutually exclusive, and when describing market participants, 'stockjobber' remained the favoured catch-all term, especially when expressing disapproval, as in Samuel Johnson's famous definition of 'stockjobber' from his 1755 *Dictionary*: 'A low wretch who gets money by buying and selling shares in the funds.'[69] But as 'stockbrokers' began to emerge as distinct figures, it was clear that they also had image problems. An early example was the picaresque 1759 novel, *The Life and Real Adventures of Hamilton Murray*, in which the protagonist has dinner with a group of stockbrokers. They spend the evening boasting about the fortunes they have made by manipulating the market, through such ruses as planting false stories in the press. Looking round the table, Murray observes their faces, which were 'so haggard, that they seemed more like infernal harpies than men'.[70]

The choice of the female image of the harpy is interesting here, suggesting again the feminizing dangers of the financial market, but stockbrokers were nevertheless imagined as male in public discourse. It was even claimed that stockbroking first developed as a means of catering to large numbers of women investors who could not be expected to transact their own business. 'The original design of employing brokers must certainly have been for the conveniency of the ladies, for whose service these gentlemen are always ready', wrote Thomas Mortimer in his bestselling guide to the market, *Every Man His Own Broker*, first published in 1761.[71] Later editions of the text made clear Mortimer's feelings about women's financial capacities, when he elaborated that stockbrokers derived much of their income 'from the management of the fortunes of women, whose ignorance, joined to a propensity for gaming (become of late years a female passion), renders them the easy dupes of Stock-jobbing brokers'.[72] Mortimer intended his volume as an instruction manual to enable the public to conduct their own business in Exchange Alley, rendering stockbrokers—whom he insisted charged unnecessary commission and could not be trusted—obsolete. But the gendering in the book's title was deliberate: he did not believe women capable of becoming *their* own brokers. Instead, he urged his male readers to take the time to assist their female relatives whenever they needed to buy or sell.[73]

Mortimer's text, which went through fourteen editions and was for a long time the only thorough guide to the stock market, thus entrenched the gendering of market participants.[74] At the same time that women were being conceptually excluded from stockbroking, institutional barriers were also being erected. The first attempt to restrict the market came in 1760 when a group of brokers and jobbers contracted with the owner of Jonathan's coffee house for exclusive rights to use the premises in return for an annual fee. Historians have represented their motive as being to exclude 'the disreputable hangers-on of the market', though there may have been other reasons.[75] Some reports claimed that the brokers were trying to exclude rivals who had undercut their attempts to drive up the price of lottery tickets. The result was that 'those Biters, the Brokers, have been bit'.[76] In other words, the brokers were motivated as much by a desire to control the market as to improve its respectability. But the scheme was successfully contested in the courts and, as the press reported, Jonathan's 'is now a free and open Market, and all Combinations there destroyed'.[77] The verdict put 'the Bulls and Bears in the Alley…greatly out of Humour', however, and they threatened to move their business elsewhere.[78] They resolved to fund construction of new premises, but it was not until 1772 that work began, tearing down houses at the bottom of Sweeting's Alley, not far from Exchange Alley.[79] The building was going to be called 'New Jonathan's', but in July 1773, days before the opening, the members decided to paint 'The Stock Exchange' over the door instead. The name stuck.[80]

This was not a closed market. Perhaps mindful of their recent legal reverse, the organizers stipulated that entry was open on payment of a daily fee of sixpence.[81]

22 SEXISM IN THE CITY

But it is unclear whether women were among the public who were admitted, since sources are sparse. A satirical print of 1785 depicted the exterior of the Stock Exchange with a total of nineteen figures outside or on the threshold, all of them male.[82] We might surmise that if women were known to frequent the area, it is likely that the artists, Elizabeth and William Phelps, would have included some.[83] Firmer evidence comes from an intriguing episode in 1793. The Bank of England posted a £200 reward to locate a young man, named Donaldson, who had gone to the Stock Exchange to give a stockbroker, Mr Martin, £16,000 in 3 per cent 'scrip' (subscription receipts) to sell. Martin did not know Donaldson, but another broker, Lyons, vouched for him. Only after Martin had sold the bulk of the scrip was it discovered that they were forgeries. The description the Bank circulated of Donaldson described him as 'slim made, fair Complexion, rather dark Hair, very effeminate, remarkably small Feet, about five Feet two or three Inches high'.[84] Donaldson proved elusive for several days, in which time rumours grew that the Bow Street Runners should in fact be looking for a woman.[85] This was confirmed when the authorities arrested Mary Lyons, a servant and sister of the broker who had vouched for 'Donaldson' at the Stock Exchange. On interrogation, Mary confessed that she was the mysterious Donaldson. Her brother James had inveigled her into the scheme on bogus grounds. Critically, he told her that 'as at the Stock Exchange no business was transacted by women, it was necessary that she should attire herself in man's apparel'.[86] This helps to clarify why women who wanted to operate a brokerage, like Anne Craggs (discussed earlier), needed male agents to transact business for them at the Stock Exchange.

The Stock Exchange became still more exclusive in 1801 when it ceased to be an open market and converted into a subscription room. In part, this was to deal with the growing problem of overcrowding: the national debt was ballooning during the wars with France, generating ever more business. But it was also to exert greater control over market participants. Only those who were approved by the Committee for General Purposes, paid an annual subscription of ten guineas, and agreed to abide by its rules and regulations, would be admitted.[87] Overcrowding remained a problem, so the following year the market relocated once more, this time to much larger premises in Capel Court, Bartholomew Lane.[88] The rules for admission did not include a specific clause barring women's membership. But they gendered members as male, and one clause made this very explicit: 'No new applicant for admission is admissible if he, or his wife, be engaged in business.'[89] This rule, though admitting that women might be involved in business in their own right, made it very clear that only men were envisaged as members of the Stock Exchange. It also accelerated the move towards specialization among brokers.[90]

Despite these exclusionary pressures, women were still able to access financial markets. The establishment of the Stock Exchange in 1773 did not end at a stroke the trade in stocks and shares that had traditionally been done in the coffee houses of Exchange Alley. It is likely that women continued to frequent these locations, even if there is little evidence that they were acting as intermediaries. Moreover, they were visibly present at an alternative market. In the 1760s, the Bank of England constructed a large new east wing, consisting of four transfer halls and a Rotunda, to accommodate the growing trade in government securities alongside Bank stock. The halls were staffed by clerks who managed the registration of transfers and the payment of dividends, while the Rotunda, or Brokers' Exchange as it was also known, was a public trading space, free to enter.[91] Designed to invest the traffic in the funds with something of the grandeur of Ancient Rome, the domed Rotunda was as high as it was wide (over eighteen metres), and decorated with Corinthian columns.[92] On opening to the public in 1768 it swiftly became a busy location, business often spilling out into the transfer offices. This was, and remained, a mixed crowd. Thomas Rowlandson's illustration of the Rotunda dating from 1792 (Fig. 1.1) depicts three women among the throngs of men, none of them seemingly much disconcerted by the activity going on around them. That this was a female-friendly space is suggested by a report the year before that several 'new mahogany seats' were being fixed between the pillars 'for the accommodation of the Ladies who come to transact business in the funds.'[93]

Though the evidence is vanishingly slight, a few women may have been acting as dealers as well as customers. The Bank authorities were periodically concerned by the way in which trading activity would spill out from the Rotunda into the

Fig. 1.1 'The Bank', Thomas Rowlandson (1792), Metropolitan Museum of Art, Open Access. Credit: The Elisha Whittelsey Collection, The Elisha Whittelsey Fund, 1959

24   SEXISM IN THE CITY

transfer halls, disrupting the work of the clerks, and several times considered ways of containing or even shutting down the market altogether. They sometimes consulted with 'the respectable Jobbers and Brokers', people who claimed status by distinguishing themselves from less reputable market actors, whom they represented as 'being of a description to interrupt business and a nuisance'.[94] In 1806, a Bank of England committee of inspection discussed with the respectable element an ultimately abortive plan to close the Rotunda and establish a new market elsewhere. The jobbers and brokers consulted were keen, reporting that 'the persons who attend in the Rotunda are by no means of a reputable description, consisting in general of persons who will not subscribe to the Stock Exchange, or who have been excluded; female Jobbers, and idle persons'.[95] Writing in the 1960s, the authors of an official history of the London Stock Exchange express disbelief that these women could have genuinely been 'jobbers', stating that there was 'some doubt as to how far they were dealing in stock and how far plying an even older trade'.[96] This view clearly says more about male prejudices in the 1960s than it does about the state of the market in the early nineteenth century. At the same time, it is clear that if women were working as intermediaries, their activities were on a very small scale, likely diminishing, and escaping public comment altogether.[97]

A Peep into the Stock Exchange

These assorted financial marketplaces were early on associated with noise, disorder, and—increasingly—violence. Eighteenth-century proponents of commercial society posited a link between economic development and social virtue, arguing that the function of commerce was, as J. G. A. Pocock summarizes it, 'to refine the passions and polish the manners'.[98] But if a culture of politeness came to characterize many aspects of middle-class life, then the stock market bucked this trend. For a start, those involved were of lowly social origin, in the view of critics like Thomas Mortimer, who was scathing about this throng of 'Barbers, Bakers, Shoe-makers, Plaisterers and Taylors, whom the mammon of unrighteousness has transformed into Stock-Brokers'.[99] For Mortimer, Jonathan's was a 'jarring' place, around which 'a medley of news, quarrels, prices of different funds, calling of names, adjusting of accounts, &c. &c.' constantly swirled 'in an intermixed chaos of confusion'.[100] Once trading ceased at 3 p.m., the brokers and jobbers indulged 'in the most childish and monkey Tricks, such as knocking off each other's Hats, picking of Pockets in joke…flinging of Dish-clouts at the Candles, burning of Wigs, slapping of Faces, &c.'[101]

Such unruly activities increasingly came to typify trading hours. Already labelled 'bulls' and 'bears' in popular parlance, brokers' and jobbers' behaviour was often described in bestial terms, as in the account of one disgusted visitor to the Stock Exchange in Sweetings Alley in the 1790s:

The noise of the screech-owl—the howling of the wolf—the barking of the mastiff—the grunting of the hog—the braying of the ass—the nocturnal wooing of the cat—the hissing of the snake—the croaking of toads, frogs, and grasshoppers—all these, *in unison*, could not be more hideous than the noise which these beings make in the Stock-Exchange.[102]

At the Rotunda things were little better, noise and confusion the hallmarks of the space, and members of the public complaining of 'the rude Manner in which the Stock-Brokers daily take Possession of the principal Door-Way', and of being 'hustled and ill-treated' by them.[103]

At the Stock Exchange, the brokers and jobbers prided themselves on the welcome they gave any member of the public who evaded the waiters (the staff responsible for security and for delivering messages to members) and wandered onto the trading floor.[104] Journalist James Grant, a popular chronicler of London life in the 1830s, described that when detected, such an intruder 'feels some ten or a dozen hands, as if the paws of so many bears, pulling him about in every direction. Possibly he feels them tearing the clothes off his back; and from the rough usage he receives, he very naturally fears they will tear himself in pieces.' One friend of Grant's who experienced such treatment told him 'he would as soon enter a lion's den as again cross the threshold of the Stock Exchange'.[105]

Closed to public view, but growing ever more vital to the national and international economy, over time the Stock Exchange became a place of legend, the subject of mythologies and fantasies. It was 'the temple of Mammon', a 'secret place' where 'prime mysteries are enacted'.[106] Though such terms were often deployed ironically, they nevertheless entrenched the sense that this was a place apart, that had its own unique rituals, routines, and culture. And while attracting much scathing criticism, there was also an abiding curiosity about this epicentre of financial capitalism.[107] One anonymous author in the monthly magazine *Metropolitan* in 1831 promised readers 'a peep into the Stock Exchange' to satisfy their curiosity as to what *actually* went on there. This article, and a follow-up, 'a second peep', are worth considering in depth to understand the psychology of the nineteenth-century Stock Exchange and its members. Though freely admitting the validity of much criticism of the institution, the author was in fact a former member, and clearly fond of its idiosyncrasies.[108]

Throughout both articles, the author emphasizes the adversarial nature of the trading floor, host to a daily contest between 'two opposed parties', the bulls and the bears.[109] In one, he reaches for a series of military metaphors, describing them as 'like two approximating armies on the eve of a battle, separated only by a ravine, or a stream—a single night: they muster in all their strength'.[110] Realizing he is in danger of labouring it, he promises to 'drop the long metaphor of war', but struggles to depict the confrontation in any other terms, ending by reflecting on the hardening impact on the feelings of the participants. Just as the soldier 'sees

26 SEXISM IN THE CITY

unheedingly his comrades fall beside him in the day of battle', so it was on the Stock Exchange, 'where sympathy is exhausted and deadened by the rapidity and frequency with which men drop ruined beside us, and are thrown overboard out of sight'.[111] Though admitting that his account is somewhat tongue-in-cheek, it nevertheless betrays a concerted determination to frame the buying and selling of stock as a manly pursuit.

In his other article, there are fewer references to war, but a greater focus on the corporeality of the marketplace. Describing the scene when important news reaches the exchange, he explains, 'suddenly all quit their quiescent state, and rush simultaneously into one dense cluster—shouting, struggling, and vociferating with deafening clamour; some offering to sell; others bidding to buy; each party saying and doing whatsoever they think calculated to produce their own effect on the market'. Such scenes could go on for hours, though few could endure for any length of time the 'heat, noise, and pressure of this raging group'. Some retired, 'hoarse and pale, to recover their strength', and once recuperated, 'rush again into the arena and resume the fray'. But, without warning, the mood turns:

> Hitherto all has been keen, intense seriousness, heightened sometimes by disputes and personal feelings into wildness and fury, when it frequently happens that the whole scene becomes changed in a moment, as if by magic or the effect of a sudden phrensy—every one knocks off his neighbour's hat, turns the flaps of his coat over his head and shoulders, or pelts him with paper-bombs charged with saw-dust; they slap, bump, and jostle each other: Bartholomew-fair, or the most exhilarating moment of a breaking-up for the holidays, presents nothing equal to it for noise or extravagance; and the whole frolic generally ends with 'the Black Joke', or some other popular tune, sung in full chorus by all present.[112]

Such behaviour sits uncomfortably with nineteenth-century ideas about normative masculinity. Rather than being innate, true manliness could only be acquired through effort: it was 'a hard-won state of self-mastery', as Ben Griffin puts it. 'Men were not expected to be unfeeling or unemotional but they should not be at the mercy of their emotions: the opposite of manliness was an aptness to be swayed by sentiment.'[113] But while the market as described here is ostensibly a place where participants are locked in deadly combat, where emotions have no place, the market is in fact made up *entirely* of emotions. It is an enchanted place where men are allowed to indulge their passions to excess, experiencing the mood-swings of the market, and submitting themselves to exhilarating highs and lows, the result of which is a scene of utter instability. The 'masculine' signifiers of moderation, self-restraint, and rationality are conspicuous by their absence. Far from mastering a feminized market, the brokers and jobbers are yielding to its unpredictable frenzies. Though not explicitly feminizing in this account, it is infantilizing. But rather than 'mere childish folly', their jokes and japes represented 'an instinctive effort of nature to recover from the effects of the violent and overstrained action to which their spirits have been exposed'.[114] The long-term impact on health was considerable. Muscles and sinews 'are shattered to pieces by the constant anxiety and agitation of this pursuit: pale, anxious faces crowd the canvas'.[115] The would-be masters of the market are in reality its victims, nerves shredded, bodies drained, spirits broken. Hence the over-compensatory military metaphors, shrouding the insecurities and fragilities that lay just beneath.

This market culture developed in response to social concerns about the feminizing effects of speculative activity, but it came to act as a potent justification for women's exclusion. For women to intrude on these rituals would be unthinkable. Without women present, men could tell themselves that this was a warzone, a violent and merciless pitched battle for which they, and only they, were physically equipped. If women were allowed to observe, let alone participate, however, the illusion would be broken. With women absent, men could display the most conventionally feminized qualities—volatility, duplicity, hysteria—without having their masculinity called into question. Exposing these behaviours to the female gaze would introduce a self-consciousness that would hamper the free play of the emotional currents that made up the market, ruining its delicate mechanisms. The viability of the financial market therefore depended upon keeping women out. Allowing voyeuristic readers an imagined 'peep' inside was as much as could be safely permitted.

These imperatives transcended national boundaries. France, like London, had been rocked in 1719–20 by a speculative mania fuelled by a debt-for-equity swap, focused on the shares of the Mississippi Company, the brainchild of Scotsman John Law. Stock-trading had centred on the Rue Quincampoix, a narrow, winding street where the company had an office issuing its shares. The tumultuous scenes there, featuring men and women of all ranks feverishly buying and selling shares, and immortalized in plays and prints after the crash, became the symbol of a population losing its mind to speculative frenzy.[116] One of the consequences of the mania was a royal edict of 1724 establishing a regulated stock exchange, the Bourse, to replace the unregulated street trade. The aim was to restrict participants, order the market, and restore financial trust, and it was therefore revealing that while the Bourse was open to local brokers, bankers, and merchants, and certificates could be obtained granting admission to other Frenchmen and foreigners, women were explicitly prohibited from entering.[117] As in England, women were stigmatized as disruptive to the market.[118]

In time, women gained access to the galleries overlooking the trading floor, but their presence even here became contested, partly because it was claimed that from this vantage point they transmitted orders to buy and sell to the brokers' clerks below. As a result, the Paris police made efforts to remove them in the 1830s, before a law of 1848 excluded them altogether.[119] Women remained a visible presence in the vicinity of the stock exchange, however. Typically described as 'female jobbers', and their numbers estimated by one observer at around a hundred or more, it is unclear how far they were trading for others or simply speculating on their own account, but their presence, as in London, was objected to for unsettling the market, and they remained subject to police action.[120] One American stockbroker who visited Paris in the 1850s was scathing about the 'petticoat operators' he saw outside the exchange, who he thought 'looked like rusty old maids, with sharp tongues'. They were thrown out of the exchange, he claimed, because 'they made such a noise that…the brokers could not tell whether stocks were up or down'.[121]

So, stock exchanges purged women from their precincts and coded the activities that went on inside as a manly battle between opposing armies. By and large, the military camouflage worked, and even though the London Stock Exchange continued to suffer a reputation as a glorified gambling den, few questioned its masculine credentials.[122] Whereas the Bank of England had been 'the Old Lady of Threadneedle Street' ever since James Gillray's 1797 caricature depicting the unfortunate Bank being ravished by Prime Minister William Pitt the Younger, greedy for war funding, no similar nickname emerged for the Stock Exchange.[123] True, an 1860 satire, *Smash: A Sketch of the Times*, did feature the character 'Miss Stock-Exchange', who encouraged 'enormous speculations, dressing herself to-day gaily and alluringly in Railway Scrip; to-morrow in Consols…on Friday in Spanish Stocks—a flimsy attire'. By manipulating rumours, she often succeeding in spooking 'the great General Public, who is an exceedingly nervous man in all money matters', causing him to sell his stock, so 'as to transfer from his pockets to those of Miss Stock-Exchange, one to five, or even ten per cent. of his capital'.[124] Such explicit feminizing of the behaviour of dishonest stockbrokers was very rare, however. Much more common was the opposite idea: that villainous male stockbrokers preyed upon naive and vulnerable female clients, a linkage between financial and sexual peril that proved enduring in the popular imagination.[125]

As the nineteenth century wore on, the Stock Exchange grew in importance, whereas the Bank of England's Rotunda fell in status. The City of London Corporation was particularly concerned that it was becoming a haven for unsworn brokers, and believed it should be suppressed.[126] Consequently, the Bank expelled the brokers from the Rotunda in 1838, thereby eliminating a rival trading space to the Stock Exchange.[127] While there were repeated attempts to establish alternative venues through the century, these usually proved short-lived and none managed to challenge the Stock Exchange as the centre of the London securities market.[128]

The Blind Leading the Blind

Women's position in the stock and share market remained the subject of contestation in the nineteenth century, the rhetoric and assumptions changing very little. Historians have found plenty of evidence that women could be independent, assertive, and risk-taking in their share dealings, but these traits were repeatedly condemned by male commentators.[129] In a lengthy polemic in his *Weekly Political Register* against those 'greedy and lazy wretches' who sought to make money by investing in South American bonds, radical journalist William Cobbett reserved special contempt for what he called 'petticoat speculators'. 'How many greedy, gambling women are there in England', he wondered, 'who cannot sit with you five minutes without your hearing some of their slang about fives and fours and threes and consols and reduceds and India and Greek and so on.' After meeting one such, who tries to make conversation with him about the stock market, Cobbett has to refrain from telling her that she was 'a nasty, gambling, grovelling, mercenary, sordid, merciless devil in petticoats'. Cobbett was so upset because the woman's interest in speculation offended his notions of appropriate femininity. 'As women are better than men in good qualities, they are worse in bad qualities. A stock-jobbing man is the worst of men, and a stock-jobbing woman is fit for Lucifer's wife.'[130] Notorious for his inflamed rhetoric, Cobbett might not seem the most representative voice of early nineteenth-century 'middle England'. But this section of his essay resonated, at least with newspaper editors, being reprinted under the heading 'Gambling Women' in rafts of London and provincial papers.[131]

Cobbett's diatribe came in the wake of a crash following a mania for foreign loans and company ventures in 1825 which evoked parallels with the events of 1720. The pattern was repeated again and again: in times of speculative excess, and particularly in their aftermath, women were singled out and made to bear a disproportionate share of the responsibility. All speculators were bad, but female speculators were worse. The rapid development of the rail network in the 1830s and 1840s was fuelled by a popular investment boom in which women participated. As the market heated up in 1845, commentators affected surprise at women's involvement. Sometimes this took a sexualized form, as in William Thackeray's poem for *Punch*, 'A Doe in the City', which sees the author both shocked and seduced by the presence of a young, financially independent woman in the City:

> With a sweet perplexity,
> And a mystery pretty,
> Threading through Threadneedle Street,
> Trots the little KITTY....
> What! are ladies stagging it?
> Sure, the more's the pity;
> But I've lost my heart to her,
> Naughty little KITTY.[132]

More often, men framed women's speculations as entailing a loss of femininity. 'The Railway Queen', a comic story in *Bentley's Miscellany*, is a prime example.

Though the 'Queen' is 'one of the finest young women in England', her preoccupation with shares does not show her to advantage. Her conversation revolves solely around the various railway schemes on the market, and she fires questions about the prospects of each of these at the narrator of the tale 'with a fidgety laugh that I did not relish'. The defeminizing theme is explicit, most strikingly when, to the narrator's surprise, she announces emphatically, 'If I were a man…I should be secretary to a new railroad before a fortnight. I wish I were a man.' The image she uses to describe how she would go about fleecing gullible investors with tempting prospectuses—'Point your guns…and then shot them to the muzzle'—underlines her unhealthily masculine fixations.[133]

Railway speculation was a nationwide phenomenon, encouraging the development of stockbroking communities outside London. The first railway boom in the mid-1830s had seen the establishment of stock exchanges in Liverpool and Manchester as centres for trading in railway shares. In the bigger boom of 1844–5, stock exchanges were founded in fifteen more towns, including Bristol, Glasgow, and Leeds, with several institutions often forming within a single town.[134] In Leeds, it was reported, 'share brokers' offices spring up, like mushrooms, in a night'. Those who had 'failed in every other branch of business' were drawn to the trade due to the easy profits that could be made by exploiting the 'reckless spirit of gambling' which 'has pervaded all classes, from the merchant to the shopkeeper—ay, even the shopkeeper's wife'. With talk of speculation to be found everywhere from tap-room to drawing room, one of the town's papers predicted that the mania would 'carry affliction, sorrow, and ruin into the bosoms of tens of thousands of families'.[135]

Indeed, the railway boom's slow but sustained puncture from the end of 1845 furnished plenty of real-life morality tales, such as the Marchioness of Ailesbury, whose husband reportedly needed to find £200,000 to make good her account.[136] 'Gambling', moralized the City editor of *The Standard*, 'whether attended with success or not, is not the sort of amusement which should occupy the mind of a lady'.[137] Dublin paper *The Pilot* similarly castigated the Marchioness for engaging in the 'masculine game of gold-seeking'.[138] The case captured imaginations so much as it seemed to confirm male anxieties surrounding speculating women. Of course, this was partly due to the liability husbands bore for their wives' debts. But it was also to do with the idea of the corrupting effects of speculation or, worse, that speculation *exposed* women's true natures: the mask of presumed innocence and respectability slipping to reveal sin and depravity.[139]

These kinds of attitudes could be seen as owing much to the ideology of 'separate spheres'. Prescriptive literature increasingly insisted upon a strict division of life into a public sphere of work and politics, and a private sphere of domesticity and family, with women imagined as belonging naturally to the latter. Middle-class women's horizons, it was argued, were stunted to fit the limited role accorded to them by this ideology.[140] But historians have long questioned the extent to which the ideology, despite its seeming ubiquity in nineteenth-century print culture, actually shaped the lived experience of Victorian women.[141] In particular, as Nancy Henry comments, the 'simultaneously public and private nature of financial acts seems to obviate the distinction between a public/male sphere and a private/female sphere'.[142] Likewise, Hannah Barker argues that the model 'leaves little analytic space in which to consider women in business'.[143] Barker, among others, has emphasized that in the nineteenth century, women continued to be active entrepreneurially, a visible and industrious presence in the growing urban economy. Family firms were critical: they were not only important drivers of economic expansion, but also 'a crucial site for female economic activity'.[144]

Though this was most observable in the retail sector, family firms could also facilitate women's involvement in finance. Private banks were typically family-run affairs, and women could be actively involved in such businesses, especially on the death of a husband. When Thomas Coutts died in 1822, he left the controlling interest in Coutts Bank to his widow, Harriot, who ran it successfully until her death fifteen years later. In turn, her fortune went to Thomas's granddaughter, Angela Burdett-Coutts, who continued to exercise influence on the bank's affairs, though was denied a partnership.[145] Women's active participation in banking was not quite as rare as we might think. Research by Margaret Dawes and Nesta Selwyn has identified seventy-six women who were partners in private banks in England and Wales across the long nineteenth century.[146]

With stockbroking, however, the picture was very different. Though likely making the kind of 'hidden investments' in family firms identified by Davidoff and Hall, women were not visible presences in brokerages either in London or in the growing numbers of firms operating in other towns and cities. As in London, the membership rules of the provincial stock exchanges did not bar women, but this is seemingly because there was no need to: the possibility of their membership was simply unthinkable. Public discourse on women and the stock market is likely to have played a part here. When it came to stocks and shares, the acceptable roles for women consisted of the passive provision of capital for low-risk, low-yield investments, and the passive receipt of male advice. This can be seen in the publication of the first investment manual targeted specifically at women, Emma Galton's *A Guide to the Unprotected in Every-day Matters Relating to Property and Income*, first published in 1863. Galton urged her readers to avoid risky ventures, to shun any investment based on the principle of unlimited liability, and to be content with modest returns. The idea of female financial capacity was—somewhat ironically—not countenanced. When specific advice was needed, 'a good man of business' should be able to provide this. The gendering here was deliberate. 'Seldom consult ladies in business matters', Galton warned: 'they usually know little or nothing of business. It is much like the blind leading the blind'.[147]

Though Galton believed that women—provided they read her book and followed her principles—could learn to manage their own finances, Victorian cultural commentary framed women as the most likely victims of corporate fraud and market crashes. While certain kinds of men, such as clergymen on small stipends, were also regarded as innocent of finance, widows and spinsters were frequently cited as the most vulnerable investors.[148] Attracting much sympathy when they had invested in an appropriately 'feminine' way—that is, passively, trustingly, without seeking unreasonable profits—women risked censure when overstepping these limits. A devastating crash in 1866, triggered by the scandalous collapse of Overend, Gurney, and Co., a well-known and much trusted financial institution, offers an example.[149] In the aftermath of the crisis, one contributor to *The Times* argued that 'every poor widow' and 'every industrious man' who had placed their small savings in the firm believing it was safe was a victim of a cruel and criminal abuse of confidence.[150] But women who saw opportunities in the situation were regarded differently. Months after the crash, with share prices still depressed, a bargain-minded female reader of the *Weekly Dispatch* wrote to its 'Answers to Correspondents' column enquiring whether this was 'a good time to buy a few shares in various companies'. The editor sternly rebuked her, highlighting the big risks involved, and extended the warning to any 'widow or spinster who believes she can safely turn her small income into a large one by becoming a sleeping partner in a joint-stock company'.[151] Women must avoid taking risks they did not understand and could not afford.

These kinds of attitudes turned to outright scorn if it were suggested that women could become active financial agents. If women needed protecting in the financial jungle, then the idea that they could establish their own enterprises was patently farcical. *Punch's Pocket Book* for 1867 featured a spoof prospectus for the 'Ladies' Joint-Stock Bank (Limited)'. Because the recent spate of bank failures had created a crisis of trust in the sector, it explained, 'a number of ladies have resolved to form a joint-stock bank amongst themselves in which, knowing how careful women are in everything, the public will have confidence'. Realizing that they needed to start business with a substantial sum of money behind them, the 'directresses' resolved to raise 'no less than a CAPITAL OF ONE HUNDRED POUNDS', with every farthing paid up. They would conduct the business 'according to common sense, by really taking care of their customers' money, and not gambling with it': as a result, they would place all money deposited in a fireproof strongbox with a Chubb lock, rather than lending the money at interest and 'running the risk of losing all'. For added security, a woman would sit up every night in the bank to watch the strongbox, armed with a watchman's rattle and 'a little dog that always barks whenever he hears the least noise'. The bank would be furnished with a drawing room 'where dances and soirées will take place after the hours of business, and musical notes only will be issued'.[152]

The whole skit played on the patent absurdity of the idea of women in finance: their inability even to conceive of banking on a large scale, their failure to grasp the concept of an intangible economy, their excessive and literal concern with security, and the incompatibility of genteel femininity with the realities of business life. Of course, as we have seen, women had for some time been involved in private banking, but the sketch unwittingly signals how the growing turn to joint-stock banking, which took the control of banks outside family structures and placed them in the boardroom, meant the curbing of women's financial opportunities.

Warming to its theme, *Punch* published another, related, piece around the same time, inspired by an advert placed by a reader of *The Queen*, the popular women's magazine. The ad, which appeared in a list of similar notices, offered to swap a host of unneeded objects—including some badges, seals, and used postage stamps—for a canary. *Punch* facetiously held this up as evidence of the existence of 'THE LADIES' STOCK EXCHANGE', where young women could buy, sell, and barter 'such valuables'.[153] Again, the humour rested on the incongruous juxtaposition of the perceived smallness of women's day-to-day concerns—badges, used stamps, canaries—with the grand institutions of male finance. Any female readers who, given the financial disasters of 1866, imagined that they might be able to do better were put firmly in their place.

Conclusion

Far from being marginal to early stock markets, women were in fact important sources of capital both for government and for joint-stock enterprises. Women invested in their own right, but they also managed the investments of others: family members, friends, and occasionally business clients. When the market was fluid, informal, and largely unregulated, there seem to have been few obstacles to this kind of intermediation. But as the eighteenth century progressed, the situation changed, events supporting what economic historian Joan Thirsk posited as 'Thirsk's law'. This holds that, in new enterprises or occupations, women are often prominent participants, but that this situation only lasts 'until the venture has been satisfactorily and firmly established, when it has been institutionalised, formalised, and organised. Then, when the formal structure hardens, the direction, and the style as well, always fall under the control of men.'[154] The organization of the stock market, especially its relocation out of Exchange Alley, raised barriers which it seemed impossible for women to negotiate.

Just as important as this institutionalization, however, were ways of imagining the stock market that made the participation of women impossible to contemplate. The emphasis on the tumult and turmoil of the market was one means of justifying excluding women, mirroring strategies that were also present in other environments. Anti-suffragists demarcated politics as 'an exclusively male arena', argues Ben Griffin, by locating 'masculine authority and autonomy' in the male body, 'presenting the energy and strength required for struggle in the public

sphere as too great for the supposedly delicate female constitution'.[155] The authority of the House of Commons rested on the idea that as an all-male assembly, it
was rational and unemotional. The claims to manliness of individual members
therefore depended upon a careful performance demonstrating 'self-control and
mastery of impulses'. This meant that their conduct in the chamber was constantly under scrutiny: politicians and commentators 'interpreted parliamentary
activity in terms of a complex semiotics of masculinity'.[156] In the Stock Exchange,
by contrast, behaviour regularly fell far short of masculine ideals of self-control
and restraint. This made it all the more important for its members to construct
manly identities, a project which depended upon the exclusion of women. The
strategy allowed men to keep women in their place: as passive providers of investment capital and compliant followers of male advice, rather than seeking to
become independent market actors or intermediaries themselves.

Though the London Stock Exchange grew to become the centre of the securities market, it never succeeded in monopolizing this market. Outside the capital,
the nineteenth century saw the formation of other stock exchanges, much smaller
than London but still providing a parallel institutional framework for the business of buying and selling stocks and shares. However, these exchanges did not
yet contest the gendered assumptions of London. Rather, the first challenge to the
idea of stockbroking as an exclusively manly pursuit was to come in London's
'outside' market: the brokers and dealers who operated beyond the London Stock
Exchange, whose activities were to assume a new scale and importance from
the 1870s.

Sexism in the City: Women Stockbrokers in Modern Britain. James Taylor, Oxford University Press.
© James Taylor 2025. DOI: 10.1093/9780191990397.003.0002

2

Being a Female Stockbroker in Late Victorian and Edwardian Britain

One Thursday in January 1870, the *New York Herald*'s financial column noted the presence of two 'fashionably dressed ladies' buying and selling shares on Wall Street. Attracting attention due to the scale of their transactions, the identity of the pair was the subject of some conjecture, as was how they had acquired their seemingly extensive knowledge of the stock market.[1] The mystery was quickly solved. Reading the *Herald*'s report, the women wrote to the editor offering an interview, which duly appeared two days later. Victoria Woodhull and Tennessee Claflin were sisters who had been offering brokerage services from their rooms in the exclusive Hoffman House Hotel. With business booming, they planned to shift operations to new premises on Broad Street in the heart of the financial district.[2] The *Herald*'s coverage thus acted as a useful advertisement for the sisters' new enterprise, helping to ensure that the opening of Woodhull, Claflin, & Co., bankers and brokers, in early February caused a sensation. Passers-by were desperate to see what this new being, a woman stockbroker, looked like. Crowds 'peered anxiously through the doors, and uttered expressions of surprise and pleasure if they could but catch a glimpse of one of the members of the firm'.[3]

Keen to establish their business credentials, the sisters claimed that they had the backing of 'the shrewdest and most respectable financiers in the city', and were happy to encourage rumours that railroad magnate Cornelius Vanderbilt had helped them set up their business. They also declared that they had made the huge sum of $700,000 through their financial operations, and predicted they would make much more once their business was established.[4] Women's rights campaigners were enthusiastic, leading activist Susan B. Anthony seeing their arrival on Wall Street as 'an augury of better times to come for women'.[5] After an interview with Tennessee for her periodical *The Revolution*, Anthony left highly impressed by the sisters' 'pluck, energy and enterprise', and the 'clear-sightedness they show in financial matters'.[6] But the mainstream press was equally struck, the *Herald* concluding that the example set by these 'Queens of Finance' demonstrated that women 'can ably deal with large monetary interests as well as do mere shopping'.[7]

But uncomfortable reports about the sisters' past were beginning to spread. Though claiming to come from a rich family, prior to arriving in New York they had in fact made a living travelling the country as 'magnetic physicians and

36 SEXISM IN THE CITY

clairvoyants' peddling miracle cures.[8] Though they did know Vanderbilt, and he may have helped them financially, this seems to have been more because of his interest in alternative medicine than his recognition of the sisters' financial capacities.[9] Their brokerage was—it was increasingly rumoured—more show than substance, 'a cheap attempt to win notoriety' ahead of Victoria's sensational announcement that she was planning to run for president in 1872.[10] Indeed, it seems that Victoria's second husband was in charge of the actual day-to-day running of the business, with the sisters soon switching their attentions to journalism, establishing *Woodhull and Claflin's Weekly* to promote Victoria's political career and other progressive causes.[11] Their increasingly radical politics—including attacks on high finance—and their insistent advocacy of women's rights alienated mainstream opinion, while their support for 'free love' meant that they became increasingly tarred with claims of sexual impropriety, a thinly disguised Victoria even appearing as the predatory Audacia Dangyereyes in Harriet Beecher Stowe's 1871 novel *My Wife and I*.[12] By the time their brokerage failed in 1873, the sisters' reputations and finances alike were in ruins.[13]

Woodhull and Claflin's venture therefore left a mixed legacy. The male financial establishment naturally drew conclusions that supported their prejudices. Speculator and chronicler of Wall Street life William Worthington Fowler declared that the 'profession of a stock broker would seem to be almost the last one that woman would aspire to fill, or could fill successfully.'[14] Yet the sisters' experiment did help to make careers in finance for women seem a possibility, and not only in the United States, for it did not take long for news of their venture to reach Britain.[15] Popular British weekly the *Ladies' Treasury* carried portraits of the sisters (see Fig. 2.1), and called their experiment 'extraordinary'. It believed that after this first step had been taken, 'the example of these ladies will in some degree be followed.'[16] Yet it was in America that successors to Woodhull and Claflin first emerged. The early 1880s saw women opening stockbroking ventures in New York and Chicago, though not always seeking the publicity that Woodhull and Claflin had courted.[17] These projects were occasionally noted in the British press, yet this was more about highlighting the differing financial cultures of the two nations than indicating what might actually come to pass in the City of London itself.[18] Indeed, it is telling that in Anthony Trollope's 1878 comic novel *Is He Popenjoy?*, it is an American feminist, Dr Olivia Q. Fleabody, who works up her London audience of 'strongly-visaged spinsters and mutinous wives' to believe 'that a glorious era was at hand in which women would be chosen by constituencies, would wag their heads in courts of law, would buy and sell in Capel Court, and have balances at their banker's.'[19]

So it was probably with some surprise that readers of a widely syndicated ladies' column in October 1885 read an intriguing announcement. 'The lady stockbroker is an accomplished fact. Miss Amy Bell has come to London to take up her residence, and in a few weeks' time will be ready to receive clients and

MRS. VICTORIA C. WOODHULL,   MRS. T. C. CLAFLIN,

STOCKBROKERS OF NEW YORK.

Treasury of Literature,
May 1, 1871

Fig. 2.1 Victoria Woodhull and Tennessee Claflin, *Ladies' Treasury*, 1 May 1871, 161. From the British Library Collection, shelfmark P.P.6004.o

advise them, ladies and gentlemen, upon investments and business matters generally.'[20] The author of the report, 'Aurora', the penname of pioneering female journalist Catherine Drew, welcomed Bell's arrival on the investment scene, and over the next few weeks, there were small follow-up notices in a handful of other publications.[21] By January, Bell had taken offices in Bloomsbury and was open for business, a fact which again attracted a modest trickle of press attention.[22] Another ladies' columnist, 'Penelope'—the alias of popular scientific writer Phebe Lankester—devoted several paragraphs to her. Initially doubting the wisdom of her actions, having met Bell, Lankester was won round to the idea that this 'well informed and quiet little lady stockbroker' could successfully forge a career in the world of stocks and shares.[23] As we shall see, Bell continued to attract sporadic attention in the press over the coming years.

In time, Bell's presumed uniqueness came to be regarded as peculiar, given the progress women were beginning to make in other fields, one paper wondering at the end of the century why 'no other woman has ever followed her example'.[24] Yet Bell was not, in fact, a one-off, her relative renown obscuring the fact that the 1880s and 1890s saw a number of other women venture into stocks and shares. While representing only a tiny fraction of the total population of stockbrokers, this mini boom underlines the growing opportunities for entrepreneurial women in the late nineteenth-century urban economy.[25] With the late Victorian years marking such a break with previous eras, several questions arise which this chapter seeks to answer. What were the conditions that made it possible for women to become stockbrokers when they had for so long been inactive in this field? Who were these pioneer businesswomen, and how—and why—did they get into stockbroking? What kinds of business did they establish, and what clients did they attract? Did they take risks or were they, as is often contended, risk-averse? And did they make a virtue of their sex, or did they seek to conceal it? This chapter will answer these questions by reconstructing the biographies of ten female stockbrokers, hitherto unexplored by historians, who tried to build careers in that most inhospitable of environments for women, the world of finance.

Becoming a Female Stockbroker

The City of London in the later Victorian years was an overwhelmingly male environment. With its residential population rapidly departing for the more salubrious suburbs, the City was increasingly defined by its financial and commercial functions.[26] At a time when other public space was opening up to a greater feminine presence, most notably the shopping districts of the West End, this gave the City a distinctive atmosphere. As one (fictional) visitor put it when journeying into the district for the first time, 'all the women folk melted out of the streets and gave place to one long string of men'.[27] More than a few of these men would have been members of the London Stock Exchange. With the nominal value of securities quoted on the Stock Exchange's official list increasing eightfold between 1853 and 1913, there was much work, both for the brokers who dealt with the public and for the jobbers who made the markets.[28] By 1876, there were 1,900 members of the Stock Exchange, more than double the figure for 1851. Though fluctuating with market conditions, the overall trend continued sharply upwards. By 1884, there were over 2,500 members, and in 1904 the number passed 5,000.[29] This rapid growth also necessitated the physical expansion of the Stock Exchange itself, with major extensions in 1885, 1896, and 1905.[30]

Not only were these brokers and jobbers all male, but their clerks were too. A clerkship was the typical route to membership, an apprenticeship during which young men learned how the investment business worked. Indeed, by the early twentieth century, around 80 per cent of new entrants had previously worked as a clerk in a member firm.[31] In common with clerkships across the financial sector, these posts were customarily for men only. Elsewhere in the City, however, employment practices were beginning to change. Inspired by the example of the United States Treasury, which had started employing women during the Civil War (1861–5), the Prudential, a rapidly expanding life assurance company, experimented by hiring ten 'lady clerks' in 1871.[32] Satisfied with the results, the firm increased its female workforce to fifty, and some other large City firms began to follow suit, notably merchant bankers Barings and Rothschilds.[33] The Bank of England took longer, establishing a women's department in 1894 which, two years later, was employing a staff of forty.[34]

Driven by the huge increase in routine office work, the decision to employ women was made with the intention, as Ellen Jordan explains, of creating 'an unpromotable category of clerk' to handle the lowest-grade tasks, safeguarding the pathways to advancement for men, and protecting their status.[35] Women became particularly associated with the new technology of the typewriter, it being conceded 'even by the young men whom they supersede, that they are quicker and neater in the manipulation of the machine'.[36] The fundamental distinction between female and male work was underlined spatially, with most firms adopting a policy of strict segregation, involving separate entrances and eating facilities. Though salaries for women typically exceeded those of office boys, they were far lower than the rates paid to men of their own age, and there was little for the ambitious to aspire to, other than becoming head of the women's section.[37] And turnover was high, in part due to a strict 'marriage bar' which terminated women's employment when they married.[38] Nevertheless, such were the limited options at the time that late Victorian employment guides for women warned eager readers how difficult it was to find jobs with firms like Barings, Rothschilds, and the Prudential.[39]

Despite the financial benefits of hiring cheap female labour, stockbroking firms were very slow to do so. The London Stock Exchange's rules were designed to prevent larger firms from driving smaller rivals out of business, with restrictions on the number of partners and on the number of clerks each firm could have working for them on the floor of the exchange, and a ban on branching.[40] These restrictions on economies of scale discouraged member firms from expanding: one of the leading brokerages, Heseltine, Powell, & Co., employed only seven clerks in the late 1870s.[41] Such businesses were in no hurry to adopt the new experiment, and it was only by the end of the 1890s that commentators began to note the presence of female clerks on the staff of some of the larger London brokerages.[42] Even then, many firms remained opposed to the practice. One guide for young clerks hoping to land a job in stockbroking published just before the First World War noted an enduring prejudice against employing women in Stock Exchange circles. A major consideration was that on busy account days, all staff members needed to be able to visit brokerages and banks in the vicinity of the Stock Exchange to collect and deliver cheques paying for stock. 'For this work, obviously, the lady shorthand-typist is unsuited', the author observed.[43]

Though becoming a stockbroker's clerk was not an option for women for much of this period, entrepreneurial opportunities were nevertheless arising in the development of the outside market.[44] The traditional licensing system for brokers managed by the City of London Corporation was still in operation in the 1860s and 1870s. Unsworn brokers continued to face the risk of prosecution: indeed, the list of sworn brokers published annually in *The Times* came with the offer of a £50 reward for members of the public providing information on anyone acting as a broker without authority.[45] But the system was coming under growing pressure from Stock Exchange members who had long resented paying annual fees to the Corporation, eventually leading to parliamentary interventions scaling them back and then abolishing them altogether in 1870 and 1884 respectively.[46] Though it was not the intention of legislators, this gave a boost to the outside market: those brokers who through choice or necessity operated beyond the rules and regulations of the London Stock Exchange. Another unintended effect of the removal of the City of London gatekeepers was that stockbroking began to seem a realistic proposition for women. This section introduces six of the best-documented women who worked at the more reputable end of the market between the 1880s and the 1910s. Their biographies reveal the diverse back-grounds of women attracted by a career in finance, and give a sense of the cir-cumstances that could lead women to take up stockbroking, a career which had for so long seemed out of reach.

A family background in stockbroking was not necessary to enter the outside market, as illustrated by the case of **Amy Elizabeth Bell**, whose arrival in London 'Aurora' had announced in the press in late 1885. The daughter of Charlotte and Charles Bell, the Vice-Consul of Siam, Amy lost both parents to fever when an infant in 1859.[47] She was sent to Bristol where she was brought up by her great-uncle on her mother's side, Dr Henry Hurry Goodeve, formerly a surgeon for the

East India Company and now a prominent local figure.[48] Childless, Henry involved the young Amy in all his interests, including the daily study of *The Times*. She developed an interest in the financial column, becoming fascinated, as she later put it, by 'the rise and fall in various kinds of stocks and shares'.[49] Wanting to learn more, she would listen in on 'the conversation of business men and gradually grew to understand what I heard; what I did not understand I asked about'.[50] Academically minded, at 17 she had been among the first cohort of female students at the newly formed University College, Bristol. One of her lecturers here was Mary Paley Marshall, wife of economist Alfred Marshall, who encouraged Bell to sit the entrance exams for Newnham College, Cambridge.[51] Bell won a scholarship, but within weeks of starting her studies, her great-uncle Henry fell seriously ill, and she decided to give up her studies in order to care for him.[52]

When Goodeve died in 1884, Bell, now 25, enjoyed independent means, but wanted to find an occupation. 'I had always said I would be a stockbroker', she later recalled, 'and my friends used laughingly to say I was cut out for one, because I studied the markets so much.' But what her friends took as a joke was a serious proposition for Bell. She had already demonstrated skill in managing the financial affairs of others, with several relatives, including her great-uncle, entrusting her with this role.[53] Moreover, a family connection had joined a large London brokerage and had done well for himself. She concluded that 'what cousin so-and-so does I can do', and so resolved to move to London in 1885. For a stockbroker, Bell later recalled, 'early training is a great help'. But for her, 'such training was not to be obtained, and for some years I felt the want of it. I could not, as a young man could, enter a stockbroker's office as a clerk, and so become gradually initiated into the work of each department'.[54] As a result, after picking up what technical training she could from her relative, she started trading from Russell Chambers, a redbrick residential block in Bloomsbury, learning as she went.[55]

Bell was single and relatively young, but women in very different circumstances could also gravitate towards stockbroking.[56] Widowhood has long been recognized as a spur to women's entrepreneurial activity, with wives often playing an active role in family businesses and taking control of them when their spouses died.[57] As we saw in Chapter 1, this had been the path taken by several women in the eighteenth century prior to the formalization of the market, but the London Stock Exchange's rule against the wives of members being engaged in business seems to have curbed their entrepreneurial spirits. This was certainly the view of one journalist, who criticized the rule as 'tending to make the wife of a member a butterfly of fashion rather than a useful helpmeet and mother capable of assisting her husband and children in case of need...every channel is closed to her except pleasure and domesticity'.[58] Consequently, widows of members do not feature among the ranks of women stockbrokers in this period. A near-exception was Frances Abbott, the widow of William, a broker who had once been a member before developing a successful career as an outside broker.[59] After William's death in 1888, Frances did briefly attempt to keep his business going through an arrangement with William's former clerk, who had recently set up on his own.[60] But this seems to have been motivated entirely by temporary financial necessity, as William had left Frances and her daughters unprovided for.[61] A subscription in the City, where William had been a popular figure, raised funds to rectify this, and Frances seems to have rapidly withdrawn into private life.[62]

However, widowhood did propel another woman into stockbroking. **Emma Patience Robson**, née Swanton, was born in County Cork, Ireland, in 1862 to a wealthy merchant, James Swanton, who had extensive mining and other business interests both in the south of Ireland and in England.[63] In 1886 Emma married engineer William Robson, who had been involved in several bridge construction projects in the area.[64] The couple moved to Africa when William was hired as chief engineer on a major railway project, the Delagoa Bay Railway, ending up in Johannesburg, a town that had just been founded as a result of gold discoveries in the Witwatersrand region. Though William was offered a post on the Natal Government Railway, the pair decided to try their luck at the goldfields instead. They lived 'a life of excitement' for a year, Emma later recalled, but everything came to a sudden halt when William contracted typhoid fever and died in 1890.[65] Emma returned to the UK, bringing with her a new interest in the stock market. The Johannesburg Stock Exchange had just been established when they arrived in town, and Emma had been inspired by meeting 'men of vast ambitions and great wealth': the so-called Randlords.[66] William had left just £800, and with a young daughter to support, Emma tried several lines of work, without much success.[67] But in 1898, aged 35, she 'finally decided to follow my natural inclination and set up as a stockbroker', taking offices in Broad Street House on New Broad Street in the City.[68]

Whereas marriage often signalled the end of women's paid work, the extent to which this was the case was exaggerated by census recording practices which underreported wives' active contributions to family businesses.[69] Moreover, marriage could in some cases be a stimulus to women's entrepreneurial activity, allowing wives to tap into new social networks and capital.[70] A few years after their New York broking venture failed, Victoria Woodhull and **Tennessee Claflin** emigrated to Britain with their parents and siblings. Both sisters thrived in their new environment, Victoria marrying successful banker John Biddulph Martin in 1883, and Tennessee wedding Sir Francis Cook, a superrich textiles merchant twenty-eight years her senior, in 1885.[71] Tennessee, now styled Lady Cook, enjoyed a newfound respectability, press reports rarely raising the more scandalous features of her earlier life.[72] She remained busy, becoming involved in charitable work and writing syndicated articles for the press on political and social issues.[73] But she retained an interest in finance, and in 1898, now in her mid-fifties, decided to return to stockbroking, opening an office in St Mildred's Court, opposite Mansion House and 'three doors from the Bank of England'.[74] Of course, her interest in broking predated her marriage, but she also benefited from Francis's contacts. When establishing her new business, he arranged for her to 'have the supervision, the advice, and the aid' of his brokers, support which she valued, remarking that she 'should not have gone into the City by myself'.[75]

Another married woman taking up stockbroking in later life was **Gertrude Isabella Brooke**, née Goodeve. Born in Malta in 1866 to a military father, in 1895 she married an army colonel, Lionel Brooke, a widower seventeen years her senior.[76] Over the next few years, Gertrude and Lionel continued to live a peripatetic military life, while bringing up three daughters.[77] After being badly wounded in the Battle of Colenso during the Boer War, Lionel had further appointments in Ireland and Lancashire before he retired, having reached the rank of brigadier general, and the couple settled in Chelsea in London.[78] A few years later Gertrude, now in her mid-forties, began on a stockbroking career. Her introduction to broking had nothing to do with her husband, however, but was due to her cousin, Amy Bell. Gertrude's father, Colonel Henry Hills Goodeve, was the nephew and adopted son of Henry Hurry Goodeve, who had raised Amy. When Bell elected to retire in 1910, she handed the business over to Gertrude, seven years her junior.[79]

The women discussed so far were operating in London. But around the turn of the century there were the first signs that women—at least those with family connections—were becoming more involved in stockbroking outside London. In the west of Ireland, Daniel Scanlan Bulger had been a prominent figure in the commercial community of Kilrush, but sold up in 1883 to embark on a midlife change of career.[80] Moving his wife **Anne Bulger** (née Delaney) and children across country to Dublin, he set himself up as a stockbroker and joined the Dublin Stock Exchange.[81] In time, one of their children, Daniel Delaney, joined the firm, now styled D. S. Bulger & Son, while Anne threw herself into Dublin philanthropic life, singing in charity concerts and becoming an active committee member.[82] Daniel Delaney left in 1894 in order to set up his own business, which meant that when Daniel senior's health collapsed in 1902, it was Anne, now in her late fifties, who took on the running of the family firm.[83]

Brokers' daughters were also beginning to play more prominent roles in family firms. H. Bazett Jones & Sons was a Preston stockbroking firm that had grown out of the activities of its founder, railway company secretary Henry Bazett Jones, in the 1840s. When Henry died in 1866, the firm was taken over by his two sons, Richard and Frederic, with Frederic assuming sole control in 1876.[84] In due course, two of Frederic's five children took an interest in the business: his son, Henry, and his daughter, **Marianne Bazett Jones** (b. 1867). As she later told a journalist, 'she had been brought up to stockbroking and loved it...she did not think she could do anything else'.[85] By 1900, both siblings were working at the firm, but Marianne—at 33, eleven years Henry's senior—was the chief assistant.[86]

44 SEXISM IN THE CITY

The three subsequently went into partnership, but when Frederic fell seriously ill in 1909 and died shortly after, the firm passed entirely to Marianne.[87]

How Women May Keep Their Money

It is no coincidence that this cohort of female stockbrokers emerged at a time when women were becoming a more important and visible element of the investing public, a factor which presented new opportunities to women to build businesses catering to female investors. The investing public was both broadening and deepening in the later nineteenth century, as those with money increasingly took it out of real property—land and buildings—and put it into the stock market. Estimates of the size of the investing public suggest an increase from around 250,000 to 1 million between 1870 and 1914.[88] The gender composition of this public was also shifting significantly, influenced in part by the large and growing gap between the female and male populations which made the so-called 'surplus woman problem' a major topic of debate in Victorian society. Without men to support them, these women needed to invest in order to maintain themselves.[89] Those who did marry also had more freedom to invest independently following the Married Women's Property Acts of 1870 and 1882, which greatly extended wives' economic rights within marriage.[90] One major quantitative study suggests that where women may have represented just 15 per cent of shareholders in the 1870s, this had grown to over 25 per cent by the 1890s, and reached nearly 34 per cent in the 1910s.[91]

Viewing this mass investing public from the stockbroker's perspective, some clients were undeniably preferred over others. Most desirable were those clients who knew what they wanted to invest in and did not require much in the way of guidance. There was a longstanding reticence when it came to recommending investments, with brokers believing that if such tips did well, they were unlikely to be thanked, while if they went badly, they were sure to be blamed.[92] Complaining about the unreasonableness of clients was one of their favourite pastimes, and female clients attracted the most scorn. Needy, unreliable, and prone to panic, they were often dismissed as more trouble than they were worth. As one anonymous broker put it, whenever the market dropped, he was plagued by letters, telegrams, and personal calls from female clients demanding to know whether prices would continue to fall and whether they should sell up. 'You can't be rude to lady clients, you know. You must try and answer all their questions, and calm down their fears. And that's pretty hard.'[93] At the same time, women's assumed naivety and desire for unrealistic profits was frequently thought to leave them particularly vulnerable to exploitation by the unscrupulous.[94] So prone were they believed to be to falling for frauds that some contended that 'the law ought to shield them even from themselves.'[95]

Women stockbrokers were able to capitalize on both of these discourses, presenting themselves as best-placed to cater to the particular needs and idiosyncrasies of female investors. This idea was enthusiastically promoted by women journalists who were gaining more of a voice in the later Victorian newspaper press.[96] The very first press paragraph noting Amy Bell's appearance in London, penned by Catherine Drew, welcomed the protection she would bring female investors.[97] 'In these days of bubble companies, it would be very desirable to teach women to be cautious and not plunge into schemes which they do not understand. Sound advice from a professional would have saved many a woman from the workhouse in old age.'[98] Days later, a writer for leading feminist periodical the *Englishwoman's Review* struck a similar note when hailing Bell's arrival, observing that there were 'many ladies of small means and entire ignorance of business' who 'sorely need the advice of another woman on their investments'.[99]

Women's lack of financial education, and their often-limited resources, meant that they required specialized help, creating space in stockbroking for women. As Phebe Lankester, another journalist, put it, Amy Bell's 'special function' was 'to be consulted about feminine finance, just as a lady doctor hopes to be consulted about feminine digestions'. Such women were put off by male brokers' severe reputation, Lankester noting

> how few women have the courage to enter a grand business office to consult a formidable looking gentleman as to what they should do with their nest egg of fifty or a hundred pounds, and if they did, I fear they would get but scant attention unless through a special and personal introduction.[100]

Bell, by contrast, presented an altogether more sympathetic face. As she put it to one of *The Echo*'s journalists: 'I am always taking trouble, and am constantly explaining to women left alone in the world, and perfect babes in business matters, the fidgety little minutiae which few men will have the patience to repeat to them.'[101]

Another journalist, Charlotte O'Conor Eccles, gave a detailed account of the difference Bell could make to women's financial lives. A friend of Eccles was brought up in comfortable circumstances but, as was common for young women, 'in entire ignorance of business and business methods'. When her father died, she could make little sense of his papers, so she took them to her father's stockbroker for help. Not understanding his answers, she asked more questions, but 'obviously bored and dismayed by her ignorance', the broker advised her to get her brother-in-law to explain things to her before returning to him. Mortified by the broker's rudeness, and not trusting her relative, she tried to find a woman who could help her, but without success, until one day someone chanced to mention Amy Bell. Bell 'understood her difficulties, and, sitting down beside her, with endless patience explained to her the meaning of every word that perplexed her

Fig. 2.2 Amy Bell, from Margaret Bateson, *Professional Women upon their Professions* (London, 1895), facing p. 70. From the British Library Collection, shelfmark 8415.ee.43

until my friend grasped it perfectly. There were no more difficulties.' Rather than returning to her father's broker, she made Bell her broker, and 'for her capability for managing her affairs she always thanks Miss Bell who has been useful to hundreds of her sex'.[102]

These kinds of accounts written by female journalists allowed Bell to secure valuable publicity without incurring the cost (or stigma) of advertising. Interviews with Bell sometimes even featured her portrait, as with Fig. 2.2, which originally appeared in *The Queen*.[103] This rendered her more visible than most male brokers of the period, as well as making her seem more approachable. In addition to the interviews, 'Answers to Correspondents' columns steered female readers towards Bell, while letters from readers praising her services were also published.[104] Though she argued that personal recommendations were far more valuable to her than anything that appeared in the press, such coverage clearly helped Bell to build a client base.[105] By late 1888, she was doing well enough to move from Bloomsbury—a peripheral location for a stockbroker—into 'finely furnished' new offices in Bucklersbury, a few steps from Mansion House in the heart of the City of London.[106]

BEING A FEMALE STOCKBROKER   47

Bell also established a presence as a public financial authority through publishing financial advice for women. Though investment advice had been a booming business since mid-century, practically none of this was tailored to a female audience. Emma Galton's *A Guide to the Unprotected*, discussed in Chapter 1, reached its seventh edition in 1900, its success demonstrating the market for such advice.[107] Bell capitalized on this by producing a series of signed articles for the *Englishwoman's Review* in 1892 on 'How Women May Keep their Money'.[108] The following year she followed up with further pieces on saving strategies for women in *Work and Leisure*.[109] Other stockbrokers who followed in Bell's wake also benefited from the support of the women's press to publicize the specialist help they could offer female clients. When she made her return to stockbroking in the late 1890s, Tennessee Claflin (now Lady Cook) enjoyed exposure from an interview and accompanying sketch in *Woman's Weekly*, while around the same time Emma Robson was interviewed for *Woman's Life*.[110] In the latter, Robson explained that women liked her 'because I am more patient than the surly male, who will not condescend to explain the stock and share "lingo"'.[111]

The kinds of counsel these brokers gave their female clients was overwhelmingly cautious. The columns Bell was commissioned to write for the women's press were full of ultra-conservative advice. 'Be content with moderate interest; high interest must mean bad security.' Three per cent was all that could be had in perfect safety, the desire to get 5 or 6 per cent was 'the bane of so many women. They will not realise that the risk is altogether disproportionate to the advantage'.[112] In keeping with this emphasis on moderation, Bell made it clear to clients that she refused all speculative business, only handling long-term investments.[113] This hard-line stance was echoed by others, including Lady Cook, whose business card was unequivocal: 'No speculative accounts will be entertained, but bona fide investments will be carried out with care'.[114] Robson too underlined that the mainstay of her business was 'legitimate broking'.[115] Marianne Bazett Jones in Preston took the dimmest view of women's financial behaviour. Women lacked the 'calm judgment' of men, were bad losers who always blamed the broker when an investment went wrong, and generally had 'very funny ideas' when it came to money. This meant that while she accepted speculative business from male clients, she never did so for women.[116]

By emphasizing women's limitations and framing their services as educational, women brokers risked entrenching dominant ideas about female financial ineptitude, as well as 'ghettoizing' themselves within the occupation, rather than establishing themselves as equals to their male peers. A letter Bell wrote to the London Stock Exchange's Committee for General Purposes, in response to a proposed change to the rules on splitting commissions with outside brokers that threatened her business, is telling. 'A great deal of my work is explanatory and instructional, and not in the strict sense commercial at all', she wrote. In other words, her services complemented rather than competed with male brokers.

If she were driven out of business, most of her clients would be lost to the Stock Exchange.[117] This strategy confirmed the idea of a gendered hierarchy: as a woman, Bell was taking on the troublesome and unprofitable clients male brokers could not be bothered with.

On the other hand, this was a viable means of carving out a niche in an overwhelmingly male business, a method successfully deployed in other occupations including accountancy, medicine, and even farming.[118] Journalist and suffrage campaigner Margaret Bateson, who interviewed Bell for *The Queen*, realized this. Women were not seeking to oust men in the professions, she observed, 'but they make places for themselves that men have hardly known to be places at all.'[119] As well as the professions, there were also parallels with women entrepreneurs in sectors like the beauty business who specialized in appealing to female consumers. Though trading in this way can be framed as diminishing their achievements—relying on their sex more than their skills—this misses the point, as Margaret Walsh has argued. 'They succeeded as entrepreneurs who saw an economic opening and they developed a different approach to that traditionally deemed as essential by men.'[120] With most of her clients 'women of moderate and inelastic means', possessing a few hundred pounds in savings, Bell explained her purpose as a stockbroker in terms that most men in the profession would likely have rejected.[121] As she put it when talking to Bateson, 'I want to make women understand their money matters and take a pleasure in dealing with them. After all, is money such a sordid consideration? May not it make all the difference to a hard-working woman when she reaches middle life whether she has or has not those few hundreds?'[122] Her approach—working with every client to determine the best investment strategy—'humanised her profession', as a friend later put it. 'One great secret of her success was her happy art of turning clients into personal friends.'[123]

Though it may have seemed that Bell and others were unhelpfully echoing male discourses about women investors, there was an important distinction. Rather than talking about women's innate limitations, they saw these as the natural—but entirely avoidable—result of the inadequate opportunities they were given to learn. By providing this instruction, they were giving practical application to popular novelist Dinah Craik's call for women's financial education. In an 1886 essay, Craik argued that

> every woman who has any money at all, either earned or inherited, ought to keep it in her own hands, and learn to manage it herself, exactly as a man does. There is no earthly reason why she should not.... Ordinary business knowledge and business habits are just as attainable by her as by him.[124]

Craik thought financial education would be far more liberating for women than political enfranchisement. It could certainly be gently subversive. Women brokers argued that by educating women, they were teaching them to be independent from men, and from the bad financial advice they often gave. Bell wanted to tutor her clients to be less susceptible to what she termed 'dinner-table advice'. As she explained, women would 'meet a gentleman at dinner—an entire stranger—who tells them that some mine or another is doing wonderfully well. Forthwith they put their money down that mine, and probably never see it again.'[125] Every time a woman consulted a broker of her own sex, she was challenging the masculine monopoly on financial expertise. Women who wanted to invest but did not know how were no longer compelled to place their fate in male hands.

Moreover, this approach to stockbroking did not preclude doing business for male clients. Every female broker active in these years had a mixed clientele. Even Bell had a handful of male clients, 'a very few old friends', likely from her Bristol days.[126] Other brokers claimed more extensive sets of male clients. Robson had 'many folk of both sexes' on her books, while Lady Cook went further still, insisting that she had more male than female clients.[127] Bazett Jones—her antipathy to them noted above—said that she had 'not many women clients'.[128] Bell's successor Gertrude Brooke was outspoken in claiming not only to have 'many' male clients, but in suggesting that they were not always well versed in financial matters. 'I notice that many of the men who come to consult me know nothing about finance, whereas my women clients are as keen as Saladin's sword and as cool as linen.'[129] These brokers were thus confidently embodying the principle that it was possible for a woman to advise a man on his investments, and that there were plenty of men who might need their expertise.

In doing so, they were contributing to a growing realization that financial ability was not solely determined by sex. Though clergymen had long figured in debates alongside widows and spinsters as archetypically naive and vulnerable investors, writers were increasingly highlighting men's financial limitations more generally.[130] To return to Craik, who was driven to authorship early in life because of financial pressures created by her spendthrift father, she believed that 'very few men know how properly to use money. They can earn it, lavish it, hoard it, waste it; but to deal with it wisely, as a means to an end, and also as a sacred trust…is an education difficult of acquirement by the masculine mind.'[131] Women's broader sense of responsibility, plus their 'infinite capacity for taking trouble', made them, so Craik argued, better money managers than men, if given the right training.[132] The growing profile of women stockbrokers in these years made it possible to imagine that Craik might have a point.

The Bucket Shop Brigade

The stockbrokers discussed thus far were operating at the more respectable end of the market. But there was another, less reputable, side to this market, which

50 SEXISM IN THE CITY

was undergoing significant development in the second half of the nineteenth century. Until this point, outside operators had been seen as fairly ephemeral figures, scraping marginal livings.[133] But the repeal of the 'taxes on knowledge'— duties on advertising, newspapers, and paper—between 1853 and 1861 made advertising much cheaper and much more potent. With the penny press, newspaper readerships boomed and most titles carried adverts placed by brokers. The removal of paper duty, combined with advances in print technology and falling postal rates (reduced to a halfpenny from 1870) also made mass circulars possible. Firms sprang up to harvest the names and addresses of potential clients from public registers and to address envelopes by the thousand. The pioneer in this field, George Septimus Smith, was boasting as early as 1871 that he had compiled a list of 300,000 shareholders—'a first-class investing public'—which could now be reached by post.[134] With minimal outlay, therefore, stockbrokers could harness the power of print to advertise their services to legions of investors. But it was only the outsiders who benefited from these changes. In keeping with its anti-competitive policies, and keen to emulate professions like law and medicine, the London Stock Exchange imposed a strict ban on advertising by its members.

As well as print, another technology was also transforming the market. From 1872, the London Stock Exchange allowed the Exchange Telegraph Company to broadcast stock prices from the trading floor via telegraph wires. The prices were received on machines—nicknamed 'tickers' because of the sound they made— which printed them on spools of tape.[135] Members and non-members alike could subscribe to the tape service, but it was the latter who harnessed its full potential. With prices now ticking out in close to real time, their offices were transformed into surrogate stock exchanges, in which members of the public could buy and sell directly in response to market conditions, just like the brokers and jobbers in the actual Stock Exchange. Those unable to come to a brokerage in person still benefited, able to place buy and sell orders by telegram or telephone. No longer fringe operators, these entrepreneurially minded brokers were increasingly becoming the public face of the stock market by the 1880s and 1890s.

The activities of the 'outside brokers', as they were increasingly known, conse-quently became a matter of extensive public debate. Their supporters claimed that they were democratizing the market for stocks and shares, providing wel-come competition to a complacent Stock Exchange.[136] But their critics stressed the dangers of dealing with the outsiders, and dismissed their businesses as 'bucket shops', little better than gambling dens.[137] A particular problem, according to the critics, was the lack of regulatory oversight. Those wanting to set up as outside brokers were not subject to vetting by the Stock Exchange's Committee for General Purposes. And from 1884, nor did they need to obtain a licence from the City of London Corporation. The absence of any kind of screening process led to concerns that the sector was becoming a haven for undischarged bankrupts and other disreputable chancers. Yet it was also to prove a magnet for some

BEING A FEMALE STOCKBROKER   51

ambitious and entrepreneurially minded women, four of whom we will now meet, who were drawn by the prospect of sizable profits.

The earliest adopter on record was **Jane Anne Walker**.[138] Born in Edinburgh around 1841, Jane had been living at a fashionable Piccadilly address since the late 1870s.[139] Previously a music and singing teacher, she had married but was now widowed, and by the time of the 1881 census, she was sharing her house with two live-in servants.[140] Jane seemingly became convinced that there was money to be made in catering to the growing appetite for speculation in stocks and shares. So, in July 1884, using £3,000 of her own money, she established the St James's Stock Exchange, on St James's Street, a few steps from her home address.[141]

It is unclear whether Walker had any male assistance in setting up her business, but in other cases, relationships with men helped women to establish themselves. **Alice Matilda Beauclerk**, née Cressey, was born in 1866 in Childerditch just outside Brentford, Essex, to Elizabeth and Benjamin, an agricultural labourer.[142] The youngest of a large family, Alice had moved to London at the age of 14, and was working as a housemaid to a printer in Marylebone.[143] How long she remained in this position is unclear, but by the mid-1880s, she had become a habitué of the upmarket Holborn Restaurant, where she met a young bucket shop keeper, Sidney Cronmire.[144] The pair hit it off and lived together for around a year before marrying in October 1885.[145] Though Sidney took this step partly because Alice 'had inspired another gentleman with a warm attachment' and he wanted to secure her affections, there was also a financial motive. Facing lawsuits from clients who were owed money, Sidney took the precaution of vesting all his property in Alice's name as part of the marriage settlement.[146] As it turned out, he successfully thwarted the legal actions by pleading that he was under 21 at the time of the transactions—earning him the mocking nickname 'The Infant Stockbroker' in the press.[147] But his relief was short-lived. His creditors now pursued a criminal prosecution, against which his age was no defence. Convicted of misappropriating his clients' money, he received an eighteen-month jail sentence.[148] Released in August 1887, still owing his creditors over £5,000, he was subsequently lost sight of, but a few years later the Official Receiver was tipped off that Sidney, who had since changed his name to Beauclerk, was running profitable bucket shops in the City of London under the names of W. Freeman and T. Nelson. If his creditors could prove that Sidney was behind these firms, they could get their hands on the assets. But when he was examined in court in 1894, Sidney claimed that these were his wife's businesses.[149]

In view of Sidney's track record—and as such devices were not unheard of— the Official Receiver found this implausible, and the matter was thoroughly sifted before Justice Vaughan Williams.[150] It seemed an open-and-shut case, as framed by Solicitor General Sir Frank Lockwood, representing Sidney's creditors. The use of Alice's name in connection with the businesses, Lockwood claimed, was nothing more than a cynical stratagem for thwarting the creditors.[151] But when

Alice was called to give evidence, she told a very different story. After his release from prison, Sidney was without means and was doing little to support himself or her. In early 1888, Alice met James Kotchie, a company promoter, financial agent, and gambler, in a City restaurant. The two became friends, Kotchie taking Alice to race meetings and lending her money from his winnings, which she used to buy cottages in East London. In 1889, he suggested she set up an outside brokerage, the profits from which she could use to pay him back his money. He advanced her £150 to establish the business and provided her with a list of names and addresses of potential clients. But when he started explaining what to do next, he quickly found out 'that she knew as much about the business as he did'.[152] Likewise, the journalist Alice hired to write her advertising copy, James Hawkes, told the court he judged her 'a particularly shrewd and business-like woman'.[153] After listening to Alice's account of her career, Justice Vaughan Williams agreed. At the conclusion of the case, he ruled that these bucket shops were indeed her businesses.[154]

In court, Hawkes had remarked that though Alice was the first female broker he had worked for, 'he was aware that there were now other women who carried on business as outside brokers'.[155] One such was **Olivia Jane Bingham**, née Masters. Born in Somerset in 1863 to Mary Ann, a butcher's daughter, and Henry, a farmer, at the time of the 1881 census, when Olivia was 17, she was still living at home.[156] But by the following year she had moved to London, marrying Frederick Bingham, a 16-year-old grocer's assistant who was living in Westminster.[157] It is unclear whether the couple separated or Frederick died, but by 1890 Olivia was in a relationship with another man. Arthur Frederick William de Courcy Bower was an adventurer who had spent time in Chile in the 1880s as an associate of the famous 'Nitrate King' Colonel John North.[158] An enthusiastic speculator, gambler, and drinker, Bower was full of schemes for making money, but it seems his biggest talent was spending it: 'he floated Companies that he never finished, he threw money away as if it were so much dirt', recalled a friend.[159] Just as James Kotchie helped Alice Beauclerk establish herself as a bucket shop keeper, so Bower seems to have played a similar role for Bingham. In the early 1890s, Bingham became the proprietor of the Holborn Stock Exchange, on High Holborn.[160] This was a job she combined with motherhood as—though not marrying—Olivia and Arthur had two children together, a daughter in 1891 and a son three years later.[161]

Just as the outside sector was a space which offered women scope to set up as brokers, so outside brokerages were quicker than member firms to provide opportunities for women to work as clerks. By 1890, the staff of the Universal Stock Exchange Company (Limited), a bucket shop established by an American, Howard Montague Mackusick, was allegedly made up of 'nearly 60 young ladies', a fact which the firm drew attention to in its advertising. Explaining the policy, management explained that women were 'more attentive, more precise, better writers, and quicker workers than men'. And rather than simply being employed to take care of the rudimentary office work, the firm boasted that the women 'fully entered into all the intricacies of a stock dealer's business'.[162] Indeed, by 1894, besides its clerks, it was also employing a manageress, named Mrs Mitchell.[163] This was not the first outside firm to employ women. In 1888, Frederick Spencer Guy, a Fenchurch Street broker, added a 'Ladies' Drawing-room' to his premises, where 'proficient Lady advisers are always in attendance'.[164] It seems likely that one of these advisers was Alice Beauclerk, Guy having employed her husband Sidney as a clerk. Moreover, Guy knew Alice and had introduced her around this time to James Kotchie, the man who would become her financial backer.[165]

As we have seen, Alice graduated to running her own firm, but for others, too, there were opportunities for progression. Born in 1865, **Lizzie Matilda Beech** was the daughter of a Drury Lane haberdasher, and by the time of the 1881 census, when she was aged 15, she was working as a primary school teacher.[166] Sometime after this she joined the Universal Stock Exchange as one of the company's platoon of female clerks, and seems to have won a position of trust with her boss, Mackusick.[167] Limited companies needed to have at least seven shareholders by law, and it was common for sole traders wanting to secure the benefits of limited liability to reach the legal threshold by giving single shares to relatives, friends, or employees.[168] In 1888, Lizzie was listed as one of just nine shareholders in the company, along with Mackusick's business partner, Henry Lowenfeld, Lowenfeld's wife, and Reginald Hodson, the company's secretary.[169] But she had bigger plans, and left the firm in 1892 along with Hodson in order to form a rival company, the Union Stock Exchange, Limited. Hodson was the managing director, on £6 10s. a week, while Beech was co-director, on £4 10s.[170] It is unclear whether Beech subsequently fell out with Hodson, or whether she merely wanted to be in charge of her own company, but the following year she departed to form a new venture, the Central Stock Exchange, Limited.

A Perfectly Easy System

Making a living from the commissions earned on small and occasional investments was no pathway to riches. In interviews, Amy Bell had warned readers that stockbroking was 'excessively hard work for a very modest remuneration'.[171] But the bucket shop phenomenon created more lucrative options for would-be brokers. Though most bucket shops also offered standard investment services, their speciality was facilitating gambling in stock prices. Clients would choose the stock they thought would go up, then deposit a small fraction of its price—often just 1 per cent—as 'cover'. If the price rose on the tapes, they could close the transaction, taking the profit together with their cover, or keep the bet open, hoping for bigger gains. If the price fell by the percentage they had staked, their cover 'ran off' and the transaction closed. The brokers who ran such businesses were not really brokers at all, their detractors claimed, but dealers. Rather than buying and selling shares for their clients as agents on commission, they were principals in these transactions, much like bookmakers. This meant that it was in their interests that their clients lost.[172] And whereas investment brokers did not advertise, bucket shops thrived on publicity, sending their circulars to thousands of households, advertising in a wide range of newspapers and periodicals, and publishing longer 'how-to' guides to investment, often distributed gratis.

It was a form of business that several women enthusiastically embraced, undercutting ideas that women shied away from riskier sectors of the economy.[173] They deployed bold publicity methods to promote the craze for speculation. Whereas the minimum cover advertised by many outside brokers was £5, several bucket shops run by women accepted smaller sums, enabling them to tap a broader speculative market, including women in straitened circumstances.[174] Jane Walker's St James's Stock Exchange advertised that it accepted £1 and £2 cover stakes, promising magical increases in wealth to readers: 'SPECULATION—One Sovereign invested as margin on a speculative account frequently doubles itself in the course of a single day.'[175] Lizzie Beech's Central Stock Exchange went further, advertising that it accepted ½ per cent cover on £100 stock—that is, just ten shillings—terms matched by Olive Bingham's Holborn Stock Exchange.[176] No one could approach a member broker with such small sums. And at a time when the commission charged by inside brokers was a common cause of complaint, Walker was an early adopter of commission-free dealing, when even many of the most successful outside brokers were still levying fees.[177] And though Bingham's Holborn Stock Exchange did charge its customers commission, it made a strong pitch to novice speculators, its ads offering to provide 'plain and simple instructions for successful speculation', and 'twelve simple rules for the guidance of speculators' which it claimed were particularly valuable 'to country operators'.[178]

Women's abilities as outside dealers were highlighted by the legal proceedings determining whether Alice Beauclerk or her husband Sidney owned the bucket shops W. Freeman and T. Nelson. Alice certainly benefited from the support of her mentor James Kotchie who, as well as helping to fund the brokerage and furnishing her with a client list, assisted her with correspondence. But much of the business Alice conducted herself, operating bank accounts under the names Winifred Freeman and Theodora Nelson, signing her own cheques, and placing orders for circulars with firms of stationers.[179] Though the judge and prosecuting barrister clearly found the idea of a lady stockbroker amusing, Alice kept her composure in the face of extensive and occasionally patronizing questioning, calmly explaining the business of outside broking (which she called 'a perfectly easy system when one understood it') to the judge. As the case progressed, the amusement continued, but its source shifted, no longer deriving from Alice's pretension in claiming to be a stockbroker, but from the fact that she was patently a much abler stockbroker than her husband. Far from it being Sidney's business, he did not even know about W. Freeman for a couple of weeks, and was, Alice remembered, 'so jealous' when he found out.[180] Employed as a clerk at rival bucket shop Frederick Spencer's, Sidney eventually lost his job there, and so Alice employed her husband as a clerk on £3 a week, his main responsibility being to watch the quotations on the ticker tape and copy them out. When asked what kind of clerk he made, she replied, to much laughter, 'a very bad one indeed', complaining that he 'thought only of pleasure'. Other witnesses corroborated her account, one noting that when spotted in the office, Sidney was 'generally smoking with his hat on.'[181] When Alice was away, it was not Sidney but another woman, the manageress Miss Bennett, who saw clients and signed the cheques.

Under Alice's direction, W. Freeman thrived, starting off at Bishopsgate before moving to larger premises on Billiter Street. After a marital row, Alice barred Sidney from the office, at which point he tried setting up his own brokerage off Bishopsgate, but he did not have enough money even to furnish the premises, so she took it on under the name T. Nelson. Sidney was not allowed to have anything to do with it.[182] With her earnings she was soon able to repay Kotchie his initial investment, and was ploughing her profits into property in East London. By the time of the bankruptcy hearings, the Freeman and Nelson firms had folded, but she remained in business, now trading as the National Securities Company, Bishopsgate, which she told the court she planned to float as a limited company. When asked whether Sidney had any chance of becoming a director in her new venture, she replied, to loud laughter, 'None whatever.' She did, however, still allow Sidney £3 a week 'pocket money'.[183]

Despite her intentions, Alice did not succeed in registering her National Securities Company venture. As with the 'stock exchanges' of Jane Walker and Olivia Bingham, her businesses were unincorporated. Lizzie Beech took a different path, however. Having been a clerk in one limited company, the Universal Stock Exchange, and having co-founded another, the Union Stock Exchange, with Reginald Hodson, she registered the Central Stock Exchange herself in November 1893, with a nominal capital of £20,000 and a modest issued capital of £2,000.[184] As managing director of the Central Stock Exchange, she successfully deployed most of the techniques in the bucket shop playbook. Start-up firms needed to persuade the public that they were not fly-by-night enterprises, so its earliest adverts in 1893 falsely claimed that the business had been established in 1890.[185] It sought to reassure readers that, far from being a gamble, speculation on the cover system offered 'QUICK and SAFE PROFITS'.[186] From January 1894, the company published a free weekly four-page circular, *Finance*, carrying a market report and the latest share prices. It also published explanatory booklets for novice speculators—*Pounds Sterling: How to Make Money and Use it*, and *Motives and Methods*—which presented stock market speculation as a sure path to riches, and acted as advertisements for the Central Stock Exchange's services. It then paid provincial newspapers to publish favourable reviews of all of these

56 SEXISM IN THE CITY

publications, quotes from which could then be reprinted in its own advertising, serving as seemingly objective testimonials.[187] While disclaiming 'blind pools' (operations where customers stumped up cash which the brokerage then pooled and used to speculate in stocks of its own choosing), this was precisely the system the Central Stock Exchange favoured, duplicity which earned it particular censure in the press.[188]

Though advertising on a grand scale, these bucket shops did not use gender as part of their sales pitch. To be a woman publicly encouraging speculation would have risked offending late Victorian sensibilities at a time when traditional ideas about feminine respectability still structured women's options.[189] As a result, they preferred to use the anonymity of the bucket shop to trade incognito. In all of the Central Stock Exchange's promotional materials, the managing director was given as 'L. M. Beech', whom press commentators took to be a man.[190] Beauclerk's advertisements adopted a form of literary cross-dressing, shielding her identity. A typical one ran: 'W. FREEMAN DOES NOT PROFESS to be infallible, neither does he insure success; but those who follow his advice are almost invariably enabled to secure GOOD PROFITS, his FORECASTS being SOUGHT AFTER by the keenest of operators.'[191] Only when a customer asked to speak to the principal did they see her.[192] Likewise, she remained in the background with the National Securities Company. There was nothing in the 'circulars, letters, and telegrams galore' with which it flooded the country to hint at its originator's sex.[193] As a result, press commentators assumed its operator was male.[194] It was only her husband Sidney's unpaid debts that set off the chain of events that led to her secret career being exposed. In the cases of the St James's Stock Exchange and the Holborn Stock Exchange, too, the sex of their founders was only uncovered in courtrooms.

Trading anonymously, these bucket shop proprietors were also trading audaciously. Surveying the various touting outside brokerages active in 1895, the *Financial Times* awarded 'the first prize for impudence' to the Central Stock Exchange.[195] Even the company's name was seen as brazen, signalling that it 'evidently intended to take the place at present occupied by the Throgmorton-street establishment'.[196] Similarly, advertising circulated by Beauclerk's National Securities Company revelled in hyperbole, promising to share with clients details of 'the doings of the inner circle', and claiming that its predictions were so accurate that they were 'sought after by giant speculators'.[197] There was therefore something more than a little subversive about these women, hidden in plain sight, using all the tricks of the trade to place themselves imaginatively at the very centre of the late Victorian speculative economy.

Conclusion

The majority of women who worked as stockbrokers in the late Victorian and Edwardian years took entrepreneurial, and sometimes independent, routes into the business, often establishing their own firms, rather than simply participating in or inheriting businesses run by husbands or fathers. Prevented, at least initially, from gaining experience by working as clerks, women were obliged to take this entrepreneurial route. But the booming outside market, unregulated and without gatekeepers, presented unprecedented opportunities for women to establish their own businesses. Several women benefited from advice, assistance, or funding from men, and clearly connections within the stockbroking world were advantageous. Likewise, an affluent background helped. Amy Bell and Gertrude Brooke both came from a well-off family steeped in imperial service. Tennessee Claflin had married the wealthy industrialist Francis Cook, Emma Robson was the widow of a railway engineer, and Jane Walker, too, seems to have come from a comfortable background. But others had more modest antecedents. Olivia Bingham was a Somerset farmer's daughter who had married a grocer's assistant, while Lizzie Beech was the daughter of a haberdasher, and before starting at the Universal Stock Exchange had been a primary school teacher. And Alice Beauclerk was an Essex's labourer's daughter who had worked as a housemaid before graduating to the world of stocks and shares. Clearly, with its relatively low start-up costs, late Victorian stockbroking presented opportunities for social mobility to a small number of women as well as to many men.

Beyond background, stockbroking also offered opportunities to women with a wide variety of personal circumstances. With greater freedom to focus on their careers, it is perhaps unsurprising that several women stockbrokers remained single, such as Beech—at least for the period that she ran the Central Stock Exchange—while Bazett Jones and Bell remained unmarried their entire lives. Beech resided with her parents in Dulwich, while Bazett Jones also lived in the family home until the death of her father, when she set up a new household with her aunt. When asked by a reporter about her life outside broking, Bell replied: 'I live quite alone...and find it a great rest.'[198] All three entered stockbroking at an early age, but widows such as Walker and Robson turned to stockbroking much later in life, the latter motivated by the necessity of supporting a daughter. Being married was not an insurmountable obstacle to business activity. Claflin returned to stockbroking after marrying, and children could also be juggled alongside stockbroking, as the cases of Bingham and Brooke indicate. In an interview, Brooke gave a glimpse into her daily routine, commuting from her Chelsea home to the City. 'My office hours are from ten to four. My husband...stays at home, and the children have gone to school by the time I leave.'[199] Women could therefore cross boundaries between 'feminine' and 'masculine' spheres much as middle-class businessmen did, rather than being confined to a rigid model of behaviour.[200]

This diversity of backgrounds and circumstances extends to the kinds of businesses these women ran. Just as historians have rejected the idea that there was a single 'type' of female entrepreneur, so there was no sole way to be a female stockbroker in late Victorian Britain.[201] Offering conservative financial services to women of modest means, seeking a more mixed clientele, or running speculative bucket shops where customers could bet on the rise and fall of share prices were all paths pursued by women in this period. Some women built their business around their gender, offering niche services to women investors, whereas others acted covertly, operating under institutional or male aliases. Though the businesses female brokers established were mostly small-scale affairs, this does not diminish their achievement: as business historians have recently stressed, 'the vast majority of male businesses were also small'.[202] In founding these businesses, they were demonstrating independence, courage, and sometimes entrepreneurial flair. That they managed to do so in a field overwhelmingly coded as masculine makes their achievement all the more remarkable.

But how did wider society respond to these daring innovations? And what would happen if it were suggested that these women might join their male counterparts inside the nation's stock exchanges? These questions are the subject of the next chapter.

Sexism in the City: Women Stockbrokers in Modern Britain. James Taylor, Oxford University Press.
© James Taylor 2025. DOI: 10.1093/9780191990397.003.0003

3

Not in the House?

Attitudes to Women Stockbrokers in Late Victorian and Edwardian Britain

'Do you really care about business and such things?'

She nodded assent.

'But why do you care?' he asked.

'For money, money, money!' She snapped the word at him like three shots of a revolver. They shocked him. He saw her eyes shining with no fictitious meaning. Now at least she was not in jest.

Julian Sturgis, A Master of Fortune (New York
and London, [1896]), 117

Thus speaks Millicent Archer in Julian Sturgis's 1896 novel, *A Master of Fortune*. A 'female amateur stock-jobber', Archer has risen from humble origins to a position of fame for her financial prowess on the London market.[1] The novel is sketchy on the details of her financial activities, but while she does not offer her services professionally, we learn that she handles the investments of her friends alongside her own speculations.[2] The novel, an instalment in Hutchinson's 'Zeitgeist Library' series, offers a picture of financially liberated femininity in the age of the 'New Woman'.[3] For all its self-conscious modernity, however, its depiction of Archer owes more than a little to traditional portrayals of women and the market. Her financial success is presented as the result not of rational calculation, but of feminine intuition: 'she is like a highly sensitive tape', explains one admiring friend: 'she feels the imminent fluctuations of stocks'.[4] Her confidence and forwardness are signs that the market has compromised her womanliness. At the end of her first meeting with the novel's protagonist, Alan Carteret, she invites him to her flat for tea. Taking his wrist, she writes her address on his cuff in pencil, leaving him feeling 'as if he had been taken possession of, branded like a stray pony'.[5] Though unusually beautiful, she tells Alan, 'You needn't take me for a woman... it bores me. I demand to be talked to as if I were a man. I'm unsexed.'[6] While her market operations are initially successful, she is unable to repress indefinitely the female propensity to gamble, embarking on a huge speculation in silver. 'I am going to run a big risk, and win a big prize', she tells Alan excitedly.[7] This is her undoing, and as she faces ruin, Alan bails her out, backing her exposed position in the market until the price of silver can recover.

60 SEXISM IN THE CITY

What is modern about the novel, what makes it part of the 1890s 'zeitgeist', is its refusal to criticize Archer's financial agency or her embrace of risk. Sturgis, an American by birth whose father headed Barings Bank, seems fascinated by the gendered play involved in a woman's navigation of the market.[8] When we first encounter Archer at a party, she cuts an extravagant figure, '[t]all, serious, superb, with her dark eyes full of dreams', so that Alan mistakes her for an actress; when she enters the City, by contrast, she dresses 'with puritanical severity'.[9] This sartorial flexibility reflects her ability to switch effortlessly between feminine and masculine codes, interspersing innocuous chatter with serious financial questioning to disorientating effect. It is after some inconsequential badinage at afternoon tea that she tells Alan of her money motivation, the words fired at Alan 'like three shots of a revolver' underlining her ability to keep men off-balance. She is not the 'Doe in the City' of William Thackeray's imagination, but 'a brand-new lioness' with 'the grace of a panther'.[10] Her financial expertise feminizes the men around her. She manages the investments of a friend, the effete artist Hubert Hobart, and the way he describes the arrangement ('She is good enough to invest my little moneys for me') accentuates the gendered reversal at play.[11] Likewise, when her financial partnership with the slick young financier Bertram Grosshart goes wrong, she tells him he is a fool and his petulant response—to try to bring about her financial ruin—feminizes him. He does it, she says, '[b]ecause he is spiteful as a pretty cross cat, or as a sort of woman'.[12] She even has this effect on Alan, whose rugged masculinity has been emphasized throughout the novel. As they plan how to shore up her position on the market, Alan's mind is more on his growing love for her than on the calculations she impatiently explains to him ('Look here! Do attend! I've been doing it on paper.'[13]) Archer's other suitor, Alan's childhood friend Tommy, is disconcerted by her talent for speculation—'it's wonderful, but I don't like it'—and would make her give it up if they were to marry.[14] But it is Alan who wins her, as he will not try to change her, despite her warning that 'I should not be submissive; I should gamble again; you would hate me'.[15]

Many reviews of the novel focused on the character of Millicent Archer, revealing significant division of opinion. *The Sketch* appreciated the fact that the book featured 'a lady stockbroker who is neither the villain nor the laughing-stock of the piece, but the very likeable heroine'.[16] The *Liverpool Mercury* found Millicent 'distinctly attractive, and her character remarkably well-drawn'.[17] Similarly, the *Daily News* appreciated Sturgis's 'brilliant sketch of an amazing woman', while *The Bookman* observed 'we like her very much'.[18] Others were less impressed, however. In a culture in which female knowledge about finance was often regarded with distaste, the *Morning Post* seemed slightly unnerved by Archer's 'remarkable eccentricities', while *The Athenaeum* was more specific, observing that she has 'a taste for speculation and a fair (and unfeminine) knowledge of "markets"'.[19] The *Saturday Review* wrote that the 'lady stock-gambler, who supplies the serious love interest of the tale, does not strongly attract us', a sentiment

NOT IN THE HOUSE? 61

shared by *The Times*'s reviewer.[20] *The Academy* noted that Millicent 'may seem a trifle too "bold"', but, thankfully, 'in the end her true womanliness asserts itself'.[21]

Such divergent views suggest that the figure of the modern financial woman had a remarkable power to polarize opinion in late Victorian Britain. While the laws on married women's property had undergone significant revision between 1870 and 1882, the legal climate remained in some ways frosty on the principle of female financial autonomy. This was vividly illustrated just weeks after the publication of Sturgis's novel. A stockbroking firm was suing two female clients, one married and one widowed, for unpaid losses the duo had racked up by speculating in South African mines during the boom of the previous year. When the case reached the Court of Queen's Bench, the ladies received short shrift from Lord Chief Justice Baron Russell of Killowen, who ruled in favour of the plaintiffs. In his closing comments he asked: 'What business had they to go speculating on the Stock Exchange; especially what right has a married woman to go speculating on the Stock Exchange? It is monstrous.'[22] His scolding words were widely recycled in the press—apparently approvingly—under headings like 'To LADIES WHO SPECULATE' and 'LADIES AND SPECULATION'.[23] Yet, just as the figure of Millicent Archer had her admirers in the press, so Russell's opinion was challenged in some quarters. *St James's Gazette* muttered that this was 'the first time that we have heard of sex distinctions in gambling', while Dublin's *Social Review* insisted that 'if gambling is bad in itself', then 'it is equally as bad for a man as for a woman'.[24] *The Echo* made the strongest case for equality, seeing no reason why women should not have 'an equal opportunity in engaging in money market transactions as men'. Inverting the traditional argument that women should confine themselves to speculations on the matrimonial market, it argued that married women, thousands of whom brought fortunes to their husbands, 'have as much right to speculate with their own money as men who have nothing, but who speculate in marrying rich women'.[25]

In a climate in which the very presence of women on the stock market as investors and speculators could be questioned by a Lord Chief Justice, how would the arrival of the altogether more disturbing figure of the female stockbroker be regarded? Though some were willing to argue the principle of gender equality on the financial markets, would they continue to do so when it came to the prospect of women's membership of stock exchanges? Answering these questions provides important new perspectives on the gendering of finance at a critical point in the expansion of the stock and share market. Facing persistent stereotypes about the defeminizing impact of finance, stockbroking women had to think very carefully about the public image they projected. At the same time, they had a surprising amount of freedom to operate within male business networks. Yet it was one thing for a woman to deal with members of stock exchanges, and quite another for her to become a member herself, as this chapter will show.

Changing Places

Fin de siècle debates about the 'New Woman' pointed to a growing 'instability of femininity', as traditional gender roles came under new levels of scrutiny.[26] Driven in part by the growing demographic imbalance between the sexes, which meant that—in the words of *The Queen*—there were 'not enough husbands to go round', there were signs of a significant cultural shift.[27] Though tensions between older and newer ideas about 'womanliness' continued to fizz, cruder ideas about 'separate spheres' certainly weakened as advice literature and popular fiction, both long-time exponents of this creed, became much more positive about girls' education and work.[28] The popular press weighed in too, 'What Shall We Do with Our Daughters?' proving a topic editors could rely on to generate heated debates among their readers.[29] From an early point, women's advances into stockbroking were understood as one facet of a broader move towards middle-class women's emancipation in the world of work.[30] Amy Bell's relatively high profile meant that the 'lady stockbroker' was frequently cited as a marker of progress. At the annual meeting of the Mid-Northamptonshire Liberal Association in 1890, for example, Winifred Lady Robinson enthused that 'there were two lady aldermen...then there were innumerable lady doctors; a lady lawyer; a lady stockbroker...Woman's sphere would soon have no limit.'[31] Similarly, the *Woman's Suffrage Calendar* for 1894 observed approvingly that 'London has its lady landscape gardener, lady dentists, lady record agent, lady insurance agent, and lady stockbroker with her office in the city.'[32]

By contrast, most men's responses to the earliest reports of female brokers ranged from flippancy to disbelief. When Bell's arrival in London was first noted, the *Western Mail* joked that similarities between the language of markets and of romance—'engagements', 'settlements', 'advances', and 'declinations'—would make her vulnerable to practical jokes played by young male brokers.[33] Around the same time, when Jane Walker's identity as the proprietor of the St James's Stock Exchange became known, *St Stephen's Review* observed that '[a] lady lawyer is a phenomenon calculated to shake the strongest male nerves, but a Stock Exchange in petticoats is still more startling.'[34] Some had trouble accepting that the lady stockbroker really existed. Echoing Thackeray's 'Doe in the City' from half a century earlier, *The Globe* could not 'believe that the rough spirits of bulls and bears have so far been softened as to enable a gentle deer...to live happily in their midst.'[35]

Such jokiness masked an undercurrent of nervousness. The woman stockbroker embodied several ideas—feminine financial competence, the prospect of financial independence, and freedom to pursue new careers—that challenged some deep-seated prejudices. Citing 'lady stockbrokers' among other novelties, one columnist bemoaned 'the feverish eagerness with which women hasten to proclaim their equality with men in almost every profession, business, or recreation'.[36] 'What shall we do with our boys when our girls shall have ousted them from their present occupations?' asked another, prompted by the news that the Bank of England was to start employing female clerks.[37] These anxieties were crystallized in 1895 by the legal proceedings which uncovered Alice Beauclerk's career as an enterprising bucket shop proprietor, which attracted much press coverage. Perhaps surprisingly, it seems journalists had little difficulty believing her account. Reports of the case were typically headlined 'The Lady Stockbroker', and one courtroom sketch was captioned 'The Lady Stockbroker & her husband-clerk' (see Fig. 3.1).[38] In this image, Alice takes centre stage, with Sidney relegated to a small inset. This reversal of traditional spousal roles—troubling enough in itself—had another dimension. The tight correlation in Victorian discourse between gender roles and sexual identity meant that challenges to men's primary economic status were experienced as emasculating. 'Women's claim to the "masculine" roles of breadwinner and independent self', argues Margaret Beetham, 'threatened not only men's economic power but their sexuality'.[39] Asked to clarify Sidney's role at W. Freeman, Alice explained that his duties were strictly in the public office, not in her private room. The Solicitor General pressed her:

Fig. 3.1 Alice and Sidney Beauclerk, *Penny Illustrated Paper*, 20 April 1895, 246. From the British Library Collection, shelfmark MFM.M40509

'The man you had sworn to honour and obey, do you mean to say that if you saw him in your private room writing a letter you would be so hard-hearted as to say out you go?' (Laughter.)

'I should certainly.'

'He knew his place too well?'

'Well, if I went out I used to lock the door and take away the key.'[40]

The vision of a dominant wife and emasculated husband may have generated laughter in court, but there was an underlying tone of unease, perhaps sharpened by the timing of proceedings, running almost in parallel with the trials of Oscar Wilde and their challenge to dominant sexual codes.[41] Moreover, although ruling that Alice was telling the truth, Judge Vaughan Williams could hardly have been more scathing about the type of business she ran. It was 'of a very unpleasant character, a mere gambling business, a business carried on avowedly merely for the purpose of inducing people to gamble in stocks and shares.'[42] That women should be behind such schemes was considered deeply distasteful. The *Westminster Gazette* sarcastically subtitled one of its reports 'ANOTHER CAREER FOR THE NEW WOMAN', while the *Sussex Agricultural Express* thought that Alice's story, and the revelation that there were other women doing a similar business, was 'calculated to astonish even those who are "in the City".'[43] Getting to the heart of the matter, an anxious *Coventry Evening Telegraph* enquired: 'Are men and women changing places?'[44]

The hostility unleashed by the case indicated the problems female bucket shop proprietors faced when their dealings were made public. This was true, too, of Lizzie Beech. In running a publicly registered company, Beech had to file details of her business with the Joint-Stock Companies Registry, which left her vulnerable to exposure by different means. The City editor of *The Sketch* became aware of the Central Stock Exchange when it kept sending its circulars to a clergyman friend, even after he died. He visited the Registry to do some digging, and found, to his surprise, that the firm's 'managing director'—he insisted on placing the title in inverted commas—was a woman. Worse, this self-proclaimed 'experienced company' was made up of just seven shareholders, the minimum required by law, and all were women. Of the company's £2,000 paid-up capital, £1,994 was held by Beech herself. Sarcastically noting that this was 'all so interesting—from the point of view of the "higher education of women"', *The Sketch* clearly hoped that publicizing these details would be sufficient to discredit the company.[45] Yet other newspapers failed to pick up on the story, and Beech managed to preserve her anonymity, important for the continued viability of her business. The mid-1890s proved a turbulent period for the bucket shops, their access to the ticker tape cut by the Exchange Telegraph Company on the orders of the London Stock Exchange, resentful of the competition posed by the outsiders.[46] Though two of the biggest outside firms, George Gregory & Co. and John Shaw, folded, the Central Stock Exchange survived. Switching address several times, beginning on Fetter Lane, moving to King William Street, and ending on Cannon Street, its advertising in the Edwardian years continued apace, foregrounding the firm's longevity ('The "Central" was founded in 1893, and the present managing director has controlled it from the first'), using bold headlines to grab attention ('MONEY SAVED IS MONEY EARNED', 'GOOD TERMS ON ALL METHODS'), and riding the wave of the latest trends in speculation ('OPTIONS ON THE FRENCH METHOD').[47]

Of course, those stockbrokers who traded openly as women did not have to worry about exposure, but they did have to be very aware of their gender image. Longstanding fears about the defeminizing effects of involvement with finance were sharpened by fresh concerns about the 'mannish' and 'masculine' New Woman.[48] Even Sturgis's more positive portrayal of Millicent Archer rested on the assumption that women's involvement in finance entailed a complex, self-conscious, and ever-shifting performance of gender. The supporters of women stockbrokers were therefore at great pains to stress that stockbroking had not made them any less wholesomely feminine in appearance and manner, a tactic later adopted by militant suffragists for similar reasons.[49] The *Women's Penny Paper* described Bell as 'young and fair, with a bright cheerful manner which betokens absence of worry'; her features looked like they 'belong to one who spent her days studying art or in the fresh air, rather than watching the rise and fall of stocks and shares in London'.[50] A sympathetic paragraph in *The Star* noted with relief that she 'has a voice free enough from the City metallic ring, nor has the contemplation of figures at all interfered with the pleasantly round outlines of her face'.[51] These efforts to stress femininity could be somewhat heavy-handed. A profile of Emma Robson in *Woman's Life* was headlined 'CAN A PRETTY WOMAN SUCCEED IN BUSINESS?'[52] Other times they verged on the ridiculous. An interview with Lady Cook in *Woman's Weekly*, in which she emphasized that she was 'essentially a womanly woman, devoted to my husband and home', was interrupted by the entry of a servant, and the interviewer overheard the stockbroker 'with all a wife's tender solicitude, giving instructions about Sir Francis's slippers being warmed ready for him on his arrival'.[53] Readers familiar with Cook's radical feminist positions in the 1870s might have been surprised at the different note she was now striking.

The considerations that went into the curation of an appropriate public image are particularly clear in the case of Gertrude Brooke. Journalists described her in terms similar to her predecessor, Bell: one recounted being 'agreeably surprised' on paying her a visit. 'She is not at all the kind of woman one would expect, being gentle and pretty and quiet.'[54] A photograph of Brooke which appeared in *The Sketch* was a clear attempt to project authority, expertise, and femininity

66 SEXISM IN THE CITY

Fig. 3.2 Gertrude Brooke, *The Sketch*, 13 November 1912, 167. © Illustrated London News Ltd/Mary Evans

(Fig. 3.2). The telephone held to her ear suggests her mastery of new business technologies and her connection both to the market and to clients, while the hat, scarf, and frilly cuffs reassure viewers that she retains her feminine sensibilities.[55]

Indeed, the need to 'perform' femininity in this way did not necessarily hamper women's stockbroking activities in the masculine City. Historians of businesswomen in other sectors have rejected the idea that women traded 'in a semiprivate way, outside of the networks of male traders'.[56] This certainly applies to women stockbrokers, who very much operated within the same business ecology as men. Trade directories were an important means of attracting business, and women appeared in these volumes alongside men. Jane Walker was the first woman to list a stockbroking business in the *Post Office Directory*, her St James's Stock Exchange featuring in the 1885 edition, along with the more specialist *Stock and Sharebrokers' Directory*.[57] Most other women who traded as brokers followed suit, though several emulated Walker in giving no clues as to their sex, as was the case with 'W. Freeman', 'Central Stock Exchange Lim. (L. M. Beech, man. dir.)', and 'E. P. Robson'.[58] The first woman to list openly as a woman was 'Mrs Olive Jane Bingham' in 1894.[59] Amy Bell—whose business was so reliant on word-of-mouth recommendations—chose not to list till 1900.[60]

Some women also proved able to navigate a changing regulatory landscape in order to protect their businesses. Legislation in 1891 exempted contract notes between brokers from stamp duty, but in 1899 this exemption was restricted to members of stock exchanges.[61] In response to lobbying from aggrieved provincial stockbrokers, the Board of Inland Revenue established a register of outside stockbrokers at Somerset House, members of which would, for the purposes of the Act, be treated 'as if they were members of a Stock Exchange'.[62] To get themselves registered, brokers had to give as a reference the name of a broker belonging to a stock exchange, and provide any additional information requested by the Board to prove that their business was genuine.[63] Registration thus conferred respectability on outside operators, and it was therefore significant that some women brokers—first among them Bell—successfully had themselves registered with the Board. It seems likely that this is what prompted Bell to start listing in the *Stock and Sharebrokers' Directory* in 1900, registered brokers receiving an asterisk next to their names to distinguish them from those who remained unregistered. When Brooke took over the business in 1910, she retained this registered status, while in Preston, Marianne Bazett Jones enjoyed the same standing.[64]

All outside brokers depended on developing connections with London Stock Exchange brokers to transact their business on the official market. As suggested by their ability to register with the Board of Inland Revenue, several women brokers did this. Amy Bell forged a strong and lasting working relationship with the inside firm Messrs Whiteheads & Coles, a connection which she passed on to Brooke.[65] Brooke claimed that the male stockbrokers she did business with treated her 'splendidly': 'I have never found my invasion resented.'[66] The well-connected Lady Cook painted a similar picture, claiming that bankers were happy to send customers her way and that she had 'met with no opposition in the City'.[67] Cultivating good relations with institutions outside the capital in order to reach more distant investors was also important. Many London brokers relied on provincial banks to put business their way, splitting the commission on the deals, and Lizzie Beech exploited this system successfully. Some customers in the north of England ended up doing business with her Central Stock Exchange as a result of 'a casual conversation' with their bankers.[68]

Women dealt with City authorities in the course of their businesses on similar terms to men. Those women who ran bucket shops transacted with the Exchange Telegraph Company to rent the ticker tape machines which fed them market prices through the day. Beauclerk, Beech, and Bingham were all clients of the company at various points in the 1880s and 1890s, until the London Stock Exchange pressured the company to cut off non-members.[69] Though there was nothing they could do about this, on other occasions, women negotiated directly with the London Stock Exchange itself on matters concerning their businesses, albeit not always successfully. When a dispute arose between a client of Jane Walker and the member broker she had employed to transact the client's business, Walker wrote to the Committee for General Purposes asking them to adjudicate, a request which they declined.[70] And, as noted in the previous chapter, Bell—along with many other male brokers—wrote to the Committee when a proposed rule change on splitting commission threatened her business.[71] Women were also employers of men in various capacities. As we have seen, Alice Beauclerk engaged pen-for-hire James Hawkes to write her promotional materials, and it is likely that Lizzie Beech had similar assistance to produce her weekly circular, *Finance*.[72] When Alice took on a second brokerage, T. Nelson, she hired a man, a Mr Bolton, to manage it, while Jane Walker also employed a man to manage the St James's Stock Exchange.[73]

Yet operating in a masculine business environment was not incompatible with a strong feminist identity. Bell had deep links with women's causes: when she wrote to the Committee for General Purposes, it was followed up a few days later with a letter of support from leading suffragist Millicent Fawcett.[74] She was involved in the Women's Protective and Provident League which promoted trade unions for women, gave talks to the Women's Progressive Society and the Gentlewomen's Employment Bureau, participated in suffrage marches, and on her death was recognized by the *Woman's Leader* as one of the pioneer 'workers for the women's cause'.[75] Though she did not refer to these activities when talking about her professional work, others were more vocal advocates of equality. Lady Cook, who had a long pedigree of campaigning for women's rights, explained to the press that she had decided to return to stockbroking because she wanted 'to show women that they are quite as capable of undertaking such work as men are'.[76] Women were entering fields like law and medicine. 'I would show them that they are capable of finance.' She hoped her example would encourage parents to put their daughters 'into the world'.[77] Gertrude Brooke echoed these sentiments, arguing that there was 'an interesting career in the financial world for women. They have more intuition than men and as a rule are more persuasive. They are not lacking in caution, and they certainly are the best bargainers'.[78]

These were not empty words: several women brokers used their position to give employment opportunities to other women. From as early as 1888, when such a thing was almost unheard of in the stockbroking world, it was noted that Amy Bell employed a 'lady clerk'.[79] This soon became common practice among women brokers: Lady Cook only employed 'lady clerks', while an interview with Marianne Bazett Jones noted that, 'in keeping with the firm', her 'office boy' was 'a young lady'.[80] In the bucket shop sector, where it was common to take on larger teams of clerks to process the high volume of transactions generated by frequent trading, female proprietors were also early employers of women. When Beauclerk first established her W. Freeman brokerage, she employed two or three women as clerks, and when she moved to larger premises on Billiter Street, the business expanded so much that she claimed she was soon employing 'thirty or forty lady clerks' (and just one office boy).[81] Beech, who started as a clerk at the Universal Stock Exchange, appears to have had several female clerks as both employees and friends. The 1901 census shows three clerks staying with her and her father in

Bournemouth, at least one of whom, Edith Minnie Charles, seems to have been a clerk with the Central Stock Exchange and was also one of the company's shareholders.[82] Ten years later, the Wheeler family were living with Lizzie in Dulwich, including Jane Wheeler, who since at least 1900 had been the Central Stock Exchange's chief clerk, responsible for filing the company's annual returns with the Board of Trade.[83] In several cases, women stockbrokers were keen to train clerks to develop independent careers in stockbroking.[84] Beech's protégé, Edith Charles, set up as a stockbroker in 1902, while later Edith Maskell, one of Bell's clerks, also became a stockbroker in her own right.[85] Thus, women stockbrokers were helping, albeit in a modest way, to bring other women into the City.

The Men of the Stock Exchange

The huge growth in the securities market in the nineteenth century rendered the centre of this market, the London Stock Exchange, the subject of increasing comment. Though regarded as a 'great financial machine' and 'the pulse of the country', it nevertheless continued to attract criticism.[86] The 1870s saw two parliamentary investigations prompted by concerns over fraudulent market practices. While their reports largely backed the Stock Exchange's method of self-governance, the second did recommend reforms to restore public trust, including opening the building to visitors, and incorporating the Stock Exchange by royal charter to make the institution more publicly responsible.[87] Correctly surmising that there was little political appetite to enforce these measures, however, the Stock Exchange ignored them. Yet this meant that it remained vulnerable to being painted as a monopolistic institution hostile to the public interest.[88]

One of the Stock Exchange's main tactics to deal with such criticism was to maintain a liberal admission policy. Unlike Paris and New York, there was no restriction on the number of members until 1905, and even then, at over 5,500, the cap was set at a considerably higher level than these other exchanges.[89] Moreover, very few applications—between 1886 and 1903 only 1 per cent—were rejected by the Committee for General Purposes.[90] This was a major factor behind the 'endemic fluidity' of the Stock Exchange, with a constantly fluctuating membership and large numbers of modesty capitalized firms.[91] The lack of entry barriers led to a degree of ethnic diversity, which consolidated timeworn antisemitic critiques of the stock market: in the 1870s there were reportedly around sixty to seventy members of foreign birth, mostly German, and among them many Jews.[92] The Stock Exchange was also seen as a magnet for the upwardly mobile: as one disdainful critic put it in the late 1870s, the modern stockbroker 'has decided social aspirations', setting up 'a showy establishment' and becoming a member of 'one or two good though not always first-rate clubs'.[93] But in a sign of its growing respectability, the Stock Exchange also started to attract a new class of member, stockbroking rapidly becoming, in the words of novelist John Galsworthy, 'the chief glory of the upper-middle class'.[94] And it began recruiting from even further up the social scale: by the turn of the century, up to thirty sons of peers were members.[95]

Though liberal in its admission policy, the culture inside the Stock Exchange was anything but, and became increasingly dominated by a particular type of 'hegemonic masculinity': conformist, conservative, and competitive.[96] Back in the 1840s, one chronicler of City life had noted the sartorial boldness of younger stockbrokers, many of whom dressed to 'make a sensation'.[97] By the end of the century, however, the Stock Exchange had become famous for its conservative dress code of tailcoat and top hat. Anyone tempted to flout it—by wearing a light-brown suit, for instance—found themselves frogmarched out of the building and invited to reconsider their outfit.[98] With this came a staunch Conservativism. One Edwardian observer of the Stock Exchange noted that 'the overwhelming majority of its members are Tories, of the bluff, boyish, breezy type, always ready to cheer and demonstrate and sing "God Save the King" on the shortest notice'.[99]

The longstanding association of the Stock Exchange with rowdiness remained, and for some continued to be evidence of the moral turpitude of its members.[100] But it was more often understood as a sign of healthy boisterousness, and increasingly linked with the public-school ethos of physical toughness. At the start of the nineteenth century, the nation's seven public schools catered to a tiny aristocratic elite, but by 1890 there were seventy-two of them, shaping middle-class masculine norms along very particular lines.[101] Hierarchical, conformist, and often cruel, the public-school culture was designed to promote both group loyalty and self-reliance. Manliness was displayed through athletic prowess rather than intellectual ability, and certainly not aesthetic sensibility. Boys were taught to prefer the company of males, and behaviour associated with the opposite sex, such as emotional disclosure, was condemned as effeminate.[102]

This homosocial culture was increasingly exported to other contexts, whether places of leisure such as gentlemen's clubs, or work environments such as the Stock Exchange. Members moved seamlessly between these settings, one jobber, Murray Griffith, describing the Stock Exchange as 'the Best Club in London'. Joining 'the House'—as the Stock Exchange was familiarly known—as a clerk in the 1880s, Griffith was initially overawed by the 'giants' of the markets with whom he was now trading, but was surprised to find that 'all the big men acted more like fathers to me than competitors'. He valued this 'schoolboy comradeship in the hard battle for success', and learned that a simple code of values prevailed: the public school ethos that everyone must 'play the game'.[103] 'Playing the game' had a literal dimension, with the public-school love of sports thoroughly assimilated into the House. One admiring observer, the journalist Roland Belfort, stressed the varied sporting pursuits of members, and doubted whether 'any other Stock Exchange could present such a brigade of fine athletic men as the London establishment'.[104] When markets were dull, Belfort elaborated, members organized 'weird sports and indulge in antics which would delight the denizens of any smart nursery', a form of cricket with bats and balls crafted out of the morning newspapers proving a particular favourite.[105] Nicknames, another feature of school life, were also enthusiastically adopted, often highlighting members' appearance or habits ('Teeth and Hair', 'The Amorous Goldfish', 'Annual Bath', 'The Animated Flea'). In the public schools, name-calling was one facet of the culture of bullying, a 'gendered practice' which involved rejecting anything linked with femininity. The weak or the studious were invariably given female names to mark them out as 'not real boys'.[106] That so many Stock Exchange nicknames were also feminized suggests that something very similar was taking place here: 'The Gaiety Girl', 'Lady Godiva', 'Fairy Footsteps', 'The Bearded Lady', 'Nun Nicer', 'Mary', 'Lucy', 'Polly', 'Miss', 'Virgin', and 'Charley's Aunt'.[107]

Hegemonic masculinity was also enforced through brute force. As with earlier periods, the violence of the trading floor in busy times remained a defining feature of how the Stock Exchange was popularly imagined, propagated as much by members as outsiders.[108] Being able to withstand the rough and tumble, and treat it as simply part of the fun, was core to Stock Exchange masculinities. In an essay on the Stock Exchange written for a popular guide to London, one member, Godefroi Ingall, wrote with some relish that during a panic, the scenes on the floor were 'most exciting':

> Jobbers throw themselves into a central melee, haul each other out of the margin of the mass of members, shout each other down, bid for, or offer stocks or shares in the most frantic manner. Instances have occurred where perspiring members have had to change their collars and even their shirts several times during business hours; others have had clothes torn, and so on. The vocal organs, too, are often seriously affected for a considerable time.[109]

This was not the abstract, rational market described by the economists, but an emphatically corporeal market, where elbows, fists, and larynxes were the tools of the trade. Though much smaller, provincial stock exchanges were presented in similar terms by their members: 'if times are good, pandemonium reigns, brokers yelling their offers and bids, telephone bells ringing, members banging their desks to attract attention; hundreds, thousands of pounds' worth of securities changing hands in a minute'.[110]

Looking back on his career in the 1920s, Murray Griffith regarded the London Stock Exchange as 'the real and true example of a socialistic institution, inasmuch that it gives everyone a chance of getting on, if he has the energy and brains so to do'.[111] Such presentations of the Stock Exchange as a meritocracy hinged, of course, on ignoring women, and the way in which the very culture of the market depended upon their exclusion. The idea that women could have any legitimate

THE STOCK EXCHANGE OF THE FUTURE.

Fig. 3.3 'The Stock Exchange of the Future', *The Sketch*, 8 November 1899, 131.
© Illustrated London News Ltd/Mary Evans

place in such an environment was widely regarded as an absurdity, even by those who knew that women were already operating successfully as outside brokers. During the bankruptcy proceedings that confirmed Alice Beauclerk as a bucket shop proprietor, Alice's counsel claimed that several other women were running similar businesses in the City. Judge Vaughan Williams interjected, 'Not in the House?', prompting laughter from the court. The lawyer replied, 'They have not got there yet', to further laughter.[112] The courtroom hilarity echoed in the press whenever the subject of women stockbrokers came up. In 1899, an illustration on *The Sketch*'s financial page of 'The Stock Exchange of the Future' (Fig. 3.3) depicted a number of women on the floor of the exchange engaging in polite conversation with brokers and jobbers. The ironic accompanying commentary 'hoped that the view of the House as it might be will commend itself to the Managers'.[113] The institution's dress code means that the incongruity of women's presence among the men in their top hats and tailcoats is immediately obvious. The joke was that allowing women into the Stock Exchange would transform its character, and thus undermine its purpose. The battleground has been turned into something resembling Hyde Park on a Sunday afternoon; the masculine market has been neutered.

Indeed, visualizing women on the trading floor was so difficult in part because of conventions of dress. Anticipating the arrival of Walker, Bell, and company by several years, the 'lady stockbroker' first appeared in Victorian Britain in fanciful form, as a suggestion for an outfit in Ardern Holt's 1879 guide, *Fancy Dresses Described: Or, What to Wear at Fancy Balls*:

> Short pink silk skirt bordered with white satin, on which are printed the several kinds of stocks and gold coins; low bodice of pink silk, over it a low polonaise of star-spangled gauze, caught up with roses, the top of the bodice trimmed with gold coins and fringe; gold belt at the waist; gold net on the head with coins; a cornucopia carried in the hand, out of which stocks, money, and roses seem to spring; high-heeled pink shoes; black mittens.[114]

A popular pastime in Victorian society, fancy dress balls often engaged with social as well as sartorial trends, and the inclusion of this outfit in Holt's guide—probably inspired by Woodhull and Claflin's efforts in New York—underlines that it was becoming possible to imagine women in this role. Yet, as Rebecca Mitchell notes, though fancy dress balls allowed women and men to play with contemporary trends in a mildly subversive way, there was a clear distinction between representation and impersonation in such outfits.[115] The 'lady stockbroker' dress incorporated *representations* of finance—stocks, gold coins—rather than allowing its wearer to inhabit the world of finance. The cornucopia, or horn of plenty, links the 'lady stockbroker' to Lady Fortune, who was traditionally depicted holding a cornucopia scattering coins.[116] And the financial aspects of the outfit are feminized by the inclusion of the pink skirt, roses, and high-heeled shoes. Thus, women—as ever—can symbolize the speculative economy but cannot occupy it. Wearing this outfit would only serve to highlight the difference between the 'lady stockbroker' and an *actual* stockbroker. As one review of Holt's guide unnecessarily remarked, 'it is quite clear that this dress could never be worn on the Stock Exchange'.[117] The outfit thus neutralized the woman stockbroker's threat to gender norms.[118] Without doubt professional authority was—as historians of other occupations have argued—intimately associated with the body and its clothing.[119]

The logic of exclusion also depended upon differentiating the market for stocks and shares from other types of market in which women were already very visible. The developing consumer culture of the late Victorian years, epitomized by the luxury department stores of London's West End, was giving women a greater public presence.[120] Though their activities as shoppers were subject to constant male scrutiny and criticism, one thing upon which most commentators agreed was women's innate 'propensity for bargaining'.[121] While this risked driving women to buy things they did not need or which were of inferior quality just because they were cheap, haggling was at the same time recognized as a 'skilled process'.[122] As a result, Stock Exchange members and their supporters had to draw a distinction between women's bargain-hunting expertise and the kinds of skills required on the trading floor. In an article complaining of widespread public

74 SEXISM IN THE CITY

ignorance of the mechanics of the Stock Exchange, the *City Leader* ridiculed the idea that, when dealing with jobbers, the broker was

> expected to beat down the price quoted, with the threat of going to an opposition shop. If this were the process, or anything like it, we should be strong advocates of a Ladies' Stock Exchange. Not only would they be extremely successful in this sort of dealing, but they could have such delicious talks at lunch and after-hours over 'such a bargain in Mexican Rails', or that 'wonderfully cheap remnant of Trunks'.[123]

The masculine realities of Stock Exchange dealing—a subtle and high-stakes game of bluff between broker and jobber—did not play to feminine strengths, such writers insisted.[124] Another columnist supposed that the idea that the Stock Exchange could be opened to women 'can only be intended as a joke'.[125]

The prospect of admitting women did not seem entirely foolish to all commentators, some of whom poked gentle fun at the view of the Stock Exchange as a 'sacred' masculine space.[126] More pointedly, though lukewarm on the issue of women's suffrage, the *Lady's Pictorial* thought that if women proved that they could trade successfully outside the House, 'there seems no reason why their admission to Capel-court should be long delayed'.[127] Some rejected the idea that admitting women would undermine the market; others were bolder still, arguing that women would actually improve the 'atmosphere' of the House. One *Woman's Herald* columnist believed that 'by their conscientious rectitude and high principle', women would 'do much to sweep out the Augean stables' of the Stock Exchange.[128]

Women stockbrokers themselves had mixed feelings about membership. Lady Cook was enthusiastic, stating in an interview that she looked forward to joining and anticipated little opposition: 'I shall be so businesslike and shall show such strength that they will want me amongst them.'[129] Bell was probably the most credible candidate, but she seems not to have seriously entertained the idea of membership. After her death, a friend claimed that her diffidence was a result of her delicate health.[130] Even among their advocates in the press, there were several who believed that women would be a disruptive presence in the masculine market. Though Phebe Lankester was supportive of Bell's endeavours to help women investors, she thought her joining the Stock Exchange was not a realistic proposition. 'Of course no lady would be admitted within this charmed circle', she wrote. The merest glimpse 'of a petticoat on the flags of the great emporium of stocks, bonds, and debentures, would put to flight all thoughts of business, or, perhaps, dissolve the whole assembly of black-coated brokers'.[131] If these comments were laced with irony, the journalist who took on Lankester's 'Penelope' penname from the late 1890s was less ambiguously conservative, doubting that women brokers would have 'the requisite nerve to face the odds in a time of panic'. She concluded that they were 'far better out of the heat and turmoil of the Stock Exchange'.[132]

If such views were chiefly based on preconceptions about the London market, then they applied equally to the nation's other stock exchanges. Memories of half an hour once spent inside the Liverpool Stock Exchange on the invitation of a broker friend made one unnamed female writer for *The Echo* 'shrink from the bare idea of a lady spending her days in the midst of such an excited and boisterous throng'.[133]

But what was regarded as a humorous fantasy—or dreadful nightmare— threatened to become an imminent reality in June 1904 when a woman applied for membership of a stock exchange. This was not in London, or indeed Liverpool, but Dublin. Daniel Bulger, a member of the Dublin Stock Exchange, had been incapacitated through illness for a couple of years and during this period his wife, Anne, had kept the business going. To allow her to continue running the firm more effectively, Anne now wanted to join the Stock Exchange. Aiding her case was her reputation for 'exceptional business capacity', and the high profile she enjoyed more generally through her involvement in charitable causes.[134] Indeed, elements in the Irish press were supportive of Anne's bold move, arguing not only the specific case but the more general one. Here, ideas about women's bargaining skills came to the fore. Dublin's *Evening Telegraph* thought that there should be 'no difficulty about her admission' since women were 'specially qualified for business dealings; they have often an instinct for a bargain and a caution in securing good value that the mere man can only envy'. Bulger deserved 'all encouragement and a hearty welcome'.[135] And though causing something of a 'sensation' in Dublin business circles, it was reported that her application 'was not unfavourably received so far as individual members are concerned'.[136] Despite this, the institutional response was less sympathetic. Although it allowed her application to hang on the wall of the exchange for the customary ten days, the committee informed her that it was 'impossible for them to entertain it'.[137] At the end of the ten days, she was summoned before the committee and invited to withdraw her application, which she did.[138]

Nevertheless, the episode pointed to somewhat divergent business cultures in Dublin and London. If Bulger had won at least some support among local brokers and journalists, the view from London was less sympathetic. The *Financial Times* did not take Bulger's application at all seriously, playing with the familiar zoological imagery of the market to dismiss the idea out of hand. 'We have already "bulls" and "bears" and "stags". Apparently we are now going to have "dears"', it sighed.[139] Though the paper did not see fit to mention the topic again, the *Daily News* was more interested, sending a reporter to canvass the opinions of the brokers and jobbers of the London Stock Exchange on the question of female membership. The responses he received were 'exclamatory rather than explanatory', with the respondents speaking 'briefly and in italics'. 'Preposterous and impossible!…No lady has ever applied, and it would certainly be [a] waste of time.…No, sir, never! Never! Never!! Never!!!'[140]

London's attitude was consistent with other major financial centres which remained determined to exclude women. In New York, women continued to set up brokerages in the 1880s and 1890s, yet they remained as firmly outside the official exchanges here as in the UK.[141] Marie Pollard, a widow who had established a New York brokerage in 1890, announced her intention to apply for membership of the Consolidated Stock Exchange, the main rival to the New York Stock Exchange. Described in the press as a 'Female Jay Gould', she claimed that male brokers were jealous of her success, and feared that as a result they would oppose her application.[142] If she did go through with it, she was seemingly unsuccessful, and by 1892, she had ceased broking.[143] Indeed, the culture of Wall Street was as aggressively masculine as in London, brokers and their clerks cultivating a rakish, sporting persona hostile to women.[144] Over in Paris, though the Bourse was open to male members of the public, the authorities waged a constant campaign to keep women out.[145] Those wanting to gain entry were left with only one option, described by journalist and economist Mathilde Méliot in 1897. Arriving at the Bourse in order to take notes for a financial column only to be turned away, she returned home and changed into a male outfit, including a bowler hat. So attired, 'I proudly came back ... and no one suspected anything. Until the sound of the bell, I shouted, I debated, I assessed, I quoted, I bought, I raised funding, I sold, I delivered, I switched, I made arbitrage, I traded, I swindled like a true man.' Understandably, Méliot did not make a habit of such ruses, and subsequent attempts to get close to the trading floor in ordinary dress remained fraught with difficulty.[146] Stock exchanges, it is clear, remained heavily gendered spaces hostile to incursions by women.

Invasions

Although the masculine sanctity of the nation's stock exchanges was defended as successfully in the United Kingdom as elsewhere, there were some small exceptions. History was made in 1897 when the wives and sweethearts of members were allowed onto the floor of the London Stock Exchange for the Diamond Jubilee celebrations, an event considered so remarkable that it was remembered by a *Financial Times* columnist forty-five years later.[147] The same columnist also recalled when the celebrated actress, Ellen Terry, after a visit to the Bank of England with her broker to transfer some stock, decided that she would like to see inside the Stock Exchange. Despite being told such a thing was impossible, Terry wandered up to the door and, finding no waiter on duty, stepped into the House, looking around with great interest. The members recognized her immediately 'and cheered her heartily'. After a minute or two, she 'bowed herself out with her irresistible smile'.[148]

Of course, these infringements posed no threat to masculine authority, but more serious challenges were to come in the Edwardian period when radical supporters of the campaign for women's suffrage targeted stock exchanges as appropriate sites for disruption. In May 1908, during Winston Churchill's by-election campaign, members of the Women's Social and Political Union, led by Mary Gawthorpe, made 'a great raid' on the Dundee Stock Exchange. Gawthorpe then proceeded to hold a meeting at the door of the Exchange Hall, making a speech then fielding questions from the assembled merchants. Though facing plenty of heckling, at the conclusion of the meeting, Gawthorpe 'was cheered again and again'.[149] The following year, a small division from the Women's Freedom League 'invaded' the Exchange Flags, the open-air trading venue for Liverpool merchants. Armed with a large chair for a platform, they gave speeches to a throng of businessmen, many of whom came down from adjoining offices to listen. Muriel Matters, who had recently gained notoriety as one of the women who had chained themselves to the grille in the Ladies' Gallery of the House of Commons, so impressed members of the Stock Exchange that they invited her into the building to continue her speech. She was allowed to mount 'the sacred rostrum' where she spoke vigorously, making free use of the hammer for emphasis, and winning a resounding ovation and praise for her 'argumentative prowess'.[150] The London Stock Exchange was not subjected to even this kind of temporary incursion, however. In June 1908 a small party of suffragettes held a demonstration in Throgmorton Street outside the exchange before attempting to gain entry, but were thwarted.[151]

A more successful—though purely imaginative—invasion had been achieved earlier that year with the publication of Olive Malvery's novel *The Speculator*. If Sturgis's heroine, Millicent Archer, was only an amateur dabbler, then Malvery's has professional aspirations, and the novel deals with the question of gender and the stock market in ways that warrant close attention. As Nancy Henry, the first scholar to study the novel, notes, this is a 'transgressive' text which 'dramatizes the possibilities, limitations, and dangers' of a woman's movement between private and public spheres.[152] Malvery, who had relocated to Britain from her native India in 1900, had sprung to fame in 1904 with her sensational series of undercover reports for *Pearson's Magazine*. Adopting a variety of disguises—flower girl, organ grinder, barmaid—Malvery offered the middle-class readers of *Pearson's* a titillating glimpse of 'the hard and unhappy lives' of 'London's poorer daughters'.[153] Copiously illustrated with photographs of Malvery in her various costumes, the reports were positioned 'somewhere between serious social enquiry and play-acting'.[154] Indeed, it was the latter element that distinguished Malvery from the legions of other 'lady explorers' of urban poverty.[155] And it was an idea that she translated into fiction with *The Speculator*, her first novel.

The protagonist is Helen March, a former actress and now wife of Richard, British consul at 'a remote Arabian port'.[156] Richard's eyesight is deteriorating and he has been warned that if he continues to work, he faces the prospect of blindness, but he has no choice in the matter after losing his life's savings in a

78 SEXISM IN THE CITY

bank failure. Reading about 'the success of various men who seem to have built fortunes by astute transactions on the Money Market', Helen, who lives in Surrey because her constitution will not tolerate conditions in the Middle East, hatches a plan to retrieve the family's fortunes.[157] She will become a speculative stock-broker, and make enough money to allow her husband to return home and to support their two young children. Her friend and confidant Paul, who works in a bank, hates the idea: she would find herself 'in competition with the most astute and unscrupulous brains that modern life produces. How on earth could a woman hope to profit by becoming a stock-broker, even supposing such a thing to be possible?'[158] She demurs, reasoning that if a woman could 'educate herself for a business life, what would there be to prevent her from following such a life successfully?'[159]

To that end, she subscribes to a dozen financial papers, and gets a job as a typist at a large outside brokers, where the pay is poor, but the work gives her insights 'into the whirlpool of the Money Market'. She takes evening classes at a school of accountancy to give her a grounding in arithmetic, and tops up her knowledge by employing a stockbroker to coach her 'in finance and business routine'.[160] It is hard work, for her 'ignorance was simply colossal'.[161] But after four months, she is ready to become a broker, which—echoing Mathilde Méliot's strategy for entering the Bourse—involves discarding her own identity and inventing a new one: 'the immaculate and somewhat dandified Otto Martini', a Greek man with a 'trim little black moustache', shiny boots, and spats.[162] Paul asks why she cannot just make money by speculating as a woman, but Helen explains: 'I must have a prosperous office, I must be my own broker, thereby saving the enormous fees these men charge'.[163] Her ultimate aim is to become a member of the London Stock Exchange, for an outsider 'could not, she thought, hope for the chances that might fall to those actually within the magic circle'.[164] This strategy makes the question of gender central to the novel's storyline.

Malvery, a supporter of the constitutional wing of the suffrage movement and a member of the Pioneer Club for women, stresses that Helen is up to the daunting challenge she has set herself. When describing her activities in the City, Malvery refers to her as Otto, not Helen, and uses masculine pronouns, underlining the success of the transformation and the mutability of her protagonist's gender identity. She takes an office on the Strand and kits it out to look 'like the private office of a successful City man'.[165] The walls are covered in maps and plans of railways, while directories and reference books sit on the mantlepiece and line the shelves. She hires a young clerk, Frank, who does not know her secret, and places the following short advert in the London papers: 'A gentleman of financial experience advises ladies and gentlemen on money matters, and the purchase of stocks and shares, on a system which is likely to lead to handsome profits'.[166] The results exceed her expectations: she receives over a hundred letters in three days, mostly from women desperate for advice, 'who seemed born into the world to be the victims of any adventurous scoundrel they might chance upon.[167] Little do these clients realize that they are victims of a double deception: not only are they not dealing with 'a gentleman of financial experience', Helen having taken the briefest of crash courses in finance, but also they are not even dealing with a gentleman. The irony is that although they would feel tricked if they knew they were dealing with a woman, it is this which guarantees their safety. Her clients have been badly treated by male brokers before: one complains that she had 'yet to find the stock-broker who doesn't want to make money out of women'.[168] Helen, by contrast, though appalled by her clients' naivety, vows that even if her advice turns out bad, she will sell all her possessions to compensate them. But her investment advice is in fact highly profitable, and bonus payments she receives from grateful clients, including a rich Peruvian speculator, enable her to open a second office in the heart of the City, and to stump up the capital needed to join the Stock Exchange.

This is the crowning moment of her plan, but it is curiously underplayed in the novel. Her entry to the floor is not described; indeed, only one scene is set inside the Stock Exchange, where 'Otto' wanders around the various markets listening to talk and checking prices. All of a sudden, there is a cry of 'stranger' and a journalist who had somehow gained access to the floor is spotted and violently set upon. Panicked and confused, 'Otto' is caught in the middle of the action, and is carried

> like a straw on the flood towards the door. There he saw a group of men drag-ging at a figure which looked broken and limp....He looked wildly round; a sort of bestial fury seemed to flame from the sea of faces round him, and a horrible hot darkness fell over him.[169]

Helen staggers outside and collapses in the street where a crowd gathers. She fears her disguise has been exposed, but it has not, and she departs in a cab, escaping back to her office, bruised and exhausted. 'What brutes men are!' she exclaims to Frank, her clerk.[170]

Malvery's melodrama reinforces the belief that women are vulnerable figures in the masculine maelstrom of the Stock Exchange. Though Helen rejects Paul's argument that the incident proves the Stock Exchange 'is no place for a woman', we do not see her there again.[171] Soon after this incident she meets the powerful American financier, Ransom P. Hill, and the stockbroking plotline is eclipsed by Helen's quest to locate secret papers in the possession of the half-mad, drug-taking, Anarchist confidential secretary to Hill's business rival, which will enable Hill to thwart a Russian conspiracy against Japan. Now Helen is recast in a sup-porting role: 'She thrilled to the thought that she might be to this man a friend and helper.'[172] Doing so involves shifting the scene of action away from the City and into the mean streets and opium dens of the poorer districts of London, which are described in much more vivid detail than the inside of the Stock Exchange.

80   SEXISM IN THE CITY

Whereas other novels of the time used cross-dressing themes to present masculinity and femininity as socially constructed roles based more on costume than biology, *The Speculator*, as Silvana Colella notes, is 'preoccupied with reasserting Helen's adhesion to femininity even as the plot traces her numerous ventures into masculine territories'.[173] The novel therefore serves to reinforce traditional gendered ideas about finance. Though the plot holds that a woman, if sufficiently determined, can educate herself about stockbroking, for Malvery this is unnatural. Early in the novel she explains that 'a woman is not by nature fitted for a business career unless some untoward circumstance throws her out of her natural surroundings and thrusts her into a position where it must be fight or fall'.[174] Indeed, Helen's exceptionalism is stressed throughout: as Paul says after her initial stockbroking success, 'you have done what one woman in a million could hardly have accomplished'.[175] Helen successfully disguises her femininity in the City but she cannot suppress it, which means she runs the constant risk of exposure. Overwhelmed with relief at a tense but successful speculation, she drops her head on the table and starts sobbing. ' "Hold on to yourself, sir", said Frank with that contempt which a man feels for any exhibition of emotion.'[176] Ransom Hill's arrival—he reminds Helen of 'a perfectly sighted rifle, slim, grim-looking, and capable of dealing death strokes'—unambiguously recodes finance as masculine.[177]

Towards the end of the novel, as Helen winds up her broking affairs and plans to 'disappear from the financial horizon for ever', she has mixed feelings about the resolutely domestic future that lies ahead of her with her husband, now returned from the Middle East.[178] But by its final chapter, the novel has done nothing to suggest that the broker's office, let alone the Stock Exchange, is a more appropriate location for Helen than the kitchen, cooking mince pies with the children.[179] For Malvery, then, becoming a stockbroker necessitates becoming a man, but this can only ever be a temporary performance, dependent on an exhausting suppression of woman's natural femininity. By relying on the gender-swap device, she ultimately makes stockbroking seem a fantastical impossibility for women. This is certainly how most reviewers at the time interpreted the novel: 'a highly, not to say wildly, improbable tale'; 'an exciting, impossible, enthralling story'; 'much seems singularly unreal'.[180] Subsequent commentators have agreed: in her analysis of the novel, which she calls 'a fantasy of success and empowerment', Colella concludes that 'a great deal of fictionalizing was necessary in order to imagine the protagonism of women in the money market'.[181] Yet framing women's presence on the Stock Exchange as a fantasy overlooks the activities of those women who had, either covertly or openly, been working to gain a toehold in the world of finance for the previous quarter of a century. Malvery's tale, though transgressive in its imaginings, ultimately served to reinforce some very traditional ideas about women and finance.

Professions for Women

The ideology that insisted women had no place in the world of finance paradoxically equipped them to make progress in another fast-developing domain of the business world. Bookkeeping had long been seen as an essential component of women's domestic duties, and household advice manuals familiarized middle-class wives with increasingly rigorous and demanding accounting systems which inculcated frugality and economy.[182] To an extent, such training reinforced patriarchal authority in the home, designed as it was to deter perceived feminine extravagance in spending while leaving male assets and liabilities unaccounted for.[183] Yet, as Stephen Walker argues, accounting also 'represented a calculative medium which permeated the boundary between the private and public spheres', with women performing bookkeeping roles in family firms long before companies like the Prudential began employing female clerks.[184] Because it had long been associated with women's 'natural' roles and aptitudes, there was scope for bookkeeping to become accepted as a legitimate public occupation, and feminist groups capitalized on this. From the early 1860s, the recently established Society for Promoting the Employment of Women began offering bookkeeping classes, and its efforts contributed to the extensive 'feminization' of bookkeeping by the late nineteenth century.[185]

These growing pools of female bookkeepers—like women clerks more generally—were attractive to employers because of their cheapness, and their existence was fundamental to the gendered professionalization of accountancy in the later nineteenth century. Men began forming associations to demarcate their functions and elevate their status, first the Institute of Chartered Accountants in England and Wales (ICAEW) in 1880, and then the rival Society of Accountants and Auditors (SAA) five years later.[186] But at the very moment that they were formalizing the gendered distinction between male accountancy and feminized bookkeeping, it was being challenged. One early alumna of the Society for Promoting the Employment of Women's bookkeeping classes, Mary Harris Smith, became the accountant for a large incorporated company. She began receiving so many offers of work that in 1887 she took offices and established herself as a public accountant.[187] Whereas her contemporary Amy Bell was content to trade outside the London Stock Exchange, Harris Smith applied to the recently established SAA for membership as soon as she started business on her own account. Though rebuffed, Harris Smith did not quietly accept the decision, and campaigned tirelessly over the coming years for her right to recognition.[188] The two main English associations of accountants were eventually forced to concede the principle of admitting women to ensure that the Board of Trade did not oppose their statutory registration bill in 1909.[189] Though the measure was not enacted, which meant that the societies did not actually start admitting women,

82 SEXISM IN THE CITY

the prospect remained within reach. Indeed, a newer organization, the London Association of Accountants, admitted its first female member, Ethel Ayres Purdie, later that year.[190]

Evidently, women stockbrokers had made significantly less progress than their accountant sisters in the battle for institutional recognition and status. Moreover, simply finding an entry point into a stockbroking career remained very difficult for women. Though Bell and some others did employ female clerks, as we have seen, there were obvious limits to the opportunities they could offer. That demand for such jobs far outstripped supply was vividly illustrated in 1892, when an advert appeared in the London dailies that the well-known outside firm George Gregory & Co. was hiring twenty-five 'lady clerks' at £5 per month, and that applicants should apply at the company's offices at 11 a.m. that morning.[191] Before that hour, the premises were crowded with women, and the 'unwonted spectacle of throngs of petticoats in a City by-way soon attracted the attention of the police', who stationed officers at the end of the road to turn away other applicants. A *Financial Times* reporter estimated that between 400 and 500 women showed up in person, with many more who were unable to come to the offices writing in.[192] Yet all were destined for disappointment: the advert turned out to be a hoax, the firm offering a £25 reward the next day for information on the parties responsible.[193]

By the Edwardian years, even some suffrage supporters were beginning to criticize the number of young, middle-class women who were gravitating to the City. Novelist and playwright Constance Smedley disparaged their lack of 'business sense', which she believed doomed most of them forever to remain clerks. 'The business which is being transacted round them seems to float over their heads while they tap out letters and take down notes in absolute ignorance of and indifference to the sense of what they are doing.'[194] Annesley Kenealy, active in the suffrage movement and an advocate of, among other things, ju-jitsu for women, was keen to reroute such women's ambitions.[195] Rather than aspiring to becoming 'stockbrokers or insurance agents', and ending up stuck in badly paid jobs as typists, they should seek business opportunities which played more to their inherent strengths. The City offered profitable 'domestic possibilities', Kenealy explained, because all of its offices, warehouses, and shops needed cleaning. The City's charring businesses were currently run—badly, Kenealy believed—by men, many of them 'Poles and Russians', and this presented enterprising women with an opportunity. If the *Woman's Herald* had thought that women stockbrokers would cleanse the 'Augean stables' of the Stock Exchange, then Kenealy's vision of women's purifying effect was both more literal and more prosaic: a female-run charring business would ensure 'the disappearance of that general air of domestic dishevelment so apparent in City premises', introducing 'a hundred dainty domestic touches…to the business man's surroundings'.[196]

Eventually, the lack of progress on the stockbroking front began to seem disappointing. In a 1909 article for *The Queen*'s weekly feature on 'Public Work and

Women's Employment', Mary Greenwood wondered why there were not more women stockbrokers. She believed that though women started 'from zero' due to their lack of grounding in business basics, it was likely that the 'business instinct' was latent in the minds of many, and only needed encouragement. But by spending so much of her article listing the numerous essential and desirable attributes of the successful stockbroker—she must be energetic, with an alert mind and the habit of watching 'human action and thought', tactful, courteous, shrewd in bargaining, of good, sound health, with 'more than an ordinary good education', particularly in economics, and possess a substantial capital—Greenwood may have inadvertently deterred any budding stockbrokers who happened to be reading. Moreover, she was unhelpfully vague on the practicalities of starting out. The best advice to a beginner was 'be sociable', since many of a broker's clients were former school friends and relatives. And though stating that the '"raw" girl' would have to spend at least two or three years 'in the office of an experienced person' in order to learn the business, Greenwood had no idea whether Bell or any other female stockbroker who might be in business would take pupils. She speculated that there might be more opportunities for women stockbrokers 'in the northern centres'.[197]

Indeed, by this point, Marianne Bazett Jones had taken over the running of her father's Preston-based stockbroking firm. But Bazett Jones, a Conservative-supporting anti-suffragist, was not at all keen to act as a recruiting sergeant. For a woman like her, 'brought up to stockbroking', any other occupation was unthinkable. But she seems to have discounted the possibility that a woman not steeped in finance since childhood could pick it up, flatly informing the *Preston Herald*'s interviewer that as a career for women, stockbroking was, 'generally speaking, unsuitable'.[198] Even women who had a family connection to stockbroking could lack confidence in their prospects. In 1904, a widow of a Glasgow stockbroker wrote to Frederick Dolman's syndicated column 'How to Succeed in Business', asking whether he thought she could establish herself as a broker in her own right. Dolman replied that he knew of 'two or three London ladies' doing such a business, but admitted that 'Glasgow is not London'. His advice—'Why not sound some of your late husband's clients as to whether they would entrust their commissions to you'—seemed little more than common sense, but that she asked the question at all hints at the uncertainties women felt in this context.[199] Taking stock of the range of employment opportunities opening up by 1911, *The Englishwoman's Year Book and Directory* published a table detailing '80 Professions for Women'. It included accountancy, dentistry, and lecturing, but, tellingly, stockbroking was not mentioned.[200]

To be sure, only a minority of those women who turned their hand to stockbroking in these years managed to establish viable and long-lived businesses. The most obvious success story was Bell, who traded continuously from the start of 1886 till 1910, when she handed over her business to her cousin Brooke. Bell

84 SEXISM IN THE CITY

seems to have been able to support herself comfortably in the final ten years of her life, staying in the luxury Ivanhoe Hotel in Bloomsbury with her lady's companion at the time of the 1911 census.[201] She did not make a fortune from stockbroking, however, leaving just £850 when she died in 1920.[202] Lizzie Beech also enjoyed a long broking career. After fifteen years in operation, her Central Stock Exchange finally ran into difficulties at the end of 1908. Facing multiple legal actions from customers she was unable to pay, Beech took the last resort of pleading the Gaming Act, arguing that as these were gambling transactions, they were unenforceable in law.[203] The strategy failed and the company closed its doors.[204] Yet this did not signal the end of her career. She found a job as a clerk in the Investment Registry, a business run by Henry Lowenfeld, one of her former employers at the Universal Stock Exchange Company.[205] She also found love, marrying William Berghoff, a German-born language teacher and widower, in late 1911, aged 46.[206] Marriage did not limit Lizzie's independence: she did not give up work, continuing at the Investment Registry into the 1920s, where she ended up managing a department.[207] She seems to have enjoyed a comfortable standard of living, remaining in her Dulwich home until her death in 1945, a few months short of her eightieth birthday, leaving £1,869.[208]

Though not in stockbroking for as long as Bell or Beech, labourer's daughter Alice Beauclerk profited far more from it. The National Securities Company appears to have been her third and final venture, ceasing to advertise in 1895.[209] But ploughing her bucket shop profits into property paid off handsomely. By the 1901 census, she and Sidney were living comfortably on their own means in Essex, with their infant son Gerald, a cook and two live-in servants.[210] When Alice died in 1922, she left the substantial sum of £29,175.[211] But if Alice quit broking having made good money from it, others were seemingly less successful. Jane Walker's St James's Stock Exchange soon swallowed the initial £3,000 investment she had put into it, and she borrowed a further £8,000 from friends to keep the enterprise going. But after less than two years' trading, the business failed and Walker petitioned for bankruptcy. Her failure, she told the court, was due to her (male) manager, who 'neglected to take cover from clients, made bad debts, and incurred liabilities in her name without her knowledge'. After declaring bankruptcy, she returned to her former career of teaching music.[212]

Several entrepreneurially minded women who tried stockbroking seem to have found better opportunities elsewhere. Olivia Bingham's Holborn Stock Exchange ran into financial problems in the mid-1890s, leaving her needing to raise further funds on a bill of sale in 1894, and an attempt to sue a fellow outside broker in a dispute over £38 deposited as cover for speculation failed.[213] Though the business continued into early 1895, it seems to have faded thereafter, and a break with her lover Arthur, who married a rich widow in 1895, encouraged her to try a different path.[214] While Arthur remained a resolute speculator, later acquiring fame as one of the first men to 'break the bank' at Monte Carlo, Olivia switched to a more typical—and respectable—occupation for her sex, establishing a lodging house in Kensington, and remained in this line of work in the long term.[215] Emma Robson's stockbroking career was also brief, though possibly in part because of a turbulent private life. Months after establishing her business, she married Thomas Renwick, a clergyman's son, who deserted her soon afterwards and emigrated to the United States.[216] By 1901, Emma was living in Wimbledon with her sister and daughter from her first marriage, and had certainly quit stockbroking, listing her occupation in that year's census as 'medical gymnast and electrician'.[217] These did not work out either, and she subsequently ran a London–New York Tourist Agency, became secretary of the Ladies' Kennel Association, and worked as a journalist before emigrating to Canada, where she became involved in politics, successfully securing election as president of the Women's Voters' League.[218] Tennessee Claflin's first spell as a broker in New York had not lasted long, and though attracting plenty of publicity, her return to stockbroking in the late 1890s as Lady Cook does not seem to have lasted much beyond the death of her husband in 1901.[219] 'Clients were not numerous', a journalist later noted, and in widowhood, Cook redirected her considerable energies into the campaign for women's rights, addressing huge crowds of supporters on platforms in London and New York.[220]

Anne Bulger also thrived after she quit stockbroking following her rebuff from the Dublin Stock Exchange. The firm took on a new partner, Patrick Kirwan, son of the former manager of Dublin's National Bank, who had no problems joining the Stock Exchange, and the firm continued as Messrs D. S. Bulger & Kirwan.[221] Soon after this, her ill husband died and Anne, now in her early sixties, decided on a daring new venture. Moving to the spa town of Lisdoonvarna in the west of Ireland, she bought up a hotel, renovated and expanded it, and reopened it as Thomond House, a luxury hydro complete with golf links.[222] Taking on the management herself 'as a kind of hobby', she made a success of the venture, and continued to manage the hotel till her death in 1923.[223] Meanwhile, her husband's brokerage might have fared better had the Dublin Stock Exchange accepted Anne's application to join. As it was, Kirwan made heavy losses in 1912 by speculating in Marconi shares, and fraudulently converted clients' money to try to plug the financial holes. His defalcations discovered, he was jailed for three years.[224]

In Preston, Marianne Bazett Jones traded successfully, despite a rift that developed between her and her younger brother Henry. Possibly resentful at Marianne taking control of the firm when their father fell ill, Henry departed in 1908, establishing a rival firm, H. Bazett Jones Junior, a couple of minutes' walk from his sister's office.[225] Undaunted, Marianne continued to run the main firm as sole partner until her retirement in 1919, when in her early fifties.[226] At this point, the two firms amalgamated under Henry's sole control.[227] Her decision to retire may well have been due to ill health, given her death soon afterwards in 1922.[228] When Henry died in 1933, his obituary incorrectly noted that on leaving school 'he joined his father's business, together with his sister, and since his father died had

86 SEXISM IN THE CITY

been in full control of the business.'[229] Marianne's own stockbroking career was thus erased from the record.

Conclusion

Marianne's erasure points to a broader process of discovery and forgetting in these years. Though attracting episodic press attention on account of their novelty, their small numbers meant that women stockbrokers often drifted out of public consciousness altogether. It was telling that in 1904, the author of a survey of women's 'invasion' of the world of work stated: 'As far as I have been able to ascertain, we must go to America for the woman stockbroker.'[230] The few women who remained in the public consciousness, such as the successful American speculator Hetty Green, were taken to be exceptions that proved the rule of female financial incompetence: as one paper argued, 'Mrs Green is one among a million of her sex.'[231] Exacerbating this tendency was the fact that many female-run brokerages were short-lived affairs, women often finding better opportunities elsewhere. Among the disadvantages faced by women, one of the biggest seems to have been the attitude of clients, most of whom expected to be advised by a man. This was certainly the view of one journalist, who argued that women stockbrokers struggled more to establish themselves in London than in New York because of 'the more conservative view of financial affairs taken by British investors', who felt 'that ladies were not, for various reasons, adapted to the business of stockdealing.'[232]

This in turn underlines a broader failure in these years to reframe traditional public discourse on women and finance. To be sure, there were signs of change towards the end of the period. Farrow's Bank—a self-styled 'people's bank' founded by energetic entrepreneur Thomas Farrow—attracted much press attention in 1910 by establishing a bank for women, staffed entirely by women.[233] The bank was managed initially by May Bateman, then by Kate Reilly, who, argued the *Daily Herald*, refuted the idea 'that women are incapable of competing with men under ordinary banking conditions.'[234] At the same time, women were establishing themselves as financial authorities, most notably journalist and suffragist Lucy Helen Yates, who graduated from writing cookbooks to authoring popular investment guides including *The Management of Money: A Handbook of Finance for Women* (1903).

Yet there were clear limits. None of the big joint-stock banks were interested in following Farrow's experiment, at least not until war forced their hands.[235] And there were also signs of a subtle male backlash against the idea of women's financial authority. Keen to capitalize on the growing importance of women investors, in 1910 the *Financial News* started a new weekly column called 'Marjorie and Her Money', catering to 'lady investors'.[236] Not to be outdone, one of the paper's rivals,

The Financier, quickly followed suit with a rival column, 'Finance for Women'.[237] Yet both series were penned by men. 'Marjorie' was not the author of the *Financial News*'s column but its intended reader; the advice was dispensed by Ellis Powell, the paper's editor.[238] Indeed, Powell held very traditional attitudes on women and money, complaining in 1912 that 'I have been unable to discover ladies able to write about finance'.[239] If women were at last being acknowledged as financial subjects with the capacity to learn about money, they were nevertheless being told that what they needed was male expertise.

In this climate, the exclusionary policies of the nation's stock exchanges were uncontroversial, seeming little more than common sense. The issue of women's membership of these institutions existed on the periphery of the movement for women's suffrage which exploded in the Edwardian period. Though suffragists sometimes contested the arguments of the male brokers, they did so in ways that risked entrenching the idea of gendered difference in the market. To what extent these circumstances would survive the dislocations of the First World War and the achievement of votes for (some) women in 1918 is the subject of the next two chapters.

Sexism in the City: Women Stockbrokers in Modern Britain. James Taylor, Oxford University Press.
© James Taylor 2025. DOI: 10.1093/9780191990397.003.0004

4
Careers for Your Daughters
Women Stockbrokers, 1914–1939

> The very appearance and atmosphere of the City seem to have changed, and many of the young men now serving at the front would find it difficult to recognise their old 'City', as they knew it, in the altered conditions. Strange indeed would they find the London stations during the hours at which they were wont to arrive and depart. The dozens of typists of those days have been replaced by thousands of neatly-dressed, bright young women, who appear to have become an integral part of the life of the City.
>
> *Daily Telegraph*, 21 October 1916, 12

The demands of the First World War had a major impact on the gendered make-up of the nation's workforce.[1] Though the presence of women in munitions factories and the uniformed services has often seemed the most noteworthy transformation to historians, the clerical sector actually saw the greater rise in female employment.[2] Nowhere was this more apparent than in the City of London. Marked for some time as more-or-less exclusively male space, the rapid feminization of the district by the middle of the war was becoming the subject of much comment. The 'bright young women' observed by the author of the *Daily Telegraph*'s women's page were visible not only during rush hour: at lunchtimes, the City's restaurants and cafés were 'now so filled with women customers that a man enters shyly and abashed', according to the *Daily Mail*.[3] New ventures were established to cater to this fresh market: the Rainbow, a women-only self-service restaurant providing hot meals for eightpence opened on Upper Thames Street in August 1916, while by 1918, it was remarked that shops supplying 'feminine fineries' were 'springing up in the City in all directions in order to cater for the woman clerk.'[4]

The perceived merits and failings of the female clerk—especially the bank clerk—became a favourite talking point in the press. Working under trying circumstances, and given ledger or counter work after a month or two's training 'which the average youth rises to in his second or third year', they were initially criticized in certain quarters for being slow and making mistakes.[5] But though some bankers continued to argue that women were unfitted for all but the most basic tasks, many managers found their new workers intelligent, conscientious, and quick to learn.[6] Their qualities astounded a manager of the London and

South-Western Bank. 'I do not think the war has brought a more remarkable development—in fact, it is a miracle—than the revelation of the capacity of women in banking.'[7] Banks consequently hired women in large numbers: by war's end, women represented 29 per cent of Lloyds Bank staff, while even the staid Bank of England had over 1,000 female clerks.[8] And though their pay did not typically reflect it, they were trusted with more and more responsibilities by their employers.[9] In 1916, it was announced that the London City and Midland Bank was appointing a woman as a branch manager, albeit 'in a remote country district'. Though the bank's rivals were disinclined to follow suit, a representative of the Midland confirmed that thirty to forty additional women were being trained up for management in case of further losses of male staff.[10] Added recognition came in 1917 when the Institute of Bankers opened its examinations to women. The following year, over a quarter of the 1,218 candidates were female.[11]

But after the war, as servicemen were gradually demobilized, there was a concerted push to purge banks of women.[12] Though many women were in fact able to stay on, they found themselves relegated to the bottom of the pile: opportunities for progression became much scarcer as traditional attitudes reasserted themselves.[13] Even the Midland Bank renounced its wartime experiment with female branch managers. Giving evidence to a Royal Commission on the Civil Service, the bank's general manager, Frederick Hyde, was adamant that the typical female employee could not be trained for higher positions. 'She likes a job where she knows exactly what she has to do', he explained. When pressed on the point, he blamed the public: 'this is a country with very old prejudices and a bank has to be the servant of the public, not the master. We discovered that when we had women managers there was a good deal of reluctance on the part of the customers to go and discuss business with them.'[14]

To some extent, as this chapter will explore, stockbroking presented a similar picture over these years, of a temporary increase in employment and opportunities, followed by a post-war backlash. Yet there were also differences. Whereas banks were large centralized and bureaucratic institutions, whose branches were responsible to head office, brokerages were much smaller private firms embodying the attitudes of their partners. Although these attitudes were often traditional when it came to women's capabilities, brokers occasionally proved more open to female talent. Furthermore, if a female clerk found her employers unwilling to promote her, it was possible to set up her own business, a course that was no longer feasible in the highly capitalized world of joint-stock banking. As a result, the years from 1914 represented a turning point in the history of women stockbrokers. Family firms now became a more common pathway into stockbroking for women, and at the same time, a number of clerks successfully made the transition to establishing their own businesses. Moreover, several London firms began hiring women as commission agents, who were tasked with bringing in extra business on a split-commission basis.

90 SEXISM IN THE CITY

As well as growing numbers of women involved in stockbroking, there was also significant geographical diversification. Whereas women's stockbroking activity had until now been mainly confined to London, the interwar years saw female-led brokerages in—among other locations—Bradford, Burnley, Bury, Leeds, and Rochdale in the north, and Bath, Exeter, and Nuneaton in the south and midlands. It is striking that much of women's stockbroking activity was focused in small to medium-sized towns and cities, rather than the metropolis, or the large urban centres of the midlands and the north. These tended to be towns without stock exchanges, and this was not coincidental, as the absence of a stock exchange, and the gendered prejudices that went with them, created a more open business climate in which women could establish themselves.

The financial world thus offers a valuable if unfamiliar vantage point from which to evaluate the course of women's rights following enfranchisement. The interwar period was once regarded as witnessing the demise of the drive for equality, the radicalism of pre-war women's movements dissipating after the attainment of partial and then full enfranchisement in 1918 and 1928 respectively, replaced by a 'new' feminism which accepted rather than contested ideas about sexual difference and separate spheres.[15] More recently, historians have questioned such narratives, arguing that though activism may have changed, it did not disappear, instead adapting successfully to altered circumstances. The nature of the debate shifted, partly due to a 'mainstreaming of feminist and equalitarian principles after suffrage' that is itself a measure of the significant progress that had been made.[16] Much of this revisionist work concentrates on political activity and associational life.[17] But shifting the focus onto finance provides further evidence supporting the idea of the interwar years as a period of dynamism and development when it comes to the options open to women. As we will see in this chapter, which introduces eleven women who worked as stockbrokers in the interwar years, financial careers were becoming more viable, and some of these women were developing a public profile enabling them to advocate for finance's ability to emancipate their sex.

Routes into Stockbroking

Though, in the early twentieth century, London remained the country's chief market for stocks and shares, stockbrokers were to be found all over the country. As the range of possible investments grew, the role of the stockbroker as an expert intermediary expanded, with investors increasingly seeking out those who could give specialist advice, rather than bankers or solicitors who lacked the same detailed grasp of the market.[18] The major towns and cities had substantial populations of stockbrokers, the majority of whom belonged to the local stock exchange. But towns which lacked stock exchanges also boasted smaller numbers of professionals, who often combined stockbroking with the work of an insurance or estate agent, accountant, or auctioneer.[19] In the early 1920s, Falkirk was home to three such brokers, Fleetwood in Lancashire two, while Falmouth in Cornwall had just the one.[20]

Once established, it was rare for a provincial stockbroker to move to a different town. Though, like London brokers, they could have a geographically scattered clientele, they were primarily dependent on local custom, people who valued personal contact. Being known and trusted locally was therefore a precious commodity.[21] This allowed provincial brokers to buck the broader business trend whereby, though family firms were common, 'very few...survived for more than one generation'.[22] Brokerages could become longstanding presences in a town, outlasting their founders and being handed down through several generations.[23] Sons and nephews were the mostly likely relatives to become involved in a family stockbroking business, but there is evidence of growing involvement from women, at least outside London. The death of the head of a firm could prompt his widow to keep the business going. When prominent Leeds stockbroker John Lawson died in late 1914, his widow Annie Lawson (b. 1860) continued the firm, John Lawson & Co., with her husband's old partner Walter Lofthouse.[24] Yet there is little evidence that she was active in the firm, and by 1921, her partnership with Lofthouse was 'dissolved by effluxion of time', with Lofthouse subsequently continuing the business on his own.[25]

Daughters, however, were more clearly participating in provincial stockbroking businesses. This had been a rarity in earlier years, with Marianne Bazett Jones in Preston an exception discussed in Chapters 2 and 3, but it was becoming more common. For these women, as with Bazett Jones, growing up in a stockbroking environment set them on financial careers. Fig. 4.1 shows **Doris Ellen Mortimer**, who was born in 1898 into a stockbroking family, her grandfather William having founded W. Mortimer & Son in Exeter in 1842.[26] The firm had subsequently passed to her father, Thomas, and Doris joined the business as a clerk just before the First World War, soon after leaving school. She later recalled that she was 'born and bred in the business': for her, stockbroking was 'hereditary in the family'.[27] It was similar for **Oonah Mary Keogh** (b. 1903), shown in Fig. 4.2. Her father Joseph had established a brokerage, Messrs Keogh & Co., in Dublin in 1902.[28] Oonah later described being 'soused' in stocks and shares growing up, learning about the business from Joseph, with whom she regularly played golf and tennis.[29] Despite this, she did not initially plan to follow her father into stockbroking. She considered careers in art—briefly studying at the Metropolitan School of Art in London—and politics, but changed course when her father invited her to join the family firm.[30] **Phyllis Moscrop Robinson** (b. 1895) was another who grew up in a financial environment, her father Hugh, who was the

Fig. 4.1 Doris Mortimer, *The Vote*, 18 April 1924, 121. From the Women's Library, London School of Economics

son of an accountant, having begun offering stockbroking and insurance services in Bury in Lancashire in the early 1890s.[31] By 1921 Phyllis had started working as a clerk at her father's firm.[32] In nearby Rochdale, **Adela Taylor** (b. 1898) was brought up by her uncle Enoch Dawson, who had established a brokerage in 1900. On leaving school in 1913, Adela worked in office jobs, latterly as a bank clerk, but in 1917 she left to join her uncle's business.[33]

Absence of competing male siblings smoothed the passage into stockbroking for these women, making fathers more likely to encourage them into the family business. Bury stockbroker Hugh Moscrop Robinson had three daughters but no sons, while Oonah Keogh had seven living siblings, all of them female except for Arthur, six years her junior, who was still a child when Oonah was invited into the family firm.[34] Doris Mortimer did have an older brother, Thomas, but he elected to train for a medical career instead of following the family profession.[35] In Rochdale, the situation was slightly more complex. Enoch Dawson had no children of his own, and adopted his niece Adela when she was 4 years old, making her the only child in the household. Dawson did also employ Adela's older brother Samuel, who had remained living with his parents, as a clerk, but—as we shall see—this did not impede Adela's advance in the firm.[36]

CAREERS FOR YOUR DAUGHTERS 93

Fig. 4.2 Oonah Keogh, *The Vote*, 5 June 1925, 177. From the Women's Library, London School of Economics

For these women, instruction in stockbroking happened early and informally. But for those without a family background in finance, secretarial training increasingly became the means of securing employment in a brokerage. As seen in Chapter 3, Victorian women's organizations had done much to improve educational and training opportunities, and they quickly saw the potential of the new technology of the typewriter to leverage further openings. The Society for Promoting the Employment of Women was instrumental in founding the country's first typing agency in London in 1884, and provision of training rapidly proliferated.[37] By 1892 the feminist periodical *Shafts* noted that there were 'hundreds of typewriting offices, mostly run by women', offering training in the 'twin arts' of typewriting and shorthand.[38] Other women's periodicals like *The Englishwoman's Yearbook* and the monthly *Work and Leisure*, both founded by leading campaigner Louisa Hubbard, also publicized typewriting as a suitable opportunity for educated women to develop careers as clerks.[39] The impact can be seen in the career of one of Hubbard's followers, **Edith Mary Maskell** (b. 1860). The daughter of a Westminster clergyman, Edith supported herself as a daily governess, but became increasingly involved in Hubbard's activities, sub-editing *The Englishwoman's Yearbook* and acting as secretary for the United Sisters' Friendly Society.[40] It was almost certainly through these activities that she met stockbroker

94 SEXISM IN THE CITY

Amy Bell, who contributed articles on money matters to Hubbard's *Work and Leisure*. At some point in the later 1890s, when Maskell was in her thirties, she started work as a clerk with Bell.[41] When Bell's cousin Gertrude Brooke took over the business in 1910, Maskell continued at the firm, and she assumed outright control when Brooke retired four years later.[42]

By the early 1900s, office work was becoming an attractive proposition to a growing number of young women, an alternative to joining the ranks of 'down-trodden factory-girls' and 'brow-beaten shop assistants'.[43] With as little as six months often sufficient for training in typing and shorthand, office work was the 'best and easiest to enter' option for many young women, according to the *Girl's Own Paper*.[44] Moreover, it was perceived as 'clean' and 'dainty' work that would not compromise the femininity of those who did it.[45] A wide range of educational providers were entering the market, increasingly catering to women as well as men. By 1900, Pitman's School, founded thirty years earlier for male pupils, was offering 'a complete commercial education' to both men and women. 'The demand for youths and young ladies with a good business knowledge is greater now than it has ever been', its advertisements declared.[46] A rival, Cusack's Business Training College, promised 'Success in Life': 'Day and Evening Classes for All', including a 'Practical Commercial Course' open to both sexes.[47]

This kind of training could set women up for financial careers, as illustrated by one of Cusack's students, **Beatrice Gordon Holmes**. Born in London in 1884, Holmes's father was an Irish doctor and amateur classical scholar with a limited income; her mother came from South African mercantile stock, but the family had lost its money in the 1866 crash. Beatrice's education had been patchy, more home schooling than formal teaching, but when she was 18, she persuaded her father to lend her the four guineas required to enrol at Cusack's. There she spent ten months not only learning typing and shorthand but also receiving 'mild cramming in English composition, commercial subjects, business correspondence' and other topics.[48] This enabled her to land a job as a £1-a-week typist at the London office of Odense Aegforretning, a Danish egg merchants, in 1904.[49] Though her responsibilities multiplied during eight years at the firm, her salary hit a ceiling of £2. Her desire to earn £2 5s. a week priced her out of the typing market, and as she later recalled, 'there were hardly any other jobs for women in the business world in 1911'. Eight months of replying to newspaper advertisements yielded little.[50] But finance provided Holmes with her opportunity. Despite liking to declare that women were 'incapable of understanding financial matters', the Canadian journalist-turned-financier William James Thorold gave Holmes a three-month trial in August 1912 at his Canadian and General Trust, an issuing house which specialized in selling North American securities in the British market. Holmes quickly impressed Thorold and secured a permanent position at the firm.[51]

Fig. 4.3 Edith Midgley, *Leeds Mercury*, 7 February 1936, 4. Reproduced with permission from National World Publishing Ltd

Training opportunities were also becoming more available outside London. Alongside local institutions catering to small numbers of students were larger enterprises like Skerry's College, which had originated in Edinburgh in 1878, but rapidly expanded into towns across Scotland and the north of England from the 1890s. Colleges like Skerry's offered day and evening classes, as well as correspondence courses, making training widely available to those already in work.[52] This kind of flexibility benefited **Edith Midgley** (see Fig. 4.3), born in Bradford, Yorkshire, in 1887. Edith's father was a railway clerk, her mother was a blacksmith's daughter, and on leaving school at 14 she began work in a Bradford drapery store, working sixty-four-hour weeks, only ending at 7.30 p.m. on weekdays and 9 p.m. on Saturdays. The lack of opportunities for progression eventually drove her to pursue extra qualifications, so she found work that would give her enough time to attend evening classes, which she did three evenings a week.[53] In time, this enabled her to obtain a clerkship, first at a printing works, then in 1911 at a stockbroker's office, aged 24.[54]

As we have seen, the First World War drove a significant increase in opportunities for women in office work, though the dislocations it brought about initially made the employment situation more precarious for women.[55] This was particularly true in the world of stocks and shares. The London Stock Exchange was exceptionally hard hit by the rush to enlist that swept the country on the declaration of war. By October 1914, nearly 30 per cent of brokers' clerks had signed up, patriotism given a further boost by the fact that the Stock Exchange had closed at the end of July to prevent panic selling.[56] Though it reopened in January 1915, the volume of business remained low and employment was slack.[57] But facing a further squeeze on male staff, the Committee for General Purposes promoted the employment of women clerks among its member firms.[58] By the final year of the war, observers were noting that 'Lady clerks in stockbrokers' offices have ceased to be a novelty, and are as familiar there as in banks.'[59] As with banking, such was the drain of male staff to the front that brokerages had little option but to entrust women with positions of considerable responsibility. The number of members of the London Stock Exchange fell by 1,000 during the war, and of the 4,000 or so who nominally remained in November 1917, it was estimated that 1,500 were not active because of military service or other war work.[60] Outside London, the membership of other stock exchanges saw a similar depletion, Liverpool—one of the larger exchanges—losing 199 clerks and forty-seven members by 1917.[61] Here too, women were employed on a larger scale than hitherto, and enjoyed opportunities to do more than the routine office work that had mainly been their lot before the war.

One woman who transitioned to finance during the war was **Amy Hargraves Moreton** (b. 1893). Her parents, Arthur and Betsy, ran a small chain of boot shops in Nuneaton in the Midlands. These had initially been operated by Betsy's aunt, but when she died, the pair took them on, Arthur having previously been a commercial clerk. This was a joint venture, Betsy being listed in the 1911 census as 'assisting in business management', as well as being prominent in local Conservative politics and philanthropic work.[62] As a teenager, Amy displayed literary talents, writing a play, *Freedom in Happy England*, in support of the tariff reform cause, which was widely performed in 1911.[63] After that, she worked on a local newspaper, but the war presented her with an opportunity to switch from journalism to stockbroking by deputizing for a man on military service in a London stockbroker's office.[64]

Similar opportunities opened up outside London. **Ellen Rose White** (b. 1891) was the daughter of a lock gas fitter and plumber in Bath. While her older sister became a dressmaker, Ellen took a different route, and by the time of the 1911 census she was working as a typist.[65] In April 1916, once conscription had begun to bite, Ernest Jefferis, a Bath stockbroker and accountant, found himself short-staffed, and placed an advertisement in the Situations Vacant column of the *Bath Chronicle* for 'a Bright Young Girl' to work in his office.[66] Though impossible to know for certain, it seems likely that this is how Ellen made the transition to finance. She was certainly working at the firm as a clerk by the time of the 1921 census, and she remained with Jefferis long after the war.[67]

Women who were already in stockbroking prior to the war could find their responsibilities—and workload—dramatically increasing. In Exeter, Doris

Mortimer had started work in her father's stockbroking firm just before the war began. When the drain of male staff began, and her father fell ill, she had to take on a leading role in the business, despite still being in her teens.[68] More striking still is the example provided by Beatrice Gordon Holmes at the Canadian and General Trust. At the start of the war, her boss Thorold returned to Canada, while other directors and senior staff enlisted, resulting in Holmes becoming 'company secretary, sales manager, and managing director combined'. As she later recalled, 'I found myself with a handful of girl typists and office boys in charge of the business, either to keep it open or close it down'. Working on her pre-war salary of under £4 a week, and despite 'half kill[ing] myself with the strain of doing it', she was proud to be able to hand the business back to her boss Thorold in a flourishing condition.[69] As she put it: 'in 1918 every man had his job to come back to at a better salary than when he left'.[70]

Though female clerks shared in the general backlash against working women after 1918, facing strong pressure to give way to returning servicemen, many did hold on to their jobs.[71] Indeed, in 1921 there were more than three times the number of female clerical workers that there had been in 1911 (564,000 as opposed to 179,000).[72] After the war, stockbrokers continued to hire women, and this could offer significant social mobility. **Helen Gladys Tyrrell** (b. 1898) was the eldest daughter of Charles, a London postman, and Rebecca, who came from agricultural labouring stock.[73] After Charles died, Rebecca took the family to Burnley in Lancashire, where she established a small boarding house. Helen's brother got a job as a sheet metal worker, her younger sister worked as a shop assistant, but Helen secured a clerkship at local stockbroking firm, A. C. Robinson & Co.[74] Undoubtedly, female clerks remained popular with employers because they could be paid less than men and could be given the most mundane office work. But there is evidence that at least some stockbrokers recognized their capabilities, one Leeds stockbroker observing that women 'were highly capable in all that had to do with the office work of a broker's business and in the work that went on over the telephone lines with London and the various provincial exchanges'.[75] Such women were not therefore automatically confined to the lowest-level office tasks, which—as we shall see—allowed them to gain the skills and confidence needed to set up their own firms.

If family firms and clerkships were the main routes into stockbroking, then a third path emerged in the shape of the half-commission system. Barred from advertising, London member firms instead employed outside agents to drum up new business, splitting the commission they received with them. Half-commission agents were often well-born society men who found themselves strapped for cash: they were ideally placed to bring in lucrative new clients from their social circles.[76] In journalistic accounts, women were frequently cast as the victims of such charmers, ignorant of the financial motives that lay behind their attentiveness.[77] But in the years before the First World War, commentators began to note the growing numbers of women who were working as 'touts' for stockbrokers and company promoters. The 'superb creature' who charms with 'the sparkle of her wit' at the dinner table might in fact be a broker's agent waiting for the right moment to furnish 'alluring details' of some stock guaranteed to rise, wrote one journalist.[78] That men were thus vulnerable to market seductions, a reversal of the typical situation, was highlighted, one sensational account warning its male readers to be wary of these 'brainy, fascinating *financières*'.[79] Nevertheless, half-commission women were particularly valued for their ability to reach investors of their own sex. Brokers' touts could be found in ladies' clubs, restaurants, and shops: milliners and dressmakers in fashionable West End shops were paid by brokers to facilitate stock exchange flutters 'for fair clients suffering from the gambling craze'.[80]

In the interwar years, the system intensified, becoming a recognized hazard at 'smart lunch and dinner parties'.[81] Even the acclaimed actress and theatre producer Auriol Lee appears to have been employed by a broker for a time in this capacity.[82] If, before the war, these paid agents were not directly concerned with the actual business of stockbroking, in the interwar period some London brokers began bringing them inside their firms and formalizing their position. They saw such agents as a particularly effective way of catering to female investors. The numbers involved were not large, but the practice was becoming more widespread by the later 1930s, one paper reporting that several member firms 'now employ one or two women as "commission men" [sic] on their staffs, dealing in particular with women clients'.[83]

One such was **Mabel Gosnell** (née Fox), born in 1897 to Maria and Charles Fox, who was a successful businessman and leading figure in the entertainment industry of the Isle of Man.[84] Mabel married twice, first when she was just 18 to Charles Lockwood Tatham, a second lieutenant in the Cheshire Regiment, and when this marriage failed after the war, she married another military man, cavalry officer Harry Theodore Gosnell, who had been the co-respondent in her divorce.[85] As a military wife, Mabel would have developed useful links among the officer class, the stigma of divorce notwithstanding. She was also heavily involved in the early motorsports scene centring around the wealthy racers and adventurers known as the 'Bentley Boys'.[86] Mabel was one of several women who raced cars and motorbikes around the Brooklands circuit, and she contributed articles to *Autocar* and the *Motor Cycle*, as well as penning a series on 'Motoring and the Woman' for the *Yorkshire Post*.[87] After marrying Gosnell, she gravitated away from motorsports and developed an interest in finance, extensive travel giving her the chance of studying it abroad. In time, she began investing on behalf of her friends. 'Perhaps it is a flair, but I have done very well', she later remarked, and her business grew to such an extent that she decided to 'turn professional', joining member firm George J. Ascott & Co. in the mid-1930s as a half-commission agent.[88] Women had been managing the investments of friends for centuries, but the opportunity to 'professionalize' by joining a firm of inside brokers was entirely new in the interwar years.[89]

Outside brokerages also turned to female agents in the interwar years to drum up business. The theme of seduction was often to the fore, at least in accounts in the popular press.[90] Under the headline 'BLONDES BRING BUSINESS TO BUCKET SHOPS', the *Daily Herald* described how outside brokers were hiring 'attractive young women with jobs that bring them into contact with large numbers of men', such as actresses, chorus-girls, receptionists, and hostesses.[91] Interwar bucket shops increasingly turned to pressure selling—'share-pushing' as it was dubbed— employing salesmen to travel door-to-door offloading overvalued or worthless stock.[92] These kinds of fraudulent activities were attracting the attention of the authorities, with an increase in criminal prosecutions in the 1920s and 1930s. But these prosecutions confirmed that men were the main movers behind such scams.[93] Though women had run their own bucket shops in the pre-war years, they seem to have played less of a leading role in such enterprises in the interwar period. And when they did do so, they were peripheral and short-lived affairs.[94] Undoubtedly, women enjoyed much greater success at the more legitimate end of the share market in interwar Britain.

Developing a Career

Whereas the majority of women who had ventured into stockbroking in the late Victorian years had struggled to establish much of a foothold in finance, longer-lasting careers were becoming more possible in the interwar years. Daughters of brokers who entered family firms did not remain in supporting roles. Tending to remain single and living in the family home, they developed close working relationships with their fathers. Having joined Hugh's Bury firm by 1921 as a clerk, Phyllis Moscrop Robinson entered into partnership with her father in 1925.[95] As well as stockbroking, the firm also provided insurance broking services, and Phyllis accordingly qualified as an insurance broker in 1927, reportedly the first woman to do so.[96] In Dublin, Oonah Keogh's rise within her father's firm, Messrs Keogh & Co., was even more rapid. Having joined the business in 1925, she became a partner the following year.[97] Daughters could also take control of family businesses, either formally or informally. In Exeter, when Doris Mortimer's father died in 1922, she succeeded him as senior partner in W. Mortimer & Son.[98] After joining her uncle (and adoptive father) Enoch Dawson's Rochdale firm in 1917, Adela Taylor quickly rose to a position of responsibility, accelerated by Dawson's recurring health problems. Her older brother Samuel looked after the cotton side of the business, and attended the Oldham Exchange as Dawson's authorized clerk, on a weekly salary of £6. Adela, despite being paid £4 a week, was actually the senior of the two, being in charge of the firm's day-to-day running, signing cheques on Dawson's behalf, and quickly assuming 'complete control' of the office.[99] In the 1921 census, whereas Samuel was recorded as 'Clerk & Representative', Adela was 'Stock & Sharebroker'.[100]

Of course, for women clerks working outside the context of family firms, progression was far less certain. As mentioned above, Edith Maskell took on Gertrude Brooke's business when she quit in 1914, and women clerks could also occasionally succeed to male-run businesses. In Bath, Ellen White clearly developed a strong working and personal relationship with her boss Ernest Jefferis. When Jefferis died in 1931, aged 70, White was named as one of his executors alongside his widow, and was listed among the family mourners in the local newspaper's report of his funeral.[101] White took over the business, initially trading under the Ernest Jefferis name, and continued doing business from the same address.[102]

It was more common, however, for women to run up against limits to advancement in such firms: a problem that could lead to entrepreneurial solutions. At the Canadian and General Trust, Beatrice Gordon Holmes found her boss William Thorold unappreciative of her exceptional efforts to keep the business going during the First World War. Recalling Thorold's return in 1917, she wrote that 'when he strode into the office he would barely shake hands with me'.[103] Though she managed to negotiate a salary increase, putting her on £500 a year, relations with Thorold remained tense, especially as she found herself becoming the buffer between the rest of the staff and Thorold's 'crazy, irrational temper'.[104] A row led to her quitting 'sixty seconds before he sacked me', but within months personal circumstances—combined with the broader economic climate—caused her to return, reluctantly.[105] As she put it, 'starting all over again elsewhere in my midthirties with my mother to support and post-war unemployment looming' was an unappealing prospect.[106] Despite another pay increase, to £1,000 a year, she grew thoroughly disillusioned with work. 'Starting a financial house of my own had never occurred to me as a remote possibility', she later recounted, but when her former boss from her days as a typist, Ludwig Ravens, suggested she do just this, she excitedly broached the idea with Thorold's company secretary, Richard Sefton Turner, with whom she had always been on good terms.[107] Holmes had imagined that raising the £10,000 start-up capital they needed would be impossible, but Ravens and a colleague agreed to stump up half, while Turner secured the remainder from his business contacts.[108] They left Thorold and established the National Securities Corporation, Limited, 'in two small rooms with two typists'.[109] The business was a direct competitor of the Canadian and General Trust, one of a growing number of houses specializing in new share issues, while also advising clients on investments. Holmes and Turner were its joint managing directors, appointed for life.[110]

Other women also struck out on their own to develop their careers independently. Amy Moreton left her London clerkship after the war, moving back to her parents' home in Nuneaton. By 1921 she had set up her own firm, a few doors down from Nuneaton's only other brokerage, in the commercial centre of town.[111] In Burnley, Helen Tyrrell served a much longer apprenticeship as a broker's clerk, having worked in that capacity since the early 1920s. But in 1935 she took the step of starting her own firm, the fifth brokerage operating in the town.[112] By contrast, Bradford was a larger centre with a stock exchange, and Edith Midgley, who had joined a member firm in 1911 as a clerk, worked there till 1930, when she switched to another inside firm. But in 1933 she left to establish her own business, becoming only the second outside brokerage operating in the town, trading from the prominent and prestigious location of Britannia House on Leeds Road.[113]

These stockbrokers were working in a cultural environment in which traditional attitudes to women in business died hard. Ostensibly progressive but actually somewhat equivocal was the short story, 'Claudia's Business', penned by popular author Marie Corelli in 1916 and reprinted in her final collection of short stories in 1920.[114] Concerning the doomed courtship of an American stockbroker, Claudia Strange, by a young English aristocrat, Lord Francis Markham, the story juxtaposes traditional and modern ideas about femininity. Proudly conventional, Francis expects women to be 'half drudge, half toy', and does not think them sufficiently intelligent 'to have any control of finance'. When he discovers Claudia's profession, he is both fascinated and repelled ('What an unwomanly career!'), and also confused, clumsily referring to her as 'a man of business'. Claudia quickly corrects him: 'It isn't necessary to be a man in order to have a little plain judgment and common sense.' She criticizes society's hypocrisy on money and gender. It was acceptable for women to entrust their money to a male broker, who might give her bad advice, or cheat her: in such cases, it was her fault—'women shouldn't speculate!'

> But when a woman takes the trouble to study and to learn the ins and outs of the world's money-markets, and uses all the foresight and instinct nature has bestowed upon her to win success for herself as well as for others without making herself physically hideous in the process—that's unwomanly!

Indeed, Corelli is determined to show that a woman can be devoted to business *and* adhere to feminine beauty standards. The text is peppered with references to Claudia's appearance. She dresses 'exquisitely', with 'extreme daintiness and elegance'; at a party, she presents a 'dazzling vision of fair hair, blue eyes, laughing lips, white arms, and delicate snowy chiffon attire…a jewelled chatelaine dangling at her waist'. She has 'pretty hands, small, well-shaped, white as milk, and adorned with one or two choice and sparkling rings'. For Claudia, a business career is not incompatible with traditional femininity: 'I can pin an hour's pure joy on a hat, and I revel in a pretty frock and lovely jewels. But there are other things.' Yet Corelli's unrelenting focus on Claudia's appearance problematizes her presence in the financial district. Her Wall Street office is a thoroughly masculinized space, Markham noting that 'There was nothing to indicate the presence or influence of a woman anywhere', only 'the strictest office necessities and documentary paraphernalia of the money-making male'. Claudia's presence is therefore rendered incongruous: 'at a big desk, sat the small and *mignonne* Claudia, arrayed in a neat, dark navy serge costume and holding a telephone receiver to her pretty little ear'.[115] Admittedly, this was different from Olive Malvery's *The Speculator*, discussed in Chapter 3, where the heroine has to turn herself into a man in order to become a City stockbroker.[116] Ultimately, however, rather than serving to normalize the idea of women stockbrokers, Corelli's story presents them as exceptional. We are expected to find Claudia as remarkable as Francis does: typical of Corelli's heavy-handed symbolism, the lady broker is literally designated 'Strange'.[117] And by locating her tale on Wall Street, Corelli implies that financial careers for women were only viable in the more progressive United States.

Though in many ways an eccentric figure, and by now approaching the end of her career, Corelli's concerns were not atypical. The time-honoured idea that involvement with finance was dangerously defeminizing remained commonplace in the interwar years. The popular stage revue *Yoicks!* which ran in London and the provinces in the mid-1920s, featured a role-reversal sketch in which a 'simpering he-flapper' is wooed by a 'mannish girl' in plus-fours, encouraged by the youth's 'cigar-smoking and rum-quaffing, be-trousered, stockbroker mother'.[118] Even female journalists fretted over whether women's professional involvement in finance would come 'at the cost of our good looks and the hair on the top of our heads'.[119] The woman stockbroker therefore remained resolutely 'strange', likely inhibiting young women from imagining financial careers for themselves. The pre-war pioneers had not succeeded in normalizing the presence of women in finance; indeed, they had been largely forgotten, a *Westminster Gazette* journalist commenting in 1923: 'To the majority of us it comes as quite a surprise to learn that a woman stockbroker existed even before the war'.[120] Establishing a public presence was further complicated by stock exchange rules. Long anxious about the competition posed by outside brokers, stock exchanges were imposing ever more restrictions on their members' dealings with non-members. Outsiders who wanted to do business with a member broker had to follow stock exchange regulations against advertising.[121] To pre-empt accusations of advertising, newspaper articles discussing women brokers usually refrained from stating the firms they worked for; some went further still by not even mentioning the brokers' names.[122]

Nevertheless, the interwar press showed a fascination for female stockbrokers which gave the topic of women in finance a far higher profile than it had enjoyed before the war. In part this was a consequence of the interwar 'feminization' of the daily press, with editors keen to appeal to newly enfranchised female

CAREERS FOR YOUR DAUGHTERS   103

readers.[123] Rather than defining women's content narrowly around domestic concerns, newspapers made a strong pitch to 'modern' women. This meant recognizing—and in some cases celebrating—women's newfound opportunities in the public sphere. Newspapers were particularly excited by their 'discovery' of the female stockbroker in the 1920s. A speech given by Holmes in October 1924 describing her early career attracted particular attention. She later recalled, 'That evening all the newspaper placards in London broke out in a rash "Woman Stockbroker tells her Secrets!"' When she returned home, Holmes found the press pack 'camped on the doorstep'.[124] Newspapers the next day were full of accounts of the '£1 a Week City Typist Who Rose To Be a Stockbroker' and was now a '£1,000 A YEAR GIRL'.[125] The attention was not fleeting, Holmes remaining in the public eye thereafter, using the press as numbers of other female celebrities did in these years to destabilize traditional assumptions about women's capabilities.[126] She even enjoyed sufficient fame to write an autobiography, *In Love with Life*, published in 1944.

Despite celebrating the achievements of women like Holmes, newspapers proved ambivalent allies, their engagement with the subject of women in business often proving highly superficial.[127] Though newspapers sought Holmes's views on a range of issues after discovering her in 1924, these were frequently frivolous, such as whether women were playing too many sports, proper fashions for female clerks, and the importance of good looks in business.[128] Not strictly speaking a stockbroker, but head of an issuing house, Holmes did not face such severe restrictions on publicity, but others had to be wary about garnering media attention.[129] Journalists could use underhand methods to get stories. In 1936, an 'interview' with Burnley broker Helen Tyrrell appeared in the *Daily Express*.[130] But the journalist obtained the information by phoning Tyrrell and posing as a client, asking for her opinion on cotton shares.[131] Journalists did not mind inventing details to embellish their accounts, as with alleged interviews with Edith Midgley in the national press. A local reporter who knew Midgley remarked that her friends 'must have been astonished and amused to read that she is a blonde (her hair is dark), and that she often works 14 to 16 hours a day upon snacks and cups of tea (also pure invention, of course)'.[132] It was not always possible, therefore, for women brokers to decide whether or not to 'go public', and to control their image if they did.

The press was also responsible for recycling traditional ideas about women as investors. Conventional attitudes were propagated as much by female journalists as male, who argued that women paid little attention to financial news and had 'magical' ideas about the growth of money.[133] Familiar fears about the vulnerability of women intensified with the advent of door-to-door share-pushers, since housewives were thought to be their preferred prey. These 'well-dressed and glib-tongued hawkers' called when husbands were at work, and used a mixture of intimidation and seduction to persuade their targets to buy their wares.[134] As had

104 SEXISM IN THE CITY

been the case before the war, these kinds of beliefs were as much an opportunity as a hindrance to women seeking to carve out financial careers. *The Vote*, the journal of the Women's Freedom League (WFL), presented female stockbrokers' main function as catering to timid women investors, who, 'entirely ignorant of the mysteries of stocks and shares, and the money market generally, are only too glad to consult and entrust their business to one of their own sex'.[135] Likewise, in an article on stockbroking for *Good Housekeeping*, Helena Normanton QC, who had become the country's first practising female barrister in 1919, explained that it was 'the gullible, elderly woman' who was the chief victim of share-pushing outside brokers. She was shy of taking her 'rather paltry affairs to an eminent broker', so she fell for the convenience of the share-pushers who came to her door. Women brokers, 'capable but kindly', who actually took an interest in someone with just £25 to invest, would protect them from fraud. Only they had the 'infinite patience' to deal with the kinds of 'elderly and pernickety ladies' who exasperated male stockbrokers.[136]

Capitalizing on this discourse, women could—following in the footsteps of Amy Bell in the 1890s—use the press to disseminate financial advice for women. Holmes contributed advice columns to *The Graphic* which echoed Bell's prudence, instructing her readers not to believe claims made by 'wild-cat' schemes that would double and treble their money. 'Be cautious; keep your purse-strings tight; seek the advice of those who know', she urged.[137] Holmes was alert to opportunities presented by new media as well, giving a radio lecture on stockbroking in 1925.[138] Nuneaton stockbroker Amy Moreton also harnessed the new technology to boost her profile, discussing 'Women and Finance' on Birmingham radio in late 1926.[139] This clearly went well, as she was commissioned the following year to deliver a series of talks on 'Women and Investment', with episodes covering 'The Fascination of Money', 'Safety First', 'Capital in Industry', and 'For the Adventurous'.[140] These were broadcast at 4.45 p.m., perhaps allowing Moreton to reach housewives before their husbands returned from work, and rescuing them from the clutches of the door-to-door share-pushers.

The varied titles of Moreton's talks repudiate the idea that female investors were all the same, recognizing instead that they might legitimately take a variety of approaches, from those who put 'safety first', to women who adopted more 'adventurous' methods. In doing so, she was contributing to an interwar rethinking of women and the stock market, in which the stereotype of the nervous and vulnerable old lady in need of perpetual help and reassurance was challenged by a new idea of professionalized female investment. This modern female investor was increasingly glimpsed in the pages of the interwar popular press, where economic emancipation was often presented as moving hand in hand with new political freedoms.[141] Some women stockbrokers were keen to harness this idea as a means of enhancing their own status. As half-commission agent Hilda McKean put it to a *Daily News* reporter in 1928: 'To-day the business woman as much as the business man needs her own stockbroker.'[142]

Traditional prejudices certainly continued to circulate, and came to the fore when the market began to overheat in the late 1920s. Just as in the year of the South Sea Bubble, women bore a disproportionate blame for the speculative fever, 'the feminine temperament' supposedly predisposing them to gamble recklessly on the stock market.[143] But such preconceptions were challenged by data pointing to very different conclusions about women's financial behaviour. Historians' estimates based on detailed analysis of registers of publicly listed companies suggest that whereas women had represented just 15 per cent of shareholders in the 1870s, this had reached over 45 per cent by the 1930s.[144] Though such systematic surveys of shareholder populations were not available in the interwar years, commentators were beginning to grasp that the realities of women's investment were very different from the clichés. When *Truth*'s City editor obtained investor registers in seven leading industrial companies in 1930, he was 'amazed' to discover the high proportion of women shareholders. That women were in the majority in two of the largest, he found 'astonishing.'[145] Likewise, the *Daily Mirror*'s City editor confessed his surprise when he discovered the large numbers of women shareholders in first-class industrial enterprises, even those 'whose business is in no way connected with feminine requirements'. But he continued that, judging by the letters in his postbag, 'I can certainly vouch for the fact that women take a very intelligent interest in their investments', closely studying the undertakings in which they held shares.[146] So, rather than throwing their money at share-pushers, many women were investing their money quietly, cleverly, and profitably.[147] They were also becoming more seriously involved in corporate governance, attending general meetings and attempting to influence boardroom policies.[148]

Despite the growth of female participation in interwar markets, it is striking that the women stockbrokers of this era did not specialize in catering to women investors. Indeed, rather than highlighting their sex, women stockbrokers nearly always effaced it. The clearest example was Holmes. Dispensing with her first name, she went by 'Gordon Holmes' throughout her career, and published her autobiography under this name. Other women preferred to use their initials rather than their full names in the names of their firms: E. Midgley, A. H. Moreton & Co., and H. G. Tyrrell & Co. Whereas New York in this period saw brokerages established exclusively for women, there were no analogues in interwar Britain.[149] Investors who consulted trade directories or lists of brokers would usually have had no means of telling which ones were women. Helena Normanton identified this as a problem, and as a solution suggested that women go to a library to check the Law List, find a female solicitor, and contact her to ask to be put in touch with a woman stockbroker.[150]

Effectively a system of exclusive dealing, Normanton's method was a way of tapping into women's professional networks to promote the cause of female stockbroking. But women stockbrokers themselves were more preoccupied with forming good relationships with clients of both sexes. When embarking on her career in finance, despite being initially anxious about her reception, Holmes proved instantly popular with investors. 'So far from objecting to doing business with a woman, practically all the men and women clients, large and small—and some of them were very substantial—regarded me as a fascinating novelty, something no other financial House could offer them.' Later, when she was heading her own firm, a manager told her she should not meet with clients, 'as after an initial interview with me it was such hard work for him to get them accustomed to dealing with a man'.[151]

Holmes's experience was not unique: it seems that despite initial prejudices, women stockbrokers could quickly make a positive impression, with clichés about women's distinctive qualities even proving an asset rather than a hindrance. At Enoch Dawson's in Rochdale, Adela Taylor was quickly recognized as a boon to the business, clients valuing her 'womanly intuition' and believing that she had 'a flair for the markets, a Midas touch'.[152] Consequently, as was later reported, 'clients who came to do business with Enoch Dawson desired to be advised by her. It was not so much that Enoch Dawson left the business to her because of his illness, as it was that he left it to her because of her ability'.[153] Likewise, Helen Tyrrell noted how she was able to overcome early scepticism in Burnley. 'At first some men were inclined to sit back and smile at the idea of a woman running a stockbroking business', but after eighteen months in business, 'now they are coming along as clients'.[154] Over in Bradford, Midgley had 'many well-known Yorkshire business people' on her client list, while in London, Edith Maskell observed that she had 'quite a large number of men who entrust their investments to me'.[155] In part, this was a matter of practicality: with the majority of women stockbrokers operating in the provinces and catering chiefly to local communities, it would have been unrealistic to ignore male investors, even with the numbers of female investors growing. But it was also a result of how women stockbrokers viewed themselves: not content with occupying a subordinate niche in the profession, they rather sought to trade on equal terms to their male counterparts.

Professional Identities

Indeed, besides the gendered prejudices that women in business had to deal with in this period, many of the hazards they encountered were similar to those faced by male stockbrokers. At the Canadian and General Trust, Holmes credited herself with pioneering simple and transparent literature for inexperienced investors, whether female or male. Finding the postcards sent out by the firm to prospective clients with prospectuses overly complex, she rewrote them, which—she claimed in her autobiography—had the effect of quadrupling business. She then applied this approach to the firm's communications with clients, writing clearly and avoiding jargon. Though her boss Thorold was sceptical, informing her that other City firms were mocking them for their 'simple explanations of the obvious', the strategy proved successful, and she asserted that her plain style was later adopted during the First World War by the government, which had to sell war loans to 'a financially illiterate public'.[156] The reality was a little more complex, however. In 1915 the Metropolitan Water Board sought an injunction against the Canadian and General Trust for a circular and prospectus which gave the false impression that it was acting as agents to the Board in offering fresh 3 per cent stock in the Board. In fact, there was no new stock and the Trust was not an authorized agent of the Board. Justice John Astbury granted the injunction, labelling the firm's communications 'grossly misleading'.[157] The scandal-hunting journal *Truth* commended the verdict, reporting that many of its readers were 'pestered with speciously worded touting circulars' from the same firm.[158] Indeed, the reprimand was not a one-off. Towards the end of the war, the Trust again attracted criticism for its 'hawking' circulars, with City journalists finding the circulars disconcertingly vague on details, 'sufficient to give any wise investor pause'.[159]

When Holmes established the National Securities Corporation, she continued with the same methods of attracting business, earning further rebukes. Shortly after its formation, *Truth* mocked this new firm of 'City philanthropists who desire to make us all rich', with its seductively titled magazine, *Making Money*.[160] Through the 1920s, its circulars continued to attract sporadic criticism, City articles often lumping the firm in with the 'share-pushing' businesses which were attracting growing criticism.[161] As late as 1939 the firm's circulars were being cited in parliament as proof of the need for legislation to protect investors.[162] Yet critics rarely mentioned Holmes's sex, and the criticism does not seem to have hampered the firm's advance.[163] As had been the case with the earlier generation of bucket shop proprietors—male and female—who used aggressive marketing techniques to drum up business, circulars offered women the means of competing with men for capital on a level playing field.[164]

Running a brokerage inevitably meant dealing with the risks posed by clients. Many firms had strategies for mitigating these risks, which some women brokers followed. Maskell was one such, explaining: 'I only deal with people who have been recommended. Clients are always introduced, and those who have transacted business with me introduce others.'[165] But other firms, particularly in the provinces, had to be more flexible, making rapid judgements on whether strangers could be trusted, which could leave brokers vulnerable if their confidence was misplaced. This was demonstrated in Bath in 1934, where Ellen White was defrauded by a male con-artist. Henry Lesser was an undischarged bankrupt who had a criminal record stretching back to 1908. Professing to seek work as a half-commission man, he asked White to sell some shares on his behalf, which were being sent over from India by his wife. White arranged for her London brokers to purchase the shares, and over the next few weeks, Lesser placed three other sales orders with White. But he never produced any of the share certificates, eventually admitting that he did not own any. This was a simple scam: when the delivery date arrived, if there had been a profit on the transaction, he would have taken it, but as there was a loss, he refused to pay it.[166] In court, White admitted that perhaps she should have asked Lesser for references before agreeing to sell his shares, but denied that she had been negligent. She explained that 'we treat people as if we trust them', and she believed Lesser to be 'quite straight'. His angling for work as a half-commission man had confirmed her impression that he was 'a man of means'.[167]

Falling for Lesser's trick does not mark out White as gullible or incompetent for she was by no means the only stockbroker to extend credit to Lesser, who was a prolific and very persuasive swindler. His transactions with White totalled £1,500, but police claimed he had speculated to the extent of £20,000 with a range of other brokers across the country over the course of a couple of months, and had served short prison sentences in 1932 and 1933 for fraudulently obtaining credit. Indeed, the police noted that he was a man 'of ability and plausibility' who was regarded by the London and New York Stock Exchanges as a 'menace'.[168] White's evidence against him was sufficient to secure a twelve-month sentence with hard labour.

Of course, trust was a two-way street, and one case showed that women stockbrokers could succumb to the same temptations as their male counterparts when dealing with confiding clients. In Rochdale, Adela Taylor's reputation for financial acumen derived from events that happened not long after she joined Enoch Dawson's brokerage. Dawson had, against Taylor's advice, invested personally in several local concerns which, when the cotton slump of 1920 hit, resulted in a loss of over £10,000. Taylor had 'by careful investment' managed to recoup the whole amount for the firm. Around this time, Dawson gifted Taylor shares worth £6,000, and she used these to begin playing the market on her own account. Though initially successful, over time she lost money and began borrowing from the firm, with her uncle's knowledge, in order to continue speculating. By the end of 1934, Taylor owed the business over £6,000. Two years later she assured the firm's accountant that she would stop, but instead she doubled down and her losses grew to £49,000. On 'a mad impulse', she began misappropriating clients' money in a desperate bid to retrieve her losses. But she fell further into the red, ultimately driving the firm into bankruptcy in November 1937. Dawson died the following month, and investigations by the liquidator showed that Adela owed the firm over £84,000. She was criminally prosecuted at Manchester Assizes in 1938 for fraudulently converting clients' money, and pleaded guilty, admitting, as her barrister put it, that she 'had been extremely foolish' in her speculations.

Though declaring himself 'old-fashioned enough to think that some allowance ought to be made for a woman' in his sentencing speech, Justice Croom-Johnson focused far more on her professional status. 'You are an experienced business woman, and I must deal with you on that basis', in order to shore up 'the trust and confidence which are reposed in people like you by the public in general'. The sentence, four years' penal servitude, was three years short of the maximum permitted, but was broadly consistent with the kinds of sentences given to men guilty of similar crimes.[169] Indeed, at the same Assizes, Croom-Johnson sentenced a male stockbroker from Stockport who had misappropriated clients' money on a smaller scale than Taylor to three years.[170]

Interwar women stockbrokers thus operated in the same commercial environment, ran similar businesses, and faced the same risks—and temptations—as their male counterparts. Though few in numbers, they were part of the financial landscape, more of them succeeding in getting listed on the Somerset House register of outside stockbrokers that had been operated by the Board of Inland Revenue since 1899.[171] The initial requirement that applicants had to provide the name of a single stock exchange member to vouch for their *bona fides* had been increased to three names by the interwar years, so women's ability to get themselves registered speaks to their growing acceptance by stockbroking communities.[172] Indeed, by the late 1920s, Amy Moreton had, by her own account, established 'a large clientele, spread over England and Ireland, and agents at the various Stock Exchanges'.[173] In several cases, rather than going it alone, women enjoyed successful working relationships with male brokers. In London, Edith Maskell continued the connection with Whiteheads & Coles, the member firm with whom Amy Bell had done business since the 1880s.[174] In other cases, such close relationships developed into formal partnerships. When Doris Mortimer took over her father's firm on his death in 1922, she took into partnership Walter John Way, a much older man who had been at the firm since his teens, and had worked his way up to the position of manager.[175] The partnership proved durable, lasting until Way's death in 1940.[176] In Bradford, when Edith Midgley established her own firm, she initially traded on her own, but by 1937 had taken a man, W. E. Dear, into partnership, the firm becoming 'E. Midgley & Co.' This arrangement did not last, but a later partnership with another man, Robert Chaloner, proved more durable.[177] Equally stable was Holmes's relationship with her business partner Richard Turner. Having successfully established the National Securities Corporation, the pair set up a string of further companies: J. W. Fisher and Co., the Guardian Securities Company, and the Stock Exchange and General Securities Corporation, all operating out of the same City offices.[178] Modelled on Thorold's Canadian and General Trust, they were chiefly involved in issuing stock for a wide range of international businesses, and Holmes and Turner developed strong links with Budapest, taking up directorships of several Hungarian companies.[179] By the 1930s, Holmes was earning 'a steady £4,000 or £5,000 a year'.[180]

110   SEXISM IN THE CITY

Despite their embeddedness in male broking communities, gender was an important element shaping women stockbrokers' professional identities, encouraged by the new business and professional networks for women that were developing at this time. As a young clerk in the 1900s, Holmes had joined the Women's Social and Political Union, selling *The Suffragette* outside Westminster, and proudly wearing the movement's purple, green, and white badge every day in the City. Though she admitted to not having been the most active member, her involvement influenced her greatly, as she later recalled: 'It gave us pride of sex, helped to stop the everlasting apology within us for being women, [and] taught us to value ourselves and our abilities.'[181] She was also involved in organizing to protect the interests of female clerks, becoming an early member of the Association of Shorthand Writers and Typists in 1904, which developed into the Association of Women Clerks and Secretaries. Though drifting away from such activity once she started working at the Canadian and General Trust, in 1924 she was invited to join the recently established Soroptimist Club of London, which was to have major repercussions for her life and career.[182]

Reflecting a new type of middle-class associational culture, the Soroptimists were a feminine analogue of the Rotary Club. Originating as an informal luncheon club in Chicago in 1905, and reaching Britain in 1911, the Rotary movement promoted an ethos of public service and progressive citizenship. Admitting one representative member of each business and profession after a rigorous vetting process, the idea was that the clubs would be well placed to engage with contemporary problems in their local communities.[183] A rapid success on both sides of the Atlantic, the model was soon adopted by business and professional women, with the first Soroptimist Club established in the United States in 1921 and in London two years later.[184] Clubs rapidly formed across the country, and the Federation of Soroptimist Clubs of Great Britain and Ireland was set up in 1930, reaching a total of 3,500 members by 1939.[185] As well as remaining a keen Soroptimist, Holmes played a critical role in the establishment of another club movement, the National Federation of Business and Professional Women's Clubs, in 1938.[186] As the federation's first president, Holmes worked in collaboration with Lena Madesin Phillips, the founder of the parent organization in the United States, to oversee the rapid establishment of a large branch network, which comprised 109 local clubs and over 6,500 members by 1945.[187] Some provincial stockbrokers were involved with these club movements, as well as other women's organizations. For example, Phyllis Moscrop Robinson was a founder member and president of the Bury Soroptimist Club.[188] Edith Midgley, meanwhile, was prominent in the Bradford branch of the Business and Professional Women's Club, as well as joining the National Council of Women and the WFL, and being active in local Liberal politics.[189]

Membership could have a profound impact. Joining boosted businesswomen's confidence by reminding them that they were not unique, providing opportunities for sociability and networking among their peers. Holmes later recalled of joining the Soroptimists the 'shock of happy surprise at finding myself surrounded by women who had pioneered as successfully in other directions...as I had in finance. I rediscovered women after years of daily living in a world of men.'[190] The clubs had an ambivalent relationship to feminist ideology, preferring to promote women's citizenship, reflecting, as Helen McCarthy argues, 'the desire of professional women to claim for themselves an identity that was not solely defined by gendered political struggle.'[191] In the wake of enfranchisement in 1918 and 1928, the clubs underlined to members that they had a serious role to play in the social and political questions of the day. As Holmes put it in 1941, her Federation sought to encourage women, 'from the £2 a week typist to the £1,000 a year executive, to co-operate in intelligent thought and responsible action on public questions, war problems, and post-war problems.'[192] This emphasis avoided conflict and adopted a collaborative view of relations with men based on gendered difference. Indeed, it was common for Soroptimists to disavow 'claims of equality with men', and instead urge members to 'claim co-operation with them in mutual undertakings, where each has a unique contribution to make.'[193]

The implications for understanding of women's role in finance were ambiguous, which can be seen in Holmes's public pronouncements. On the one hand, she sought to normalize the idea of women in finance by challenging conventions of talking about it in exclusively masculine terms. She rejected the idea that 'deadly accuracy at figures' was essential for a financial career, on the grounds that there were 'more ways of twisting figures than of trimming hats.'[194] Women's domestic monetary role, she argued, naturally equipped them for careers in finance: 'every woman has to handle situations at home similar to those arising in finance. For instance, she has her "settlement day" when she pays her bills. She calls it "seeing to things".'[195] However, perhaps mindful that such a strategy risked relegating women to a subordinate role in finance, Holmes also played down the idea of gendered difference. She argued that 'the question of sex' was 'of no importance whatever in business'. The essential characteristics—'strong personality, good judgment, willingness to take risks, enthusiasm, and a quick, alert intelligence—are found equally in both sexes.'[196] In her autobiography, she wrote: 'if I am asked what women, as women, can contribute to finance, my candid reply would be "Nothing." There is no sex in discounting a bill or in judging a balance sheet.'[197] When financial capacity was so persistently seen in heavily gendered terms, this bold vision of financial equality had subversive power.

The service clubs gave women a public platform to express such ideas, for the press tracked their development and proliferation enthusiastically and often reported speeches given at their meetings. Indeed, the talk which first sparked public interest in Holmes in 1924 was given at a Soroptimist luncheon meeting. Before the war, female brokers, together with some of their supporters in the press, had tended not to present stockbroking as a viable career path for more than a few specially qualified women Some brokers continued to sound a note of caution, Edith Maskell warning would-be women brokers that 'a life of hard work and business anxiety' awaited them.[198] But others were more encouraging. Talking to the *Daily Mirror* in 1936, for example, half-commission agent Mabel Gosnell was convinced that there were 'many women with financial brains who will want to choose the same career as I have.'[199] Holmes, though, was the most consistent and high-profile advocate of women in finance. Her own rags-to-riches tale—which she recycled endlessly in speeches and interviews, and told at greater length in her autobiography—successfully packaged for a mass audience the idea that women could succeed in the financial world. The message was reinforced visually, a photo of her appearing in the press sitting at a busy desk surrounded by the paraphernalia of the 'Woman Chief of "Big Business"' (see Fig. 4.4).[200] Though her story's atypicality was tacitly recognized in one newspaper's description of it as 'a romance of the modern commercial world', it nevertheless placed the possibilities of finance in the minds of thousands of readers.[201] As she put it, 'with proper encouragement and suitable training, girls can go far, very far—in fact, all the way.'[202]

Fig. 4.4 Gordon Holmes, *Birmingham Gazette*, 9 January 1937, 5. Reproduced with permission from Reach Licensing

Holmes did not deny that 'firmly rooted prejudices' made it harder for women to succeed in commerce: her own experience suggested 'that a woman must be ten times as efficient as a man to hold the same position, and then very often the salary is not as large'.[203] But finance, she argued, was 'the one opening for women where there is no expensive training, and in which they can earn as they learn'.[204] These ideas received wider endorsement, particularly in the press, which began highlighting financial careers as a viable proposition for women.[205] Stockbroking was included, alongside aviation, engineering, and Angora rabbit farming, in a 1928 *Daily News* article on 'Careers for your Daughters?'[206] Others were admittedly more cautious, stockbroking meriting only one sentence in Ray Strachey's 1935 guide, *Careers and Openings for Women*.[207]

Indeed, the business culture in the United Kingdom was often compared unfavourably with the situation in the United States, which was typically framed as the progressive 'other' to the more conservative UK.[208] When the British author May Edington travelled to the USA in 1924 to negotiate the movie rights for one of her novels, she discovered that women were 'given a wider scope, more responsibility, and higher salaries than English business women', and that women stockbrokers were particularly successful there.[209] Gordon Holmes expressed the same idea more colourfully following an American trip. In New York, she said, women stockbrokers were 'almost as numerous as blackberries in Autumn'.[210] US census statistics supported these impressions. Already, the 1910 census counted 207 women it categorized as stockbrokers, dwarfed by the 13,522 male brokers, but still a significant force. By 1930, the number had leapt to 1,793, compared to 69,157 men, an increase from 1.5 per cent to 2.5 per cent.[211] The bare statistics for England and Wales did not chart a similar story of growth. The 1921 census, the first which captured granular occupational data, counted 5,817 male stockbrokers and jobbers, and nineteen female (0.3 per cent).[212] Ten years later, while the male total had risen to 6,058, only eight women brokers and jobbers were enumerated (0.1 per cent), with three more listed as retired.[213] Even with the necessary caveats—half-commission agents may not have been counted as stockbrokers; provincial stockbrokers who combined broking with other commercial services may have described themselves under different headings; the data exclude Scottish stockbrokers—the numbers suggest the barriers that remained.[214]

Women stockbrokers and their allies were well aware of the wider culture shift required to create more opportunities. Holmes urged parents to 'put their girls in business careers' rather than options they perceived to be safe, but which offered poor pay and poorer prospects.[215] Helena Normanton, too, placed the onus on parents, particularly stockbroker fathers, whom she argued should encourage their daughters as well as sons into business.[216] Following the example set by several female stockbrokers before the war, Holmes sought to give as many young women as possible a start in finance in her own firm. She and Turner employed mostly women, not only to extend opportunities, but also as a practical demonstration of women's 'business efficiency'.[217] Beginning fresh out of school as office girls at £1 a week, the ambitious and hard-working ones could be promoted to heads of department on £6 8s. a week, while 'those who only think of a "safe" job' were weeded out.[218] Holmes explained that one woman, under 20, 'handled the entire securities of the company, and...had three juniors whom she had trained herself'.[219] In 1924, the company employed sixty 'girl clerks', while by 1930, the office had nearly a hundred staff, 'the majority women'.[220] The convention that women staff would leave when they married—the 'marriage bar' which curtailed so many women's careers in the interwar years—did not apply here. 'Sometimes our girls stay on after marriage, sometimes they don't; but we regard it as entirely their own affair as to which course they pursue'.[221]

Opportunities in male-run houses were also increasing. Though recognizing the new degrees in commerce being offered by London University, as well as degrees in law and economics, Normanton argued that the best route into stockbroking for an ambitious woman was to get a lowly position in a member broker's office—typist or filing clerk—where she could gain a practical education, absorbing 'everything possible about the methods and scope of the business itself'. Showing intelligence in the role could lead to promotion, or if not, she could switch to a firm that would give her opportunities, 'explaining quite clearly to her new employers that she was ambitious and desired to advance along the main route'.[222] If this sounded optimistic at a time when clerical work for women was typically viewed as 'a stop-gap between school and marriage', then at least one 1930s careers expert affirmed that in business, employers were becoming more open to the idea that 'girls' who proved they had 'the brains and personality of a future executive' should be promoted.[223] Around the same time, women were also placing their own adverts seeking work in brokerages. Though most common were adverts from women searching for secretarial work, a few were pitching their ambitions higher. One 'business woman' boasting an extensive grounding in Stock Exchange affairs, including 'advice on investments', advertised in *The Times* for a 'situation where payment is in accordance with results'.[224] Later, the *Financial Times* carried the notice, 'Competent Woman seeks Senior Post Stock Exchange business'.[225] While it is impossible to know whether such advertisements got results, their existence would have been hard to imagine in the pre-war City.

Though many of this generation of women stockbrokers were forging long-lasting careers, traditional constraints continued to limit their options. Few women combined a stockbroking career with marriage, let alone children. For Dubliner Oonah Keogh, marriage to Bayan Giltsoff in 1933 signalled the dissolution of the partnership with her father and the end of her broking career, though she did develop a building and restoration business with her husband in Somerset.[226] At a time when the marriage bar was very much the norm in banking, Mabel Gosnell was unusual in combining marriage and finance.[227] She spent four days a week in London, returning at weekends to her country home in Hampshire and her husband. 'My husband does not object, and I like the work as a career', she told reporters, hinting at the uncommonness of such an arrangement.[228] Indeed, Holmes, Maskell, Midgley, Moreton, Mortimer, Robinson, Taylor, Tyrrell, and White all remained single through these years, living with parents and, in some instances, siblings. For some, a single life and the good income generated by a successful brokerage facilitated a flexible and rewarding lifestyle. Amy Moreton, for example, was able to combine stockbroking with her many other interests. She closed her office in Nuneaton in the late 1920s to spend a year in the south of France. When she returned, she took up a role with a Birmingham brokerage.[229] As well as more travel, including an extended trip through Africa ending in Durban with her father in 1938, she returned to her former literary pursuits, having a one-act play about post-war conditions performed in Birmingham in 1931.[230] She was also increasingly active in local Conservative politics, securing election as Nuneaton area chairman of the women's branch of the party in 1935, before being elected to the Warwickshire County Council in 1937, and to the Nuneaton Town Council the following year.[231]

Others experienced less freedom, however, especially those living with a stockbroker father. Keogh's exit from broking was accelerated by a deteriorating relationship with her father Joseph. Though the terms of the partnership were that both would share equally in the profits, Joseph did not honour this agreement. The relationship was further strained by Joseph's personality: Oonah found him 'very difficult' and 'self-opinionated', and he would make decisions without consulting her. By the end of 1930, she was going less frequently into the office, and the following year she moved to England, though remaining a partner.[232] Shortly afterwards she met her future husband. More stable, though still perhaps tense, was the relationship between Hugh and Phyllis Robinson in Bury. Father and daughter were still working and living together into the 1950s: indeed, Hugh only stepped down from Bury magistrates on his seventy-fifth birthday in 1943 under the age rule.[233] In 1952, aged 84, he celebrated sixty years as a stockbroker, and told the press that he had no intention of retiring. 'The more leisure a man has, the greater opportunity he has for indiscretions', he confided. So he continued to come into work every day, and while Phyllis was office manager, Hugh remained head of the firm.[234] That she may have lived somewhat in the shadow of her father is suggested by the fact that, just weeks after his death in 1954, Phyllis, now in her late fifties, announced her engagement to the vicar of her local church.[235] Hugh, it seemed, had not approved.

Gordon Holmes also had a complex relationship with a parent—in this case, her mother Maria, with whom she lived until the latter's death in 1939. Maria was 'entirely dependent...emotionally as well as financially' on her daughter, who found her mother's behaviour controlling and manipulative.[236] Though this got in the way of her own friendships and relationships, it did not preclude a lavish

116   SEXISM IN THE CITY

lifestyle. Holmes enjoyed the luxuries that went with her large earnings, becoming a familiar face at opulent hotel Claridge's, where she was known as 'The White Queen' on account of her all-white outfits. In the United States, where she was a frequent visitor, she became a high-profile figure, acquiring the nickname 'Miss John D. Rockefeller'.[237] Even if most other female stockbrokers lived less extravagantly than this, finance was clearly beginning to offer women significant opportunities for independence and fulfilment.

Conclusion

Though the numbers of women stockbrokers remained small, this fact should not obscure some notable interwar developments. Women were gaining a foothold in the financial world outside London, operating in towns and cities across the country. Several demonstrated considerable entrepreneurial spirit in establishing their own businesses, and were undoubtedly more successful than their predecessors, some careers spanning several decades. They also experienced a growing visibility and status, sometimes participating in wider debates about professional and businesswomen, and encouraging girls to follow in their footsteps. But while some women were hired by London firms specifically to cater to female investors, most resisted being seen in gendered terms, trading under androgynous or masculine names, not challenging existing business norms, and not going out of their way to seek a female clientele. They therefore demonstrated a kind of 'gender-blindness'—a rejection of the importance of gender in business—that scholars have presented as a characteristic of much more recent generations of female entrepreneurs.[238] Driven by a desire to avoid being 'othered' and marginalized within the financial system at a time when they were widely viewed as 'strange', this gender-blindness may have helped women to operate effectively in many ways. But gender became impossible to ignore when it came to the issue of access to the nation's stock exchanges, whose exclusion of women clearly undermined claims regarding the gender-neutrality of business. Several of the women discussed in this chapter attempted to change this, with mixed results, as we shall now see.

Sexism in the City: Women Stockbrokers in Modern Britain. James Taylor, Oxford University Press.
© James Taylor 2025. DOI: 10.1093/9780191990397.003.0005

5

Angels in the House

Women Stockbrokers and the Stock Exchanges, 1914–1945

On Monday, 30 June 1919, to mark the signing of the Treaty of Versailles the previous Saturday, the London Stock Exchange opened the day's proceedings with singing of the national anthem followed by a peace ceremony. With attention focused elsewhere during the singing, two women sneaked into the building and managed to reach the floor of the exchange.

> Some members, observing the strangers, at once treated them to good-humoured banter and began to bid boisterously for 'the two lots'. By this time the waiters got wind of the intruders, and escorted them out of the building amid shouts and laughter, this being the first appearance of women on 'Change during office hours.[1]

Though an inconsequential episode in itself, by succeeding where the suffragettes had failed before the war, the women's prank was freighted with significance in the context of the Stock Exchange's exclusionary policies. Indeed, one paper headlined its report 'Coming Events? Women Invade Stock Exchange'.[2] The members themselves attempted to defuse the challenge of the invasion by reducing the women to the level of commodities, bidding for 'the two lots' as they might goods at an auction. If women had made it to the floor of the exchange, then it was not as traders, but as objects to be traded. Nevertheless, some commentators used the incident to reflect seriously upon women's prospects in finance in the post-war world, looking forward to a time when they could become members of the Stock Exchange.[3]

The subject of women's professional opportunities was very much in the air in the summer of 1919. The war had completely recast the suffrage debate, allowing patriotic service and sacrifice—the experience of millions of women during the war—to replace sex as the key test for citizenship.[4] The result was the Representation of the People Act of 1918, which enfranchised nearly 8.5 million women over 30 who met a property qualification.[5] But there was recognition that legislation on a wider basis was needed, and the Coalition Government went to the polls in the November 1918 election pledged 'to remove all existing

118 SEXISM IN THE CITY

inequalities of the law as between men and women'. The result was the Sex Disqualification (Removal) Act of 1919.[6] This stipulated:

> A person shall not be disqualified by sex or marriage from the exercise of any public function, or from being appointed to or holding any civil or judicial office or post, or from entering or assuming or carrying on any civil profession or vocation, or for admission to any incorporated society (whether incorporated by Royal Charter or otherwise).[7]

Long regarded as 'a broken reed' or 'a dead letter' by historians who pointed out that it did not contain provisions for enforcement, and that it had little effect on the marriage bar, the Act has undergone something of a re-evaluation more recently.[8] It certainly had an immediate impact: having been rejected as a student by the Middle Temple in 1918, Helena Normanton successfully reapplied within hours of the Act's passage, and others swiftly followed. By the time Normanton was called to the Bar in November 1922, Ivy Williams had already qualified in May, and Frances Kyle and April Deverell in Ireland in November 1921.[9] Women made swift progress in other areas of law, with Carrie Morrison becoming the first female solicitor in 1922, while women began sitting as Justices of the Peace in magistrates' courts, giving them an immediate and significant position of power in the public space of the courtroom.[10] In accountancy, the 72-year-old Mary Harris Smith finally won her decades-long battle to gain admittance to the Institute of Chartered Accountants in England and Wales, while north of the border women could now enter the Institute of Accountants and Actuaries in Glasgow.[11] Other institutions were also now legally obliged to admit women, including the Royal College of Veterinary Surgeons and the Royal Institution of Chartered Surveyors.[12]

These victories had, according to one *Daily Express* columnist, produced 'a slight air of nervousness' on the London Stock Exchange. 'Is the woman stockbroker coming—or, rather, how much longer can this most conservative of bodies keep her out of the House?'[13] In fact, the issue had already arisen during the war. In December 1914, John Lawson, a long-time member of the Leeds Stock Exchange, died, and his widow Annie took over his place in the firm alongside John's business partner. But in May 1917, the Stock Exchange's managing committee spotted an irregularity. Though the firm consisted of two partners, since 1915 only one annual subscription had been paid, in contravention of the rules. The solution decided upon by the committee was a surprising one: Annie Lawson would be elected a member of the exchange.[14] A special meeting was ordered for the following month at which Lawson was duly elected: the first woman to become a member of a British stock exchange.[15] This seemingly momentous event was motivated entirely by monetary considerations. The same day that Annie was elected, the secretary of the Stock Exchange wrote to her ordering payment of the £25 entrance fee, £15 annual subscription for the remainder of 1917, and a nominal backdated subscription of two guineas for 1915–16.[16] Nevertheless, the occasion was noted positively in a few newspapers, the *Financial News*—somewhat unexpectedly—among them. Underlining women's involvement in business 'for nearly seven centuries', it argued that it was 'about time woman passed from the generalities of mercantile life to the special opportunities of the Stock Exchange'. Though admitting the exceptional circumstances of the war, it hoped that 'the officials of other provincial exchanges will be disposed to follow the chivalrous example'.[17] Indeed, *The Accountant* believed that now one stock exchange had 'broken the ice', it was likely that others would follow. It predicted, however, that London would be 'the last to surrender', but that it could 'hardly hold out indefinitely'.[18]

But the precedent set in Leeds was largely symbolic. The minute books show that Lawson never attended any general meetings of the Stock Exchange, nor does it seem that she went on the trading floor prior to withdrawing from the firm and resigning as a member at the end of 1921.[19] Other provincial exchanges did not follow Leeds's example, and the idea that London would consider changing its policies appeared far-fetched. Interviewed by the *Daily Graphic* in 1919, Edith Maskell said that although several members had assured her that 'they have no personal objection to women stockbrokers', she feared that 'it will be a long time before we gain admission to the House'.[20] It was even alleged that older members were 'disturbed' by the mere presence of women in the vicinity of the exchange, as it was now common 'for a girl secretary to deliver documents at the "House", or to call a broker or jobber to the doors'.[21]

The wider public was encouraged to see the London Stock Exchange as its members themselves regarded it. The opening line of *The ABC of Stocks and Shares* (1925), penned by leading financial journalist Hargreaves Parkinson, explained to readers: 'The London Stock Exchange can best be described as a peculiar and exclusive club'.[22] If the broker-journalist Walter Landells, who wrote the chatty 'Round the Markets' column for the *Financial Times* under the pen-name 'Autolycus', was representative of wider Stock Exchange opinion, then the prospect of women joining the club was remote.[23] Usually dealing with the subject under the ironic heading 'Angel in the House'—referencing Coventry Patmore's 1850s paean to feminine domesticity—he was confident that 'there is not a single Stock Exchange in the United Kingdom which would elect a lady as a member'.[24]

Nevertheless, in the wake of the 1919 Act, and the progress being made by women in other professions, the issue remained a live one through the interwar years. Buoyed by support from women's organizations and—increasingly—from the press, more women were willing to apply for membership, forcing stock exchanges to define and justify their exclusionary policies. Some breakthroughs were made, especially outside London, but most exchanges remained antagonistic to women. By the mid-1930s, growing concerns about the fraudulent activities of outside brokers raised the possibility of sweeping legislative action to curb the

120   SEXISM IN THE CITY

sector. The implications for women stockbrokers were uncertain. On the one hand, restrictive intervention threatened the livelihoods of women who were obliged to work outside the exchanges; on the other hand, it raised the possibility that parliamentary power could be deployed to abolish the sex bar.

Exclusionary Strategies

The late nineteenth and early twentieth centuries saw the continuing expansion of the stock and share market outside London, with the memberships of provincial stock exchanges continuing to grow, and new exchanges being formed in cities like Dundee and Nottingham.[25] In 1890, the three largest exchanges—Liverpool, Manchester, and Glasgow—were the main movers behind the formation of the Council of Associated Stock Exchanges, designed to promote joint action and assimilate rules across the country. By 1922, the organization comprised twenty-two stock exchanges with a total of over 1,000 members.[26] Stockbrokers in towns without a stock exchange were also beginning to see the benefits of greater collaboration. Following successful joint action in 1912 to lobby the London Stock Exchange to rethink changes to its rules on commission which would have made it harder for London members to deal with outside brokers, they formed the Provincial Stock and Share Brokers' Association, which was incorporated by a Board of Trade charter in 1914.[27] The Association aimed to give its members a voice and a shared identity, and it was well supported. By 1923, it boasted a membership of over 250, doing business in 102 towns across the UK.[28]

Anxious to gain credibility, and to foster good relations with the London Stock Exchange, the Association strove to mirror London's rules and regulations. In particular, this meant adopting by-laws curtailing members' freedom to advertise and circularize the public, distancing itself from the activities of the less reputable outside brokers, measures which caused significant ructions.[29] This made it all the more notable when, in May 1923, Doris Mortimer, who had taken over as senior partner in her father's Exeter firm W. Mortimer & Son on his death in April 1922, was welcomed as a member.[30] By admitting a woman, the Association was diverging from the practice of the established exchanges in a noteworthy way, at a time when it was lobbying for uniform national standards for stockbroking.[31]

The Association's openness to gender equality was in part pragmatic: its incorporated status brought it under the terms of the 1919 Sex Disqualification (Removal) Act, meaning that rejecting an application from a woman would place it on doubtful ground. But its stance was likely also due to attitudes among its early leaders. Hugh Moscrop Robinson was one of the founders and first presidents of the Association, and having brought his daughter Phyllis into his brokerage, he clearly had no prejudices against the idea of women brokers. Moreover, the fact that the Association was a professional body rather than a physical stock exchange may have made it easier for members to contemplate female brokers: arguments about women not being able to tolerate the harsh conditions of the trading floor were clearly irrelevant.

But Mortimer's admission was nevertheless significant. The idea that the Association was a kind of stock exchange in its own right was strengthened by its foundation of the Provincial Brokers' Stock Exchange in 1924.[32] Though headquartered in Hull, it did not possess a trading floor. Nevertheless, its establishment was a further step towards the official status and recognition of its members.[33] Indeed, as a member, Mortimer quibbled with descriptions of herself in the press as an 'outside broker'.[34] Women's groups recognized Mortimer's success as important—she was 'the first woman to enter the stockbroking profession by the front door', argued the *Woman's Leader*, which was a step towards the ultimate goal—admission to the London Stock Exchange. Mortimer's admission meant that 'an attack has been made on the circumference of the profession, and the citadel becomes in consequence more easy of approach'.[35] And though the Association had abandoned its charter when it became the Provincial Brokers' Stock Exchange, it did not use this as a pretext to alter its admissions policies, with Phyllis Moscrop Robinson joining Mortimer as the second female member in 1925.[36]

That year, an even bigger milestone was reached in the new Irish Free State, established under the Anglo-Irish Treaty of 1921. Having been invited by her father, Joseph, into the family stockbroking firm, Oonah Keogh soon afterwards applied for membership of the Dublin Stock Exchange in May 1925. Aged just 22, Keogh's application divided members. Opponents cited the Dublin Exchange's rejection of Anne Bulger's application in 1904 as sufficient rationale for blocking Keogh, but the context had changed significantly since then.[37] Article 3 of the 1922 Constitution of the Free State bestowed equal rights on its citizens 'without distinction of sex', and as a chartered body, whose new members were licensed by the Minister of Finance, the exchange's ability to ignore this was in doubt. Though scholars have highlighted the 'fundamental weakness' of the Constitution as a guarantee of equality, in this instance, it did have a significant impact.[38] Political eyes were trained on events, one member of the Irish parliament writing to the President of the Stock Exchange reminding him of the Constitution. The exchange's legal counsel agreed, advising the governing committee that rejecting Keogh on the grounds of sex would be illegal. Keogh's opponents now changed tack, proposing a change in the rules to insist that all new members serve a three-year apprenticeship in a broker's office before being admitted. But her supporters signalled that they would pressure the Minister of Finance to veto such a patently cynical rule change.[39] The governing committee interviewed Keogh and found no reason to question her 'fitness and means' to act as a broker: it certainly helped that one of her sureties was the Minister of Agriculture, while Joseph Keogh was a popular long-time member of the exchange.[40] The ultimate decision was handed back to the members, who voted in favour by a majority show of hands.[41] This was not an enthusiastic embrace of equality, one member telling the press 'we had no alternative but to admit her.'[42] But it did firmly establish women's right to join the exchange, which amended its rules to clarify that 'any words which import the masculine gender shall be understood to indicate the feminine gender wherever the context so permits.'[43]

The success of Mortimer and Keogh raised questions for London.[44] When in 1924 there were rumours—false it turned out—that Mortimer planned to move to London and apply for membership of the London Stock Exchange, the Committee for General Purposes was unconcerned.[45] A *Financial Times* reporter was told by the Secretary's Office 'that if a lady applied for membership her application would be placed before the Committee, but the result would be—(the remainder of the answer was expressed by a shrug of the shoulders.)'[46] But events in Dublin— which were widely reported in the United Kingdom—sufficiently spooked the Committee into seeking the opinion of its solicitors on the implications of the Sex Disqualification (Removal) Act for the Stock Exchange.[47] In response to a query from the solicitors, Messrs Travers Smith Braithwaite & Co., the Committee made it clear that they wished 'to exclude women from membership.'[48] The solicitors accordingly produced an opinion that suited the agenda of their clients. Though the Stock Exchange's rules on membership did not explicitly bar women, the language throughout gendered members as male, 'and there is nowhere any Rule or definition that the masculine includes the feminine'. Consequently, Travers Smith Braithwaite advised that women were not eligible as candidates, and the Committee 'would be quite in order in refusing to accept a nomination of a female if put forward'. The Sex Disqualification (Removal) Act did not change this because the London Stock Exchange, unlike its Irish counterpart, was not an incorporated society. Moreover, London did not possess a monopoly. There was nothing to prevent women from operating as brokers outside the House: membership of the London Stock Exchange 'only enables persons to carry on such profession or vocation in a particular place, which is a private building.'[49] Armed with this legal opinion, the Committee directed the secretary to refuse any application by a woman.[50]

There were hints that a few London brokers had different views on the gender question. The London Correspondent of the *Sheffield Daily Telegraph* reported in 1928 that 'some London stockbrokers are preparing for the day when women will be admitted to the "house". They are training young women in their business just as they do the men clerks who will eventually become partners.'[51] Yet the question of women's membership would be tested first not in London but in Bradford, though metropolitan attitudes would shape the outcome. By 1930, Edith Midgley, now in her early forties, had worked for the same firm of stockbrokers for nineteen years. She had trained young men who had subsequently joined the Bradford Stock Exchange, and saw no reason why she should not follow the same course, especially as membership would open the door to a partnership. She soon encountered difficulties, however, in securing nominations: even her employer, despite having promised to back her, reneged at the last minute, citing her sex as the reason. Midgley enquired directly with the Bradford Stock Exchange as to its policy on women. Uncertain as to what it should do, the committee solicited the opinions of other exchanges. The secretary then wrote back to Midgley, claiming to have received 'a definite ruling' from the London Stock Exchange that 'such applications should be refused'. Undeterred, Midgley eventually managed to secure nominations, but the committee refused to accept them, the secretary writing to her in January 1931: 'There has been no change since the previous inquiry, nor is there likely to be, so long as the ruling of the London Stock Exchange Committee obtains.'[52] To try to put the issue to bed, later that month the committee passed a new rule stating that so long as the London Stock Exchange refused applications from women, 'the same shall be incorporated and form part of the rules and regulations of this Exchange'.[53]

London's own stance was put directly to the test in 1936, when Mabel Gosnell signalled to the Committee for General Purposes that she wanted to apply for membership so that she could become a partner in George J. Ascott & Co., the firm for which she worked as a half-commission agent. She understood that the secretary had previously been instructed not to accept an application from a woman, but 'would respectfully ask that the Committee reconsider the matter & allow me to apply for membership in the ordinary way'.[54] Gosnell's approach led the Committee once again to check its legal position, consulting Frederick Branson, a partner in commercial law firm Linklaters and Paines. Combing through the Stock Exchange's foundational deed of settlement, Branson quickly encountered a problem: in the first clause, it was laid down that 'words importing the masculine include the feminine gender'. The implication was that the clause dealing with the admission of members 'would allow of the admission of women'. Yet the clause went on to say that the persons admitted to membership would be those the Committee 'shall think proper' which, Branson argued, entitled the Committee 'to refuse admission to women if they think fit to do so'. Moreover, the rules subsequently passed to elaborate the processes for admitting members did distinguish between the sexes, and there was nothing in them 'to make the masculine include the feminine'. He concluded that 'a woman seeking admission is not a "candidate" within the meaning of the Rules, and that the Committee are not bound to recognize, or in any way to act on her application'. Nothing in the Sex Disqualification (Removal) Act, Branson assured the Committee, affected this judgement.[55] As a result, Gosnell was informed that 'the Committee were not prepared to vary the instructions given in July 1925'.[56]

London thus excluded women informally, based on legal advice, rather than passing a rule explicitly discriminating on sex. Though Bradford referred to a 'ruling' of the London Stock Exchange, its policy lacked even this status, since a ruling was 'an interpretation by the Committee of a rule [which] usually follows a query regarding the rules and is communicated to members for their guidance'.[57] The London Stock Exchange preferred to continue quietly excluding women without drawing attention to the issue by dealing with it more formally. Bradford's rule made it the only stock exchange in the country to have adopted a formal bar.[58] There were suggestions that members of other provincial exchanges had different views on the matter. One leading member of the Leeds Stock Exchange, which, as we have seen, had admitted Annie Lawson during the war, claimed that if they received an application, 'we should not consider ourselves bound by London, but should consider the application on its merits'.[59] Likewise, the secretary of the Glasgow Stock Exchange said that no woman had applied, but if one did, she would receive the same treatment as a man.[60] Yet feminists were sceptical about such expressions of independence, arguing that Bradford proved that 'Stock Exchanges, though "nominally open", quickly shut up when a qualified woman approaches for admission.'[61]

Confirmation came in 1936 in the form of an enquiry sent by the Soroptimist Clubs of Great Britain and Ireland to twenty-two stock exchanges across the British Isles regarding their policies on admitting women. Remarkably, given Midgley's efforts to join the Bradford Stock Exchange, the Council of the Associated Stock Exchanges advised its members 'to reply that as the question put was purely hypothetical no opinion could be expressed'.[62] Others were less diplomatic. At the annual meeting of the Council, a member of the Newport Stock Exchange, Harold Griffiths, expressed his outrage that 'a lot of chits of girls...chose to write to us and ask us a question of this sort', and advised his fellow brokers that 'the only proper way of dealing with that is to put the letter in the waste-paper basket, as I did. It is perfectly absurd.'[63] Nevertheless, besides Dublin, which of course admitted women, fifteen other responses were received. They did not offer much encouragement, however: 'four stated they did not admit women and the remaining eleven declined to say that they would admit women'.[64] London's preferences, though not codified, undoubtedly set the tone for the nation's exchanges.

Mixed Stockbroking?

However, male stockbrokers were not able to silence women on this issue. The question of the stock exchanges' discriminatory policies remained a live one in the interwar years largely thanks to the efforts of women stockbrokers, with the support of women's organizations. Despite a growing focus on domestic and welfare issues, feminist groups remained deeply concerned with women's opportunities outside the home, and female stockbrokers were able to tap into these networks to publicize their cause.[65] Early on in her attempt to obtain entry to the

Bradford Stock Exchange, Edith Midgley won the backing of Alderman Kathleen Chambers, the city's Deputy Lord Mayor.[66] A member of the Labour Party and of the Women's Freedom League, Chambers was able to help Midgley make contacts in London, including radical Labour MP Ellen Wilkinson. In 1930, Wilkinson gave a lunchtime talk to a large gathering of Rotary Club members, tackling the question 'Are Business Men Wasting the Talents of Women?' Though not mentioning Midgley by name, she referenced her case, highlighting that despite having worked in a stockbroker's office for nearly two decades, she had been rejected by the Bradford Stock Exchange, 'while a man who had trained under her was given membership after only seventeen months' experience'.[67] Midgley also talked to the Open Door Council, founded in 1926 to promote equal rights for women in the workplace.[68] But it was the WFL which most enthusiastically took up her cause.

At a time when the WFL's president, Emmeline Pethick-Lawrence, was particularly concerned by what she saw as a determined male counterattack on women's position in the workplace driven by rising unemployment in the early 1930s, Midgley's predicament resonated deeply.[69] The WFL's weekly paper, *The Vote*, began reporting on Midgley's situation, and encouraged its readers to influence the debate, suggesting they consider 'ventilating the question with any stockbrokers of their acquaintance'.[70] Delegates debated the subject at the WFL's annual conference in April 1931, and passed a resolution calling on the nation's stock exchanges to remove their ban on women.[71] Midgley joined the WFL that year and her presence kept the issue firmly on the organization's agenda. In 1932, members passed a resolution protesting against 'the continued sex differentiation shown by the Bradford Stock Exchange' and calling on it 'to bring its rules more into line with modern practice in other professions'.[72] Such votes became fixtures at subsequent WFL conferences.[73]

The WFL's secretary, Florence Underwood, who also edited *The Vote*, was particularly engaged in this campaign. In the early 1920s the London County Council had established a course of classes and lectures for clerks of the London Stock Exchange: an early example of professional training.[74] The classes proved popular, and it became customary for the Stock Exchange chairman to present prizes and certificates to the successful students every year. At the prizegiving in December 1932, chairman Sir Archibald Campbell praised the 'great moral training' provided by the Stock Exchange, and its democratic approach: 'all young men practically started with the same advantages. There was no favouritism towards class or circumstances'.[75] A *Times* report of the speech, headlined 'Equality of Opportunity', infuriated Underwood, who pointed out the obvious hypocrisy in an article in *The Vote*, in which she regretted 'that no women were present to ask him why women were excluded from admission'.[76] She followed up with a letter to Campbell protesting against the Stock Exchange's stance on women, and threatening legal action.[77] Its policy, argued Underwood, was illegal

126 SEXISM IN THE CITY

under the Sex Disqualification (Removal) Act, and she signalled that the WFL was 'prepared to fight that point'.[78] She was bullish about the strength of their case, reportedly saying that if it reached the House of Lords, 'she was certain that it would go in Miss Midgley's favour'.[79]

Such a legal challenge never emerged, however, and it would be easy to see Underwood's threats as empty bluster. Indeed, Catriona Beaumont characterizes the WFL and the Open Door Council as 'small and somewhat ineffectual pressure groups throughout the 1930s'.[80] With just sixty to seventy delegates attending the WFL's annual conferences, their resolutions would hardly have caused the nation's stock exchanges much anxiety.[81] Yet their backing was highly significant. For one thing, they provided Midgley with valuable moral support in her quest to win membership. In 1931 she wrote to the WFL to say that she appreciated 'more than I can say the help of the various organizations, as without their help I couldn't have pressed my claim nearly so far'.[82] Two years later, she renewed her thanks to the executive committee at the annual conference, saying: 'I do not think I should have been able to keep on so far if they had not been behind me. It really does hearten one on.'[83] Buoyed by their support, she established her own brokerage in Bradford in 1933, and kept on applying to the Bradford Stock Exchange, notching up her sixth rejection in 1936. Such was their opposition that when she took on a male partner, and he applied for membership, he was rejected on the grounds that a woman was the head of the firm.[84] The WFL did not try to conceal its exasperation, issuing an official statement condemning the Bradford Stock Exchange for 'emulating the insufferable arrogance, blind prejudice, and cowardly fear of women's competition of the London Brotherhood'.[85]

Moreover, the WFL's persistence helped to make the exclusion of women by the nation's stock exchanges a matter of public debate. Once Midgley had made contact with the WFL, it got in touch with the press, which immediately took up the story.[86] With interwar newspapers making a more systematic pitch to female readers than previously—and showing particular fascination for the 'modern woman'—they proved far more interested in the subject than they had before the war.[87] At the same time, as a study of interwar reporting of women barristers argues, satirical approaches poking fun at both sides allowed papers 'to sell more copies than would unreserved support for any particular interest group'.[88] This strategy can be seen in *Daily Mirror*'s resident cartoonist W. K. Haselden's contribution (see Fig. 5.1). Haselden mocked male brokers' extreme opposition to admitting women, the first panel of the cartoon showing a harassed City man with his back to the door of the Stock Exchange, blocking women's entry, and exclaiming 'NEVER!'. Yet the rest of the cartoon suggested that Haselden shared their sense of the absurdity of the prospect of 'mixed stockbroking'. This is reflected linguistically, with the term 'stockbrokeresses' subtly 'marking' women stockbrokers as frivolous and divergent from the masculine norm.[89] More obviously, the absurdity is conveyed visually, with panels depicting an oxymoronic

ANGELS IN THE HOUSE 127

Fig. 5.1 W. K. Haselden, 'Women on the Stock Exchange', *Daily Mirror*, 19 May 1933, 11. Reproduced with permission from Reach Licensing

female bull on the telephone, and a 'she-bear' clutching a parasol and share certificates. The last two panels contain a gendered reversal of the traditional stockbroking and seduction trope, with a female broker smoking at a dinner table with a male client, leaning forward and confidentially advising him which shares to buy. The final panel shows the advice turning out bad, and the female broker insouciantly admitting that she may have accidentally recommended the wrong stock.

The press latched onto women and stock exchanges as a polarizing topic generating good copy and engaging reader interest. Haselden's cartoon was a response to a *Mirror* article two days earlier describing Midgley's struggles with the Bradford Stock Exchange. His cartoon in turn prompted a series of readers' letters on 'stockbrokeresses', all recycling various gendered clichés, and amplifying ideas in Haselden's cartoon. One, written by a stockbroker's clerk, stated that he 'should hardly like to risk financial ruin at the hands of women stockbrokers. Unlike men, they would not stop to think seriously before recommending the purchase or selling of shares.' Another held that women were 'too vague-minded to run a business which requires an essentially business mind.'[90] A little later, the topic featured in the *Daily Herald*'s 'Controversy Corner'. Popular novelist Gilbert Frankau vigorously opposed women's membership of stock exchanges on the grounds that women 'have no sense of money at all. The average girl is brought up with no knowledge of money and she receives no training in any of the many aspects of finance and business.' Men, by contrast, 'have an inherent aptitude for handling money. They have done it for centuries.' Apparently, Frankau believed it would take centuries more to remedy the situation.[91]

As in the earlier period, journalists sometimes solicited the views of male brokers on the issue, and, as previously, they sometimes felt that no reasons for excluding women needed to be given. One exclaimed: 'A woman in the Stock Exchange! It's unthinkable. It would cause a revolution.'[92] Another simply described excluding women as 'common sense'.[93] Others advanced more concrete reasons. Some focused on women's perceived intellectual limitations: working 'by instinct rather than by reason', and unable to master the technicalities of stock exchange jargon, they would struggle on the stock exchange.[94] But arguments increasingly emphasized women's supposed physical frailty. In a range of fields, including medicine, law, and academia, exclusionary strategies highlighted 'the physically tiring and arduous nature of the job' to justify women's exclusion or relegation to subordinate roles.[95] As we have seen, such arguments were present in late Victorian stockbroking, but they became even more prevalent with the development of the Stock Exchange's cult of athleticism in the early twentieth century, which became a growing part of the institution's public image. The year 1903 saw close to a hundred members compete in a fifty-two-mile walk from London to Brighton.[96] Enormous crowds gathered to watch the start, and the race became an annual tradition, garnering much media attention. The Brighton Walk was seen as proof of 'the health and athleticism of the Stock Exchange', an impression deepened by its formation of an athletic club in 1911.[97] From this point the various sporting pursuits of members—rugby, boxing, swimming, football— were extensively reported.[98] Physical prowess was not simply celebrated for its own sake, but was seen as a reliable indicator of moral character, as in this judgement by a *Financial Times* journalist:

> The House is proud of its athletic reputation, for 'the glory of a man is in his strength', and whatever detractors may have to say about the London Stock Exchange, its virility is unquestionable. A man is soon sized up in the market, and it is very seldom that this collective estimation of a member's character has to be revised.[99]

This linkage was deepened by war service: the closure of the Stock Exchange in July 1914 expedited the formation of what became known as the 'Stockbrokers' Battalion', one of the first 'pals' battalions of the war.[100]

Athleticism, virility, and moral character were thus increasingly bound up together in the identities of members. The institution became a forum in which men sought 'to have their manhood validated by other men'.[101] Borrowing from more recent gender theorists, it is possible to see stock exchange masculinity as a relational 'homosocial enactment', performed for—and assessed by—other men.[102] This made it all the harder for stock exchange members to imagine women in their midst. At a time when women were beginning to make inroads into other professions, members latched onto the idea that stock exchanges were fundamentally different, posing uniquely physical challenges which made women's participation impossible. Working on the floor of the exchange was 'not like acting as a principal in law, or business, or accountancy, or even like getting up and pleading as an advocate in the courts', explained one broker.[103] Life on the stock exchange floor was 'far too strenuous' for them.[104] When Mabel Gosnell's application was refused in 1936, a London broker explained that it was for her own good, for 'a woman would be at a grave disadvantage when markets are active and brute strength is an important asset'. Their presence would—ironically—upset the democracy of the trading floor. Male brokers might, for example, feel obliged to behave courteously towards them, which was an unfair benefit. 'On the floor of the House all men are equal. But a woman would be either worse or better off.'[105] Either way, the smooth working of the market was undermined. 'Emphasis on physical difference', as Beth Jenkins argues, rather than supposed intellectual failings, therefore became an increasingly useful tool for exclusion.[106] This was spotted by novelist Virginia Woolf, who highlighted the shift in emphasis in interwar exclusionary strategies: 'whatever the brain might do when the professions were opened to it, the body remained'.[107]

The press did not allow these views to go unchallenged, and counterarguments were given a far greater airing than before the First World War. Of course, *The Vote* was in the forefront of efforts to rebut the reasoning of male brokers, taking particular exception to the contention that the floor of the exchange was too hazardous an environment for women. Such arguments carried little weight in the modern age, 'when the whole world is accustomed to women's feats of energy and endurance'.[108] But readers of a variety of other newspapers would also find brokers' contentions challenged. The *Daily Telegraph* reported Ellen Wilkinson's rejection of the physical frailty argument, Wilkinson pointing out that female MPs had proven that they could work for twenty-two and a half hours at an all-night sitting in the House of Commons without problems.[109] Readers of the *Manchester Guardian* learned from Midgley that the rough and tumble of the London Stock Exchange was not representative of the nation's other exchanges, many of which were smaller, more sedate spaces. Bradford's had fewer than twenty members, who met for less than half an hour twice a day; arguments used to exclude women from the London Stock Exchange were therefore irrelevant elsewhere.[110]

With its focus on human interest, the popular press was keen to highlight the personal stories involved in women's battles to become inside brokers, and to present their point of view to readers. Gosnell's rejection in 1936 made headlines, with journalists besieging her London flat eager to interview her. A reporter for the *Daily Express* gained access, and described 'a tall, handsome figure in a chiffon gown [and] a little white "halo" hat'; the *Daily Mirror* had even more success,

SHE WANTS TO BE ON THE STOCK EXCHANGE

Mrs. H. T. Gosnell, of Mount Royal, Oxford-street, London, who applied for membership of the London Stock Exchange. Her application has been refused, but Mrs. Gosnell hopes to be successful at some future date.

Fig. 5.2 Mabel Gosnell, *Daily Mirror*, 26 June 1936, 19. Reproduced with permission from Reach Licensing

persuading her to have her photograph taken (see Fig. 5.2). Yet she had little control over how the press represented her situation. The *Express* and *Mirror* correspondents portrayed two completely different Gosnells: one 'very distressed' by all the media attention and wanting to let the matter drop, the other much more self-possessed and vowing, as the headline ran, that 'SHE WILL NOT TAKE STOCK EXCHANGE "NO".'[111]

The overall tenor of coverage in the popular press, however, was sympathetic. The *Daily Mail* was particularly supportive, an editorial predicting that women 'will quickly demolish' all arguments against their entry.[112] The paper thought the brokers' case so weak that there must be other reasons why they were so determined to keep 'the mysteries of finance' secret from women.[113] One possible reason, thought a male columnist in the *Somerset County Gazette*, was dread of competition. 'Do the members fear the cleverer brains of the female sex will prove their undoing, and show up women's subtlety where finance is concerned?' He argued that women's 'intuitive gift' made them excellent financial advisers, and 'there is no reason why investors should not be allowed to benefit therefrom in finance.'[114] 'Olive', author of a syndicated women's column, agreed that men feared competing with women. The 'whole art' of the successful stockbroker lay in concealing whether he was a buyer or seller from the jobber with whom he was dealing. 'The more inscrutable he is in this respect the better he is at his job, and women are not less acute than men in personal concealment of their thoughts and intentions if there is reason for doing so.'[115] Some women went further, arguing that feminizing the City would improve commercial standards. High-profile cases of financial fraud emboldened one anonymous 'Business Woman' to write to the *Daily Mirror* to ask 'Would women be so trusting with the Kreugers and Hatrys?'[116] Speaking in the Commons, Conservative MP Mavis Tate agreed, arguing that since the Stock Exchange, made up entirely of men, panicked much more often than the country as a whole, women must have a beneficial effect if admitted. 'Then we might see less panic and a greater spirit of calm.'[117] Tate's viewpoint grabbed headlines: 'No jitters if women were brokers', as the *Daily Express* had it.[118]

The financial press generally took a different tack. Titles like the *Financial News*, *The Economist*, the *Investors' Review*, and the *Investors' Chronicle* mostly ignored the question through the interwar years, not seeking to question the internal arrangements of the nation's stock exchanges. The *Financial Times*—by this period the best-selling financial paper—paid slightly more attention, though usually adopting a neutral or gently sceptical stance.[119] Yet it occasionally presented a more encouraging front. The author of the 'Saturday Causerie' column cited the American examples of Tennessee Claflin and Hetty Green to argue that women 'with special aptitude for the work can easily beat the average man'. Liberalizing the rules would hardly cause 'a general invasion by women of the Stock Market', and with other professions now open to women, the onus was on those wanting to maintain the status quo to justify their position.[120] Indeed, women's progress on other fronts began to make the London Stock Exchange's stance seem unjustifiable. In 1928, the *Daily Express* observed that women could

> instruct a woman solicitor to draw up their wills disposing of all their possessions, have a woman barrister briefed to represent them in the highest courts of the land, employ a woman chartered accountant to keep their money in order, consult a woman physician or a woman surgeon on life and death matters, and help send a woman to take her seat in the mother of Parliaments to make new laws—but when it came to buying shares this must be done through a man.[121]

As well as marking out the stock exchanges as anti-progressive, the restriction on the options available to investors was attacked on the grounds of economic freedom. It was 'thoroughly bad business', argued *The Vote*. 'A woman's money is as good as a man's money, and it is ridiculous to shut out women who have money and brains as well.'[122] Ultimately, argued *The Accountant*, the issue should be decided by the individual investor, not the exchanges. 'He naturally selects his own broker, and, as it seems to us, is entitled to complain if undue restrictions are placed upon his selection.'[123] In this case, the typical gendering of the investor as male had subversive implications, by suggesting that some men might prefer to deal with a female stockbroker.

132   SEXISM IN THE CITY

Moreover, reformers were increasingly able to contrast the situation in the United Kingdom with what was happening in other nations. Women were achieving partnerships in New York Stock Exchange firms at an impressive rate, an option not available to their counterparts in London. There were three in 1914, nearly twenty in 1927, and by 1936, sixty-six of the 3,000 partners of member firms were women, twenty-eight of them active partners.[124] The New York Stock Exchange appointed its first woman to an executive role in 1928, a purchasing agent, in charge of buying supplies for the Stock Exchange and all its subsidiaries.[125] Such successes led some to believe that the New York Stock Exchange did not discriminate by sex.[126] The reality was somewhat different, however, as New York's female brokers began to find out in the 1920s. In the highest-profile case, actress-turned-broker Peggy Cleary, who had reputedly made $500,000 in successful speculations, announced in 1928 that she was willing to stump up $300,000 for a seat, but received a 'curt rebuff' on account of her sex.[127] Elsewhere, however, stock exchanges were proving more flexible. Dublin was not the only, or even the first, European stock exchange to open its doors to women. The Hamburg Stock Exchange reportedly changed its rules in 1919 to admit women.[128] The Berlin Stock Exchange followed in 1922, while the following year, Amsterdam admitted its first female member, Henriette Deterding, niece of Royal Dutch Shell director general Sir Henri Deterding.[129] By 1932, *The Vote* was claiming that stock exchanges in Norway, Bulgaria, Hungary, and Austria had also liberalized their rules.[130] The attitudes of UK exchanges could thus be painted as increasingly out of step with more enlightened attitudes elsewhere.

How the hypothetical arguments about the effects of admitting women related to the reality can be gauged by the experiences of Oonah Keogh in Dublin. Though not discussing the subject at the time, given the stigma regarding publicity, she did describe her time on the trading floor in later interviews. Her father had certainly been sensitive to the multiple ways the presence of a female body on the stock exchange might disrupt proceedings, making it clear to his daughter that it was her responsibility to manage herself so as not to disturb either the market or gendered conventions. She was under strict instructions not to wear too much make-up, while at the same time being 'careful not to have a shiny nose'; perfume was completely off-limits, on the grounds that it would 'profane the sacred precincts of the exchange'. Some brokers had been resolutely opposed to Keogh joining, and had warned her that 'they would never acknowledge her, would push past her in doorways, and do "terrible things" to her'. Consequently, on her first day she arrived at the exchange 'nearly sick with fright'. But she was introduced to her fellow members and even her former antagonists were polite. The Dublin Stock Exchange was spatially very different from its London counterpart, with brokers sitting in chairs, one for each firm, arranged in two concentric circles. Brokers would call out the stocks they wanted to buy or sell, and any broker wishing to deal would reply, 'and you look at each other like two cats ready to spring'. Aside from the shouting, telephones would ring constantly, 'each call liable to turn the market from a buying to a selling market' and back again. At first, Keogh's main role was to stand behind her father and keep the books, but when he fell ill, she traded for several months on her own. The work was demanding, and 'sometimes at home she wept under the strain', but she adapted to the 'daily battle of wits' and came to enjoy it. Her 'girlish voice' put her at a disadvantage in more frantic periods of trading when it would not carry across the floor, but in such cases, 'brokers on either side would shout up gallantly' on her behalf. On another occasion, 'a young broker blushed and stammered on her speaking to him'.[131] Whether any of this undermined the efficient working of the market, as opponents claimed, seems unlikely.

Yet despite being accepted into the exchange, Keogh encountered other obstacles. The culture remained masculine, which meant subtle exclusions, such as when a vulgar joke was told. 'The men would turn round, see me standing there and they would become embarrassed. But I didn't mind.' A more literal constraint was the gendering of many of the social spaces where deals were done. As she later recalled, 'women did not socialise with men in lounges of pubs', while when she went to the races, her father would go to the bar for a drink, whereas she 'would have to slip off for afternoon tea'.[132] Keogh ceased to be an active member of the exchange in the early 1930s, and other women did not follow her into the market in this period, years which saw the erosion of the Free State's early commitment to gender equality.[133] The only other woman visible as a broker in Ireland in this period is Violet Condon, who also worked in her father's firm, John Condon and Son, in Youghal, County Cork. As with growing numbers of women brokers in the United Kingdom, it was the Provincial Brokers' Stock Exchange, rather than a physical exchange, which offered her official recognition, and she became the first Irish female member in 1942.[134] Stockbroking culture in Ireland was ultimately not significantly different from the United Kingdom's.

Ousting the Outsiders

Obliged to deal outside UK stock exchanges, women stockbrokers' position became potentially precarious from the mid-1930s when outsiders became the subject of unprecedented official scrutiny. In April 1935, Attorney General Sir Thomas Inskip took the unusual step of delivering a warning to listeners on BBC Radio about share-pushers who were inducing the unwary to speculate in stocks and shares. He read a letter he had received from a small tradesman who had lost his life's savings of £500, and claimed that there were 'scores' of similar cases every day. He urged the public to resist promises of easy wealth: those who had money to invest should write to a stockbroker they knew or consult their bank manager.[135] Though attracting much favourable press comment, the broadcast did little to abate the tide of share scandals. By the summer of 1936, the government was facing growing cross-party pressure to act to protect the 'women and old people' who were the chief victims of bucket shops and share-pushers, according to Labour MP Robert Morrison.[136] After consulting with the London Stock Exchange, the Bank of England, and the Director of Public Prosecutions, President of the Board of Trade Walter Runciman announced the appointment of a departmental committee to investigate the share-pushing activities of outside brokers in November 1936.[137]

Helmed by former Director of Public Prosecutions, Sir Archibald Bodkin, and comprising leading legal and City figures including Robert Wilkinson, deputy chairman of the London Stock Exchange, the Committee heard evidence from over fifty witnesses from the worlds of business, law, government, the police, and the press.[138] Already convinced of the seriousness of the problem before it had finished taking evidence, the Committee urged the Board of Trade to issue a warning to the public about the share-pushing menace. Consequently, no fewer than 15 million pamphlets were published and distributed by the Post Office and the nation's banks from April 1937, declaring that the government intended 'to take all possible steps' to curb the activities of the share-pushers. In the meantime, the pamphlet reprinted Justice William Finlay's words when sentencing a gang of share-pushers the previous month, advising the public that they should 'only take advice with regard to their investments from their bankers or members of the Stock Exchange'.[139] Finlay had said that he wished 'my words could be heard in every house in the country'. The Board's pamphlet came close to making this a reality.[140]

As the rhetoric against outside brokers ramped up through 1936, some women brokers began to feel vulnerable. Edith Midgley worried about the viability of continuing to do business outside an exchange. 'The fact that one is refused admission to an exchange', she argued, 'casts a certain reflection.'[141] The Bodkin investigation threatened to make the situation worse, as one proposal was to grant a monopoly of the trade in stocks and shares to the existing stock exchanges. However, a formal monopoly, granted by a royal charter, would mean regulatory oversight, a curbing of the London Stock Exchange's freedom of action which it had long opposed. Stock Exchange chairman Robert Pearson was quite open about this during his questioning before the Bodkin Committee. Adumbrating reasons for London's opposition to a monopoly, Committee member Lionel Cohen asked Pearson, 'I suppose that another difficulty would be that all other professions have been thrown open to women, and you would not very much welcome women members, would you?' Pearson replied, 'Not yet.'[142] Rather than a monopoly, the Bodkin Committee quickly came to favour a different solution: a system of compulsory registration. However, this also came with risks to women brokers, especially in the form initially favoured by the Committee: a registration authority composed of representatives of the country's stock exchanges. This would not only compromise women's freedom to establish their own businesses; it would also subject them to the authority of a body of men, many of whom actively opposed women's right to compete on equal terms.

As the Bodkin Committee was forming, Midgley mobilized her contacts to try to ensure women's concerns were heard. She urged the WFL to write to the Committee to offer to give evidence; an offer which was accepted.[143] Midgley's idea was that the WFL would be able to represent women stockbrokers collectively, and to this end, she gave them the details of about twenty women involved with stock and share dealing and suggested writing to them to ask for cooperation. The issue had also drawn the interest of Gordon Holmes, and in January 1937 the WFL leadership met with Holmes and Midgley at the Minerva Club to discuss next steps. But the results of the WFL's survey of women in finance were disappointing: they had received only six replies, with 'very few helpful suggestions, and no promise of actual cooperation'. As a result, the WFL withdrew from giving oral evidence, on the grounds that it did not possess 'sufficient technical knowledge' about the subject.[144] But it identified an alternative means of influencing the debate. Holmes's National Securities Corporation was one of several outside firms invited to give evidence, and though Holmes's partner Richard Turner was initially going to represent the firm before the Committee, the WFL successfully persuaded Holmes to join Turner in order to make the case for women.[145] On the day they attended, Holmes's presence astonished Committee member John McEwan, chairman of the Associated Stock Exchanges. He later reported at the Association's annual conference that though he had known that two directors would be attending, '[n]othing in the correspondence led us to believe that they were other than two men, but when they came into the room we discovered that one was a woman'.[146]

Though Holmes largely confined herself to a listening brief, when Turner was explaining to the committee that the proposed brokers' registration authority should not 'refuse registration to people who could produce a reasonably satisfactory reference or references as to their bona fides and as to their standing', Holmes jumped in to add: 'Or to refuse registration to women merely because they were women.' When Bodkin asked whether the London Stock Exchange had a rule against 'lady stockbrokers', Holmes said there was, but Committee member Wilkinson retorted that 'There is no rule and nothing in the constitution which prevents it.' Holmes interposed, brandishing the results of the Soroptimists' recent survey of stock exchange policies on women's membership, which proved that 'it would be necessary to make provision that there should be no exclusion on account of sex'.[147] But Wilkinson's response—that the London Stock Exchange was a club which was free to make its own decisions on membership—suggested that such a provision would be opposed by the exchanges.[148] Indeed, McEwan's account of Holmes's intervention to members of the Associated Stock Exchanges indicates how little interest leading male brokers had in the issue:

136   SEXISM IN THE CITY

She made a most eloquent appeal to the Committee on behalf of the cause of women, but, of course, as a matter of that kind was not on the agenda, no notice was taken of it. I mention that incident to show how keen these women are to put forward their case at every opportunity that they get.[149]

Though not giving evidence to the Bodkin Committee, Midgley had other ways of influencing the debate. She had won an ally in her local Labour MP, William Leach, with whom she had discussed the possibility of government intervention in the admission policies of stock exchanges.[150] Leach began highlighting the vulnerable position of women stockbrokers in the Commons while the Bodkin Committee was preparing its report.[151] Following the report, drafting viable legislation proved a lengthy process, and the Prevention of Fraud (Investments) Bill that eventually reached parliament in late 1938 proposed a rigorous licensing system for brokers, managed by the Board of Trade rather than a committee of brokers, with licences requiring annual renewal. Though the Board had initially wanted to include all brokers, members and non-members alike, on this register, the exchanges objected and the Board relented.[152] The bill thus gave stock exchanges and their members a privileged status, exempt from regulatory oversight: only non-members needed to be licensed. The threat to women brokers remained.

When the bill entered its committee stage in February 1939, Leach argued that creating a two-tier system jeopardized the livelihoods of women brokers. Because the bill gave stock exchanges official recognition for the first time, '[a]ny stockbroker carrying on business in a town where there is such a recognized stock exchange, of which he or she is not a member, might as well shut up shop'. While women could apply for a Board of Trade licence, Leach held that investors were unlikely to regard such outsiders as trustworthy, especially since the publication of the Board's warning pamphlet. Because stock exchanges had the power to block applicants on the grounds of their sex, the bill jeopardized the livelihoods of women brokers, who were facing 'very early ruin'. He therefore moved an amendment that the membership policies of all stock exchanges be regulated by the Board of Trade, thus preventing them from discriminating on sex.[153]

Before the debate, Midgley had written to the WFL asking them to use their parliamentary contacts to win backers for Leach's amendment, efforts which led to promises of support, or at least consideration, from ten MPs of different parties.[154] And Leach couched his case in terms that could appeal to a wide a range of MPs. He highlighted the changing constitutional standing of private bodies, pointing to the fact that in recent years, the law regulating the behaviour of such bodies had been tightened up. 'Whether it be the case of the doctors or the lawyers or trade unions, any unreasonable refusal of membership is conspiracy', and was actionable on the grounds of depriving a person of his or her livelihood.[155] Though two female Conservative MPs, Florence Horsbrugh and Mavis Tate, spoke in favour of Leach's amendment, the government opposed it. Parliamentary Secretary to the Board of Trade Ronald Cross argued that Leach's concerns were irrelevant to the bill's purpose. The bill trusted stock exchanges to prevent fraud among their members, and it would be counterproductive to interfere with their membership rules. More surprisingly, Cross reasserted the notion of stock exchanges as 'private clubs' which should be allowed their liberty to regulate their own affairs as they saw fit, 'provided they are properly conducted'. Though Leach pressed his amendment, it was defeated by 180 votes to 104.[156]

The episode was extensively reported in the press, which recognized it as an important moment—an attempt to use parliamentary power to end the exclusion of women—which had failed.[157] The bill passed later that session, but the livelihoods of women brokers may have been less imperilled than Midgley and Leach feared.[158] Acknowledging the legitimate business done by many outside brokers, the Bodkin Committee had recommended that they form an association to impose a stringent code of conduct on their members.[159] This association would then be recognized by the Board of Trade, obviating the need for its members to apply individually to the Board for a licence to deal. Holmes and Turner were quick to take up the suggestion. In 1938 they played a leading role in establishing the Association of Stock and Share Dealers, in consultation with the Board of Trade.[160] Holmes was one of six members on the executive, along with Turner, who was its chairman.[161] As a result, women brokers doing business in a town with an exchange could join the new association, while those who operated in a town without an exchange could also join, though they had the alternative option of the Provincial Brokers' Stock Exchange.[162] Also recognized by the Board of Trade, the latter had seven female members at the start of the Second World War.[163] Members of both could therefore continue trading after the legislation took effect without having to register individually with the Board, and enjoyed the status conferred by belonging to a recognized organization.[164] Yet their hopes of actually joining stock exchanges seemed as remote as ever.

Keeping the Financial Wheels Turning

If the attempt to use parliamentary power to force women's admission had failed, then the Second World War presented other opportunities. As had happened during the previous conflict, there was a significant gender shift in the staffing of brokers' offices, though the early phases of the war saw a drain of female as well as male personnel. Firms belonging to provincial stock exchanges employed 851 women before the war, representing 20 per cent of the total workforce. Over 500 of these women departed, but many replacements were found, bringing the total back up to 663, or just over a third of total personnel, by mid-1942.[165] Likewise, of around 1,600 women employed by London Stock Exchange firms in 1939, only

138 SEXISM IN THE CITY

609 remained by mid-1942, but hundreds more women were recruited, bringing the total back up to 1,271. Making up around 11 per cent of the workforce in 1939, women represented 21 per cent by 1942.[166]

Facing a similar depletion of staff, the London Stock Exchange itself also began employing larger numbers of women to fill gaps in the administration of several departments.[167] By September 1941, women were working in the Trustees' and Managers' Office, the Secretary's Office, and the Share and Loan Department, and a woman was even operating one of the lifts. Describing this, predictably, as a 'feminine invasion', the *Financial Times* thought it likely that the Committee for General Purposes would draw the line at admitting women to the floor of the exchange itself, despite the prospect of further call-ups of men.[168] But the Trustees' and Managers' Office proved more willing to experiment.[169] Later that month, under the headline 'NO WOMAN DID THIS BEFORE', the *Daily Mirror* reported:

> Two girl clerks, notebooks in hands, stood at the entrance of the London Stock Exchange yesterday. Then, while members gasped with astonishment, they did what no other woman has done before. They walked across the floor—hitherto exclusive masculine domain—and quietly began work recording bargains in the mining section.[170]

This was not a trading role; rather, it was a purely administrative function. The clerks, Margaret Plenty and Muriel Collins, who worked for the Trustees' and Managers' Office, received slips from brokers of transactions done and marked the prices on boards. The marking boards even doubled as a screen which 'discreetly shielded' them from the male brokers.[171] Yet the *Mirror*'s breathless report conveys an awareness of the significance of allowing women on the trading floor, while *The Times* went so far as to dub it, in all seriousness, an 'epoch-making' event.[172] The *Illustrated London News* even carried a photograph of the pair.[173]

This breach of tradition was genuinely inspiring for women in finance, making the possibility of further inroads seem a real possibility. Two days after the 'girl clerks' had walked across the trading floor, Lilian Stanfield wrote to the Committee for General Purposes. In light of the recent 'interesting development', Stanfield asked whether 'consideration may be extended to women as members of the Stock Exchange?' Having joined the member firm Knight & Searle as a shorthand typist in 1919, Stanfield had worked her way up to the position of managing clerk and was consequently 'fully in touch with Stock Exchange Rules and business'. With more men liable to be called up, allowing women into the House 'would be exceedingly useful and certainly facilitate the conduct of the business'.[174]

Stanfield's bold enquiry was seemingly not thought worthy of a reply. But the more modest proposal of allowing the clerks of member firms into the Stock Exchange was a live one.[175] Indeed, in July 1941 Haley & Co. had applied for permission to employ a female clerk to check bargains in the Settling Room.[176] This was a significant question, since male brokers typically began their Stock Exchange career with this role, which involved brokers' and jobbers' clerks meeting to confirm the details of deals and handling the associated paperwork, before they graduated to the trading floor as unauthorized clerks. After serving this apprenticeship, they could apply to become members.[177] The broker-journalist Walter Landells, writing under his 'Autolycus' penname in the *Financial Times*, seemed mildly shaken that the matter was being seriously considered, and predicted strong opposition. 'Only war conditions can be advanced as warranty for breaking with all the traditions of the past in this way'.[178]

Sure enough, when Haley & Co's application first reached the Committee for General Purposes in August, it was voted down by seventeen votes to eight.[179] But emboldened by the Trustees' and Managers' decision to employ women on the marking boards in September, the firm wrote again, asking the Committee to reconsider its decision.[180] The Committee deferred the matter, but the next month a second firm, A. Sherriff & Co. also applied with an identical request, since the firm's entire male staff, barring one authorized clerk, had enlisted.[181] Uncertain how to handle the matter, the Committee continued to procrastinate, until both firms renewed their requests in March 1942.[182] In April, the Committee voted again on the issue, and this time the vote was in favour of admitting women to the Settling Room by the narrow margin of twelve to eleven.[183]

The concession was a limited and grudging one. The Temporary Regulation subsequently drawn up stipulated that women could only be employed when no suitable male candidate was available, and were to be employed only for the duration of the war. Moreover, the Committee was careful to specify that service by women in the Settling Room could form no grounds for a subsequent application for membership.[184] These restrictions seemed to reassure enough sceptics on the Committee, the measure passing by seventeen votes to four.[185] The only remaining obstacle was the pressing issue of where women would display the red button which all Settling Room clerks had to wear. Men wore it in their buttonholes, but how would women wear it, wondered the *Financial Times*, if not dressed in a coat?[186] The problem was apparently not insurmountable, the first cohort of three women, each given a red button, entering the Settling Room before the end of May, working alongside over 600 male colleagues.[187] Their presence was quickly accepted, subsequent Committee minutes showing a steady flow of female clerks appointed to Settling Room duties.[188] Indeed, the Committee itself noted sardonically in its annual report a year later that 'contrary to certain rather alarmist prognostications the foundations of the Stock Exchange do not appear to have suffered any serious damage as a result of this revolutionary, if temporary, measure'.[189]

Women therefore played a significant role in keeping the financial markets operating during the war, helping to deflect calls for the stock exchanges to close

140   SEXISM IN THE CITY

for the duration, the case for which Minister of Labour Ernest Bevin was examining with Chancellor of the Exchequer Sir Kingsley Wood in 1942.[190] Nevertheless, stock exchanges worked hard to maintain traditional gender boundaries despite their dependence on women's labour. Though permitted in the Settling Room, and as marking clerks, going further and allowing women a more active role on the trading floor as 'blue-button' clerks was, in most cases, not on the cards. Yet stock exchanges were not quite united on this point. In March 1942, the Liverpool Stock Exchange permitted a member firm, H. Barnes & Co., to employ two authorized female clerks on the floor of the exchange, with full dealing powers. Shortly afterwards, a second firm also employed a woman in the same capacity.[191]

Liverpool appears to have been an outlier, however. The Sheffield Stock Exchange proved less flexible. Local brokerage Walter Ward & Co., as so many others, was depleted of staff during the war, in particular when Walter's son joined the Royal Air Force in 1939.[192] When Walter died in May 1941, his daughter Constance, who had been a clerk at the firm since its establishment in 1924, was left in control.[193] Being unable to access the trading floor was an impediment: as she later explained, 'I could do business on the telephone, but other brokers had to go into the stock exchange and do my dealing for me.'[194] So the following year, Constance applied to the Sheffield Stock Exchange Committee to become an authorized clerk. The Committee decided that, as the application was 'for a lady, which would be an innovation', it should give members the 'opportunity of expressing their views' on 'the admission of ladies'. A ballot was consequently held, and while four members voted for, seven voted against.[195]

This determination to maintain strict gendered boundaries went largely unquestioned, though there was one notable exception. At the end of 1943, the Prime Minister's wife, Clementine Churchill, became the first woman to make a speech on the floor of the London Stock Exchange, to raise funds on behalf of the Young Women's Christian Association for a servicewomen's hut at Aldershot.[196] 'Don't be shocked,' she wrote the next day to her husband, 'I didn't force my way in. I was invited by the Chairman.' She admitted, 'I was terrified, but I think it all went off very well.'[197] Indeed, members contributed over £4,000, and both Clementine and the chairman, the recently knighted Sir Robert Pearson, attended the opening ceremony the following March. Pearson told what he supposed was an amusing story that when the Queen learned that Clementine had visited the House to make a speech to members, she had remarked, 'Brave woman.' Perhaps resenting Pearson's smugness, Clementine responded by chiding the exchange in her speech, which was widely reported in the press:

> Women have broken into the Army, Navy and Air Force, but not yet into the Stock Exchange. I am very sorry about this, because I should like to think I had a stockbroker daughter. I must ask Sir Robert if he thinks there is any chance of my granddaughter becoming one.[198]

Since the introduction of conscription for women in December 1941, the numbers of women in the three auxiliary forces had grown rapidly, with 450,000 in active service by the time Churchill made her speech.[199] In an environment in which, even if it was widely assumed that they should be protected from combatant roles, it was no longer remarkable to see a woman in military uniform, the contrast with the strict maintenance of barriers to women in finance was striking.[200] That allies could point this out, and publicly, was perhaps an ominous sign for the nation's stock exchanges. Ultimately, however, the war did not seriously threaten their exclusionary policies.

Conclusion

The London Stock Exchange's influence on the careers of women brokers went beyond simply denying them membership. A couple of cases from 1936 illustrate the kinds of constraints London could impose upon them. After refusing Mabel Gosnell the right to apply, Gosnell wrote to the Committee for General Purposes for permission to publish a series of articles in the press 'dealing with general financial matters for women'. She had refrained until now because of her intended application, 'but as I may not be a member I presume there can be now no objection to this project'.[201] But the Committee blamed Gosnell for the publicity her membership application had received, and was in no mood to oblige. It wrote to inform her firm, George J. Ascott & Co., that 'in view of the prominence given by the Press to Mrs Gosnell's application for membership, the Committee considered the publication of the suggested articles would be undesirable'.[202] London's influence extended far beyond the capital. Not only did its exclusionary policy shape the actions of the provincial stock exchanges, as seen in the case of Bradford and Edith Midgley, but it could also influence the business practices of women forced to operate outside the exchanges. In 1936, Midgley began advertising her firm in the local press, and sending out circulars undercutting the fees charged by member firms.[203] The Huddersfield Stock Exchange contacted the London Committee to complain, demanding that Midgley no longer be allowed to deal with members on reduced terms. London immediately wrote to Midgley, successfully obtaining her commitment not to advertise or circularize in the future.[204]

In these two cases, however, London's influence did not prove fatal to women's careers. Though barred from advising women in print, Gosnell continued working for George J. Ascott & Co. into the early 1950s, eventually retiring after fifteen years at the firm. After this she continued to advise many friends on their investments.[205] When she died in 1972, aged 75, she left an estate worth more than £87,000.[206] Prohibited from advertising by the London Stock Exchange, Midgley still managed to thrive as an outside broker. Taking a Leeds stockbroker, Robert

142   SEXISM IN THE CITY

Chaloner, into partnership, she worked until 1953, when she handed E. Midgley & Co. over to Chaloner.[207] She died seven years later, aged 72, leaving £15,665 in her will.[208]

Indeed, though the business environment was becoming increasingly hostile to outside brokers due to the Bodkin Committee's investigations and the ensuing legislation, many other women built successful financial careers. By far the highest-profile operator of this period, Gordon Holmes's death aged 67 in 1951 following a long illness was a major news story. She was hailed as '[o]ne of the big success stories of the past half-century', though many notices incorrectly reported that she was the 'first woman member of the Stock Exchange'.[209] She left over £26,000 in her will.[210] Also working in London, but with considerably less press attention, Edith Maskell—by far the oldest female broker working in the interwar period—continued to run her City brokerage into the early 1930s.[211] In 1933 she died suddenly at Lewes Railway Station, aged 72. Like her mentor Bell, stockbroking had not made her rich: she left just £230.[212]

This made her something of an outlier, however, with most women stockbrokers of this period making their businesses pay. The status and institutional support offered by the Provincial Brokers' Stock Exchange may have been a factor here, even when careers were curtailed through health or other factors. In Exeter, after taking over her father's firm in 1922, Doris Mortimer traded successfully through the interwar years in partnership with Walter Way, until the latter's death in 1940.[213] But poor health seems to have dogged Doris—the 1939 Register lists her as 'Stock & Share Broker, incapacitated'—and she died in 1947 aged just 48.[214] But she had made a good living, her estate being valued at just under £20,000.[215] Careers could also be cut short by choice. From the mid-1930s, Amy Moreton was focusing increasingly on her work as a county councillor and Conservative Party activist, describing herself in the 1939 Register as 'Provincial Stockbroker (partially retired)'.[216] Besides securing election as a county alderman in 1951, she spent much time on social issues, holding a series of chairs and deputy chairs on welfare and health committees, work which earned her an OBE in 1954. By this point she had fully retired from stockbroking.[217] Continuing to serve on the county council until 1970, she died two years later, leaving a substantial estate of close to £78,000.[218]

For several others, stockbroking proved a longer-term vocation. Having finally taken over the family firm on her father's death in 1954, Phyllis Moscrop Robinson recruited a male partner, Edward Chadwick. The firm, now styled Moscrop Robinson & Chadwick, became increasingly focused on insurance services. At the end of 1959, Phyllis retired, leaving the firm in Chadwick's hands.[219] She lived another sixteen years, dying a few months short of her eightieth birthday, her estate valued at £13,427.[220] In Bath, Ellen White, like Robinson, also combined her brokerage activities with other financial work for her clients—the 1939 Register lists her as 'Accountant and Stock Broker'—and was regularly named in the press as executor for the estates of deceased local residents, as well as conducting some liquidation work.[221] She seems to have enjoyed her career, continuing to work into her early seventies, before retiring in 1964.[222] When she died four years later, she left an estate worth nearly £25,000.[223] In Burnley, Helen Tyrrell was also still in business in the 1960s and, like White, remained a member of the Provincial Brokers' Stock Exchange.[224] Her long career was particularly profitable: when she died in 1976, she left a substantial estate of £111,535.[225]

Despite London being the heart of the financial system, the best opportunities for women in finance in the interwar years lay outside the capital, particularly in towns without a stock exchange, where the business culture appeared to be less prejudiced against women. But after 1945, this began to change, as women made significant inroads in London firms, successfully contesting the limits on advancement that had largely confined them to clerical roles. Challenging the unofficial ban on membership of the London Stock Exchange, however, was to remain as difficult as ever.

Sexism in the City: Women Stockbrokers in Modern Britain. James Taylor, Oxford University Press.
© James Taylor 2025. DOI: 10.1093/9780191990397.003.0006

6

Something in the City

Women Stockbrokers after 1945

> A smart honey-blonde leans over the counter of a London West End
> bank and talks to the cashier.
>
> It's an everyday scene—with a difference. The blonde is Britain's
> first WOMAN BANK MANAGER and this is her bank.
>
> *Daily Mirror*, 29 November 1958, 7

Hilda Harding's appointment as manager of a Mayfair branch of Barclays Bank in 1958 attracted a flurry of excited press attention. This was the first time one of the 'Big Five' banks had given a female employee the opportunity to manage one of its branches.[1] Harding's chance came after much work. Joining Barclays aged 18 as a £1-a-week shorthand typist in a High Wycombe branch, she worked her way through the ranks, becoming a ledger clerk after five years, then a director's secretary, switching to head office to become secretary to the general manager, before becoming manager at the age of 42.[2]

Setting the obvious sensationalism and sexism of the popular press's coverage to one side, Harding's rise supports the idea that the post-war years saw significant changes in the employment context for women. Longer lives and the developing consumer society created what social researcher Richard Titmuss believed was a fundamentally 'new situation' for women, with paid employment now seen as a central ingredient of 'an emotionally satisfying and independent life'.[3] Titmuss made this claim in 1952, a year that also saw the publication of sociologist Ferdynand Zweig's *Women's Life and Labour*, based on interviews with several hundred women. Zweig found that paid work transformed 'the whole relationship of husband and wife', the ability to earn an independent income altering 'the woman's whole personality'.[4]

Though 'sex-typed roles and prevailing assumptions about women's central responsibilities as mothers' survived the dislocations of the Second World War, there were definite limits to the post-war reversion to the status quo.[5] Some time ago Pat Thane warned against the 'polemical stereotyping' of the 1950s as 'dull, static and uniformly conservative' when it came to the position of women.[6] Though overshadowed by the more tumultuous era that followed from the late 1960s when second-wave feminism grabbed the headlines, the earlier post-war years saw significant developments, from the substantial erosion of the marriage bar, to the achievement of equal pay in large parts of the public sector in 1955.[7] Though it was rare for women with young children to work, it was increasingly common for women to return to paid employment when family responsibilities eased, a move facilitated by a noteworthy increase in part-time working.[8]

These kinds of shifts in discourse and experience have not yet been systematically traced in relation to the history of the financial world.[9] Yet, as Kieran Heinemann has noted, the post-war years saw the growing visibility of women as financial actors, going well beyond the growth of women's investment seen in previous periods.[10] The 1950s and 1960s witnessed the tentative beginnings of what could be described as a 'feminization of finance' in which men's monopoly of the world of 'high finance' was publicly challenged on multiple fronts.[11] Hilda Harding made a success of her Mayfair branch, prompting Barclays to appoint more female managers, the second being Margaret Harwood in 1962.[12] Barclays' rivals slowly followed suit: by the early 1970s, National Westminster had two women branch managers, Lloyds and the Royal Bank of Scotland one, with Barclays on four. Though these numbers spoke to very cautious growth, women were 'quietly moving up into senior positions behind the scenes', with sixty-three women in managerial-level jobs at what was now the 'Big Four'.[13]

But it was not just high street banking which was beginning to experience changes. Financial journalism had been an almost exclusively male preserve to this point, *The Economist*—motivated by hard business logic—being very much an outlier in hiring women before the war. 'You can get a first-class woman', observed editor Geoffrey Crowther, 'for the price of a second-class man.'[14] Though statisticians like Margaret Rix (hired in 1936) and Marjorie Deane (appointed in 1947) became important members of staff, most readers would have been unaware of their work. It was not until the 1950s and 1960s that women became a visible presence in financial journalism. The leader here was Margot Naylor, who got her break in the early 1950s when Rix mentioned her to Harold Wincott, editor of the *Investors Chronicle*. Wincott gave her a job on the magazine, 'where the only women before her were secretaries'.[15] Unlike Rix and Deane, Naylor focused on personal finance, and her association with investor protection helped secure her a prestigious spot as the only journalist—and only woman—on the Jenkins Committee on company law reform in 1959. Her talents were such that she easily made the transition to the mainstream press, writing on finance for the *Daily Telegraph* and *The Observer* before being poached by the *Daily Mail* in 1967 for its *Money Mail* supplement.

By this point, the climate for female financial journalists had changed enormously. Initial appointments were seen as experiments, but quickly paved the way for more hires. The *Financial Times* took on its first female contributor, Sheila Black, in 1958, only after she had written to the editor to suggest they boost their coverage of consumer affairs.[16] Initially regarded as 'a kind of curiosity' at the paper, by the early 1970s there were 'quite a few women—enough for us to get

146   SEXISM IN THE CITY

taken for granted'.[17] As the leading dailies boosted their financial coverage, editors came to regard women journalists as essential members of their financial news teams, albeit a minority presence. In 1967, when *The Times* launched its major new business news section, the team of thirty included four women, including Margaret Allen and Gillian O'Connor, both of whom had started, like Naylor, at the *Investors Chronicle*.[18]

With this incipient feminization of financial news desks, the press became more attuned to high-achieving women in a range of City roles, from Pamela Hunt, a pension fund manager at NatWest, to Angela Howarth and Marilyn Johnston, who were prospering in local authority finance.[19] The promoters of unit trusts, a form of collective investment allowing small investors to spread risk, began to see the benefits of incorporating women's perspectives. In a move which attracted headlines in 1963, financier Oliver Jessel recruited three women, including Margaret Rix, to join the board of his new Family Savings Unit Trust.[20] The following year saw Baroness Gaitskell, the recently widowed wife of the Labour Party leader Hugh Gaitskell, taken onto the board of the Growth with Security Trust, while the prominent Conservative MP Dame Patricia Hornsby-Smith became the first female unit trust chair when she was recruited to the Western and General Unit Trust.[21]

Women were also becoming more visible presences at the annual general meetings of the companies in which they invested, where they often formed the majority of attendees.[22] Though they were not always confident enough to participate actively in these meetings, one woman made it her mission to change this. Accountant and chartered secretary Freda Spurgeon formed the Association of Women Shareholders in 1964 to encourage members to attend meetings and report problem boards.[23] So many male shareholders showed an interest that it rebranded itself the Investors and Shareholders Association and allowed them membership. By 1968, it had 4,000 members, men now outnumbering women, though Spurgeon explained that women 'do most of the work'.[24] Spurgeon herself led from the front, becoming a familiar face at general meetings, always willing to pose the awkward question on behalf of her members. Much more than an irritant, her ability to coordinate shareholder opinion and mobilize proxy votes led to a string of successes. By 1970 she could boast that she was responsible for removing around forty chairmen from company boards.[25]

By becoming bank managers, journalists, directors, and activists, women were going further in normalizing the idea of feminine financial expertise, a process which had begun in earnest in the interwar years. By 1958 the *Daily Telegraph* observed that women were becoming 'something in the City', and that they had 'better chances than ever...to achieve executive and senior supervisory status'.[26] But how far this trend would influence the world of stockbroking—especially in conservative London where women had struggled to rise above secretarial roles— was far from certain. Indeed, the 1951 census enumerated seventeen women stockbrokers and stockjobbers (compared to 5,192 men), higher than the eight recorded in 1931 but fewer than the nineteen in 1921, hardly suggesting that the war had brought about a lasting transformation.[27] Yet changes were afoot, particularly in the later 1950s and 1960s, that were making financial careers for women more viable. This chapter follows a cohort of eight women in London and three outside London to explore these changes. It identifies a professionalization of stockbroking and a move towards credentialism that undermined arguments that women were unsuited to such work. And it explores women's shifting professional identities, focusing on the implications of their growing tendency to downplay their gender at work.

People Who Fit?

In London, the decline of the outside market, prompted by the restrictions imposed by the Prevention of Fraud (Investments) Act of 1939, made setting up a business a less feasible option than it had been in the interwar years.[28] After 1945, the only realistic option for women was to work for a member firm, but recruitment policies remained conservative. A leaflet entitled 'A Career on the London Stock Exchange', obtainable from the Secretary's Office of the London Stock Exchange in the 1950s, appeared to offer women scant encouragement. It advised the 'young man' interested in such a career that the first step was to obtain an introduction to a stock exchange member 'through a friend or business acquaintance'.[29] As this implies, a culture of gentlemanly capitalism was alive and well in the post-war City, with social connections continuing to determine recruitment practices. Family was all-important in many firms: at Joseph Sebag & Co., for example, each partner could nominate a son to join the firm, while at Foster & Braithwaite, partnerships were restricted to family members.[30] Those without a familial connection to a brokerage usually acquired the necessary contacts at school or university.[31]

A careful filtering process was at work with this system of recruitment. Antony Hornby, senior partner at Cazenove's, explained his philosophy: 'we must be careful to have in the partnership people who fit and who think the same way as us'.[32] People like Hornby felt this way because of how brokerages such as his operated, thriving on the privileged information that members received from company chairmen and other City figures in the course of boozy lunches, rounds of golf, and other social events. These profitable 'tips' could then be passed on to favoured clients, in an age when insider dealing continued to be tolerated. Stockbrokers had to be 'people who fit' in order to operate successfully in these settings: class, race, and gender were everything.[33]

To a limited extent, well-connected women could benefit from these practices. With London firms still not permitted to advertise for new clients,

148   SEXISM IN THE CITY

half-commission agents, increasingly known as attachés, retained an important role.[34] Exploiting their social contacts to funnel business to the firm that employed them, such agents were highly sought after.[35] By the mid-1960s, around half a dozen women were reportedly acting as attachés for London Stock Exchange firms.[36] One was **Elisabeth Rivers-Bulkeley**, née Neustadtl, wife of Robert, a former member of the Scots Guards (see Fig. 6.1). Born in Austria in 1924, and a former champion skater, swimmer, and skier, she was friends with celebrities like playwright Noël Coward and publisher George Weidenfeld, making her and her husband prominent players in London fashionable society.[37] Cutting a stylish figure in outfits by Chanel, Elisabeth's activities made it to the pages of *The Tatler*.[38] Her address book made her a highly desirable asset for brokerages, and at a dinner party in October 1957 she was invited to join City firm Hedderwick Borthwick & Co. as an attaché.[39] Her first day was not auspicious, as she later recalled:

> I went to work with one of the partners, was given a desk, two telephones, the Stock Exchange Daily Official List reporting all marked bargains and was told to carry on and ask when necessary. It was most alarming and I must admit that I did not for a moment believe then that I would still be in stockbroking fifteen years later.

Despite the lack of training, she soon started acquiring clients and enjoyed working as an attaché, recalling that it was 'very interesting to learn about how people handled their finances and to have an insight into their lives [and] even more interesting to learn about how industrial companies and other institutions organise their affairs'.[40]

Far more common feminine presences in stockbrokers' offices, however, were secretaries. The feminization of clerical work which had begun earlier in the century continued in the post-war years, though it was slower in the City of London than elsewhere.[41] By the early 1960s, it was estimated that women made up around a third of the total workforce in stockbroking firms, a time when they were approaching parity in banking.[42] But, as in banking, a gendered division of labour remained, and hierarchies were actually entrenched by the adoption of modern techniques of scientific management, especially the innovation of the open-plan secretarial pool.[43] Computerization—a feature of the larger brokerages from the 1950s—introduced new distinctions. At Phillips & Drew, the computer room was in a basement, staffed by 'punch girls' who had to endure the heat generated by the technology, and often worked evenings and weekends. This kind of labour, argues Amy Thomas, 'was very close to factory work in character'.[44] True, male employees often started as office boys running errands, but they benefited from a clearly defined career ladder: from office boy to junior clerk in the back office, from there to working in the Settling Room as a red-button clerk, progressing to

Miss Muriel Bailey: 42 City years.

Mrs Elizabeth Rivers-Bulkeley: she does much work for institutions and trusts.

Fig. 6.1 Muriel Bailey and Elisabeth Rivers-Bulkeley, *Illustrated London News*, 11 March 1967, 32. © Illustrated London News Ltd/Mary Evans

the trading floor as a blue-button, before eventually becoming a broker or jobber and perhaps a partner in the firm.[45] Women, by contrast, were hired as typists and secretaries, and were expected to remain content with such work until they left to marry.

Nevertheless, there were examples of women who could—with difficulty, and over many years—progress to more senior roles, such as **Muriel Hayler Bailey** (see Fig. 6.1). Born in 1907 to a stockbroker's clerk, Muriel had got a job in 1925 as a shorthand typist at the stockbroking firm Chandler & Co., whose senior partner, Lionel Walter, was a friend of her father's.[46] In 1934 she switched to James Flower & Sons, where her interest in investment developed, an interest which was encouraged by the senior partner.[47] The Second World War presented her with what she later referred to as 'my big break', just as it had with Gordon Holmes in the First. With many men called up, the firm managed to get Bailey exempted from service, and she took over the running of the office.[48] She 'used to take the files home and study them at the weekend. That is the way to learn, you assimilate knowledge as you go along.'[49] In the later stages of the war, she began to develop a substantial portfolio of clients, which she built on after 1945.[50]

Even if metropolitan stockbroking seemed a traditional and somewhat closed environment after the war, changes were nevertheless brewing. Broking firms remained small, with longstanding Stock Exchange rules discouraging growth still in place: six partners was the average for brokerages in 1959, employing just five clerks.[51] Yet there were significant pressures to expand. The amount of paperwork required of firms was rapidly multiplying due to more complex and onerous taxation and audit regimes, while brokerages also had to work harder to meet the needs of new institutional investors, especially the insurance companies and pension funds which were rapidly becoming major players in the post-war equities market.[52] A series of mergers saw a significant decline in the number of brokerages in operation: just 209 by the late 1960s, less than half the 465 that had been active prior to the Second World War.[53] This trend was further encouraged by the London Stock Exchange's removal of limits on the number of partners in 1967. Sheppards & Chase, a merger of two long-established firms, Sheppards & Co. and Chase Henderson & Tennant, was the first to respond by expanding to twenty-eight partners.[54]

Larger firms not only benefited from economies of scale but could also develop more specialist services for clients, a significant driver of professionalization. The way the gentlemanly amateur had traditionally picked up business—'by being seen at the right places, like deb dances and so on', as one Old Etonian broker put it in 1967—certainly continued, but it was beginning to be challenged by changes in the market.[55] Whereas personal investors had owned over four-fifths of the shares listed on the London Stock Exchange at the start of the Second World War, this proportion was eroded year on year by institutional investors, and by 1969 it had dropped to about half.[56] Stockbrokers hoping to win the lucrative business of the institutions cultivated a modern, professional image underpinned by cutting-edge analysis.[57] As early as 1955 there was enough interest in the subject to warrant the formation of the Society of Investment Analysts.[58] The most progressive brokerages, as well as banks and investment trusts, began to establish research departments. Phillips & Drew, one of the larger brokerages in the early 1960s with eleven partners and 150 employees, became particularly associated with such research.[59] The status of these departments increased as they proved their value, giving London firms an edge over their provincial counterparts.[60] At bankers Hill Samuel, the analysis department had begun life as 'a glorified library service' but quickly became 'a hothouse for investment ideas' shaping their fund managers' strategies.[61]

The shift to specialization and investment analysis, together with the merger of smaller family firms, drove changes in recruitment practices. The traditional elitist channels were becoming insufficient for securing younger employees, recognized in 1961 when the London Stock Exchange founded an Appointments Bureau as a means of matching school leavers and graduates with Stock Exchange firms.[62] The Bureau established close links with university appointments boards, and while a degree by no means became a requirement for a stockbroking career, a growing number of employers were looking for a university education. Economics and maths degrees were often favoured, particularly for those being recruited to the new research departments, though arts subjects were also considered.[63]

But just as demand for staff was increasing, supply was in danger of drying up. There was growing evidence that stockbroking was beginning to lose its lustre among young men, who were coming to believe that they could have more interesting—and profitable—careers elsewhere, especially in industry.[64] A 1968 survey of schoolboys showed that the five most popular careers mentioned were engineering, science, administration, medicine, and law. Only fourteen boys, 0.1 per cent of the total surveyed, envisaged a career on the Stock Exchange.[65] Around this time, one office manager complained that stockbrokers were only able to recruit 'the misfits of someone else's office', and that it was difficult keeping even them.[66]

The shift to more open recruitment strategies together with stockbroking's declining appeal began to open the doors to women, especially at the larger firms. University degrees proved particularly significant here. A university education had been creating opportunities for women, albeit on far from equal terms, in fields such as law and science since the late Victorian and Edwardian years.[67] The same was to become true for finance, especially in the post-war years with the number of women progressing to higher education growing steadily.[68] Degrees were the passport into financial journalism for women such as Margaret Rix, Margot Naylor, and Margaret Allen, all of whom had graduated from the London School of Economics. University careers officers and graduate recruitment firms were increasingly likely to highlight financial careers to young women. One careers expert identified investment analysis as a field 'in which women with the appropriate skills have an equal chance with men'.[69] A degree could also allow women to bypass the traditional secretarial phase. An early example was **Audrey Geddes.** Born in 1931 into a business-minded environment, her father was director and secretary of a large paper manufacturing company, and was one of the

152   SEXISM IN THE CITY

best-known businessmen in the north-east of Scotland.[70] Privately educated at the Albyn School, Aberdeen, she went on to study economics at St Andrews, and got her first job in the City in 1956 doing statistical work with an insurance firm, moving to stockbrokers Buckmaster & Moore two years later, where she made a successful switch into private client work.[71]

Sometimes, as Susan Thomas put it in the *Sunday Telegraph*, a bit of 'cheek' was required to land a job.[72] **Hilary Root** (b. 1945), a graduate in French and Spanish from Trinity College Dublin, was planning a Foreign Office career, but given the lengthy application process, she needed something to do in the meantime. Looking at *The Times* one day, she saw a notice advertising Stock Exchange opportunities 'for young men with O and A levels' placed by an employment agency. 'So, for no reason at all I rang them up and said have they got anything for a girl with a degree in languages.' The agency secured her three interviews, resulting in two job offers, and she joined Sheppards & Chase in 1969. After a period going around the different departments at the firm 'learning what went on', she started working for one of the partners in the private client section.[73] At Sheppards & Chase she met another graduate, **Anthea Gaukroger** (b. 1941). Having studied French at University College London, Gaukroger did a secretarial course: as she explained, 'I imagined myself being a sort of bilingual secretary, but it didn't really quite turn out like that.' She got a secretarial job at merchant bankers S. G. Warburg, where her responsibilities included typing up notes on meetings between partners and clients on major projects, work which 'gave you an idea of what was going on'. One of the executives, Piers Dixon, noticed that she 'took a bit more interest than some of the others', and in 1966, when he had moved on to join Chase Henderson & Tennant, he invited her to join him as his assistant. Though she would continue her secretarial work, she now also had the chance to do investment analysis, which would soon become her specialism. 'That was a really useful breakthrough for me and got me into the stockbroking business', she said.[74] She was not the only one. By the point that Gaukroger was getting into investment analysis, financial journalists were already beginning to note the presence of 'some very clever female "backroom boys"' in City firms.[75]

Though both Root and Gaukroger found their degrees to be a big help to them in getting into stockbroking, some firms cared less about a university education. **Ellen Fraser** (b. 1942) studied anthropology at Cambridge, but this played little part in her stockbroking career. In 1966, after a brief period selling sweaters at fashionable Chelsea department store Peter Jones, and a job as assistant office manager at the Film Producers' Guild, Fraser answered a newspaper ad for a 'female typist-cum-trainee' at brokerage Fielding Newson Smith. Though she had studied at secretarial college, she admitted she was not much of a typist, but quickly picked up the mechanics of investment. After a year she moved to one of the largest stockbrokers in the City, James Capel & Co., as a valuation clerk in the pension fund department. 'It was about two years before they realised I even had a degree. They never asked and I didn't tell them', she later recalled.[76]

Fraser's next step—as Gaukroger's had been—was to work as personal assistant to one of the firm's partners. As well as having a higher status than typist, being a private secretary could open up opportunities for progression in post-war firms.[77] This was spotted by Rivers-Bulkeley, who believed that becoming secretary to a partner was a great option for young women with ambitions. In this role, 'the intelligent girl will find that clients will talk to her in her boss's absence. She will soon learn their needs, stock exchange terms, the mechanics of dealing and will eventually build up knowledge of stocks and shares as well.'[78] This was certainly Fraser's experience. When the partner she worked for retired, she took over his client list and embarked on a successful career in portfolio management.[79]

With a degree not a prerequisite for many employers, female school-leavers also entered stockbroking, often after trying other lines of work, and typically through the secretarial route. **Louise Peachey** left school with five O-levels, and began her working life as a secretary to an accounts executive in an advertising firm, but she found it 'a bit frivolous and very narrow'. Worse, her route to becoming an accounts executive herself was blocked on the grounds of her sex. She came to understand that 'the job is to put the clients at ease. If the clients like you they want to go to bed with you, and if they don't, they don't like you! I had to run round the desk six times on one occasion.' So she quit and started at a small merchant bank.[80] 'By then I was very interested in broking, but the nearest they let me get to it was taking the minutes for an investment committee.' So she hunted again for a better opportunity, working for a series of stockbroking firms through the later 1960s, training as an investment adviser at Joseph Sebag & Co., then working as an assistant to one of the partners of Strauss Turnbull, where, now in her early thirties, she developed her own private client list.[81]

Susan Pretty's route in was unique. Born in 1935, the daughter of a senior government official in what was then Malaya, when Japan invaded in the Second World War she escaped traumatically and landed in South Africa. From 1946, she experienced a peripatetic education in a string of English boarding schools. When the time came to begin work, she found the options available to young women of her class in the early 1950s decidedly limited: 'there were only three choices: you either became a nurse, or you went to university, or you became a secretary. There was no other choice. And I didn't fancy any of them.' Opting for secretarial college, stints in the Colonial Office, in industry, and as a secretary to two Members of Parliament followed, but she felt stuck. So she registered with the Lucie Clayton agency, which prepared women for more glamorous careers, notably in modelling. While Susan was not interested in becoming a model, the agency helped her get work at the Ideal Home Exhibition and the Smithfield Show. The agency then learned of a vacancy for a guide at the London Stock Exchange's visitors' gallery, and after a daunting interview with the governing

Council, she got a job there in 1961.[82] 'It was the last thing I ever really thought of doing,' she later recalled, 'but I loved it very much indeed, and was thoroughly trained to be able to answer any questions posed by visitors.' Through the work she got to know many of the members, especially brokers, who had a habit of bringing their clients to the gallery and leaving them for the guides to look after. And, keen to boost her income, she took on after-hours work, first at a jobber's office, then a broker's, from which she learned much about the mechanics of finance. On leaving the gallery after five years due to a lack of opportunity for progression, she received job offers from several Stock Exchange firms. She agreed to a three-week trial at William Mortimer & Son, working with one of the partners, Richard Bradshaw, on his private client business.[83] Her trial proved a big success and she stayed at the firm.[84]

If opportunities were opening in London, then the picture was more mixed elsewhere in the country. In the interwar years, smaller towns without a stock exchange had offered women the best opportunities. Some of the women who had been running stockbroking firms in this period carried on doing business after 1945, with both Ellen White of Bath and Helen Tyrrell of Burnley still trading into the 1960s.[85] They were joined by others, whose pathways into stockbroking were similar to the routes taken by their predecessors. Some women were born into the business, such as Elizabeth Hill (1914–2005), who joined her father's Lincoln brokerage, J. W. Hill & Co., after leaving school in the early 1930s, and eventually took it over when he died in 1945.[86] As before, it was not only family firms where this happened. The daughter of a Lancaster-based friendly society agent, Connie Whittaker (1915–98) started work as a secretary for a local brokerage, eventually rising to office manager. When the principal retired in 1962, she took over the firm.[87] White, Tyrrell, Hill, and Whittaker were all members of the Provincial Brokers' Stock Exchange, along with Joyce Kither in Taunton (1907–76) and Jean Cole in Dunfermline (1904–73), both of whom, like Whittaker, had stepped up to take on a firm when their employers retired or died.[88]

Though women remained a presence in small-town stockbroking, this presence was certainly not growing after 1945. This may have been partly because the environment was becoming more challenging. Although the Provincial Brokers' Stock Exchange reached a peak membership in the late 1940s of 360, belonging to nearly 250 firms in 140 towns, changes were on their way. The London Stock Exchange introduced new rules stipulating that only firms whose partners were full-time stockbrokers could do business with its members on preferential commission terms. This was a major problem for the many 'dual business' provincial brokers who combined broking with accountancy or other work, and prompted some to quit stockbroking. Additional membership requirements introduced by the Provincial Brokers' Stock Exchange, including the vetting of articles of partnership and annual balance sheets, and examinations for new members, may have also contributed: by 1962, the organization's membership had fallen to 248.[89]

Fig. 6.2 Helen Smellie, family photograph taken c.1960. Reproduced courtesy of Kira Mourao

In this context, it is perhaps not surprising that the entrepreneurialism shown by women like Helen Tyrrell and Edith Midgley in establishing their own brokerages before the war was not so much in evidence after 1945.

What was really beginning to change was the position of women within member firms in the larger towns and cities. In the interwar years, such firms had increasingly relied on women as secretaries and typists. As in London, however, after 1945, some women who had joined at this level were finding it possible to rise beyond secretarial work. One such was **Helen Gilchrist Smellie** (b. 1911), daughter of a mechanical engineer (see Fig. 6.2). After an education at Coatbridge Secondary School she went on to the local technical school where she received a training in shorthand, typing, bookkeeping, and business.[90] This enabled her to get a job as a shorthand typist in the Glasgow stockbroking firm of Wilson, Scott & Co. in the late 1920s.[91] She later recalled deciding 'on the first day I was going to hate it', but she soon grew to enjoy the work, and stayed at the firm in the long term, being promoted past the clerical level.[92] A second example was **Nellie Neale**, née Jones (b. 1905), the daughter of an iron worker who had progressed from the shopfloor to manage the Gadds Iron Rolling Mills in West Bromwich. Soon after leaving school, aged 15, Nellie got a job as a shorthand typist for a

Birmingham jewellers.[93] Marrying Arthur Neale, a steel casement fitter, in 1931 did not signal the end of her working life, though it did seem to signal a change of occupation, the 1939 Register listing her as a grocery store shopkeeper.[94] But during the war, Nellie Neale switched again, getting a secretarial job at Birmingham stockbrokers J. H. Sabin & Co., which quickly led to client work.[95] Constance Ward in Sheffield (1904–79), Mary Ward (no relation) in Huddersfield (1921–2013), and Muriel Melvin in Aberdeen (1918–77) were other women who started at the secretarial level in the interwar years and were to progress beyond it after 1945.[96]

As in London, firms were also beginning to take on graduates and this could help women to bypass secretarial work altogether. The daughter of Frederick, an accountant, and Millicent, a secretary, **Margaret Holt** (b. 1944) was privately educated at Cheltenham Ladies' College.[97] An only child, she was 'persecuted' by her father with figures growing up, triggering her to study English and drama at Manchester University.[98] Returning to Southport after graduating in 1966, she initially pursued a career in journalism, securing a graduate traineeship at the *Liverpool Daily Post*.[99] But she found her interest in money and investment developing 'in an amateurish sort of way', and after just five months at the paper, she left to join the investment department of Liverpool brokerage Tilney, Sing, Parr & Rae.[100]

Degrees opened doors, then, but they were hardly harbingers of meritocracy. All of the women surveyed here had middle-class backgrounds: indeed, in the late 1960s, just one in 600 working-class girls went on to study at university.[101] On the other hand, many more women had degrees than possessed the social contacts needed to become attachés. And given that UK universities recruited numbers of overseas students, the turn to graduates could promote ethnic diversity, in London at least. An extensive investor in Japan, London brokerage Vickers da Costa hired Kazuko Okura and later Haruko Fukuda, graduates from the London School of Economics and Cambridge respectively, as investment analysts.[102] Asha Wagle, the daughter of a Mumbai businessman, who graduated from Oxford with a degree in philosophy, politics, and economics (PPE), began as a trainee research analyst with the Prudential for eighteen months, before working for a series of prominent City firms, reaching Rothschilds in the early 1970s, where she became the firm's first female manager.[103] Given the City's complex history when it came to attitudes to 'outsiders', these women's ability to forge successful careers suggests the growing openness of the financial world.[104]

Proving Ourselves

The post-war investment scene was being transformed in a number of ways, though some trends attracted a lot more attention than others. For Labour's

Harold Wilson, the rise of institutional investment was 'the biggest revolution in the financial scene this century', but he was amazed how little it was discussed until the mid-1970s.[105] By contrast, the countervailing trend of wider share ownership became a major talking point after 1945. With swathes of industry being moved into public ownership by the post-war Labour government, many on the centre-right became vocal advocates of popular capitalism as a viable alternative to further nationalizations.[106] This agenda was promoted by the Wider Share Ownership Council, a pressure group formed in 1958 and dominated by Conservatives including Prime Minister Harold Macmillan's son Maurice, and future party chairman Edward du Cann. Its aim was to 'manufacture' new capitalists by promoting stock market investment, and it did much to make the small investor a subject of public debate.[107] Those who wanted to encourage wider share ownership, as *The Times* observed, had to overcome 'a feeling that share buying is a thing that only rich people do', and by the end of the 1950s, financial institutions were going to some lengths to woo the 'cloth cap investor'.[108]

How able stockbrokers were to appeal to new investors was debatable. A study commissioned by the London Stock Exchange in 1965 found that only 32 per cent of investors did business directly with a stockbroker, compared with 53 per cent who dealt via a bank. When it came to deciding which shares to buy, only 11 per cent sought the advice of a stockbroker, lagging well behind the 24 per cent who asked their bank manager, and the 19 per cent who took their cues from the press.[109] Class and connections made a big difference. Nearly all of those who did deal with a stockbroker had been personally introduced by someone they knew, while one of the main reasons people gave for not using a broker was that they believed their investments to be too small.[110] There was evidence that investors living outside London were more likely to use brokers than those who lived in the capital, suggesting the extent to which provincial stockbrokers remained embedded in their local communities.[111] London brokers, by contrast, tended to be thought of as 'remote and impersonal'.[112]

Gender also played a big role. While the figure of the 'cloth cap investor' masculinized popular investment, pitches to new investors were aimed as much at women as men.[113] Moreover, the impression that women were as engaged with the stock market as men received repeated confirmation in the form of quantitative analysis. With the politicization of share ownership, and growing sociological interest in 'affluent' Britain, these years saw a series of surveys, carried out with varying degrees of rigour, estimating the size and make-up of the investing public.[114] The first, commissioned by the *Financial Times* in 1949, estimated that women represented about 46 per cent of shareholders, and subsequent studies came up with similar numbers.[115] Some even suggested that women were numerically in the majority, a point frequently highlighted in the press.[116]

Though old habits of imagining these female investors as ill-informed and vulnerable persisted in some quarters, it became far more common to note women's financial acumen. Popular capitalist crusader and unit trust head Edward du Cann reported that nearly half his fundholders were women, 'and we find them much more exacting than men', asking the sharpest questions at meetings.[117] More colourfully, the *Daily Mail*'s Patricia Kieran claimed that once women became interested in the stock market, 'they can often beat the striped pants off male investment experts'.[118] The idea of women's financial sense seemed to be confirmed by the investment club phenomenon. Formed by groups of friends, family, or colleagues who joined together to pool their investments, these clubs were already popular in North America, and the idea took off in the United Kingdom in the late 1950s. Members enjoyed not only the economic benefits of diversification but also the opportunity to turn investment into a social and participatory activity, picking stocks over a cup of tea or a pint of beer.[119] Annual competitions were held to identify the club securing the highest returns, and though men outnumbered women by as much as six to one, all-female clubs often outperformed their male rivals, a fact which attracted plenty of press attention.[120] Further evidence of women's aptitude was provided by the results of stock-picking competitions which were part of the drive to popularize the stock market. When the *Daily Mail*'s 1959 contest was won by a woman, City editor Patrick Sergeant said the result confirmed 'that women have at least as much investing skill as men'.[121]

Even if the effect of all this was to create an environment in which women were taken more seriously as financial actors, the rise of the female investor was not automatically good news for women stockbrokers. Whether investors had preferences as to the gender of their brokers and bankers was a recurring topic in the popular press of the 1950s and 1960s. When well-known *Daily Mail* reporter Olga Franklin investigated the world of stockbroking in 1958, she made a surprising discovery. Spending a couple of days in a London brokerage to learn how the business worked, Franklin was getting on well until she had to deal with the firm's clients. 'Mr. Robinson handed me my first telephone customer. I had to hand it back though. It was a woman. She became quite hysterical at the sound of me. Didn't want to deal with a woman.' Franklin reported that the next caller was another woman who responded the same way.[122] Though the clients may have in fact been upset that they were talking to a journalist rather than a broker, Franklin's claims were borne out by others. For example, London stockbroker Richard Bradshaw, a strong supporter of equality who, after taking Susan Pretty into his office, began employing other female stockbrokers, believed that whereas male clients often preferred dealing with women, female investors tended to prefer his advice.[123]

Nevertheless, other evidence pointed to opposite conclusions. When the *Sunday Mirror* asked its readers, 'Do you like women to handle your savings? Would you deal with a woman stockbroker?', hundreds wrote in.[124] Ninety-two per cent of women answered yes, compared to a somewhat lower 66 per cent of men.[125] Despite this gender divide, the overall level of support—nearly four in five—for women stockbrokers suggested declining prejudice among the investing public, an impression supported by actual experience. Muriel Bailey was convinced that many female clients preferred dealing with brokers of their own sex. 'Women come to me with their portfolios rather than go to the partners of the firm because I understand their problems', she argued.[126] Many months after an article about her appeared in the *Financial Times*, she received a phone call from a woman who had cut out the article so that when she was ready to invest, she would know whom to approach.[127] But Bailey did not deal solely for women, building up a mixed client list of over 600.[128]

Indeed, the old idea that women's main function in a broker's office was to look after anxious female clients with small sums to invest had largely died by the 1960s.[129] Rather, women like Ellen Fraser and Hilary Root tended to begin by assisting a male partner in the private client sections of their firms, and eventually took over their client lists when they moved on or retired. They were thus operating on exactly the same terms as their male contemporaries, managing substantial mixed client lists.[130] Outside London, where there was by now a tradition of women brokers dealing for male and female clients, few prejudices were reported.[131] In Liverpool, Margaret Holt told *The Guardian* that she encountered little opposition, and even found that, as Bradshaw suggested, 'some men prefer dealing with a woman'.[132]

Nor were women restricted to dealing for a firm's smaller investors. By the early 1970s, Audrey Geddes at Buckmaster & Moore was looking after £14 million in private client money. As well as advising clients, she also provided a discretionary management service, relatively unusual at the time, whereby she would choose investments on behalf of a client. She only dealt with larger investors: the minimum account she would take on was £50,000, though she did also advise on unit trusts for smaller investors.[133] While several women focused on private clients, preferring to deal with 'real live humans and their personal problems', as Fraser put it, they were equally able to concentrate on the developing field of institutional investment, if they preferred.[134] One was Elisabeth Rivers-Bulkeley who, though starting out advising private clients, increasingly focused on the institutional side, acting for investment trusts and unit trusts.[135]

The picture that emerges in the 1960s is of a significant diversification of women's roles in brokerages. Focusing on research did not preclude women from also developing private client lists as a sideline if they so chose, as Anthea Gaukroger did at Sheppards & Chase.[136] Employers could fund sojourns abroad to pick up international broking experience. After three years, Rivers-Bulkeley's bosses sponsored a six-week US trip for her to 'have a look at Wall Street and visit San Francisco and the West Coast'.[137] Moreover, by the 1960s there was a growing amount of mobility from firm to firm, including not only brokerages but also a range of other firms which needed similarly skilled people, particularly banks, insurance companies, investment trusts, and even newspapers. Admittedly, this mobility could be seen negatively. One anonymous investment analyst told a researcher that she moved from job to job 'because she felt that any mistake she made was highlighted in a way that a man's error would not be'.[138] But it seems that overall, the mobility was driven more by opportunity than necessity, and often involved career progression.[139] Switching firms could mean reaching positions of seniority very quickly. Suzan Andrews entered the City aged 18 at Sun Insurance, but left for a job in stockbroker Paul E. Schweder & Co.'s arbitrage department. Staying there for three and a half years, she acquired extensive experience of option dealing. This enabled her to land a job at Panmure Gordon, one of the City's leading option brokers, where she led a team of nine dealers, handling six-figure option transactions. Asked by a *Mail* reporter, 'What is the attitude of City clerks under orders from a 25-year-old girl?', Andrews replied: 'There's never any trouble'.[140]

Outside London, the picture was somewhat different. Smaller firms meant fewer opportunities to specialize, though this was not impossible. In Glasgow, for example, Helen Smellie was able to concentrate on company research at Wilson, Scott & Co. 'I like the backroom detective work of investigating companies for clients', she explained.[141] More striking was the continued lack of mobility. Since a successful career depended so much upon being known and trusted locally, women hardly ever moved towns during their careers. Not only this, women tended to stay with one firm for life, even in larger towns which had competing firms. Whether this was due more to loyalty or absence of opportunity is unclear. One of the few exceptions was Margaret Holt, who started at Liverpool brokers Tilneys before moving to Manchester to become a portfolio manager at Manchester stockbrokers Charlton, Scott, Dimmock & Co.[142] Thus, in a reversal of the situation before the war, London was presenting women with the best options for financial careers.

One factor helping to shift the attitudes of employers was the rise of credentialism. Since the 1920s, the London Stock Exchange had cooperated with the London County Council in providing training courses for employees of member firms.[143] But these were not obligatory, and after 1945, the idea of introducing a system of qualifying examinations to help professionalize stockbroking and win trust with the public gained support.[144] As experienced broker and part-time journalist Donald Cobbett put it: the status of members 'must be endorsed beyond doubt in the highly specialized conditions of the modern business world'.[145] The Provincial Brokers' Stock Exchange was first to adopt compulsory examinations in 1951.[146] But elsewhere, considerable scepticism remained, the majority view being that the skills of the stockbroker were developed in the cut-and-thrust of the trading floor, not from book-learning. The New York Stock Exchange's adoption of examinations in 1963 helped change the mood, however, as did the move towards the federation of stock exchanges in the UK.[147] Proposals for examinations were first announced in 1964.[148] Consisting of a suite of papers in Stock Exchange practice, interpretation of company reports and accounts, the technique of investment, and taxation, passing the examinations would be compulsory for membership from August 1971, though exemptions would be granted for anyone who had been in continuous employment with a member firm since 1964.[149]

Would examinations trigger a meritocratic shake-up of the City? One *Daily Mail* columnist predicted—not altogether seriously—the imminent demise of 'the Throgmorton aristocrats adorned in top hats and pinstripe trousers, buttonholes immaculate, gold watch chains glinting'. But he was far from convinced that examinations would improve the services offered to investors. 'What do you want from your stockbroker—a pat analysis of Company Law or inside information that can put you on to a "good thing"?'[150] At the same time, however, he and other commentators were quick to realize the boon that examinations might represent for women. As the *Evening Standard*'s City editor noted: 'if they can produce the qualifications, it will be very difficult to refuse them full membership'.[151] Indeed, the Stock Exchange course at the City of London College had already proved a means of highlighting women's capacities.[152] Willingness to study on the course was a means for female staff to signal their ambitions to their employers. For example, it was only when Louise Peachey decided to sign up for the Stock Exchange Certificate that progression beyond secretarial work became possible, smoothing the path for her to get a job at Sebags.[153]

Certainly, for those women who had long years of broking experience, the introduction of compulsory examinations was of little significance, the prospect of cramming holding little appeal. Bailey remarked that asking her to sit an exam would feel like 'a bit of an insult'.[154] But for those who began their careers in the 1960s—several of them with university degrees under their belts already—it was very different. Anthea Gaukroger and Hilary Root both recalled that examinations were a means of 'proving ourselves', and were keen to register as soon as the opportunity arose, with the backing of their firms.[155] This was not a decision to be taken lightly, with evening classes, offered by the City of London College and some other institutions, considered a must to master the range of technical subjects appearing on the papers. When Margot Naylor, a member of the Society of Investment Analysts, took a look at the exam papers, she wrote that 'the smirk was wiped off my face', as she realized the amount of revision that would be required to pass them, and the huge effort that would be involved in taking them all in one go.[156] The first set of results confirmed that these were challenging exams, showing a pass rate of 70–5 per cent for three of the papers, dropping to just 47 per cent for the paper on Stock Exchange practice.[157] In this context, the press was very keen to publicize women's successes—like Manchester-based Margaret Holt who passed at the first attempt—as a means of underlining their capabilities.[158] Examinations thus helped refute many of the lingering myths about women, maths, and money.

162   SEXISM IN THE CITY

Don't Mention Women's Lib

A belief in women's financial capacity could go hand-in-hand with well-worn ideas about 'womanly intuition' and skills as shoppers. One thing many women found particularly irksome was the suggestion that they were only interested in buying shares in high street stores. In an interview with the *Sunday Mirror*, investment club secretary Grace Fenning conceded that 'intuition' was a factor guiding their choice of shares, but stressed that this 'doesn't mean that we only invest in stores and food'.[159] Such feelings could develop into a broader critique of the whole concept of gendered financial advice. This was picked up on by financial journalist William Davis in the *Evening Standard*:

> If you want to make an enemy, tell a woman investor that a certain share is 'just right for women'. Most of them bitterly resent the superior male suggestion that there is one investment law for men and another for women. 'There are either good shares or bad shares', they say.[160]

Davis entirely agreed with them, and questioned patronizing attempts to talk down to housewife investors which were founded on the mistaken belief that they had to be 'led by the hand through the hazardous financial jungle'.[161] Such attitudes were products of a financial environment in which women continued to be regarded as dependent on men. Married women needed their husband's permission to obtain credit, while single women or widows needed to find a male guarantor if they wanted a personal loan or a mortgage, a situation which was increasingly challenged, but which did not change till the late 1970s.[162]

It was not just men who pushed the idea of financial advice tailored to women. Prompted by London Stock Exchange chairman Lord Ritchie's suggestion that housewives should buy a few shares in the firms which made their favourite products, Margot Naylor started a column for women in the *Investors Chronicle* in 1960. Written as a series of letters to an old friend who has decided to 'take the plunge' and start looking after her own investments, Naylor dispensed elementary advice and constant reassurance to women whom she presumed were accustomed to delegating all financial matters to husbands or other male relatives.[163] After two weeks of this, a Devon reader, Violet Gladwell, wrote in to complain that Naylor's articles seemed to be addressed to 'nit wits', and were 'an affront' to women's intelligence. 'Why single them out for this infantile talk?' Gladwell wrote that 'Most of my women friends...are keenly interested in the stock market, and are shrewd investors'.[164] A few years later, Elisabeth Rivers-Bulkeley took a different approach from Naylor. Commissioned by the *Daily Telegraph* to produce a series of half-a-dozen articles on 'Feminine Finance', the stockbroker largely steered clear of any gendered stereotypes. Though dealing with the subject of the

SOMETHING IN THE CITY   163

public's ignorance about financial matters, she believed this to be as common among men as women.[165]

The idea of financial products for women was also criticized in some quarters. A *Sunday Telegraph* correspondent was contemptuous of those unit trusts which put women on the boards 'as if this, in itself, made a trust attractive to other women', as well as so-called 'shopping bag trusts' focusing on high street stocks 'which are often deemed to have a peculiar attraction for women'. The correspondent admitted there might be 'some psychological draw in buying products from companies in which you have invested, but no more for a sliced loaf than for a gallon of petrol or a screwdriver'. These kinds of trusts were part-and-parcel of an investment culture in which women were too often treated as different from (and inferior to) men. 'Shattering though it may seem, women investors are just like men—they are in it for the money', she concluded.[166]

Despite this growing denial of the importance of gender in the stock market, some financial women cultivated a gendered performance to achieve their objectives. The best example was Freda Spurgeon, activist investor and founder of the Association of Women Shareholders. Coming to prominence in the slipstream of Mary Whitehouse's 'Clean Up TV' campaign, Spurgeon similarly contrasted her housewifely common sense with the arrogance and corruption of male-dominated elites: in this case not media but financial.[167] Whenever a man was up for election to a company board, one of Spurgeon's favourite strategies was simply to ask what he was going to do. 'The chairman tends to look at me as if I'm crackers, but very often he's stuck for an answer.'[168] Gender was central to her method of eliciting the facts from male boards. 'I act the dumb innocent female and just let them talk. That way I get a lot more information than they ever meant me to.'[169] She did not share the automatic deference of most small shareholders ('They think every director is a blue-eyed boy from heaven. I think a bit differently'), and was contemptuous of what she saw as the outdated vestiges of gentlemanly capitalism. 'There's too much of this old school-tie stuff in the City', she observed.[170] City men came to detest her, dismissing her as 'that battle-axe', or worse; in response, she contended that a man doing the same job would have been called 'public-spirited'.[171]

Though Spurgeon's career highlighted the benefits a gendered performance could bring, women stockbrokers' professional identities developed along very different lines in this period. Many who talked to the press were heavily invested in the idea that their gender was irrelevant to their careers and did not view themselves as gendered actors. Audrey Geddes was broadly representative when she stated categorically, 'I've never encountered any prejudice in my job because I am a woman.'[172] Geddes and her peers did not seek to draw attention to their gender at work, and were irritated when others did. Rivers-Bulkeley did not want to be treated differently because she was a woman, reportedly 'hating the idea of being feted for her rarity value'.[173] When Louise Peachey trained at Joseph Sebag as an investment adviser, one of the male dealers 'told me I was a novelty, an oddity, and that really did make me annoyed'.[174] Another unnamed woman working as a senior investment adviser at a merchant bank explained: 'When one is in the City, one wants to be accepted on one's own worth…You don't really think about being a woman in a man's world'.[175] There was consequently little sense of a shared identity, a point picked up on by financial journalist Jean Schultz. Writing in the *Daily Mail*, Schultz observed of the women who were building careers in the City that, 'far from being organised, most of them don't know each other exists'.[176] The claim is corroborated in later interviews. 'You had your life within your firm, you didn't usually then go and meet other people in other firms', Susan Pretty remembered.[177] When there were women in the same office, there was not an automatic camaraderie. Suzan Andrews was happier working with men because there were 'no petty jealousies' to deal with.[178]

This attitude was reflected in a dwindling involvement with women's clubs and organizations. Nellie Neale, the oldest member of this cohort of stockbrokers, was an outlier here. As well as being active in Birmingham's wider civic life, for years she was an active member of the Erdington and North Birmingham Soroptimist Club, serving as its president, and later as the treasurer of the National Federation of Soroptimist Clubs for six years.[179] She also found time to join the Birmingham branch of the National Federation of Business and Professional Women's Clubs, founded in 1942, and the British Association of Women Executives, established in 1953.[180] This level of engagement seems to have become rare among women stockbrokers, especially in London.[181] While the groups themselves continued to thrive—the Federation of Business and Professional Women's Clubs had 22,000 members by 1967—stockbrokers were not prominent members.[182]

Likewise, financial women's relationship to feminist politics was also changing. Amy Bell and Edith Maskell had been deeply involved with the late Victorian and Edwardian suffrage movement, while Gordon Holmes had happily called herself a feminist. But as second-wave feminism surged in the later 1960s, and became increasingly associated with radical politics, women stockbrokers distanced themselves from the cause.[183] Bailey was perhaps the most outspoken: 'don't mention Women's Lib to me. I think they have everything the wrong way round. I believe in equal rights, but you can't have confidence in people if they behave in an irresponsible way…They have let our sex down very badly'.[184] But the younger generation was just as opposed. Margaret Holt had 'a great contempt for women's organisations who make a lot of noise about things. So many simply "*talk*" about equality', she told the *Mail*.[185] Such distancing strategies were in keeping with the disdainful way female Conservative MPs talked about feminism—or what was often a caricature of feminism—around this time.[186] Yet this rejection of 'ideological' feminism was not incompatible with support for what was later to be dubbed 'free market feminism', which called for the removal of all remaining forms of discrimination, 'leaving women and men with exactly the same rights and opportunities.[187] This aspirational, individualistic creed involved overcoming obstacles not by collective action and structural reform, but through individual 'willpower and determination'.[188] Women stockbrokers, making their way in a hostile environment, embraced this meritocratic vision of equality in which their sex was irrelevant.

This approach anticipated the kinds of professional identities assumed by later generations of businesswomen. Research by Patricia Lewis in the early 2000s identified a strong tendency for women business owners to treat the market as gender-neutral, to refuse to view themselves as gendered actors, and to argue that inequalities had been resolved, rendering gender no longer an issue. Though ostensibly progressive, Lewis argues that this 'gender-blindness' serves to conceal the gendered nature of business, rendering invisible 'the masculinity embedded in entrepreneurial activities'. Masculinity thus becomes the category against which difference is constructed, casting women as the 'other'. To escape this, women allow the attributes and standards of the majority group 'to be presented as a universal norm applied to everyone in a similar manner'. In doing so, they 'seek to secure for themselves the privilege that goes with the invisible cloak of normality and universality', but the strategy involves silencing and erasing gender when it manifests itself, and ignoring work practices which marginalize or exclude them altogether.[189] This confronts women with dilemmas, difficulties, and pressures that most men do not experience.

Denying gendered difference in a male-dominated work culture is a challenge when, as Linda McDowell puts it, 'institutional mechanisms, procedures and everyday attitudes position women within organisations' in ways that constantly emphasize their 'otherness'.[190] Based on her research into the City of London in the 1990s, McDowell argues that women had few options when it came to 'doing gender' at work, confined to limited variations on their sexual or familial roles, 'or an attempt to produce a gender-neutral performance in a parody of accepted masculine norms of workplace behaviour'.[191] This was clearly just as much the case in the 1950s and 1960s, when workplace relations could be complex. In an article surveying women's growing presence in the 'man's world' of the City, financial journalist Margaret Allen argued that men often disliked the idea of female colleagues, not because of the competition they represented, but because they 'cannot relax when working with a woman'. Allen contended that it was women's responsibility 'to prove that they can take a man's view of business and not demand special privileges as females'. This meant making behavioural adjustments. As one anonymous woman Allen spoke to explained, 'As soon as I swore, I was in. The men felt they could relax'.[192] Though Allen's take was criticized by the *Sunday Mirror*'s Sylvia Lamond, who felt that it was men who needed advice on how to behave in the office if the mere presence of women made them uncomfortable, Allen was surely right that, in practice, it was women who faced all the pressure to adapt.[193]

166   SEXISM IN THE CITY

Women tended to downplay difficulties experienced at work when talking to the press, though it would obviously have been difficult to be entirely frank when going on the record. Hazel Archer, an Oxford PPE graduate and analyst at an investment management firm, was very positive about the work culture, telling a reporter: 'I don't find it difficult working here. I reckon working in the City is a lot of fun.'[194] Others did admit the existence of tension, even if framing this as transitory. Jane Barrie came to Fielding Newson Smith as the firm's first female analyst and initially encountered 'a bit of stick' from colleagues. But she reported that 'after a year any prejudices were overcome'.[195] Isabel Drummond, a broker at Buckmaster & Moore, did not find adapting to the male working environment a challenge; nor did she think that it required women to take on 'masculine' characteristics. She did, however, suggest that well-developed social skills were essential. 'The system isn't used to women yet, but I don't think you have to be aggressive or dominating to be accepted and get ahead. You should rather be able to handle other people and be aware of what's happening in your world and the world around you.'[196] Yet the onus on making workplace relations succeed was all on women. Margot Naylor's contribution to the debate was indicative of the wider culture. She advised women who were inclined to complain at the obstacles they faced in male-dominated professions like finance that 'keeping your trap shut' was preferable. These obstacles, she suggested, 'may be created by your own characteristics and personality'.[197]

Women's perceived 'otherness' in the financial sphere was underlined by the feverish media coverage generated when Hilda Harding became a Barclays branch manager. She faced a barrage of questions from reporters which she answered patiently. What would her title be? ('manager, not manageress'). How should she be addressed? ('Madam'). What would she wear? ('whatever I feel like, including summer dresses'). Would male customers be willing to come to her for financial advice? ('I see no reason why they shouldn't'). Would she be able to say no to her customers? ('If I am approached for overdrafts there will be times when I shall have to be firm'). How would she get on with the male staff? ('I'm getting on with them very well indeed, thank you').[198] The questions—none of which would have been posed to a male manager—suggest the bafflement generated by a woman in a position of financial authority. Harding's answers highlight her desire simply to be accepted on the same terms as men.

Aspects of the wider City environment remained inhospitable for women. In 1958, when Olga Franklin spent time learning about stockbroking in a London broker's office, she discovered that lunching her 'clients' would be difficult since most of the City's most popular clubs were closed to women.[199] Similarly, a female investment analyst working at a merchant bank in 1964 noted that developing contacts outside the office was hard for her because of 'the number of eating places in the City where women just don't go'.[200] Louise Peachey admitted that finding commissions could be difficult 'because men meet in clubs and at golf, and that's when they get work'.[201] It seemed the only way the culture would change was by women deciding to go anyway. Bailey was in the habit of grabbing lunch at Slaters, described by one journalist as 'a most masculine bar in Throgmorton Street'.[202]

Outside London, the gendered nuances of stockbroking culture are trickier to gauge. Women running brokerages certainly continued to collaborate successfully with men, sometimes taking on male partners in order to ensure the long-term viability of their firms. When Elizabeth Hill took over her father's firm in Lincoln on his death in 1945, she recruited a male partner, Douglas Strange, from Sheffield to help her.[203] This proved a very durable relationship, the pair overseeing the firm's expansion, opening branches in Peterborough and Derby. In 1971 they took over the Leicester firm Cyril Osborne & Co., while three years later they established a London office, by which point two of Strange's sons had joined the firm.[204] In Lancaster, Connie Whittaker did not find such a viable long-term partner, but seems to have alternated between trading with a male colleague and alone. At some point in the 1960s she established Whittaker, Brierley & Co. with Zachry Vincent Brierley. When Brierley left in 1971, she continued under the name Whittaker & Co.[205] But within a few years, she was trading as Jackson, Whittaker & Co.[206]

Family, of course, presented women with particular challenges. As in previous periods, the majority of women stockbrokers did not marry during their working lives, and in most cases it is difficult to know whether this was by preference, or whether the demands of the job were a factor. Undoubtedly, single women encountered the fewest obstacles to advancement, but some married women, such as Nellie Neale in Birmingham and Elisabeth Rivers-Bulkeley in London, turned to stockbroking later in life and did not seem to find their married status a hindrance. Indeed, stockbroking wives could be the primary breadwinners. Rivers-Bulkeley's initial turn to the profession was triggered when her husband Richard decided to become a member of Lloyd's of London. As this meant three years without pay, Elisabeth told him 'that I would work to keep us'. But this was no short-term contingency: finding she enjoyed the work, she continued. Describing it as 'a very full-time job', Rivers-Bulkeley often spent evenings with clients, or researching the market. It was viable since her husband was 'very understanding'.[207]

Others married after embarking on stockbroking careers. Whereas in earlier periods, the expectation might have been that they would now withdraw from work, this was no longer the case, with marriage bars abandoned in most lines of work after the Second World War. Nevertheless, marriage still carried particular connotations on the London Stock Exchange. The ban on members, and their wives, being involved in any business other than broking and jobbing remained in place in the 1960s, and though women were not members, the rule raised potential issues when women began working for London brokerages in larger

168   SEXISM IN THE CITY

numbers.[208] Having a supportive boss certainly helped. Working for Richard Bradshaw, Susan Pretty married Gavin Shaw, an industrial diamond specialist, in 1968 without negative repercussions.[209] But marrying a fellow broker could be regarded differently, as Hermione Bridges found. When she married a stockbroker who worked for a rival firm, J. & A. Scrimgeour sacked her on the grounds of a conflict of interest. Scrimgeour's attitude may have been unusual, however, since Bridges soon managed to get a job with a start-up brokerage, Russell Wood, a firm which did not find her marriage problematic.[210]

Marrying within the firm was more straightforward, which happened in a couple of cases. At Capels in 1969, Ellen Fraser wed Thomas Winser, a partner. Working for the same firm was convenient: 'There are certain things you wouldn't want an outsider to know, and it would curtail our talking over the day's events if we were in different firms.'[211] Though not raising inter-firm conflicts, such marriages could pose their own problems, however. Thomas was head of the private investment department in which Ellen worked, which meant their marriage 'raised eyebrows' at first, but seems to have been quickly accepted.[212] 'He refuses to discuss my pay' and 'always leaves it to someone else to sort that out', explained Ellen in an interview.[213] At Sternberg Flower in 1971, Muriel Bailey, now in her early sixties, married an associate member of the firm, Walton Willoughby Wood. This seems to have caused little controversy: 'we'll carry on sitting at opposite desks, as we have done for years', said her fiancé.[214]

Marriage could, of course, raise the prospect of children, and the expectation that women would leave work to focus on families was one of the reasons many employers were reluctant to invest in female staff. As Michael Verey, chairman of merchant bank Schroders later explained, women 'weren't a long-term bet for our sort of business. My principal worry was having too many of them.'[215] Such attitudes were held by some women too, Margot Naylor arguing that 'the lack of encouragement offered to women in the professions is not wholly unreasonable, given the shortness of the average woman's career'.[216] Some female stockbrokers who married felt under pressure to signal to employers that, as Ellen Winser put it, they were not 'frivolous' about the job, and were 'not going to run off and have babies'.[217] Others did want to combine stockbroking and raising a family, which was clearly a challenge, especially with part-time work not common in the profession, though not entirely impossible.[218] Susan Shaw had her first child, Tania, in 1971, which did not stall her career, but the demands it imposed on her are suggested by a diary of her working week that she kept for *The Observer* in 1973. The account of her work is punctuated by the intrusion of domestic concerns ('Must remember to call Gas Board about water heater at home'), while guilt about the impact on her child of working long hours is never far away ('Mustn't be late going home tonight, insist on giving Tania her bath myself and spending some time with her. Feel like a juggler'). Working concerns impinged very directly on her home life. 'Arrive home very weary indeed. Day not finished client coming for a drink.'[219] Going on to have a second child, and working even longer hours when her husband fell ill, Susan continued to encounter challenges. 'It was always difficult, really....And there was a lot of soul-searching on my part because I wanted to be a good mother. Never having had a conventional home life myself, I wanted them to have it.'[220]

Clearly, the demands of the career were off-putting for some prospective stockbrokers. Tania Judge, like Shaw, was one of the visitor gallery guides, and landed the job having previously worked at the Bank of England. Though initially aspiring to become a broker, Judge soon abandoned these hopes as they did not fit with her broader life aims. 'Whereas there was once room for the dilettante, nowadays it is a very professional job—and I naturally wanted to get married eventually', she explained in 1970. She decided that combining marriage with working in the gallery was a more feasible proposition.[221] Those who aspired to a career on the trading floor could also lose heart. In 1968, with her hopes of joining the London Stock Exchange seemingly as remote as ever, Rivers-Bulkeley moved to New York, having accepted an invitation from Wall Street brokerage W. E. Hutton & Co.[222] Passing the required examinations, she progressed to work as a registered representative of the New York Stock Exchange.[223] This proved a temporary relocation, however: by late 1970 she had returned home, albeit now working for the London branch of US firm H. Hentz.[224] For others, exile was permanent. After six years at Phillips & Drew, Elizabeth Long, a former Olympic swimmer, found her ambitions to become an unauthorized clerk blocked, despite passing the Stock Exchange examinations with distinction. So disappointed was she that she decided to emigrate to Australia, where she had competed as a swimmer, quickly finding her prospects in Sydney much brighter than in 'Victorian' London.[225]

What has been dubbed the 'qualifications lever'—the means of gaining access to restricted occupations—was not a sufficiently powerful tool to address all the organizational barriers to women's progress that were deeply embedded in workplaces and wider society.[226] For all that women could 'get on' in City firms in ways that would have seemed far-fetched just a generation previously, there remained clear limits to what they could achieve, and the numbers reaching the higher echelons continued to be small.

Conclusion

In the post-war years, women had become 'something in the City', but what exactly they were was a matter for debate. The outside brokers of previous generations had proudly called themselves 'stockbrokers' or 'stock and share dealers'. But with the decline of the outside market, there was uncertainty over what exactly to call the growing numbers of women who worked in London brokerages, but who were, by dint of their sex, not members. This was largely a result of the 1939 Prevention of Fraud Act which, it was widely argued, meant that no one could legitimately describe themselves as a stockbroker who was not an elected member of a stock exchange or did not have a licence from the Board of Trade.[227] This point was accepted by all the women working at London brokerages. For example, Louise Peachey held that although she had passed the Stock Exchange Certificate and had a substantial client list, she could not be termed a stockbroker. 'I'm not a member of the Stock Exchange and brokers are; I really don't know quite what you would call me.'[228] Ellen Winser was in a similar position, technically 'a stockbroker's clerk' despite the large client list she ran, while Suzan Andrews at Panmure, though a senior option dealer in practice, was officially personal assistant to one of the partners.[229] The most senior of all the women, Muriel Bailey (now Wood) at Sternberg Flower, remained an 'attaché'. 'You can't be a stockbroker unless you are a member of the Stock Exchange', she argued.[230]

Women faced another, more insidious, challenge to their identity as brokers. Many had university degrees, several worked in research departments, and they embraced the new Stock Exchange qualifications as a means of proving their worth. This made it difficult to dismiss them as lacking in the calculative skills needed to succeed as stockbrokers. At the same time—and perhaps as a result— traditional brokers sceptical about the turn to investment analysis and credentialism increasingly tended to define stockbroking in terms which emphasized distinctly unmathematical qualities. The successful stockbroker, they argued, possessed qualities, described as 'a sixth sense of anticipation' or simply a 'nose', that were innate rather than taught.[231] Such views were underpinned by a conservative masculinity defined in opposition to younger men—the backroom 'boffins'—who were often feminized. Within Phillips & Drew, which pioneered investment analysis in the 1950s, a cultural divide remained, with some partners tending to dismiss the firm's research department: 'Like a lot of ballet dancers, very touchy about this and that', as Peter Swan put it.[232] Once examinations were introduced, another broker predicted that 'we are certain to end up with a lot of long-haired bespectacled youths or young men who may, on paper, know all the answers, but who won't, I am certain, make good stockbrokers'.[233]

In an ironic reversal, this growing tendency to value flair and instinct over brains came perilously close to framing intuition, that archetypally 'feminine' quality, as essential to the business of the broker.[234] In a further irony, this could prove a shock to women who arrived at brokerages with different ideas about finance. After reading history at Cambridge, Haruko Fukuda held several research posts and was briefly assistant to the Director of Economics at the World Bank before moving to London brokerage Vickers da Costa in 1972. With ten to a room, 'desks close together and telephones ringing the entire time', she found it 'a great contrast to the calm of the World Bank'.

Suddenly I was working with people who were very much at the sharp end of commerce. They were robust, they followed their intuition much more than reasoned argument, they were jumping around, always going out for long lunches and coming back having had five brandies and carrying on in the afternoon talking on the telephone.[235]

The environment did not prevent Fukuda from developing a long and successful City career. But the pivot from reason to intuition in characterizations of stockbroking pointed to men's resourcefulness in maintaining gendered hierarchies. It could be admitted, albeit grudgingly, that women, like the 'long-haired youths', had something to contribute in terms of book-smarts and diligent research. But without the 'nose', the 'vision', they were not *real* brokers, and thus stockbroking could continue to be viewed as 'men's work'.

Of course, control meant not only maintaining gendered hierarchies within firms, but also continuing the exclusionary strategy of barring women from becoming members of stock exchanges. How this played out in an era when gender discrimination was coming under unprecedented scrutiny, in parliament, in the courts, and in wider society, is the subject of the next chapter.

Sexism in the City: Women Stockbrokers in Modern Britain. James Taylor, Oxford University Press.
© James Taylor 2025. DOI: 10.1093/9780191990397.003.0007

7

Invading the Stock Exchange

The Road to 1973

> Stock Exchange members...must be men of integrity, experience, and business acumen. Their job is to serve the public, and through service to earn profits for themselves....[T]he London Stock Exchange...excludes non-members from its premises, but never has it tried to set arbitrary limits to its membership. Any suitable person can become a member, and men who have had proper training in the ways of the market can do so at relatively low cost.
>
> W. T. C. King, *The Stock Exchange* (London, 1947), 34

From 1945, the London Stock Exchange found itself in a precarious position. Facing a Labour government sceptical about the power of financiers and critical of the profit motive, and whose programme of nationalization encompassed one of the great City institutions, the Bank of England, it realized it needed to pay more attention to its public image.[1] In the interests of staving off criticism and drumming up business, the Committee for General Purposes embarked on a refresh of its promotional literature. Deciding that the existing guide, 1934's *The Work of the Stock Exchange*, was outdated and 'too technical for the man in the street', it resolved to commission a new guide for modern times.[2] The resulting five-shilling pamphlet, by *Economist* journalist Wilfred King, went all out to dispel myths about the Stock Exchange. It was no longer a private club or exclusive casino, but an important public institution whose activities in ensuring a free and fair market were essential to the prosperity of the national economy. At the same time, however, it repeated another myth of its own making, the myth of open membership. Its self-proclaimed defence of the 'spirit of freedom and competition' extended—so King insisted—to its membership policies, and he clearly assumed that readers would not detect any incongruity here.

Indeed, King was accurately reflecting wider assumptions in the immediate post-war years. With the continuing exception of the Provincial Brokers' Stock Exchange, which lacked a trading floor, the idea that stock exchanges were for men alone went largely unchallenged. The tenuous foothold women had gained during the Second World War proved fleeting. London's governing committee voted unanimously to repeal the temporary regulation allowing female clerks to work in the Settling Room in November 1945. The final women vacated the room at the end of the Stock Exchange year in March 1946.[3] Outside London, attitudes were slightly less hardline. In Liverpool, the three women employed as dealing clerks on the floor of the exchange were given the option of staying on. Two decided to leave, but one, Primrose Cornah, chose to remain, working till the 1960s as the only woman on the trading floor.[4] In early 1949, the Halifax Stock Exchange wrote to senior Liverpool stockbroker Richard Synge, who was President of the Council of Associated Stock Exchanges, seeking his advice on the admission of a woman. Synge replied that 'this was a matter for individual Exchanges and that each case should be treated on its merits'.[5] However, it does not seem that Halifax encouraged the woman, whose identity is unknown, to pursue her application.[6]

But with more women breaking into post-war finance, the question of membership returned in the 1950s and 1960s, more strongly than ever before, though as in earlier periods, it was the determination of individual women that forced the issue onto the agenda, obliging male-run institutions to respond. Women working in finance wanted membership for a variety of reasons. First, and most obvious, was the desire to work on the trading floor. Some women felt that direct contact with the market, getting a 'feel' for the way prices were going, was indispensable when advising clients. As Susan Shaw put it, on the floor 'one can find out so much more than by remote control'.[7] For others, however, this was less important. Within firms, dealing was increasingly being left to specialists, with many brokers remaining in the office.[8] 'Why would I waste my time on the floor when I can get business done by picking up a telephone?', asked Muriel Bailey.[9] For such women, status was more important. 'It is a question of becoming a recognised member of one's profession', as Anthea Gaukroger put it.[10] As seen in Chapter 6, without membership, these women could not legitimately describe themselves as stockbrokers. This was a matter of standing and also of financial returns. Attachés had to surrender two-thirds of the commission they earned to their firm, whereas members only had to remit half.[11] And—perhaps most important of all—when they could not become members, they could not hope to become partners in their firms.

At a time when women's exclusion from other spheres of work was being successfully challenged, most notably in the House of Lords, with female life peers and hereditary peers enabled by legislation in 1958 and 1963 respectively, the opposition of the stock exchanges to change remained remarkably consistent. To some extent, the reasons do not take much deciphering. Many stock exchange members felt similarly to arch-opponent of Lords reform, the Earl of Glasgow, who pleaded with his fellow peers in 1957 that 'this is about the only place left in the kingdom where men can meet without women. For Heaven's sake let us keep it that way!'[12] This was, as Duncan Sutherland puts it, the 'last desperate cry' that also 'echoed through the Oxbridge colleges, the Church, the Pall Mall clubs and the MCC'.[13] Yet why the stock exchanges held so firmly to this vision of themselves

174   SEXISM IN THE CITY

as single-sex clubs, at precisely the moment when they were in other respects anxiously tackling their image so as to be seen as modern institutions serving the public interest, requires deeper exploration. And how they were able successfully to resist accepting women as members for so long, in the face of growing opposition from the press, women's groups, and politicians, also needs investigation. At stake were not only women's rights in one sector of post-war finance, but also centuries-long habits of thinking about financial markets in gendered terms.

This Must NOT Get into the Press

Richard Synge's response to the Halifax Stock Exchange in 1949 had not signalled any opposition from the authorities to women's membership. But this stance was to be tested more rigorously by events a few years later in Birmingham, which are worth exploring in detail in order to expose the dynamics underpinning the continuing exclusion of women. In December 1955, John Sabin, senior partner of J. H. Sabin & Co., where Nellie Neale had worked for nearly fourteen years, wrote to Percy Rudge, secretary of the Birmingham Stock Exchange. Sabin argued that it was wrong 'that a woman of ability in stockbroking should be restricted indefinitely to the status of a clerk'. Neale's 'knowledge of stockbroking and her investment clientele is such that she would have been a Member of our Exchange before now, if she were a man', he continued. He therefore asked Rudge to sound out the committee of management on accepting Neale as a member.[14]

It was soon apparent that the Birmingham committee did not know how to respond.[15] They raised the matter with senior members of the Liverpool, Manchester, and Leeds exchanges, who recommended referring it further up the chain, to the Committee of the Council of Associated Stock Exchanges, which they did.[16] Their letter suggested that they had some sympathy for Neale, noting that she 'appears to be fully qualified for membership apart from her sex'. Given that theirs was 'practically the only profession to which women are not now admitted', they felt that her application should be taken seriously, but did not want to go it alone, since it was 'desirable that all Provincial Exchanges should act together'.[17] In May, the Council Committee responded, informing Birmingham that the Committee were 'personally of the opinion that...the admittance of lady members to Stock Exchanges is inevitable sooner or later', that 'all applications should be treated on their merits', and that 'admittance should be without restrictions'.[18]

The normal process was for the applicant's name to be circulated to members and posted in the exchange for a month. If no objections were forthcoming, and the candidate passed an interview, a ballot of members was held.[19] But instead of this, Birmingham's committee of management opted to canvass brokers for their views on the idea of having a female member. It wrote that they had 'received a tentative application by a lady for admission', and explained that '[a]s this is a controversial issue, the Committee feel that before proceeding further, it is their duty to place the question before the Members'. It invited them 'to say whether you have any definite objection to the admission of ladies to membership'.[20] Out of 107 members, forty-eight replied, forty of them opposing, and just eight supporting. Further enquiries on whether limited membership—without the right to trade on the exchange floor—would be a solution revealed little support.[21] As a result, the committee wrote to Sabin and Neale's sponsors that 'the volume of objection by the members is so large that the committee are unable for the time being to further consider her application'.[22]

So far as the committee were concerned, there the matter ended. But a few weeks later they discovered that a *Sunday Express* reporter was coming to Birmingham to interview Neale and others for a feature that weekend. The committee had only managed to keep the story of Neale's application out of the *Birmingham Post* on the condition that they gave the paper the scoop when they were ready to go public, and they decided they had to 'keep faith' with the paper and authorized it to go to press.[23] In a front-page splash, the *Post* acknowledged that the committee had to take into account hostility among the membership, and that if they admitted Neale's application, 'it would create a precedent which other exchanges could not easily disregard'. But it believed it was time for the profession to embrace 'new thinking'. 'It would be odd if it decided that it could dispense with the counsel of women when almost every other profession, in the end, has been glad of their assistance.'[24] Gazumped, the *Sunday Express* dropped its planned article, but the story became major national news, and it was clear that there was more support for Neale than for Birmingham's brokers. 'Why should women not be admitted as members of Stock Exchanges?' asked the *Evening Standard*, citing the examples of Edith Midgley and Gordon Holmes as successful women in finance.[25] 'This is a case of sheer pride and prejudice', claimed a *Daily Telegraph* editorial, which went on to argue that the men were trying to resist the inevitable. 'It is only a matter of time before the bulls, the bears and the stags change their sex.'[26] Members of the public joined the debate, with the large majority of letters published in the press supporting Neale.[27] Birmingham Stock Exchange chairman Alfred Jeffs' attempt at explanation did not help. 'There is nothing personal in Mrs Neale's application not being granted. It is just that a large proportion of the members did not like the idea of having lady members of the Exchange.'[28]

Nor did the members relish being in the spotlight and being subjected to such public criticism. Blaming the committee for allowing the *Post* to run the story in the first place, three members drafted a petition of protest which they presented in early September. The sixty-eight signatories were 'deeply disturbed by the ventilation in the public press of a matter which is the private and domestic concern of our Association'. As a result, they requested that the committee 'take no action

176   SEXISM IN THE CITY

with regard to the admission of women to membership of the Birmingham Stock Exchange until and unless a clear majority of all the members has expressed its definite desire in writing for such action to be taken'.[29] Articulating the written opposition of nearly two-thirds of the membership, and recorded in the minute book, the petition blocked further action.

Stung by criticism from its members, the Birmingham committee subsequently worked hard to shut the issue down. When they found that Sabin and one of his partners, Stanley Davis, had been in communication with *Daily Mail* journalist Olga Franklin, they judged Davis to be in breach of the exchange's rules on publicity and suspended him for a month. They also insisted that Sabin undertake 'that no Partner or member of his staff would in future communicate either directly or indirectly with the Press on the subject of women's membership of any Stock Exchange'.[30] Nevertheless, with Neale an active member of several women's organizations, the issue remained a live one partly thanks to their efforts. Delegates at the annual conferences of both the British Soroptimists and the National Federation of Business and Professional Women's Clubs passed motions deploring Neale's treatment and inviting the country's stock exchanges to rethink their policies.[31] Soon after, the National Federation of Business and Professional Women's Clubs wrote to the Council of the Associated Stock Exchanges asking them to clarify their position. The Council replied that 'this was a matter upon which each Exchange should make its own decision as each application for Membership of a Stock Exchange is considered on its own merit'.[32] But this was patently untrue: Neale's application had not gone through the normal process, but had been blocked by members who did not want a woman to join.[33]

When Hilda Harding hit the headlines in May 1958 as Barclays' first female bank manager, Neale's less favourable position was highlighted once more in the press.[34] Edith Pitt, Conservative MP for Edgbaston, raised the issue in a speech to the Standing Conference of Women's Organizations. Pitt called Birmingham's stockbrokers 'out of date', and argued that 'all doors should be open to those who prove they can do the job'.[35] Such public expressions of support encouraged Neale to renew her efforts. In July she wrote to the committee of management asking them to reconsider their decision.[36] Dismissing the anti-women petition as 'an agitation by three Members', she argued that, after fifteen years' service with a member firm, she deserved 'some form of recognition'.[37] Her letter clearly divided the committee. After much discussion, they initially resolved to write to members on the question, but a fortnight later, they decided instead to write to Neale that as the opinion of the majority of members was already clear, unless they received a petition altering its members' stance, they could do no more.[38]

However, two years later, there was a breakthrough. Sabin successfully persuaded the committee to reopen the matter on the grounds that the three members who had instigated the anti-women petition had no objection, and that since 1956, Neale had successfully increased her clientele 'to a point where any reasonable firm would grant her a full partnership, were it not for the member-ship bar'.[39] The committee circularized members in March 1960, asking whether they would agree to admitting women either with or without restrictions, and insisting on secrecy: '*it is essential* that no information shall leak outside as this might again start the interference of the Press', it warned.[40] The vote was indeed conducted without publicity, but this did not produce the result that Sabin and Neale wanted. With nearly all members voting, the proposition to allow women restricted membership was defeated by sixty-seven votes to thirty-one, while unrestricted membership was overwhelmingly rejected by eighty-five to fifteen. The results were sent to members, 'together with a warning that this must NOT get into the Press'. Given this clear indication of majority opinion, the committee instructed Neale's sponsors to withdraw their support for her application.[41] They regarded the matter as closed. At the annual general meeting a few months later, the chairman stated that 'if in the future this question is revived—say—by action of another Exchange, the Committee will not be able to take any action even should the opinion of the Members change at some time unless required in writ-ing by a majority of the Members'.[42] Having run out of road, Neale had no choice but to suspend her quest for membership.

The episode vividly dramatized the extent of opposition to women among male stockbrokers. Neale certainly had allies, not only in her firm, but also on Birmingham's committee of management, some of whose members seemed well disposed to her cause. But they were in a minority, and while Neale also had plenty of supporters outside the stockbroking community, they were unable to influence events. Though women's groups lobbied for a change in policy, stock exchanges paid little attention, and while the press was overwhelmingly support-ive of Neale, journalistic backing proved a double-edged sword as Birmingham's brokers were touchy about their exchange's membership policies being debated so publicly. Tactics were also critical. Though the stated policy of the Committee of Associated Stock Exchanges was that applications from women should be treated on their merits, Birmingham chose instead to trigger a debate on the question of sex. Doing so was effectively to invite opposition. If the committee had simply allowed Neale's application to proceed in the normal way with their blessing, they would have sent a clear message to members, and the outcome might have been different. But as we will see, this was a sequence of events which was to be repeated in the capital.

The Glass Wall

The London Stock Exchange remained highly sensitive about its public image even after the Conservatives returned to power following the general election of 1951. It was becoming commonplace across the political spectrum to blame the

178   SEXISM IN THE CITY

financial sector for post-war industrial decline, and traditional habits of imagining the Stock Exchange as a glorified casino persisted.[43] As a result the institution abandoned its customary aversion to publicity. In 1949, the Committee for General Purposes was superseded by a new governing Council, with experienced broker John Braithwaite elected its head. Recruiting the leading advertising agency, J. Walter Thompson, to advise on image, Braithwaite was the driving spirit behind a package of measures designed to transform public perceptions.[44] Under his leadership, the Stock Exchange constructed a visitors' gallery, circulated a range of publicity materials, including the new quarterly *Stock Exchange Journal*, and produced its first ever promotional film, *My Word Is My Bond*, narrated by journalist Richard Dimbleby, to explain the workings of the market to a mass audience.[45] Underlying the charm offensive was the aim of redefining the Stock Exchange as a public institution rather than the private club of yesteryear.[46]

Central to Braithwaite's strategy was the construction of a public gallery, emulating the New York Stock Exchange which had opened its gallery to the public in 1939 in a show of transparency.[47] When the project was delayed by the post-war shortage of building materials, the Council decided to open the trading floor to the public on Saturdays through summer 1951 as part of the Festival of Britain celebrations.[48] Attracting more visitors than predicted, the open days were repeated in 1952 and 1953.[49] Yet it was recognized that showing off an empty building was potentially underwhelming for visitors, who could 'only imagine the hum and throb of working days, when 5,000 or more are coming and going'.[50] Consequently, the Council persisted with its plans for a gallery, securing permission to build in January 1953.[51] Some members were anxious about allowing the public to observe the floor during business hours: on days when markets were slack, the absence of activity could create the wrong impression.[52] One firm wrote to the Council that 'some members would have a hard task explaining to their wives what a really hard day in the City means if their spouses were allowed to go into the gallery and see for themselves'.[53] But construction went ahead, and the gallery was opened to the public before the end of the year.[54] Now, visitors would be able to do what they had never been able to before: witness stocks being traded during business hours without risk of violent ejection. Though the sixty-feet-high gallery was enclosed by a plate glass screen, a vent at the top meant that visitors could nevertheless hear something of the 'hubbub' of the House.[55]

The gallery proved a popular draw, with women a significant presence among the crowds, including Margaret Beeby, a Shell employee who was presented with a carriage clock for being the 250,000th visitor in July 1957.[56] The gallery was to be the vehicle for a more permanent feminine presence, however. Such were the numbers of visitors that staffing—by waiters and members who gave talks in the adjoining lecture theatre—became a problem.[57] The solution adopted was to recruit a team of three women to conduct the visitors and deliver the lectures.[58]

After five weeks' training, former secretaries Joan Cressall and Gillian Evans, and Mary Crook, previously a physical education teacher, began work, amidst enthusiastic press coverage.[59] Regarded by a *Times* reporter as 'the latest and most startling step in the policy of the Stock Exchange to woo the general public', the policy was presented by Braithwaite as a concession to modern sentiment. 'The whole world has moved into an entirely new era and we in the City of London must move with it and fit ourselves to the times in which we move', he told the press.[60] Indeed, many commentators saw the move as highly significant. 'On the public side of the glass wall, at least, the monasticism of the stock exchange will be broken', noted *The Economist*.[61] Others felt the innovation had longer-term implications for activities on the other side of the glass. The *Daily Herald*'s City columnist saw it as a 'first dent in the male armour' that could eventually lead to 'the first lady stockbroker'.[62] The *Daily Telegraph* agreed, reflecting that the trio might 'go down in history as the unwitting pioneers of a successful assault on one of man's last strongholds'.[63]

Yet this was little more than sensationism, the tone and assumptions of the press reports themselves confirming that gender equality remained a distant prospect. The 'three pretty girls' in their 'smart green uniforms' and 'gay smiles' combined 'the virtues of the private secretary and the air hostess'.[64] While they had been selected from a large field of applicants for their 'intelligence and aptitude for the work', most press reports presented the women's looks as their most important attribute, one *Telegraph* columnist predicting that numbers of gallery visitors would increase sharply in the next few weeks.[65] Though the women had undergone a crash course in the history and functions of the Stock Exchange, they were not seen as potential brokers themselves. Evans revealed that the first thing they had been told during their training was that 'on no account were we to go downstairs'. Crook elaborated: 'We wouldn't dream of going on to the floor, even if we were allowed to. There are so many men.'[66] Crook warned another reporter that it was no good asking her for stock tips as she had 'no head for figures'.[67] With the Stock Exchange, the press, and the guides themselves all working to contain the potential threat, it is not surprising that the brokers and jobbers felt secure. Members, reported *The Times*, 'are said to favour the arrival of girls in the gallery'.[68] Indeed, a series of marriages between the Stock Exchange's 'hand-picked beauties' and 'well-heeled and highly eligible stockbrokers' over the next few years left the authorities on the constant lookout for replacements, especially when a fourth guide was added in 1959.[69]

Staffing its gallery with women was a way for the Stock Exchange to pose as an institution moving with the times. Indeed, its advertising agents J. Walter Thompson were heavily involved in the policy, and were alert to opportunities to gain maximum capital from it.[70] The appointment of a new guide or the unveiling of a new uniform was milked as a major PR event, reported not only in the *Stock Exchange Journal*, but in the national press as well, often accompanied by photographs.[71] Such publicity undoubtedly helped the Stock Exchange to present a modern and feminine face to the public. But this did not signal new attitudes to the question of women members. When quizzed by Olga Franklin in 1958, Braithwaite told her that 'no woman stockbroker would ever be allowed on the floor'.[72] His successor, Lord Ritchie of Dundee, who took over the following year, seemed of a similar mind. Described by journalist Anthony Sampson as 'a handsome, rather theatrical-looking stockbroker with a monocle and pearl tie-pin', he was unconscious of any irony when he brandished the Stock Exchange's meritocratic credentials in an interview for the *Sunday Times* in 1960: 'We're all looking for bright young men and we don't give a damn what school they come from'.[73] However, when asked directly about the prospects for women members in an interview shortly afterwards, he appeared cautiously supportive: 'I don't see why we should not have them. There is no rule against it'.[74] Although his words were interpreted in some quarters as progressive, this was in reality the preferred tactic for keeping women out: emphasizing that there was no formal bar, while doing nothing to facilitate women's entry.[75]

The attitude of the Stock Exchange was put to a direct test within months. Perhaps emboldened by Ritchie's words, Elisabeth Rivers-Bulkeley sought membership in early 1961. Having built a good reputation as an attaché at Hedderwick, Borthwick, she had no problem acquiring sponsors, among them the son of a member of the Stock Exchange Council.[76] But the response was disappointing. She was advised not to apply, and when she persisted, the Council manoeuvred to block her.[77] First, she was told that she was ineligible for membership as she was not British born. Her response—that she had married an Englishman aged 19, had lived in the country ever since, and had served in the Auxiliary Territorial Service during the war—was brushed off on the grounds that she had not been naturalized.[78] There were further complicating factors. One was that her husband was a partner at Lloyd's of London and therefore 'at business in risk', a problem given the longstanding rules on the business activities of members' spouses. Another was—it was widely rumoured—the lack of women's toilets in the building.[79] In an echo of the Nellie Neale affair, the Council was further offended when news of Rivers-Bulkeley's application appeared in the *Financial Times* under the headline 'The Young Lady of Throgmorton Street'.[80] The Council pressured her sponsors to withdraw their support, and 'the whole matter was quietly buried, like an unpleasant family incident'.[81] The following year Muriel Bailey also attempted an application. Her case involved fewer sticking points in that she was London-born and unmarried. But the Council's response was the same.[82]

However, change was afoot outside London. The possibility of creating a national stock exchange through a 'willing merger' of existing institutions was becoming a serious proposition, driven in part by concerns over the transformative effects, among them added competition, that would be brought about were the United Kingdom to gain admission to the European Common Market.[83]

INVADING THE STOCK EXCHANGE   181

Minds were focused by a major parliamentary enquiry on company law, chaired by senior judge Lord Jenkins, which reported in 1962. The report found serious fault with the profusion of small stock exchanges, highlighting that fifteen had fewer than forty members. This was problematic from the perspective of investor protection: small exchanges did not have compensation funds to cover defaults by their members, did not have the same powers to control their members, and were not able to subject companies' applications for quotations to the same scrutiny as larger exchanges. Consequently, the report recommended a programme of rationalization, involving the amalgamation of some of the smaller exchanges, to be implemented by the Board of Trade.[84]

Keen to stave off government intervention, the exchanges devised their own plans. As well as forming the Federation of Stock Exchanges in Great Britain and Ireland in 1965, designed to harmonize rules across the country and to improve provisions for investor compensation, they also developed a programme of regional mergers.[85] The first fruit of regionalization was the formation of the Scottish Stock Exchange, made up of the Glasgow, Edinburgh, Dundee, and Aberdeen Exchanges, in January 1964. The four constituent stock exchanges kept their trading floors, but were now under the authority of a central council headquartered in Glasgow.[86] One of the first applications for membership of the new institution was Aberdeen stockbroker Muriel Melvin.

Critically, rather than initiating a debate on the pros and cons of admitting women, as had happened in Birmingham, Melvin's application was treated the same as one from a man would have been. She had to pass a vetting stage at Aberdeen, before her proposal went on to the Scottish Stock Exchange's executive council at Glasgow.[87] The new organization's membership rules, in common with most other exchanges, did not mention sex. But this was not raised as an issue. The Glasgow council approved the application, and notified members, who had fourteen days to lodge any objections. Not even the story reaching the *Financial Times* complicated matters, and Melvin soon after became the first female stockbroker to work on an exchange floor in the United Kingdom.[88]

The regionalization project continued, the next grouping to take shape being the Northern Stock Exchange, consisting of nine members: Liverpool, Manchester, Leeds, Sheffield, Huddersfield, Bradford, Halifax, Oldham, and Newcastle.[89] Based closely on the Scottish model, the nine exchanges retained their trading floors, but were now overseen by a council dominated by the two largest members, Liverpool and Manchester.[90] In June 1965, just as Sheffield's committee was going through the process of joining the new regional exchange, it received an application from Constance Ward. As we saw in Chapter 5, Ward had unsuccessfully applied to trade as an authorized clerk in 1942. But rather than repeating the process it had followed then—ordering a special ballot on whether women should be admitted—Sheffield instead emulated the recent precedent set north of the border, treating Ward's application the same as it would a man's. The

182 SEXISM IN THE CITY

committee were satisfied with her credentials, and recommended her election. At the special general meeting of members which had the final say, Ward was duly elected a member of the Sheffield Stock Exchange.[91] This made becoming a member of the Northern Stock Exchange a formality, simply signing a form undertaking to abide by the rules and regulations of the new institution when it came into effect in August.[92]

It was not a coincidence that it was the smallest stock exchanges that were first to break with tradition on women. There were only seven stockbroking firms, with a total of sixteen members, on the Sheffield Stock Exchange by the mid-1960s, while Aberdeen was smaller still, with just nine members belonging to four firms.[93] In the context of dwindling numbers, the smallest exchanges faced an existential threat with amalgamations and mergers in the air. Maintaining the masculine purity of their trading floors now seemed less important than recruiting new members to prove their continuing viability as distinct entities within larger regional units. And as for the new regional exchanges, while not tackling the gender issue directly in their constitutions, they were aware that as new institutions, there was precious little scope to invoke tradition as a pretext for excluding women.

Arbitrary and Capricious

Though major milestones for women in finance, these admissions attracted very little press coverage.[94] Nor, perhaps predictably, did they influence the thinking of the London Stock Exchange. Labour's re-election in the general election of October 1964 had raised fears of the establishment of a body similar to the Securities and Exchange Commission that had regulated the American market for the past thirty years. The Stock Exchange's advisers at J. Walter Thompson were therefore as mindful as ever of the importance of developing 'a progressive image of an effective operation which was working in the public interest' to forestall any such initiative.[95] In meetings, reports, and letters to Council members, they regularly suggested strategies to improve London's image, persuading them to embark on a major advertising campaign in 1962, and advocating for the introduction of compulsory examinations for members as a panacea for the institution's reputational problems.[96] But they did not see the bar on women as an issue that needed addressing.[97]

This may have influenced the attitude of the Stock Exchange's new chairman, Martin Wilkinson, who replaced Ritchie in June 1965. Wilkinson was a partner in one of the City's oldest stockbroking firms, de Zoete & Gorton. His father Robert had had little time for the idea of women stockbrokers when deputy chairman in the 1930s, as shown by his run-in with Gordon Holmes during the Bodkin Committee hearings, discussed in Chapter 5. But the son came into the top job

INVADING THE STOCK EXCHANGE   183

with the reputation as a progressive, having taken a leading role in the Stock Exchange's efforts to improve its image over the previous few years.[98] Inevitably, he was quizzed about his stance on women members at his first press conference. His response—that he had 'no prejudices against women stockbrokers. I would not oppose them'—was interpreted by some as 'brave' but came with the caveat that he did not think it 'practical' that women should have access to the trading floor.[99] Indeed, *The Economist* found his stance 'non-committal', and with no action taken over the following months, it was clear that Wilkinson's priorities lay elsewhere.[100]

Yet one reform seemed to offer women cause for hope. Some member firms were struggling with a lack of capital, not helped by the rule that all partners were bound by the principle of unlimited liability for debts. The Council's proposed solution—to allow firms to recruit 'external members' who would contribute capital on a limited liability basis, but who would not take part in management or active trading—proved popular with members, who voted unanimously in favour in May 1966.[101] Though it was not the reason for the change, some commentators believed that the new membership category would make it possible for women to join the Stock Exchange.[102] Indeed, it inspired Muriel Bailey to attempt another application in October 1966 under the new rules. As she was happy to refrain from trading on the floor, the reform stood to give her the opportunity to attain what she had long wanted, to become a partner at James Flower & Sons. This time, Bailey got as far as the door of the Council. Her two sponsors were invited in while she waited outside. After forty-five minutes, they came out to tell her the verdict: because she planned to continue in active business, she was not eligible for external membership.[103]

Until this point, Bailey had followed Stock Exchange etiquette and assiduously kept her name out of the press. But exasperated by the rejection—which followed years of attempting to advance her cause behind the scenes—she now decided to break her silence and talk to journalists.[104] Frederick Ellis of the *Daily Express* wrote a sympathetic piece, while Jean Schultz, who covered financial topics for the *Daily Mail*, reported that Bailey planned 'to rally other women in the City to campaign for equal recognition with men'.[105] Going public in this way—let alone criticizing the Stock Exchange's policies—was traditionally regarded as the ultimate faux pas by City authorities, as had been seen in the cases of Neale and Rivers-Bulkeley. But the response this time was different, due to the outcome of a high-profile legal case a few months earlier in the world of horse racing.

Florence Nagle had been training racehorses for decades, but had been repeatedly refused a licence by the Jockey Club, racing's governing authority. As a consequence, she was a 'ghost trainer', her horses officially trained by her head lad.[106] Nagle decided to sue the Jockey Club in 1965, and though her case was initially dismissed, she appealed, and in February 1966, the Appeal Court judges took a strong line on the issue of sex discrimination. Rejecting the argument that

184   SEXISM IN THE CITY

racing's governing body was 'a social club' which was free to admit or refuse members as it saw fit, they held it to be 'an association which exercises a virtual monopoly in an important field of human activity'. Such associations could lay down minimum qualifications for admission, but they could not 'capriciously and unreasonably' prevent someone from earning a living. To do so on the grounds of sex was as indefensible 'as to refuse a man a licence solely because of the colour of his hair'. The Jockey Club's position was 'arbitrary and entirely out of touch with the present state of society in Great Britain'. Consequently, the judges permitted Nagle's case to proceed, much to the joy of the press.[107] The judges' position on sex discrimination was so unequivocal that the Jockey Club backed down, reaching a settlement with Nagle and granting her a licence.[108]

The relevance of the case to the Stock Exchange's position on women was clear. In the course of their ruling, the judges had even named the Stock Exchange as one of several other 'monopolistic associations', along with trade unions and the Inns of Court, which had no right to exclude people 'capriciously'.[109] It was thus entirely conceivable that Bailey, or any other thwarted applicant, might follow Nagle's example and take their case to the courts. The legal footing for excluding women had never looked so precarious. Consequently, though rejecting Bailey's application to become an external member, the Stock Exchange Council sought a solution to the issue rather than simply trying to bury it, as it had done so often in the past. In January 1967, two months after turning Bailey down, it came to what the *Daily Telegraph* called an 'almost historic decision'. It proposed a new limited category of membership especially for women who had three years' experience of working in a stockbroker's office, which would allow them to become active partners of their firms but would bar them from the trading floor. A Stock Exchange spokesperson presented this as a practical compromise, satisfying the opposition while moving the Stock Exchange 'in line with present-day thinking'.[110] But because it would require an amendment to the Stock Exchange's deed of settlement, it would have to be approved by a 75 per cent majority of members present at an extraordinary meeting.

Though the vote the previous year to allow external memberships had passed unanimously, it was clear that the gender question would be more divisive.[111] As decision day approached, chairman Martin Wilkinson wrote to all 3,400 members to make his own position clear. Arguing that women were 'rightly taking their place in a world so long the prerogative of men', he believed that there was no logical reason why the Stock Exchange should be different 'now that the old conception of a cosy club is past'. He hoped members would recognize 'the whole question as a serious one, and not one simply to be answered by prejudice', and noted that his views were shared by the majority—though not all—of the Council.[112] Wilkinson, renowned as a man with 'the ability to charm in the most outrageous way', seems to have been confident that his personal intervention would swing the vote, taking the unusual step of arranging a press conference on the floor of the exchange after trading to declare the result.[113] *The Times* believed that the chances of women becoming members 'now look to be the best in the Stock Exchange's history', though other commentators were less confident.[114]

So, there was genuine uncertainty when the press pack, including eight female journalists, descended on the floor of the exchange after trading on 28 February to hear the result.[115] They learned that 1,178 had voted in favour of the resolution and 950 against, a majority, but one that fell far short of the 75 per cent required to alter the deed of settlement.[116] The outcome was an embarrassment for Wilkinson. Delivered in the full glare of publicity, the vote attracted a slew of unwelcome headlines.[117] Establishment papers like the *Daily Telegraph* and the *Illustrated London News* highlighted the impeccable membership credentials of Bailey and Rivers-Bulkeley, further raising their public profile.[118]

Nevertheless, some saw grounds for optimism, believing that the outcome was a result of the Council's flawed strategy. By proposing a special class of membership for women, it had 'stacked the cards against itself', creating a coalition of anti-feminist diehards and those who were pro-women but who objected to admitting them on 'second-class' terms.[119] Support for women members was consequently greater than the bare numbers suggested.[120] Moreover, other leading exchanges were changing their policies. In April 1967, the longstanding ban on women entering the Paris Bourse was revoked by the Prefect of Police. Now, the female employees of brokerages would be allowed to negotiate deals on the floor of the exchange, which was seen as the first step towards admitting women stockbrokers.[121] In the United States, there were also significant developments. Back in November 1965, the American Stock Exchange, New York's second exchange, had elected its first two female members, Julia Walsh and Phyllis Peterson.[122] In December 1967, the New York Stock Exchange itself followed suit when it admitted Muriel Siebert to full membership.[123]

Siebert's achievement in particular registered with the UK press, and the publicity she received made sure the issue would not fade away in London.[124] As Bailey said in an interview: 'I feel that if New York has accepted a woman member, I don't know why London shouldn't.'[125] The initiative was now seized by broker Richard Bradshaw. He promoted women's opportunities within his firm (as we saw in Chapter 6, Susan Shaw was one of his employees), and strongly supported the cause of sex equality on the Stock Exchange.[126] He had voted against Wilkinson's compromise measure due to its discriminatory nature, but announced that he would move a resolution at the annual meeting in May 1968 calling for women's 'full and unrestricted membership'. This simpler proposition would not divide the pro-women vote, and as it did not necessitate a change in the deed of settlement, only a bare majority was required. Consequently, confidence was high that the motion would pass, especially as Wilkinson signalled that he was 'wholeheartedly' in favour of it.[127]

186   SEXISM IN THE CITY

But the ballot produced a crushing defeat for the reformers, who secured less than a third of the vote (663 versus 1,366), on a 60 per cent turnout.[128] Bailey was 'furious' and accused members of 'just not facing up to the present'. Rivers-Bulkeley was equally disappointed. 'Why don't they grow up?', she asked. But faced with such numbers, Wilkinson regarded the matter as settled. Though he wished the result had been different, he was relieved that 'the air has been cleared…in the most democratic way possible. I can't see this subject being brought up again for some time.'[129] Such hopes, however, were to prove misplaced.

A Place Like This Is for Men Only

Just as in Birmingham, the tactic of initiating debates on the question of gender had proved fatal to the objective of women's membership, acting as an invitation to members to express their opposition to change. But why did so many of them reject the case for admitting women? The scale of the opposition seemed out of all proportion to the numbers of potential female applicants involved. Journalist Margaret Rix found it hard to fathom the hostility of Birmingham's brokers to Nellie Neale given there was no evidence 'of a long queue of women waiting to enter the stock markets'.[130] A decade later, a female journalist at the *Investors Chronicle* pondered why, given that the initial ratio of men to women in the Stock Exchange was likely to be about 1,000 to 1, London members seemed so worried.[131] Stockbroker Louise Peachey was equally mystified: 'what I cannot understand is why so many men are scared of so few women'.[132]

It may partly have been because women represented the threat of professionalization in an occupation hitherto dominated by gentlemanly amateurs. As the *Daily Express*'s Frederick Ellis somewhat colourfully put it, 'I meet many male stockbrokers. And I class many of them high up my list of fools. Many of them could not earn a living in any profession that called for brains.' He predicted that 'any intelligent woman would have no difficulty in competing with many a male stockbroker'.[133] These sentiments were common. With stockbroking still 'a haven for the well-connected amateurs', the 'formidably able women' who wanted membership represented a very real threat, thought *The Guardian*.[134] This threat was felt most keenly by younger brokers struggling to establish themselves: they were often the most vocal opponents of women's entry, and this was, so some believed, on account of the competition women represented.[135]

Women may have jeopardized men's jobs to a limited extent, but—given the small numbers involved—the danger was perhaps more to the *idea* of stockbroking as man's work. In the post-war years, Helen McCarthy notes, 'the ideological legitimacy of the male breadwinner model' was beginning to be challenged by women's growing access to paid work.[136] With marriage no longer spelling the end of women's careers in the way that it usually had in earlier decades, wives' ability to earn their own income gave them a small degree of financial autonomy and a greater status within the home. Though wives, often working part-time, typically earned far less than their spouses, their contributions nevertheless subtly began to shift the balance of power within marriages. The resulting insecurity was also felt by men at work, where interactions between the sexes 'reproduced the gender relations of family life', argues Michael Roper. In his interviews with male executives in manufacturing, Roper found their dealings with women heavily influenced by 'psychic baggage deriving from family relations'. Though dominating senior management, such men felt acutely threatened by women who did not conform to the norms of domestic femininity, and struggled to conceive of women 'as autonomous actors rather than as the providers of material and emotional services'. As a result, men emphasized all the more aggressively traditional 'divisions between bread-winners and home-makers'. Their behaviour was animated by fantasies that were 'creations of the mind', but no less powerful for that.[137]

Similar dynamics can be seen in finance, with male stockbrokers advocating a gender regime based on the distant past. When the story of Neale's attempt to gain admission to the Birmingham Stock Exchange first broke, the *Stock Exchange Journal* published a poem ironically titled 'Fair Shares' in which mid-Victorian ideas of separate spheres loomed large:

> In business we'll follow
>   our separate paths:
> But sigh not, sweet Ladies,
>   nor grumble, nor grouse.
> We'll share with you gladly
>   our homes and our hearths,
> Our gardens, our flowers,
>   our off-duty hours,
> Our pleasures, our treasures...
>   THOUGH NEVER 'THE HOUSE'.[138]

Men sometimes liked to cast themselves as gentlemanly guardians of vulnerable women, displaying an exaggerated chivalric concern for the horrors they might experience on the trading floor. Anthea Gaukroger recalled that on the eve of one of the London Stock Exchange's ballots on admitting women,

the senior partner came round the office to remind the partners to go and vote. And he was standing right next to my desk and somebody said to him, 'Well Anthony, how are you going to vote?' He was the most charming man, the most delightful, the sort of man who showed old-world courtesy towards women. Instead of answering directly, he bent down and spoke to me, and he said, 'Well

188 SEXISM IN THE CITY

> Miss Gaukroger, I may be old fashioned, but I don't think the floor of the Stock Exchange is any place for a woman.' And you couldn't really take offence, because he felt he was protecting you from this dreadful bearpit of the Stock Exchange floor.[139]

For others, the idea affronted the eye, one broker explaining that, 'purely on aesthetic grounds, most members would not wish to see women in the hurly-burly of the Stock Market'.[140]

Some could get carried away with the project of hypermasculinizing the job of buying and selling shares, leading to some unlikely analogies. 'There are certain occupations best done by men—like coal-mining and stock-broking', declared one London broker, in all apparent seriousness.[141] Others contrasted the no-holds-barred nature of the market with the calmer pace of domestic life to make their point. One broker stated that 'the market floor is no place for women. When I'm there, I'm there to do business and when I'm doing business I'm not inclined to be as gentlemanly as when I'm pouring sherry at home.'[142] He seemed to believe that whereas men could modulate their masculinity according to their environment, such flexibility was not within women's capabilities. In such members' opinion, allowing women access to the floor would destabilize gender roles. 'I cannot understand their wish to do men's work. We males do not cry out to do their work and wear skirts', wrote another baffled stockbroker, inadvertently signalling how emasculating he and his peers found the idea of financial women.[143]

Though sociologists of the 1950s and 1960s found evidence that men were becoming more home-centred, historians have questioned the pervasiveness of this post-war 'domesticated masculinity'. As Martin Francis points out, many men were ambivalent about family life and nostalgic for the 'emotionally satisfying aspects of wartime male bonding'. Existing alongside post-war domestication, Francis argues, was 'a yearning for an alternative male-only "family"', which fed the immense popularity of war movies and books in the 1950s and 1960s.[144] Nostalgia for 'wartime homosocial camaraderie' certainly influenced men's leisure habits post-war, and the impact was also felt at work.[145] Studies of post-war business elites found that large majorities had experience of military service, and that it had shaped their sense of masculinity in profound ways. Completing military training, as Roper puts it, 'announced the successful achievement of manhood'. These experiences helped to perpetuate habits of understanding business—and masculinity—in martial terms.[146]

Moreover, unlike after the Great War, when conscription was stopped in 1920, the experience of military training and discipline was extended to a later generation of men after the Second World War with the introduction of national service in 1949, lasting into the early 1960s.[147] While not 'militarizing' men in a straightforward way, it did mean that direct experience of the armed services continued to mould post-war working cultures.[148] To take an example, Stephen

Raven was born in 1938, joined his father's stockjobbing firm in 1955, and was called up for national service in 1957. When recounting his earliest stock exchange experiences in an interview in 1990, it was striking that he interpreted the hierarchies within the firm in explicitly militaristic terms: 'the floor staff are very much the commissioned officers, and your non-commissioned officers may be there as well as blue-button clerks, and the office staff were very much the ranks'. When he graduated to red-button work in the checking room, he found that the waiters 'were the sergeant majors and if you did anything on that checking floor which they thought was inappropriate, they would be down on you like a ton of bricks'. He remembers it as a place of 'discipline' but also 'community spirit', with friendships forged there lasting for life.[149]

Likewise, the 1955 novel *Stone Cold Dead in the Market*, by stockbroker-turned-author Christopher Landon, testifies to the power of combat experience as a homosocial glue. It tells the story of Robert Ross, a struggling private detective, who is tasked with investigating a suspected murder in the House. Ross gets the job by dint of his friendship with Stock Exchange member Jack Poole, whom he met on the beaches of Dunkirk in 1940 amidst 'the bombs and shells...as good a way as any of getting to know someone'. Ross has to pose as a jobber in order to gain the confidence of members: initially anxious, he is reassured when he meets the young clerk 'who was to be his half section in the West African Market', known as the 'Jungle'. At several points in the narrative, the fact of shared war service helps him to win the confidence of key characters, from the Assistant Commissioner of Police to the murderer himself, former Stock Exchange member Peter Trewin. Ross having solved the crime, the novel ends with him deciding to become a jobber for real, after finding the men of the Stock Exchange 'a gutful, generous, hard-working lot...I can think of worse places than the Jungle to stand for the rest of my life'.[150]

Women threatened the tight-knit camaraderie of this male world, and habits of discussing their growing presence in finance in conflictual terms did nothing to diminish this sense of danger. Just as press coverage of second-wave feminists used a masculine language of conflict to mark them as deviant ('guerrilla fighters' engaging in a 'sex war'), women's attempts to join stock exchanges was typically described as an 'invasion', an 'assault' on a male 'stronghold'.[151] This 'citadel' was being 'stormed', and would one day 'fall'.[152] Framing the issue this way encouraged male brokers' to imagine themselves as an embattled minority, mounting a heroic defence of one of the last remaining 'male bastions'. Studies of other exclusively male workplaces have shown that as the logic of excluding women was called into question, work cultures became more aggressively homosocial, the 'performance' of masculinity more overt, and explicitly sexual.[153] Commentators noted this misogynistic turn on the Stock Exchange. 'The prejudice against women is taken for granted: boasted about rather than apologised for', remarked *Guardian* journalist Joy Melville in the run-up to the first vote.[154] Longstanding arguments that

190 SEXISM IN THE CITY

cast women as an unwelcome presence that would make the market work less efficiently were couched in increasingly sexualized terms. The delicate price-setting mechanisms of the trading floor would be disturbed by women's sex appeal, in the opinion of *Daily Express* columnist Derek Dale, one of the few post-war financial journalists backing exclusion. 'Do you honestly think a dealer would quote the same price for Courtaulds to a comely blonde as he does now to a top hat?', he asked.[155] Opportunistic firms would turn this to their advantage, some members fearing that jobbers would take on 'dolly birds' as blue-button clerks 'to woo away brokers' business from male-staffed competitors'.[156] Muriel Bailey herself recounted the line spun by her opponents that 'girls in mini-skirts would go rushing about distracting the dealers if women were allowed in'.[157] More abstractly, City men were imagining the financial economy, and money's repro-ductivity, in increasingly libidinous terms, which helped to entrench the idea of market actors as male.[158] Though more apparent in the 1980s, there were glimpses before this. When Anthony Sampson spent two months in the early 1960s talking to City figures while researching his study of elites, *Anatomy of Britain*, he was struck by 'the quasi-sexual fascination with money concealed behind large layers of humbug' he found there.[159]

Though contesting the membership policies of the stock exchanges, the media actively conspired in, and amplified, the sexualization of women in finance which justified their exclusion. With the press becoming more open about sex even before the 1960s, high-achieving women in finance were routinely objectified by male journalists.[160] The author of the *Daily Herald*'s gossip column was turned on by imagining being turned down for an overdraft by Barclays' Hilda Harding: 'The bank manager crossed nyloned legs. Her eyes were full of sympathy. "An overdraft? This hurts me more than it does you, but—no. I'm so sorry." She smiled. She had two dimples. I have never been brushed off—even in fun—so beautifully.'[161] Imagining the impact of 'lady members', the *Stock Exchange Gazette* wrote that 'if they possessed the charms of Marilyn Monroe—regular Mesdames Mata Haris!—the tophatted, carnation buttonholed characters might be left standing'.[162]

This kind of reporting was just as common in the highbrow press. From 1969, the *Sunday Telegraph* ran a feature called 'Women About the City', a series of profiles of women working in a variety of finance roles, accompanied by photo-graphs. Though celebrating the progress women were making in financial careers, the series also trivialized them by focusing on their appearance, age, marital sta-tus, interests, and hobbies.[163] Readers were invited to observe these City workers through the male gaze, and the sexualization was occasionally explicit. 'Brown-eyed, brown-haired Gillian, who measures 35-23-36, comes from Romford in Essex, and combines a taste for the arts (theatre and music) with sports (swim-ming and tennis).'[164] Though this experiment in sharing 'vital statistics' was not repeated, later profiles continued assessing the appearance of their subjects

('Maureen Smith must rank as one of the prettiest gilt edged dealers in a business in the City dominated by stripe-suited men').[165] Women in the City were thus rendered a pleasing spectacle for male eyes, the *Daily Telegraph* casually observing that, were she to win admittance to the Stock Exchange, Rivers-Bulkeley would 'certainly improve the view from the visitors' gallery'.[166] Journalistic objectification undermined women's credibility and underlined their difference, thus serving—albeit unwittingly—the project of continuing exclusion.

Nevertheless, journalists did consistently foreground what they saw as the collective irrationality of stock exchange members when it came to women. As a *Times* business columnist observed, the Stock Exchange 'becomes mildly hysterical whenever women are mentioned'. Though normal and reasonable outside the House, 'get them together on the floor of the Stock Exchange and their reactions change'.[167] For the City editor of the *Birmingham Post* their opposition was 'instinctive' and 'emotional' rather than logical.[168] The *Sunday Telegraph*'s Patrick Hutber came to a similar conclusion after asking a jobber he respected why he was against women's membership. 'His face darkened and he replied, "Because we don't want them. There are other things in life that a woman can do." '[169] Indeed, the journalistic quest for a reasoned argument was usually in vain.[170] This was underlined immediately after one of London's votes against women, when ITN journalist Jacky Gillott awkwardly stood in the corridors of the Stock Exchange—to the hilarity of passing members—in an attempt to find someone who would explain why so many of them opposed women. One who finally consented to talk to Gillott struggled to express his case:

'Well, just that I think that, er, a place like this is, is for men and, you know, men are better doing this sort of work.'

JG: 'In other words, women are intellectually inferior?'

'Er, I'm not saying that, no, by no means. Erm, but I think it's a good idea that, you know, a place like this is for men only.'

JG: 'How very extraordinary.'

'You think that's extraordinary? No, well, that's my view.'

Gillott concluded that '[t]he Stock Exchange method is not to ban women so much as to baffle them'.[171]

Consequently, women's insistence that they were robust enough to survive on the trading floor was doomed to make little impact. 'The pushing and shoving excuse is silly', Peachey told reporters. 'Those people who put it forward seem to forget that women travel on Tube trains at rush hours.'[172] Likewise, Bailey said that what male stockbrokers failed to realize 'is that any women who wanted to deal there would be tougher than they are'.[173] But she was exasperated by their refusal to listen. 'It's not like fighting an institution, it's like fighting a club', she remarked.[174] Indeed, though the official line of the country's stock exchanges was that they were no longer private clubs, it was very clear that many members continued to view them as exactly that.[175] A prime example was long-time broker and Council member Graham Greenwell, who wrote to *The Times* to condemn the paper's 'pompous' support for women's entry. He argued that the London Stock Exchange was a 'private men's club...not an institution which exists to perform a public service', and should therefore ignore pressure for change.[176] His letter prompted strong denials from Wilkinson and even Greenwell's own son, but his viewpoint was clearly representative of many members.[177] Given that their opposition was more emotional than logical, appeals to reason would fall on deaf ears. And the more the media attempted to interfere in their affairs, the stronger was their assertion of independence. As Ellen Winser rightly concluded, London members had decided that they 'jolly well weren't going to be told by a lot of newspapers what they ought to do'.[178]

Through the Backdoor

Given the depth of opposition, it was no surprise that in Birmingham, Nellie Neale's ambitions continued to be blocked. An attempt by her boss John Sabin to revive the question soon after Muriel Melvin's admission to the Scottish Stock Exchange in 1964 foundered.[179] The amalgamation of Birmingham with the Bristol, Cardiff, Nottingham, and Swansea exchanges to form the Midlands and Western Stock Exchange Association in October 1966, the third such regional grouping following the Scottish and Northern exchanges, changed little.[180] The announcement of London's vote on allowing women members did briefly reignite the issue in Birmingham, but when members were privately canvassed, there was little appetite for reform, so the committee of management decided against further action.[181]

However, inspired by racehorse trainer Florence Nagle's approach to dealing with intransigent male authorities, Neale changed tack. In October 1967, the stockbroker instructed her solicitors to write to the committee. Their letter criticized the committee's reliance on the 1956 petition as a strategy for deflecting Neale. 'We think that the Committee are under a misapprehension as to their powers and duties and must insist that Mrs Neale's application be now considered', they wrote. As the only objection ever raised against Neale was her sex, they looked forward to hearing soon that her application had been successful.[182] The committee referred the letter to their own solicitor, C. H. Harmer, and may have been surprised by the result. Harmer reported that the 1956 petition 'had no legal force', and that if the matter reached the courts, the committee's refusal to consider Neale's application 'might be regarded with disfavour'. Cowed, the committee now acted swiftly, instructing Harmer to write to members explaining the legal position ahead of an open meeting at the end of February 1968 to discuss expunging the petition from the minutes and allowing women membership.[183] The meeting, which Harmer attended in order to make clear to members the legal risks of continuing to block women, signalled approval, and when a formal vote to expunge the minute was held in March, the resolution was carried by seventy-nine votes to two.[184]

The way was finally clear for Neale's application to proceed, but in early April, days before the committee was due to meet to confirm the members' vote, Neale was taken suddenly ill at work. She died at Birmingham General Hospital two days later, aged 62.[185] Fearing negative publicity, the committee, which had until now insisted on a news blackout, hastily informed the *Birmingham Post*'s City editor Ian Richardson of the previous month's vote, stressing that Neale had been on the cusp of securing membership.[186] In his column, Richardson rightly high-lighted the significance of the Nagle judgment of 1966, which 'gave the reform a lever with which to break down the opposition'.[187] But the judges' words alone were not enough. It took a woman with the courage to threaten a stock exchange with legal action, violating the custom that stock exchange business be settled outside the courts, to force change.

If Neale had faced a distressingly protracted battle to overturn the Birmingham Stock Exchange's anti-women petition of 1956, after this, other women enjoyed a relatively straightforward route into institutional acceptance. Whereas women's prospects had been compromised in Birmingham and, to some extent, London by media scrutiny, elsewhere women were quietly admitted with next to no fan-fare. In May 1968, Huddersfield stockbroker Mary Ward became the second woman to join the Northern Stock Exchange, after Sheffield's Constance Ward.[188] In January 1969, the Scottish Stock Exchange gained its second female member with Helen Smellie, the Glasgow broker.[189] In November 1971, Nottingham stock-broker Jane Warner became the first woman member of the Midlands and Western Stock Exchange.[190] And a few months later, in April 1972, the Manchester Stock Exchange admitted its first female member, Margaret Holt, bringing the Northern Stock Exchange's tally of women to three, and the total number of female members of all stock exchanges, including the Provincial Brokers' Stock Exchange, up to thirteen.[191]

The implications were clear. The 'common sense' arguments which had been used to justify women's exclusion, until very recently mobilized by all the nation's exchanges (barring, of course, the Provincial Brokers' Stock Exchange), were now recast as the idiosyncrasies of London's financial community alone. The press outside London was certainly attuned to this, Richardson at the *Birmingham Post* arguing that it showed 'how much more grown-up the provinces are than London'.[192] But the London press agreed, *The Times* remarking that it was 'scarcely to the credit of the London Stock Exchange that it should allow its pro-vincial counterparts to set it an example'.[193]

194   SEXISM IN THE CITY

But London remained resolute against women. After the failed vote of May 1968, internal moves to challenge the male monopoly dissipated. The traditional masculine culture of the trading floor remained firmly in place, confirmed in February 1970 when the building closed to allow for a new Stock Exchange to be built on the site. On the final day's trading, the closure was celebrated 'in juvenile style', with ragging, toilet paper streamers, creative memento-hunting, one case of pyromania, and rousing renditions of 'Auld Lang Syne'. 'Like a crowd of school-boys', commented one member 'with a grin on his face'.[194] Yet two young women took advantage of the chaos, entering the building through a side entrance, and getting halfway across the floor before being spotted and, amidst wolf whistles and barracking, escorted out of the building by a waiter. The pair, Suzan Andrews and Tamara Baradon, worked for leading brokerage Panmure Gordon, but denied that they were making a political point. 'We did it because of a dare', Andrews told the press. Nevertheless, this 'raid' by 'two mini-skirted dollies', as the *Daily Mail* described them, attracted much press attention, hinting as it did at the growing vulnerability of the Stock Exchange to the forces of feminine modernity.[195]

Would the new building provide the opportunity for a fresh start? Heather McConnell of the Status of Women Committee was hopeful that 'the atmosphere of the new building' would offer the Stock Exchange the opportunity 'to move with the times'.[196] Richard Bradshaw assured her that he and his supporters 'do not intend to let the matter drop'.[197] But he seemed to have few options. When he raised the matter at the 1969 annual general meeting, he was brushed off.[198] The following June he stood for election to the Stock Exchange Council to attempt to secure reform from the inside, but he came a distant bottom of the poll, suggesting how far his campaign had made him unpopular among his peers.[199]

But political developments forced the issue back onto the Council's agenda once more. In January 1967, Labour President of the Board of Trade, Douglas Jay, had ordered a major inquiry into restrictive practices in the professions, to be conducted by the Monopolies Commission.[200] The Commission heard evidence over a period in which sex discrimination was becoming a major political issue. In 1968, Labour backbencher Joyce Butler formed a cross-party parliamentary group on women's rights, which promoted the first of several private bills tackling discrimination in employment, education, and social and public life.[201] Though the bills did not progress, they encouraged both main parties to prioritize the issue. Labour secured the passage of the Equal Pay Act in 1970, and though they went on to lose the general election in June, Edward Heath's Conservatives had already signalled a commitment to women's rights the previous year.[202] The Monopolies Commission was no doubt influenced by this climate, and when it finally issued its report in October 1970, its comments on the London Stock Exchange grabbed headlines.[203] Condemning discrimination on the grounds of sex or nationality, it underlined that the Stock Exchange was the only professional body giving evidence not to admit women to membership. Observing that 'restrictive practices in the professions have escaped the detailed and critical scrutiny' applied to other sectors of the economy, it stated that 'restrictive practices contrary to the public interest' could no longer be tolerated.[204]

The prospect of political intervention was suddenly very real. John Davies, head of the newly formed Department of Trade and Industry (DTI), which replaced the Board of Trade, confirmed that he would follow the Commission's recommendations and write to all professional associations 'inviting them to re-examine their professional practices in the light of its findings and to let me know within six months of any modifications they are proposing to make to them in consequence'.[205] As Bradshaw put it in a letter to the *Financial Times*, this was an opportunity for the Stock Exchange to 'put its own house in order' rather than having the job done for it by government.[206] Indeed, the Stock Exchange Council took the threat seriously. Not long after it received the letter from the DTI, it established a special committee, headed by Wilkinson, to decide how to respond.[207] The result was another members' vote on the issue, the third, to be held by ballot following the annual general meeting in May 1971.[208]

Bookmakers were offering short odds on a 'yes' vote, while Rivers-Bulkeley was optimistic that it would be third time lucky. 'It sounds much more as though they really mean it now', she told the *Telegraph*.[209] But the reformers were defeated yet again, securing less than 44 per cent of the vote (995 votes in favour and 1,287 against), on a turnout of 65 per cent.[210] The result sparked another wave of condemnatory headlines ('CITY MEN SNUB THE WOMEN ONCE MORE'; 'THE MONEYBIRDS GET THE BRUSH OFF').[211] *The Guardian* reported that outside the City, 'the decision was seen as so absurd as to be lighthearted'.[212] The *Daily Telegraph* thought that the Council could keep putting the issue to the vote for the next twenty years and would keep getting the same result.[213] Though Wilkinson's public position was that there would have to be 'a good breathing space' before the matter could be raised again, he knew the situation remained precarious.[214] For one, Ellen Winser had spoken to him privately, threatening to take the Stock Exchange to court, and warning him that 'he hadn't a leg to stand on'.[215] Moreover, the prospect of political intervention remained. Conservative MP Janet Fookes was considering pressing for legislation, arguing that the Stock Exchange's continuing exclusion of women was 'monstrous' and 'absolutely Victorian'. Though she would have preferred the Stock Exchange to sort out the problem itself, its refusal proved that intervention was necessary.[216]

Yet over the following weeks, it became clear that there was little ministerial appetite for action.[217] Under-Secretary of State for Employment, Dudley Smith, told the Commons that the good example set by the provincial exchanges in admitting women would eventually secure change in London, and that 'persuasion rather than compulsion is the best remedy'.[218] Smith was correct that policies outside London were critical, though not quite in the way that he thought. The creation of the Federation of Stock Exchanges in 1965 was just the first step towards greater integration, and a special committee of the Federation was tasked in August 1969 with drawing up concrete proposals for a united stock exchange.[219] This threw up a host of 'vexed questions' requiring settlement, one of which was how the merger would affect women.[220] The need for one set of rules for the new amalgamated institution meant, as one journalist succinctly put it, that 'either London would have to let women in or the regional exchanges would have to kick their women out'.[221] Those concerned were naturally anxious. In Huddersfield, Mary Ward said she was 'not sure what will happen' if London did not change its policy, while in Sheffield, Constance Ward was also wondering 'what would happen to us—they cannot go back on admitting us now'. But they had the strong support of their regional heads. The Scottish representative on the Federation's committee backed his two female members, Muriel Melvin and Helen Smellie. 'It would be absolutely appalling if London did not give in', he told a *Times* reporter, who saw this as a great opportunity for London 'to change its mind without losing face'.[222]

When the plan for amalgamation was finally unveiled in November 1971, it was clear that the terms favoured London.[223] Though the regional trading floors were preserved, London was made the vehicle for the united entity.[224] The deal gave members of regional exchanges direct access to the London floor, however, and the fact that this would grant women admittance to the House raised fears that if London members realized this, they would vote it down when it came to a poll in March 1972, especially since a 75 per cent majority was required.[225] In the event, however, 83 per cent voted in favour.[226] Either the benefits weighed more heavily with members than the women issue or—as Muriel Bailey (now Wood) suspected—many voted for it as they 'did not realise that women went with it'.[227]

Though headlines hailed the vote as a victory for women, it only applied to the members of the regional stock exchanges: what it meant for women who worked in London was far from clear.[228] But Wood seized her opportunity, writing 'a very discreet letter' to the Stock Exchange Council, pointing out 'that it was unfair that the provincial women brokers should get into the Stock Exchange when we could not', and signalling her wish to apply for membership.[229] A majority on the Council accepted that it would now be impractical to continue blocking applications from London women, and on a vote of twenty-four to five the Council agreed to begin accepting applications from women in time for the inauguration of the United Stock Exchange on 26 March 1973.[230] For women to have finally secured the right to membership 'through the back-door' was something of an embarrassment to the Council, and the early signs were that there might be a members' vote on the issue to rubber stamp the new policy.[231] But the Council ultimately decided against risking a fourth rebuff, ruling instead that the vote on amalgamation superseded the previous ballots.[232]

Fig. 7.1 The new entrants posing for the cameras on 23 March 1973. Standing L–R: Edna Stokes, Hazel Brown, Neville Priestman, George Loveday, Audrey Geddes, Martin Wilkinson, Kenneth Crabbe, Isabel Drummond, Jane Barrie, Louise Peachey, Patricia Rogers. Seated L–R: Muriel Wood, Hilary Root, Ellen Winser, Elisabeth Rivers-Bulkeley, Anthea Gaukroger. Absent was Susan Shaw. Reproduced with permission from PA Images/Alamy Stock Photo

Four women put their names forward for membership at the earliest opportunity in January 1973: Anthea Gaukroger, Audrey Geddes, Susan Shaw, and Muriel Wood.[233] Over the next few weeks, they were joined by six more: Hazel Brown, Isabel Drummond, Louise Peachey, Hilary Root, Edna Stokes, and Ellen Winser. None had any problems clearing the necessary hurdles of interview and vote by Council members.[234] On 26 March, the day the United Stock Exchange came into existence, three more women were elected: Elisabeth Rivers-Bulkeley, Neville Priestman, and Patricia Rogers, with Jane Barrie following a few days later, making a total of fourteen (see Fig. 7.1).[235] That first day, an anxious Susan

Fig. 7.2 Muriel Wood on the floor of the London Stock Exchange, 26 March 1973. Reproduced with permission from Keystone Press/Alamy Stock Photo

Shaw was the first to step onto the trading floor, entering shortly after opening in the hope that members and clerks would be too busy with early morning dealings and price checking to notice her. But her plan backfired, as she wrote in her diary:

> Enter through doors. A sea of black and white, much bustle and activity. A familiar scene—now suddenly I am part of it.... Incredulous stares from those not so busy. A brief burst of shouting as realisation dawns—a strange woman! Members familiar and unfamiliar come up and shake my hand. 'Nice to see you.' 'Welcome.' 'Congratulations.'... Feel suddenly warmed and accepted.[236]

Not long afterwards, Peachey, Stokes, and Wood (see Fig. 7.2) were also seen on the floor. As the woman most associated with the push to get women accepted, Wood, now 65, received a particularly warm welcome, crowds gathering round to shake her hand and congratulate her.[237] The men were on their best behaviour for the media. Journalists hunting for controversy found little to report, beyond one top-hatted older member who reportedly departed the floor muttering, 'I never thought I'd live to see this day.'[238]

For such members, worse was to come. When the new exchange finally opened in June 1973, jobbers had their 'pitches' inside hexagonal trading posts dotted

INVADING THE STOCK EXCHANGE 199

around the floor, and secured permission from the Council to employ female clerks alongside men inside their hexagons. The dozen or so female clerks who started work in June did increase the number of women working inside the Stock Exchange, though they were ensconced in their hexagons, and were engaged in routine office work rather than dealing.[239] Later that month, however, a more significant step was taken when the Council decreed that women could become blue-buttons, the traditional apprenticeship for a career as a broker or jobber.[240] Within days of the announcement, the application of the first female blue-button was approved: Diana Laird Craig, a clerk with brokers J. M. Finn & Co.[241]

But this did not mean that the transition to a mixed-sex trading floor would be smooth. As their presence in the Stock Exchange had been forced upon members rather than the result of a positive vote, women remained outsiders, resented interlopers, and prone to harassment, which was often focused on their appearance. A few weeks after women's admittance, Jane Barrie went onto the floor for the second time, wearing a miniskirt, which attracted the attention of a group of jobbers. 'Get 'em off!' they shouted, following up with 'catcalls and wolf-whistles'. The incident made the press, including the front page of the *Daily Mirror*, with Barrie keen to downplay its impact on her. 'This hasn't frightened me off. I'm simply ignoring it.'[242] But it demonstrated the injuries that could be inflicted quite casually in this environment, one member explaining: 'Business was a bit slack that day so we decided to liven things up a bit.'[243] It was not an isolated incident. Diana Craig, the first female blue-button clerk, quickly found her clothing the subject of male scrutiny. One senior member took exception to Craig's outfit of black trousers and (as the *Daily Mail* put it) 'dazzling, tight-fitting sweater', and wrote a note of complaint to the Stock Exchange superintendent. The note was passed to her employer, who insisted she change into 'something more suitable'. Around the same time there were also rumours that one of the 'girl telephonists' in the Stock Exchange had been ordered to wear a looser top. 'Some older members said that they were being distracted by her well-endowed figure', one dealer elaborated.[244]

Though publicizing such cases and sometimes venting criticism, the press were active partners in the sexualization of women they entailed, helping to ensure that the few women working in this environment remained marked as different. The Craig incident moved the *Evening Standard* to run a feature debating 'Should girls [sic] wear what they like at work?' The women approached unsurprisingly answered yes, but men clearly struggled to think of women as other than sexual objects or ornaments. A NatWest manager supported women's right to dress how they wanted, with the proviso that it would be 'a bit off to turn up in a bikini'. 'Women always add a touch of decoration which I am normally pleased to see', he added.[245] The piece indicated how little had changed since the 1920s, when Gordon Holmes and Amy Moreton had both been posed the pressing question, 'Are typists under dressed?'[246] The *Daily Express*'s contribution was to run a

200 SEXISM IN THE CITY

risqué (and pun-ridden) fashion feature on suggested outfits for the 'lady stocking-broker'. Though ostensibly celebrating women's newfound financial opportunities, showing 'just how a woman can play a man at his own market', the feature, complemented by titillating photographs, was all about sexualizing women. 'Putting money on his shirt and wearing it as a mini, with nothing but his tie and your legs' was 'a smart and inexpensive way of pushing your assets on holidays'.[247] The echoes of Ardern Holt's fancy dress outfit for the 'Lady Stockbroker' from nearly a century earlier were clear. Holt's 'short pink silk skirt', 'low bodice', 'gold belt', and 'high-heeled pink shoes' might have been exchanged for something more minimalist, but the message was the same: clothing marked the distinction between stockbrokers and 'lady stockbrokers'.[248]

Conclusion

The difference between the 1870s and the 1970s, of course, was that now women were on the trading floor, an achievement which several of the women of 1973 treasured, especially Shaw. 'It was the proudest day of my life', she recalled forty years later.[249] For those who had no desire to work on the trading floor, like Hilary Root and Anthea Gaukroger, the victory meant slightly less. Both 'went down for a sort of ceremonial visit', but did not return. Membership did not represent a major turning point in their careers. 'We just carried on doing what we had been doing', Root said.[250] But the right to join did pave the way for other important benefits. Ellen Winser downplayed the importance of becoming a member (telling the press it 'does not mean much'), but she was 'chuffed' when the following month she was promoted to partner in James Capel & Co., the first woman to reach this position in a London firm.[251] A little later, Root was similarly elevated at Sheppards & Chase.[252] Outside London, though women had long been partners in family firms, they were now being offered partnerships in male-run businesses. Muriel Melvin in Aberdeen, Helen Smellie in Glasgow, Jane Warner in Nottingham, and Mary Ward in Huddersfield all reached this level.[253]

Ill health could cut careers short: Melvin quit her partnership in 1972 because of illness, dying five years later at the age of 58, while soon after, Audrey Geddes died aged just 47.[254] But when illness did not intervene, long stockbroking careers were the norm. Muriel Wood continued working into the 1980s, joining Walker, Crips, Weddle, Beck & Co. as an associate member in 1981, at the age of 74.[255] Elisabeth Rivers-Bulkeley 'never really retired', remaining a City figure into the millennium.[256] Susan Shaw, having joined Bradshaw initially for a three-week trial, remained with him for over thirty years, and continued working in the City until 2002.[257]

But, as we have seen, the ability of individual women to carve out long, satisfying careers in finance was nothing new. Though on one level 1973 represented a major watershed, finally resolving a question that had been posed for the best part of a century—could women be members of stock exchanges?—in other ways, little had changed. The 'victory' had been secured outside of London by men pragmatically recognizing that it would help sustain the viability of provincial stock exchanges and stockbroking in an age of decline, a strategic switch expedited by the growing threat of legal action. In the City, it had been the price that had to be paid by an institution keen to absorb its provincial competitors, and in the face of the explicit opposition of a majority of its members. In neither instance was it achieved as a result of men's acceptance of the moral case for equality. Though women certainly had supporters, these remained in a minority, and the conflict helped to intensify the atmosphere of misogyny. In other words, the masculine culture of the City not only survived intact, but was actually strengthened by the protracted debate. Few in number, isolated from one another, and unmoved by feminist ideology, women were unable to challenge this culture. While opportunities certainly existed, women were to continue to find them shaped by their sex, limited, and unequal.

Sexism in the City: Women Stockbrokers in Modern Britain. James Taylor, Oxford University Press.
© James Taylor 2025. DOI: 10.1093/9780191990397.003.0008

Epilogue

Forever Other?

As many of their supporters had predicted, the admission of women to the London Stock Exchange in 1973 did not transform the demographics of stockbroking in the United Kingdom. A major factor was the bleak economic context. A dramatic market slump in 1973–4 saw the Financial Times All-Share Index lose nearly three-quarters of its value. Indeed, for British investors, 1974 was a worse year than even 1929.[1] As investors took flight, firms laid off staff. The numbers employed by London firms fell from around 24,000 to 17,000 by 1978, while outside the capital, the employment picture was equally dismal.[2] Some women left the sector: in Manchester, the depressed market prompted Margaret Holt—who had been the first woman to join the city's stock exchange—to look for an alternative career, successfully switching to law.[3] Those who remained could even suffer guilt at their good fortune. Susan Shaw later recalled: 'I personally felt absolutely terrible, as a lot of the men were suddenly out of work, and I was still working away there…And I thought, that is absolutely wrong. So one still had that view…that the men should be the breadwinners more than the women.'[4]

In these circumstances, the number of female members of the United Stock Exchange flatlined, with twenty-eight in 1973, twenty-seven two years later, and no discernible increase by the end of the decade.[5] When market conditions improved, however, there was some growth, the number reaching fifty-two by the start of 1984.[6] By this point, women were also beginning to be trained as jobbers as well as brokers: in the early 1980s, Wedd Durlacher, the largest jobbing firm, employed four female trainees.[7] But even so, women remained a small minority presence on the London trading floor: by 1986, of the 6,400 members and clerks who did business there, only 200 (just over 3 per cent) were women.[8] Outside the capital, where women had historically found greater opportunities, there were some notable achievements. In 1979, Carole Langley became the first female manager of the Liverpool Stock Exchange, while in 1985, Ann Green became the first female general manager of the Northern Unit, formerly the Northern Stock Exchange.[9] At the same time, however, provincial trading floors were shutting down as the market became increasingly focused on London.

Some women working in finance in these years found the culture difficult. Jane Partington started work on the London trading floor in 1975, and before she began, she knew she was entering a male domain, recalling looking down from the visitors' gallery the day of her interview and seeing 'men in top hats with white collars and not a woman in sight'. After starting, her first impressions were confirmed:

> The girls all got given nicknames by the men—I was the Night Nurse, there was Sweaty Betty, Super Bum, the Grimsby Trawler, the Road Runner, Stop Me and Pick One. They were very cruel…You had to have broad shoulders and a good sense of humour because you would be the butt of a lot of jokes.…If you were dressed in red from head to foot they'd call you Pillar-box all day and try to post letters. You'd think carefully about what you wore.[10]

While nicknames and jokes were an established feature of the market, rather than being incorporated into this culture on equal terms, women were targeted in ways that highlighted their sex. Clothing remained as much a marker of gendered difference as it had always been, women knowing that how they presented themselves on the market was constantly being appraised by men. This applied off the trading floor as well. Sarah Danes, who joined stockbrokers Vivian Gray in 1978, was not permitted to wear trousers to work until 1996.[11] For Partington, the situation was made harder to endure by what she saw as a lack of camaraderie among the few women who were on the floor. 'The thing that struck me so hard was that the women didn't stick together as I would have expected. They resented each other quite a lot, it was a little like sibling rivalry. Two or three would pair off and be friends but basically they all wanted to be Queen Bee.'[12]

Others experienced the environment differently, however. One anonymous female member, talking to journalist William Davis in 1978, said that she had no problem with life on the trading floor. 'We're not shy little girls…I think sometimes the men are embarrassed by the things *we* say.'[13] Another member, Elizabeth Sullivan, admitted that the trading floor was a challenging environment. 'The City is ruled by the law of the jungle', she observed, and 'the work is frantic and demanding', but she relished the fast pace, as well as the high pay. Yet, in comments that echoed Partington, she noted that 'The men are incredibly critical of our appearance…You have to be very determined and thick-skinned to survive here.'[14] Even once they had learned to tolerate insults, women faced other disadvantages. Wedd Durlacher's trainee jobbers found their job of picking up the rumours and gossip of the floor harder because of their sex. 'They sometimes don't think of telling you something that they would tell one of the boys', one complained about the male traders.[15] In some cases, the discrimination was overt. Linda Treacy, who worked at government brokers Mullins, found her way blocked for a peculiar reason:

> All the men wore top hats, so my first job in the morning was to brush these hats. After I'd been there for a year they had a dealing position, so [I asked to] be considered for that position. They said no because I would look silly in a top hat.[16]

While the broader employment context had changed with the Equal Pay Act of 1970, the Sex Discrimination Act of 1975, and the Equal Opportunities Commission formed the same year, legal loopholes and half-hearted enforcement by industrial tribunals meant that work cultures evolved only slowly.[17]

This did not concern many women in finance, who insisted that the attitudes of men were not a serious obstacle to advancement. They generally had faith in the idea of finance as a meritocracy in which hard work and talent would be rewarded regardless of gender. In Manchester, Ann Green argued that it was 'down to the individual to set out to achieve the goal. I have no time for these women who sit there whingeing and saying nobody recognises them.... There is no reason why you can't get there the same as any man.'[18] These women were impatient with suggestions that discrimination existed in the world of finance. 'I think it is a popular misconception that it is all run by men', said Nottingham-based stockbroker Jane Warner, who insisted that in reality, there were 'plenty of opportunities' for women.[19] At the same time, there was recognition of the limits a career placed on other freedoms. One anonymous member was particularly ambitious, aiming to become a partner in her firm, and after that, perhaps chairman of the Stock Exchange. She had decided to remain single, since '[m]arriage kills a career'.[20] Lorraine Bailey, a Liverpool stockbroker, did marry, but for her, having children was the red line. 'Taking ten years off', she explained, 'meant men were ten years ahead when a woman picked up the threads of her career.' But when asked whether she was a feminist, the interviewer reported that 'she momentarily loses her smile and suggests, with just enough firmness, that she is not one of those'.[21]

There were many who thought that by the mid-1980s, times had changed decisively, market veteran Susan Shaw among them. 'These days being a woman in the City is old hat', she argued.[22] Indeed, *The Observer* claimed that by now, women members 'receive barely a glance around the market'.[23] At the same time, journalists could still describe the London Stock Exchange as 'the ultimate male bastion—reminiscent of a new wing at a boys' public school'.[24] But changes which would transform nearly every aspect of this market were just around the corner.

Big Bangers

The 1980s saw growing fears that London risked being marginalized in an increasingly global securities market. Deregulation was viewed as the solution to uncompetitiveness, a belief that coalesced into a radical package of reforms implemented in 1986, which went by the nickname 'Big Bang'. London's traditional rules limiting outside investment in member firms, disallowing corporate membership, enforcing a division between brokers and jobbers, and fixed commission rates, were swept away, while market prices were now disseminated via a new electronic system. The changes had an immediate impact. From 1 March 1986, banks and finance houses were allowed to buy up member firms, and within six months every large brokerage bar Cazenove had been absorbed into a larger conglomerate, becoming 'financial supermarkets' offering a vast array of services to customers.[25] Many of the buyers were big international brokerages like Merrill Lynch and Nomura, who thanks to the change in the rules could now become members.[26] Indeed, by 1989, the Stock Exchange had 391 corporate members, nearly 150 of which were foreign, and three years later, individual membership was scrapped altogether.[27] This transformed the relationship between the exchange and its members, many of which 'were now far more powerful than the institution to which they belonged'.[28] The new electronic system, introduced on 27 October 1986, allowed prices to be monitored and deals made outside the trading floor, in the dealing rooms of the big firms, filled with the latest computer technology. At first, it was imagined that the trading floor would coexist with these dealing rooms, but within a few months, most business had migrated, leaving the trading floor all but deserted. 'We've got a viewing gallery and nothing to see', commented one member sadly.[29]

What would happen to the culture of the market now that, as Stock Exchange chairman Nicholas Goodison put it, the 'computer screen is the new marketplace'?[30] Ostensibly, these new dealing rooms, based on an American model, were very different spaces from the old trading floor: 'cavernous rooms' containing 'rows and rows of salesmen, traders and researchers staring into video terminals', in the words of one journalist.[31] There was a potentially feminizing effect of being 'surrounded by gadgetry and technology', which was, after all, more associated with 'the line specialist or secretary'.[32] But the dealing rooms were imagined in resolutely masculine terms. The one at Barclays de Zoete Wedd, one of the new giant conglomerate financial firms, was kitted out with £20 million worth of computers and 1,500 telephones. It looked, in the awed words of one of the directors, 'like the deck of a bloody galactic battle cruiser'.[33] Switching to screen-based trading did potentially imply a shake-up of employment, with different skills required. One senior jobber commented: 'Just because someone is a good floor trader doesn't mean he will be any good trading on the telephone from faceless screens.'[34] But firms continued to assume that men were the most effective traders. One employer bemoaned the fact that traders had to be glued to their screens ('We'll all become zombies'), but thought that his firm would be all right: 'Our young lads are brilliant. They spent so much time playing Star Wars and computer games as kids that nobody can match them for the speed at which they feed stuff into the computers.'[35]

Rather than developing new working practices, there was a conscious effort to retain the culture of the Stock Exchange floor. A *Times* journalist explained that the designers of the dealing rooms did not want to isolate dealers, who were used to 'banter on the Stock Exchange floor', from each other by batteries of 'computer screens and telephone switchgear'. Consequently, there was an attempt to recreate the 'atmosphere' of the floor by prioritizing the traditional soundscape of the market. Traders thus had 'access to both a person-to-person intercom and a general broadcast system when they wish to impart their messages to the entire room'.[36] Moreover, the space provided per dealer was deliberately less than that recommended in legislation, physical proximity designed to promote, as one report put it, 'an aggressive market and atmosphere and hence more aggressive trading'.[37] The result was an intensification rather than a moderation of the traditional competitive trading floor culture, the new dealing rooms becoming home to 'an aggressive, Americanized financial culture', as portrayed in Oliver Stone's movie *Wall Street* (1987).[38] Indeed, when Linda McDowell explored the 'world of screen-based trading' in the mid-1990s, she found 'the loud performance of aggressive heterosexual masculinity' to be one of its defining features.[39]

Moreover, the stresses of a City job were growing as a result of increasing competition, the abolition of fixed commissions, and thinner margins. 'Big Bang', the *Daily Mail*'s financial correspondent quickly perceived, would sweep away the last vestiges of 'gentlemanly capitalism', ushering in 'a much tougher, nastier world than before'. He imagined the protagonists in this world as men: the 'Big Bangers' who 'will sweat from eight until six, chasing little green numbers blinking across a bank of three or four screens, while loudspeakers blare out information as they wrestle with three telephones. It's a great life, while you last'.[40] The *Sunday Times* thought similarly. 'After a couple of centuries of peaceful, parochial, well-protected profit-making, the Square Mile is bracing itself for total war'.[41] Though somewhat sensationalist, these commentaries did identify very real changes in working culture. Even before Big Bang, longer hours and more demanding working conditions were already becoming normalized. One broker, Sue Graham, found that the working day was starting around 7.15 a.m., though people were leaving work on time. 'But there are people around the City now who work excessive hours just to be macho or out of worry', she noted.[42] With the shift to the electronic system, active from 8 a.m. to 8 p.m., trading could easily take place outside traditional floor hours.[43] Within a year of Big Bang, surveys showed stress levels in the City rising as long hours, high workloads, and overwhelming pressure to perform took their toll.[44]

Though the press identified some 'well-paid female Big Bangers' who did well out of the hiring frenzy produced by deregulation, few believed such careers were framed to appeal to women.[45] Furthermore, this intensification of the stresses and strains faced by brokers and dealers occurred just at the point where other financial institutions were beginning to rethink their working culture. Concerned in particular to recruit skilled female staff, and to retain them after maternity breaks, the big banks pioneered 'family friendly' employment policies in the 1980s and 1990s which, though falling far short of transforming the gendered division of labour, were nevertheless part of what Sarah Stoller identifies as a 'seismic shift in workplace culture'.[46] This widening gap may have been a factor behind the relatively small numbers of girls and young women applying for careers in stocks and shares. In the mid-1990s, some careers advisers were reportedly advising female graduates away from trading rooms, and this was not simply a London issue.[47] One of the directors of Midlands brokers Albert E. Sharp said he was frustrated when people asked why there were not more women stockbrokers: 'we find that out of 70 graduate applications, only two or three will be from women. If they don't apply we can't recruit them can we?'[48]

Gender difference continued to structure financial work in profound ways. In the course of her research, McDowell found that men and women understood their jobs 'in ways which are congruent with particular gender "regimes" and their own gendered identity'. Investment bankers interpreted their work in explicitly masculine terms 'of "overcoming resistance" and aggressive selling...despite the fact that the job itself might seem to demand feminised attributes of listening well and being socially available'. The way men constructed and performed their roles was 'impossible for women and so the job is reinterpreted in conventional female terms', requiring sympathy, empathy, personality, and charm: 'a version of an escort with brains'.[49] Women were thus forced into an 'adoption and exploitation of a parodic femininity' which some found demeaning. As one put it: 'Frankly you have to learn to use all your assets...it can be a form of prostitution of your sex.'[50]

Financial work thus remained deeply gendered and embodied.[51] So, while the City woman became a recognizable figure in popular culture from the 1990s, representations served to underline women's incongruity and 'otherness' in the world of finance. Literary scholar Nicky Marsh argues that the protagonists of novels featuring such women 'are deeply aware of how discordant their bodies are in a financial culture...the incongruities of a body marked by both its sexuality and its maternity'.[52] Success depends upon performing feminine roles at work. In Allison Pearson's *I Don't Know How She Does It* (2002), successful hedge-fund manager and mother of two Kate Reddy's relations with clients are described in 'a maternal language of play and "hand holding"', while in Helen Dunne's *Trixie Trader* (2001), they are couched more in 'the single woman's language of seduction and entertaining'.[53] In much of this kind of fiction, Marsh argues, the focus is on the irreconcilable tensions between the financial woman's 'sexual, maternal and professional identities'.[54] The novels ultimately confirm rather than challenge traditional ideas about the incompatibility of finance and femininity. In Pearson's novel, for example, Reddy ultimately decides to quit her job and move out of London to focus on her family. They reject a feminist critique of 'the misogynistic assumptions that render female economic power so destabilizing and female bodies so disturbing'.[55]

That popular culture, even when attempting to highlight misogyny in finance, risked entrenching traditional ideas about women and money is suggested by the plotline of the 1996 Whoopi Goldberg movie *The Associate*. Passed over for promotion in a Wall Street firm in favour of the man she trained, Goldberg's character Laurel Ayres sets up in business on her own as an investment adviser. Rebuffed by all her male contacts who don't take her seriously, Ayres eventually resorts to inventing a male business partner, Robert S. Cutty, to attract clients. The plan works too well. Cutty's advice—really Laurel's—proves so lucrative that he becomes a talismanic and trusted figure on Wall Street, while Ayres herself is sidelined. Eventually, the investors demand to meet him. Goldberg, an African American actor, dons male dress and elaborate prosthetics to pass as Cutty, a white man, in a series of increasingly farcical encounters. Though the audience sees Laurel's financial expertise, the film stresses how blind her peers are to her talent. As one character tells her: 'Everyone wants Cutty, and without him, you're nothing.'[56] The film thus echoes many of the ideas in Olive Malvery's *The Speculator*, written the best part of a century earlier, most obviously in its use of the cross-dressing device, albeit with a racial twist. To succeed in finance, both claim, a woman needs to switch genders.[57] This depiction draws on ideas about finance's 'defeminizing' impact going back at least as far as the early eighteenth century. Though the film—unlike *The Speculator*—eventually sees its female protagonist successful on her own terms, accepting this involves disregarding most of the previous ninety minutes of the narrative.[58]

Around this time, a series of legal cases involving complaints about sexist and discriminatory behaviour made it difficult to ignore the cultural barriers women continued to face in finance. In 2000, Kay Swinburne won significant damages against her firm Deutsche Bank over the 'juvenile and mean' culture she faced, culminating in being accused by her boss of sleeping with a client.[59] Soon after, Isabelle Terrillon, a trader at Japanese investment bank Nomura International, reached a settlement with the firm over her allegations of sex discrimination and unfair dismissal. Incidents she described ranged from being advised by a male executive to wear 'short, tight skirts' to being asked by another 'to strip off and give him a massage'. She found the City 'a world in itself, a clique, a closed circle that perpetuates itself'.[60] As the cases mounted, some commentators concluded that the big City firms were 'riddled with a shameful culture of machismo'.[61] Others, however, were more optimistic. Mary Ann Sieghart, who had started her career as a financial journalist in the early 1980s, thought the culture was improving, and argued that while individual cases were shocking, they were 'the last twitching of the tail of a dying dragon'.[62]

An important piece of evidence backing this view was the appointment in 2001 of Clara Furse as the London Stock Exchange's first female chief executive officer (CEO).[63] For Furse, gender was simply a non-issue in the modern City. When interviewed for the *Daily Telegraph*, she was reportedly 'horrified' when asked whether she was a feminist. 'I have worked in the City for 23 years. I love the City. There is no gender stuff. There was some in the media but I cannot say I have encountered it in my working life.'[64] Yet a little later Furse unwillingly found herself in the centre of debates about misogyny in the Square Mile when she was subjected to what was described as 'a vicious City whispering campaign about her private life'. Though her male predecessors had also been liable to intense criticism, Furse's colleague, London Stock Exchange chairman Don Cruikshank, believed that the focus on her personal life meant that these 'offensive slurs' were an unacceptable example of 'sexism in the City'.[65]

High-profile instances of misogyny seemed to support those who had queried whether a more equal gender order would naturally emerge as women gradually rose to senior positions in business. Such optimism downplayed the 'psychic dynamics' underpinning men's attitudes to women at work, argues Michael Roper. Senior women threatened 'the security of the gender order', especially when they displayed supposedly 'masculine' traits. Men 'did not just fear that ambitious career women would "lose a bit of their femininity", but that the men whose paths they crossed might lose a bit of their masculinity'.[66] In such a situation, the 'gender-blind' stance which ignored the ways in which women and men experienced work differently began to seem an inadequate method of tackling women's limited progress in the financial sector.

Not an Easy Place to Work

The global financial crisis of 2007–8—the worst since the depression that followed the Wall Street Crash of 1929—put finance on the political agenda in a way that it had not been since the 1930s. The travails of household names like Northern Rock and the Royal Bank of Scotland in the United Kingdom and Lehman Brothers and AIG in the United States, and the vast government bailouts that ensued, made averting future catastrophes a pressing question. Though the focus was on the lack of regulation that was widely believed to have encouraged the reckless lending and excessive risk-taking that fuelled the crash, there was a strand of criticism that foregrounded the issue of gender. Many saw it as a distinctly *male* crisis, identifying a testosterone-driven financial culture as the main culprit. More women in positions of authority would have introduced different perspectives, greater prudence, and better decision making into the system. Newspapers readily latched onto the idea—'Men have messed up. Let women sort it out', 'Higher heels, lower risk'—but it also influenced thinking at the top.[67] It triggered debates at the World Economic Forum in 2009, and prompted French finance minister Christine Lagarde to quip that 'if Lehman Brothers had been "Lehman Sisters", today's economic crisis clearly would look quite different.'[68]

Such sentiments catalysed parliamentary investigation into the lack of women at executive level in financial institutions, and the impact on governance. A Treasury Committee on 'Women in the City' reported in March 2010. Though it rejected claims that greater female representation would have prevented the crash, it did conclude that the lack of diversity 'may have heightened the problems of "group-think" and made effective challenge and scrutiny of executive decisions less effective'.[69] It believed that it was time for the City to take action, but preferred 'sustained scrutiny' by parliament as the tool to achieve this rather than imposing quotas or other interventions through 'legislative fiat'.[70]

But in the years that followed the crisis, there was little evidence of cultural or structural change. In the early 2010s, Dutch author Joris Luyendijk conducted a major study of City workers based on dozens of anonymous interviews. A female stockbroker he talked to entirely rejected the popular 'image of stockbrokers as boys shouting "buy" or "sell" the whole time', stressing that her job was all about serious research and giving her clients—institutional fund managers—the best possible advice. At the same time, she framed her work in gendered terms. When sitting on recruitment committees, she warned women that eleven-hour days were the norm, and impressed upon them that it was 'not an easy place to work'.

> The simple fact is that fewer women want this lifestyle than men. This job changes you. You need to become aggressive, decisive, develop leadership qualities.... If you want to last in this industry, you need to behave like a man. There's very little space for you to behave differently. Maybe that will change but currently with over 80% of the senior people around [you] being male, you still have to conform to their norms.[71]

The anonymity of the interviews allowed the women to talk frankly about the challenges of working in the City. Continuities with the past clearly remained. One told Luyendijk:

> There is a glass ceiling in finance but not in a formal sense. If you want to get to a real senior position, you have to become buddies with the senior managers, who are still all male. These men constantly hold meetings together, travel together, eat together...They need you to fit in. You need to play golf, blend in with the casual banter...When a woman joins such a team, its dynamics change. This is a very important barrier.[72]

Another highlighted the culture shift that occurred between university, where the gender split was fifty-fifty and she had not encountered problems, and the workplace. When she started in the City, men she had known from university would 'change their behaviour...influenced by older men, and their sexism'.[73] But none of those interviewed wanted affirmative action, seeing quotas as devaluing their status and undermining their authority.[74]

So, the notion that the 2007–8 crisis 'chastened' or changed the world of finance soon faded.[75] And though wider culture—most notably Hollywood—developed a significant interest in finance, this did not challenge the gendered status quo. Martin Scorsese's comedy *Wolf of Wall Street* (2013) ostensibly satirizes the culture of masculine excess, in which the anti-hero Jordan Belfort urges his team of salesmen—'my fucking warriors'—not to hang up the phone until the client 'either buys or fucking dies!'[76] But it does so sufficiently ambivalently for the film to be adopted and celebrated by its ostensible targets. Indeed, there were multiple reports of financial firms in London, New York, and continental Europe sending their staff to watch the film.[77] This was part of a longer tradition of cultural representations of City excess reproducing the behaviour they were depicting. When researching the role of Belfort, the film's star Leonardo DiCaprio found it ironic 'that we were making a movie about the debauchery of Wall Street but 80 per cent of the guys I talked to said the reason they got into the world of finance was to try to be like Gordon Gekko in *Wall Street*'.[78] Finance remained as it ever was: a cultural production. 'Through narrative, financiers can conceive of themselves as hunters', as Philip Roscoe puts it, performing masculinity through their performance of finance, just as they had been doing for centuries.[79]

Finance began to seem like an outlier in the corporate world as a whole, where the 'business case for diversity'—the argument that including women and other underrepresented groups would ultimately boost the bottom line—was gaining ground.[80] FTSE 100 companies had responded positively to a 2011 review chaired by Lord Davies calling for boards to double the representation of women from 12.5 per cent to 25 per cent by 2015, a target which was successfully reached not via formal quotas but through a voluntary 'comply or explain' culture.[81] But change was slowest in financial services, leading the Treasury to commission another review focusing specifically on women's representation at senior levels in the sector. Its 2016 report claimed that there was 'a "permafrost" in the mid-tier where women do not progress or they leave the sector'. To catalyse change, it recommended that businesses be encouraged to sign up to a charter committing them to setting gender diversity targets at senior management level, publicly reporting progress towards these targets, and linking executive bonuses to achieving them.[82] The Women in Finance Charter was launched by the Treasury in March 2016 and, though voluntary, came with the veiled threat that if sign-up rates were disappointing, government might 're-examine whether a more prescriptive approach' was necessary.[83]

Consequently, the issue remained on the political agenda. When a Treasury Committee inquiry, 'Women in Finance', was held in 2017–18 to check on the impact of the Charter, and to explore in more detail the barriers to entry and progression faced by women in financial services, it painted a mixed picture. While it was glad that 205 firms, including many of the biggest investment banks, had signed the Charter, the lack of change across the sector was clear. Women continued to be underrepresented in senior positions, gender distribution in most firms following a 'pyramid' model; women were more prominent in support roles than in profit-generating ones; the bonus culture and the culture of presenteeism were significant barriers to women; and a substantial gender pay gap remained. It concluded that 'there is a considerable way to go' towards achieving a gender balance.[84]

Indeed, though corporations' growing acceptance of the 'business case for diversity' made the issue of women's representation more prominent, the limits of this approach were becoming clear. Linking the conversation about diversity so tightly to profitability turns attention away from broader problems of inequality, argue Robin Ely and David Thomas. Rather than focusing exclusively on shareholder value, employers need to 'embrace a broader vision of success that encompasses learning, innovation, creativity, flexibility, equity, and human dignity'. Hiring more women alone does not reconfigure power relations in an organization: the policy needs to be accompanied by a concerted effort to change internal cultures, build trust, and combat systems of discrimination and subordination baked into organizational norms.[85] Without such willingness, little real progress is possible.

Examples supporting this point of view were easy to come by. Giving evidence before the 2017–18 inquiry, Amanda Blanc, Group Chief Executive Officer of AXA UK, had denied that an 'alpha-male' culture was systemic within finance. She admitted that when she had started her career fifteen years previously, there had been a chauvinistic culture at industry conferences, but said that such behaviour 'just does not exist anymore'. Yet when Blanc moved on to become CEO at Aviva, she was subjected to misogynistic comments from shareholders at the annual general meeting (AGM) in 2022, claiming that she was 'not the man for the job' and should be 'wearing trousers'.[86] In a subsequent interview, Blanc noted that it was 'a new development for me personally' that such comments could be made at a public AGM. Striking a far less positive note than four years previously, she said, 'I would like to tell you that things have got better in recent years', but in fact, 'the more senior the role I have taken, the more overt the unacceptable behaviour'.[87]

By this point, the wider context for these discussions had shifted significantly. In giving a voice to victims of sexual abuse and harassment, the #MeToo movement which erupted in late 2017 gave a new sense of urgency to demands for accountability and structural change.[88] So in the wake of fresh bullying, harassment, and abuse scandals in the financial sector, the Treasury inquiry was revived in 2023, this time under the much more pointed title, 'Sexism in the City'.[89] The evidence gathered painted a bleak picture. 'We have been quite taken aback by just how little things have shifted in the last five years', remarked committee chair Harriett Baldwin.[90] The committee heard that there were 'big pockets of no progress whatsoever', with only 12 per cent of named fund managers being women, a figure that had remained static for decades. The issue of cultural change—or lack thereof—was far more prominent this time around. The committee spoke to forty women at a private roundtable event at Westminster, and the evidence they heard was 'shocking, especially the extent of misogyny, sexual harassment and bullying, up to and including serious sexual assault and rape.' Non-disclosure agreements (NDAs) were routinely used to cover up such cases, silencing victims, protecting perpetrators, and allowing a toxic culture to persist. While the report made a series of recommendations—including legislation banning the use of NDAs in harassment cases—the emphasis remained on exhortation, urging firms to recognize the 'moral imperative' of tackling these problems as well as the business logic of doing so. Yet, as it admitted, culture was 'the most difficult area to seek to reform'.[91]

At the London Stock Exchange itself, the culture was, it seems, changing. Appointing Julia Hoggett in 2021 as its second female and first openly gay CEO, it now had a leader with over two decades' worth of experience promoting diversity and inclusion in the City of London.[92] Rather than highlighting her own achievements to claim that the City was gender-blind, she took a different approach. 'Rolling me out as an example of diversity is evidence we haven't fixed it yet', she admitted.[93] Though the Women in Finance Charter was 'a good start', she argued that bringing about genuine change required far more than this, including 'understanding historical patterns to look for embedded, often unconscious bias'.[94] This awareness of history saw the Stock Exchange host a celebration in March 2023 to mark the fiftieth anniversary of women's admission, at which two of the first cohort—Hilary Pearson (née Root) and Susan Shaw—were present. Hoggett used the occasion to encourage the industry to face up to some 'uncomfortable truths', pointing out 'the inflexibilities, inequities and resistance to change' that it had not fully addressed since the 1970s.[95]

Yet the challenge facing the sector is not simply to break with half a century of inadequate action on diversity but, as this book has demonstrated, to confront the fact that for 300 years, professional identities and institutional structures in finance have been based on the denigration and marginalization of women. Finance is not an inherently masculine pursuit but was deliberately constructed as such by institutions that sought to exclude women who—from the earliest days of the market—had shown themselves more than capable of investing for themselves and for others. The conception of finance as masculine was upheld by a wider culture that relentlessly problematized women's financial behaviour and discouraged them from imagining themselves as independent financial agents. When, from the late nineteenth century, small numbers of women began to set up their own brokerages, the institutional response was predictably hostile: stock exchanges were too heavily invested in the idea of high finance as masculine for it to be anything other. Yet some women managed to succeed in what seemed like an inauspiciously hostile environment, operating within overwhelmingly male networks, finding business partners, and winning clients, both female and male.

It was one thing for women to run stockbroking businesses successfully, but quite another to demolish traditional attitudes about women and money. There were several reasons. Restricted by professional rules against advertising, women stockbrokers had to tread carefully when publicizing their services, which limited their opportunities to normalize the idea of stockbroking for women. In any case, many preferred to trade quietly and not draw attention to their sex, meaning that they had little impact outside their immediate environment. This fed a cycle of discovery and forgetting, the press repeatedly highlighting the existence of women stockbrokers, but in a haphazard and sensationalistic fashion, stressing—with growing inaccuracy—the novelty of their endeavours rather than building any sense of a heritage. Ultimately, women stockbrokers existed in sufficiently small numbers to be presented as remarkable exceptions that proved the rule of feminine financial incapacity. And when newspapers became increasingly vocal in contesting the exclusion of women from stock exchanges, they did so in a way that trivialized and sexualized women's presence in finance. The result was that even after women finally gained admittance to provincial stock exchanges in the 1960s, and London in 1973, they remained resolutely 'other'.

Gendered interpretations of the crash of 2007–8 that sought to problematize *male* behaviour may have seemed like a turning point, but in reality they masked problematic continuities. As George Robb points out, the biological determinism of these arguments—that too much testosterone disrupted markets, that women's natural caution would stabilize them—'echo Victorian assumptions about sexual difference'.[96] And as Melissa Fisher rightly argues, though they validated women's place in finance at a moment of crisis, they 'relied on some of the same conservative definitions of femininity that had once prevented women from being viewed as traditionally successful market leaders'.[97] Such thinking underpins unhelpful assumptions about women's supposed risk-aversion that are ultimately limiting rather than empowering, as well as failing to question the dubious idea that we can generalize about women's financial behaviour at all. Current struggles to change City culture are therefore unlikely to succeed unless they appreciate the difficulty—and necessity—of confronting beliefs about gender and finance which have been embedded over centuries. Acknowledging the efforts of those women who challenged these beliefs and defied men's monopoly on high finance by forging their own careers might represent an important step towards imagining a different kind of market.

Sexism in the City: Women Stockbrokers in Modern Britain. James Taylor, Oxford University Press.
© James Taylor 2025. DOI: 10.1093/9780191990397.003.0009

Notes

Introduction

1. *Newcastle Journal*, 27 March 1973, 14.
2. Her diary for the week was published in *The Observer*, 1 April 1973, 19.
3. For the origins of the bra-burning trope, see Hilary Hinds and Jackie Stacey, 'Imagining Feminism, Imagining Femininity: The Bra-Burner, Diana, and the Woman Who Kills', *Feminist Media Studies* 1, no. 2 (2001): 153–77, at 156–62.
4. *The Guardian*, 2 February 1973, 13.
5. Iris Sloley, 'Feminism and the Women's Liberation Movement', *Women's Struggle* 2, no. 3 (1972): 111–34, at 113.
6. Margaret Coulson, 'The Politics of Women's Liberation', *Socialist Woman*, March–April 1971, 9.
7. Sally Alexander and Anna Davin, 'Feminist History', *History Workshop* 1 (1976): 4–6, at 5.
8. June Purvis, 'Women's History in Britain: An Overview', *European Journal of Women's Studies* 2, no. 1 (1995): 7–19, at 11.
9. For some key contributions, see Ellen Jordan, 'The Exclusion of Women from Industry in Nineteenth-Century Britain', *Comparative Studies in Society and History* 31, no. 2 (1989): 273–96; Maxine Berg, 'What Difference Did Women's Work Make to the Industrial Revolution?', *History Workshop Journal* 35, no. 1 (1993): 22–44; Sara Horrell and Jane Humphries, 'Women's Labour Force Participation and the Transition to the Male-Breadwinner Family, 1790–1865', *Economic History Review* 48, no. 1 (1995): 89–117.
10. Anna Davin, 'Feminism and Labour History', in *People's History and Socialist Theory*, edited by Raphael Samuel (London, 1981), 176–81. By the early 1990s, Jane Humphries believed that women had graduated from 'lurking in the wings' to 'bit parts' in the historical mainstream: Jane Humphries, '"Lurking in the Wings...": Women in the Historiography of the Industrial Revolution', *Business and Economic History* 20 (1991): 32–44, at 42.
11. Wender Gamber, 'A Gendered Enterprise: Placing Nineteenth-Century Businesswomen in History', *Business History Review* 72, no. 2 (1998): 188–217, at 200.
12. Amy M. Froide, *Silent Partners: Women as Public Investors during Britain's Financial Revolution, 1690–1750* (Oxford, 2017), 2.
13. Amy Louise Erickson, 'Coverture and Capitalism', *History Workshop Journal* 59, no. 1 (2005): 1–16.
14. Leonore Davidoff and Catherine Hall, *Family Fortunes: Men and Women of the English Middle Class, 1780–1850* (London, 1997), ch. 6; Kathryn Gleadle, 'Revisiting *Family Fortunes*: Reflections on the Twentieth Anniversary of the Publication of L. Davidoff & C. Hall (1987) *Family Fortunes*', *Women's History Review* 16, no. 5 (2007): 773–82, at 774.
15. Ann M. Carlos, Karen Maguire, and Larry Neal, 'Financial Acumen, Women Speculators, and the Royal African Company during the South Sea Bubble', *Accounting, Business and Financial History* 16, no. 2 (2006): 219–43; Anne Laurence, 'Women Investors, "That Nasty South Sea Affair" and the Rage to Speculate in Early Eighteenth-Century England', *Accounting, Business and Financial History* 16, no. 2 (2006): 245–64; Mark Freeman, Robin Pearson, and James Taylor, '"A Doe in the City": Women Shareholders in Eighteenth- and Early Nineteenth-Century Britain', *Accounting, Business and Financial History* 16, no. 2 (2006): 265–91; Anne Laurence, Josephine Maltby, and Janette Rutterford, eds., *Women and Their Money, 1700–1950: Essays on Women and Finance* (Abingdon, 2009).
16. Misha Ewen, 'Women Investors and the Virginia Company in the Early Seventeenth Century', *Historical Journal* 62, no. 4 (2019): 853–74; Barbara J. Todd, 'Fiscal Citizens: Female Investors in Public Finance before the South Sea Bubble', in *Challenging Orthodoxies: The Social and Cultural Worlds of Early Modern Women*, edited by Sigrun Haude and Melinda S. Zook (Farnham, 2014), 53–74, at 53–4.
17. P. J. Cain and A. G. Hopkins, 'Gentlemanly Capitalism and British Expansion Overseas I: The Old Colonial System, 1688–1850', *Economic History Review* 39, no. 4 (1986): 501–25; David R. Green and Alastair Owens, 'Gentlewomanly Capitalism? Spinsters, Widows, and Wealth Holding in England and Wales, c.1800–1860', *Economic History Review* 56, no. 3 (2003): 510–36.

216 NOTES TO PAGES 3–4

18. Janette Rutterford and Josephine Maltby, '"The Widow, the Clergyman and the Reckless": Women Investors in England, 1830–1914', *Feminist Economics* 12, nos. 1–2 (2006): 111–38.
19. Nancy Henry, *Women, Literature and Finance in Victorian Britain: Cultures of Investment* (Cham, 2018), 14, 43. This claim has been supported by work presented at the Women, Money and Markets Conference since 2017: <https://www.womenmoneymarkets.co.uk>.
20. Josephine Maltby and Janette Rutterford, '"She Possessed Her Own Fortune": Women Investors from the Late Nineteenth Century to the Early Twentieth Century', *Business History* 48, no. 2 (2006): 220–53; Mark Freeman, Robin Pearson, and James Taylor, 'Between Madam Bubble and Kitty Lorimer: Women Investors in British and Irish Stock Companies', in *Women and Their Money*, 95–114; David R. Green, Alastair Owens, Josephine Maltby, and Janette Rutterford, eds., *Men, Women, and Money: Perspectives on Gender, Wealth, and Investment, 1850–1930* (Oxford, 2011); Janette Rutterford, David R. Green, Josephine Maltby, and Alastair Owens, 'Who Comprised the Nation of Shareholders? Gender and Investment in Great Britain, *c.*1870–1935', *Economic History Review* 64, no. 1 (2011): 157–87; Graeme G. Acheson, Gareth Campbell, and John D. Turner, 'Who Financed the Expansion of the Equity Market? Shareholder Clienteles in Victorian Britain', *Business History* 59, no. 4 (2017): 607–37.
21. Lucy Newton and Philip L. Cottrell, 'Female Investors in the First English and Welsh Commercial Joint-Stock Banks', *Accounting, Business and Financial History* 16, no. 2 (2006): 315–40; Graeme G. Acheson, Gareth Campbell, Aine Gallagher, and John D. Turner, 'Independent Women: Investing in British Railways, 1870–1922', *Economic History Review* 74, no. 2 (2021): 471–95; Helen Doe, 'Waiting for Her Ship to Come In? The Female Investor in Nineteenth-Century Sailing Vessels', *Economic History Review* 63, no. 1 (2010): 85–106.
22. Sarah C. Haan uses this term in an American context, but it applies equally to the UK: Sarah C. Haan, 'Corporate Governance and the Feminization of Capital', *Stanford Law Review* 74, no. 3 (2022): 515–602.
23. Ann M. Carlos and Larry Neal, 'Women Investors in Early Capital Markets, 1720–1725', *Financial History Review* 11, no. 2 (2004): 197–224, at 205–8; Froide, *Silent Partners*, esp. chs. 3, 4, and 7.
24. Edward Stringham, 'The Emergence of the London Stock Exchange as a Self-Policing Club', *Journal of Private Enterprise* 17, no. 2 (2002): 1–19.
25. Amy Froide, 'Navigating the Spaces and Places of England's First Stock Market: Women Investors and Brokers during the Financial Revolution, *c.*1690–1730', in *The Cultural Life of Risk and Innovation: Imaging New Markets from the Seventeenth Century to the Present*, edited by Chia Yin Hsu, Thomas M. Luckett, and Erika Vause (New York and London, 2021), 63–79, at 78.
26. Ranald Michie, *The London Stock Exchange: A History* (Oxford, 2001), 201–3, 453–5; David Kynaston, *The City of London*, vol. 3, *Illusions of Gold, 1914–1945* (London, 1999), 346–7; David Kynaston, *The City of London*, vol. 4, *A Club No More, 1945–2000* (London, 2002), 159–60, 419–20, 425; E. Victor Morgan and W. A. Thomas, *The Stock Exchange: Its History and Functions*, 2nd edn (London, 1969), 259; W. A. Thomas, *The Stock Exchanges of Ireland* (Liverpool, 1986), 86.
27. Wendy Gamber, 'Gendered Concerns: Thoughts on the History of Business and the History of Women', *Business and Economic History* 23, no. 1 (1994): 129–40, at 129.
28. Kathy Peiss, '"Vital Industry" and Women's Ventures: Conceptualizing Gender in Twentieth Century Business History', *Business History Review* 72, no. 2 (1998): 218–41, at 220.
29. Katrina Honeyman, 'Engendering Enterprise', *Business History* 43, no. 1 (2001): 119–26.
30. A point made by Margaret Walsh, 'Gendered Endeavours: Women and the Reshaping of Business Culture', *Women's History Review* 14, no. 2 (2005): 181–202, at 189.
31. Nicola Phillips, *Women in Business, 1700–1850* (Woodbridge, 2006); Hannah Barker, *The Business of Women: Female Enterprise and Urban Development in Northern England, 1760–1830* (Oxford, 2006); Alison C. Kay, *The Foundations of Female Entrepreneurship: Enterprise, Home and Household in London, c.1800–1870* (London, 2009); Jennifer Aston, *Female Entrepreneurship in Nineteenth-Century England: Engagement in the Urban Economy* (Cham, 2016); Hannah Barker, *Family and Business during the Industrial Revolution* (Oxford, 2017). For coverage beyond Britain, see, among others: Melanie Buddle, *The Business of Women: Marriage, Family, and Entrepreneurship in British Columbia, 1901–51* (Vancouver, 2010); Catherine Bishop, *Minding Her Own Business: Colonial Businesswomen in Sydney* (Sydney, 2015); Béatrice Craig, *Women and Business since 1500: Invisible Presences in Europe and North America?* (London, 2016); Jennifer Aston and Catherine Bishop, eds., *Female Entrepreneurs in the Long Nineteenth Century: A Global Perspective* (London, 2020).
32. Carry van Lieshout, Harry Smith, Piero Montebruno, and Robert J. Bennett, 'Female Entrepreneurship: Business, Marriage and Motherhood in England and Wales, 1851–1911', *Social History* 44, no. 4 (2019): 440–68, at 441; Barker, *Business of Women*, 3.

NOTES TO PAGES 4–6   217

33. Davidoff and Hall, *Family Fortunes*, 284.
34. Kay, *Foundations of Female Entrepreneurship*, 19. For similar comments, see Phillips, *Women in Business*, 11.
35. Aston, *Female Entrepreneurship*, 99–100; Kay, *Foundations of Female Entrepreneurship*, 43.
36. Aston, *Female Entrepreneurship*, 215–25; Jennifer Aston and Paolo Di Martino, 'Risk, Success, and Failure: Female Entrepreneurship in Late Victorian and Edwardian England', *Economic History Review* 70, no. 3 (2017): 837–58.
37. Melanie Buddle, 'Gender and Business: Recent Literature on Women and Entrepreneurship', *Histoire Sociale/Social History* 51, no. 104 (2018): 401–7, at 401.
38. Craig, *Women and Business*, 4.
39. For the optimistic view, see Jessica P. Clark, '*Pomeroy v. Pomeroy*: Beauty, Modernity, and the Female Entrepreneur in Fin-de-Siècle London', *Women's History Review* 22, no. 6 (2013): 877–903, at 879. For the suggestion that women's participation may have been in decline in the early twentieth century, see Van Lieshout et al., 'Female Entrepreneurship', 467.
40. Wendy Gamber, *The Female Economy: The Millinery and Dressmaking Trades, 1860–1930* (Urbana and Chicago, 1997); Alison C. Kay, 'A Little Enterprise of Her Own: Lodging-House Keeping and the Accommodation Business in Nineteenth-Century London', *London Journal* 28, no. 2 (2003): 41–53; Jessica P. Clark, *The Business of Beauty: Gender and the Body in Modern London* (London, 2020).
41. Van Lieshout et al., 'Female Entrepreneurship', 452–3.
42. Lois Beachy Underhill, *The Woman Who Ran for President: The Many Lives of Victoria Woodhull* (Bridgehampton, NY, 1995); Mary Gabriel, *Notorious Victoria: The Uncensored Life of Victoria Woodhull—Visionary, Suffragist, and First Woman to Run for President* (Chapel Hill, NC, 1998); Myra MacPherson, *The Scarlet Sisters: Sex, Suffrage, and Scandal in the Gilded Age* (New York, 2014).
43. Sheri J. Caplan, *Petticoats and Pinstripes: Portraits of Women in Wall Street's History* (Santa Barbara, CA, 2013).
44. Shennette Garrett-Scott, *Banking on Freedom: Black Women in US Finance before the New Deal* (New York, 2019).
45. George Robb, *Ladies of the Ticker: Women and Wall Street from the Gilded Age to the Great Depression* (Urbana, 2017).
46. The literature is surveyed in Anne Witz, 'Patriarchy and Professions: The Gendered Politics of Occupational Closure', *Sociology* 24, no. 4 (1990): 675–90, at 675–6.
47. Anne Witz, *Professions and Patriarchy* (London and New York, 2004); Wai-Fong Chua and Stewart Clegg, 'Professional Closure: The Case of British Nursing', *Theory and Society* 19, no. 2 (1990): 135–72; Linda M. Kirkham and Anne Loft, 'Gender and the Construction of the Professional Accountant', *Accounting, Organizations and Society* 18, no. 6 (1993): 507–58.
48. Celia Davies, 'The Sociology of Professions and the Profession of Gender', *Sociology* 30, no. 4 (1996): 661–78, at 669.
49. Daniel Schneider, 'Gendering Profession: Experiences of Nursing in the United States' (PhD thesis, University of California, 2016), 14.
50. Witz, 'Patriarchy and Professions', 682–4.
51. Kirkham and Loft, 'Professional Accountant', 546.
52. Dina Copelman, *London's Women Teachers: Gender, Class and Feminism, 1870–1930* (London, 1996); Michelle Elizabeth Tusan, *Women Making News: Gender and Journalism in Modern Britain* (Urbana, 2005); Helen McCarthy, *Women of the World: The Rise of the Female Diplomat* (London, 2014); Patricia Fara, *A Lab of One's Own: Science and Suffrage in the First World War* (Oxford, 2018).
53. Heidi Egginton and Zoë Thomas, eds., *Precarious Professionals: Gender, Identities and Social Change in Modern Britain* (London, 2021), 14.
54. Krista Cowman and Louise A. Jackson, 'Introduction: Middle-Class Women and Professional Identity', *Women's History Review* 14, no. 2 (2005): 165–80.
55. Anne Logan, 'In Search of Equal Citizenship: The Campaign for Women Magistrates in England and Wales, 1910–1939', *Women's History Review* 16, no. 4 (2007): 501–18; Stephen P. Walker, 'Professions and Patriarchy Revisited: Accountancy in England and Wales, 1887–1914', *Accounting History Review* 21, no. 2 (2011): 185–225; Ren Pepitone, 'Gender, Space, and Ritual: Women Barristers, the Inns of Court, and the Interwar Press', *Journal of Women's History* 28, no. 1 (2016): 60–83. See also two recent special issues of *Women's History Review*: 'Challenging Women' (2020) and 'Professional Women: The Public, the Private, and the Political' (2023).

218 NOTES TO PAGES 6–9

56. Histories of British stockbroking (and stockjobbing) are thin on the ground, and gender is usually marginal to the analysis: H. V. Bowen, ' "The Pests of Human Society": Stockbrokers, Jobbers and Speculators in Mid-Eighteenth-Century Britain', *History* 78, no. 252 (1993): 38–53; Bernard Attard, 'The Jobbers of the London Stock Exchange: An Oral History', *Oral History* 22, no. 1 (1994): 43–8; Bernard Attard, 'Making a Market: The Jobbers of the London Stock Exchange, 1800–1986', *Financial History Review* 7, no. 1 (2000): 5–24; Alex Preda, *Framing Finance: The Boundaries of Markets and Modern Capitalism* (Chicago, 2009), ch. 2. A major oral history project in the 1990s, 'City Lives', did interview some women working in finance: Cathy Courtney and Paul Thompson, *City Lives: The Changing Voices of British Finance* (London, 1996).
57. Catherine Ingrassia, 'The Pleasures of Business and the Business of Pleasure: Gender, Credit, and the South Sea Bubble', *Studies in Eighteenth-Century Culture* 24 (1995), 191–210, at 191.
58. Urs Stäheli, *Spectacular Speculation: Thrills, the Economy, and Popular Discourse* (Stanford, CA, 2013), 178–9.
59. Paul Crosthwaite, Peter Knight, Nicky Marsh, Helen Paul, and James Taylor, *Invested: How Three Centuries of Stock Market Advice Reshaped Our Money, Markets and Minds* (Chicago, 2022), 242.
60. Linda McDowell, *Capital Culture: Gender at Work in the City* (Oxford, 1997); Louise Marie Roth, *Selling Women Short: Gender and Money on Wall Street* (Princeton, NJ, 2006); Melissa S. Fisher, *Wall Street Women* (Durham, NC, and London, 2012).
61. Sarah Hall and Lindsey Appleyard, 'Financial Business Education: The Remaking of Gendered Investment Banking Subjects in the (Post-Crisis) City of London', *Journal of Cultural Economy* 5, no. 4 (2012): 457–72; Penny Griffin, 'Gendering Global Finance: Crisis, Masculinity, and Responsibility', *Men and Masculinities* 16, no. 1 (2013): 9–34; Adrienne Roberts, 'Gender, Financial Deepening and the Production of Embodied Finance: Towards a Critical Feminist Analysis', *Global Society* 29, no. 1 (2015): 107–27; Helen Longlands, *Gender, Space and City Bankers* (Abingdon, 2020).
62. Elisabeth Prügl, ' "If Lehman Brothers Had Been Lehman Sisters…": Gender and Myth in the Aftermath of the Financial Crisis', *International Political Sociology* 6, no. 1 (2012): 21–35; Kate Maclean, 'Gender, Risk and the Wall Street Alpha Male', *Journal of Gender Studies* 25, no. 4 (2016): 427–44.
63. David Edgerton, *The Rise and Fall of the British Nation: A Twentieth-Century History*, cited in Egginton and Thomas, *Precarious Professionals*, 28–9.
64. Philip Scranton, 'Introduction: Gender and Business History', *Business History Review* 72, no. 2 (1998): 185–7; *Business History*, Call for Papers for Special Issue: 'Gender, Feminism, and Business History', 24 April 2019: <https://exchange-bhc.blogspot.com/2019/04/call-for-papers-for-special-issue.html>.
65. Hannah Dean, Linda Perriton, Scott Taylor, and Mary Yeager, 'Margins and Centres: Gender and Feminism in Business History', *Business History* 66, no. 1 (2024): 1–13, at 2.
66. Gamber, 'Gendered Enterprise', 191.
67. Albert J. Mills and Kristin S. Williams, 'Feminist Frustrations: The Enduring Neglect of a Women's Business History and the Opportunity for Radical Change', *Business History* 66, no. 1 (2024): 14–28, at 18; Gabrielle Durepos, Alan McKinlay and Scott Taylor, 'Narrating Histories of Women at Work: Archives, Stories, and the Promise of Feminism', *Business History* 58, no. 8 (2017): 1261–79, at 1274.
68. Gerda Lerner, 'Placing Women in History: Definitions and Challenges', *Feminist Studies* 3, nos. 1–2 (1975): 5–14.
69. Jill Matthews, 'Feminist History', *Labour History* 50 (1986), 147–53, at 148.
70. 2021 saw the creation of Wikipedia pages for three early female brokers, Amy Bell, Beatrice Gordon Holmes, and Doris Mortimer. A fourth, Oonah Keogh, has a page dating back to 2019; she was also profiled in a documentary series, *Herstory: Ireland's Epic Women*, for RTÉ One in 2020. Lizzie Broadbent is compiling a 'FT-She 100' of early businesswomen, which features Bell and Holmes; in 2024, she wrote entries for the pair for the *Oxford Dictionary of National Biography*: <https://womenwhomeantbusiness.com/the-ft-she-100/>.
71. Joan W. Scott, 'Conceptualizing Gender in American Business History', *Business History Review* 72, no. 2 (1998): 242–9, at 244.
72. Peiss, 'Vital Industry', 221.
73. Other studies of female entrepreneurship use similar strategies of source linkage: see, for example, Kay, *Foundations*, 37; Aston, *Female Entrepreneurship*, 64–6.
74. The minutes for later years have been accessed in the past by other scholars, including David Kynaston and Ranald Michie, but the London Stock Exchange did not respond to my requests for access, and it is unclear whether these archives survive.

NOTES TO PAGES 10–15   219

75. Miss Gordon Holmes, *In Love with Life: A Pioneer Career Woman's Story* (London, 1944).
76. Michie, *London Stock Exchange*, 501.
77. The title of a Treasury Committee in 2023–4 to address 'the barriers faced by women in financial services': <https://committees.parliament.uk/work/7842/sexism-in-the-city>.

Chapter 1

1. [Edward Ward], *The Picture of a Coffee-House: Or, The Humour of the Stock-Jobbers* (London, 1700), 3. For the attribution, see Matthew David Mitchell, '"The Extravagant Humour of Stock-Jobbing" and the Members of the English Body Politic, 1690–1720', *Essays in Economic and Business History* 30 (2012): 49–62.
2. Stuart Banner, *Anglo-American Securities Regulation: Cultural and Political Roots, 1690–1860* (Cambridge, 1998), 14–40.
3. Ann M. Carlos and Jill L. van Stone, 'Stock Transfer Patterns in the Hudson's Bay Company: A Study of the English Capital Market in Operation, 1670–1730', *Business History* 38, no. 2 (1995): 15–39, at 34–5.
4. Misha Ewen, 'Women Investors and the Virginia Company in the Early Seventeenth Century', *Historical Journal* 62, no. 4 (2019): 853–74, at 858.
5. Nathan Sussman, 'Financial Developments in London in the Seventeenth Century: The Financial Revolution Revisited', *Journal of Economic History* 82, no. 2 (2022): 480–515, at 483–8.
6. Bruce G. Carruthers, *City of Capital: Politics and Markets in the English Financial Revolution* (Princeton, 1999), 64–7; Sussman, 'Financial Developments', 493.
7. Charles Duguid, *The Story of the Stock Exchange: Its History and Position* (London, 1901), 15–20.
8. 'A Jobber' [Daniel Defoe], *The Anatomy of Exchange Alley: Or, A System of Stock-Jobbing* (London, 1719), 35.
9. Anne L. Murphy, 'Lotteries in the 1690s: Investment or Gamble?', *Financial History Review* 12, no. 2 (2005): 227–46, at 231; Bob Harris, *Gambling in Britain in the Long Eighteenth Century* (Cambridge, 2022), 148.
10. Anne L. Murphy, *The Origins of English Financial Markets: Investment and Speculation before the South Sea Bubble* (Cambridge, 2012), 156–8; Murphy, 'Lotteries in the 1690s', 242; Harris, *Gambling in Britain*, 187–9.
11. Barbara J. Todd, 'Property and a Woman's Place in Restoration London', *Women's History Review* 19, no. 2 (2010): 181–200.
12. Susan Staves, 'Investments, Votes, and "Bribes": Women as Shareholders in the Chartered National Companies', in *Women Writers and the Early Modern British Political Tradition*, edited by Hilda L. Smith (Cambridge, 1998), 259–78.
13. Anne Laurence, Josephine Maltby, and Janette Rutterford, 'Introduction', in *Women and Their Money, 1700–1950: Essays on Women and Finance*, edited by Anne Laurence, Josephine Maltby, and Janette Rutterford (Abingdon, 2009), 1–29, at 4.
14. Amy M. Froide, *Silent Partners: Women as Public Investors during Britain's Financial Revolution, 1690–1750* (Oxford, 2016), 68–73.
15. Froide, *Silent Partners*, 103–5.
16. Froide, *Silent Partners*, 106. See also Rosemary O'Day, 'Matchmaking and Moneymaking in a Patronage Society: The First Duke and Duchess of Chandos, c.1712–35', *Economic History Review* 66, no. 1 (2013): 273–96.
17. Bob Harris, 'Fantasy, Speculation, and the British State Lottery in the Eighteenth Century', in *Revisiting the Polite and Commercial People: Essays in Georgian Politics, Society, and Culture in Honour of Professor Paul Langford*, edited by Elaine Chalus and Perry Gauci (Oxford, 2019), 119–35, at 125; Anne Laurence, 'The Emergence of a Private Clientele for Banks in the Early Eighteenth Century: Hoare's Bank and Some Women Customers', *Economic History Review* 61, no. 3 (2008): 565–86, at 579–81; Patrick Walsh, *The South Sea Bubble and Ireland: Money, Banking and Investment, 1690–1721* (Woodbridge, 2014), 98–101.
18. Anne Laurence, 'Women Investors, "That Nasty South Sea Affair" and the Rage to Speculate in Early Eighteenth-Century England', *Accounting, Business and Financial History* 16, no. 2 (2006): 245–64; Anne Laurence, 'Lady Betty Hastings, Her Half-Sisters, and the South Sea Bubble: Family Fortunes and Strategies', *Women's History Review* 15, no. 4 (2006): 533–40.
19. Ann M. Carlos and Larry Neal, 'Women Investors in Early Capital Markets, 1720–1725', *Financial History Review* 11, no. 2 (2004): 197–224.
20. Carlos and Neal, 'Women Investors', 206.
21. A Gentleman, *A Tour Thro' the Whole Island of Great Britain, Divided into Circuits or Journeys* (London, 1724), 127–8.

NOTES TO PAGES 15–18

22. G. D. Ramsay, *The City of London in International Politics at the Accession of Elizabeth Tudor* (Manchester, 1975), 39–40; Philip Rawlings, '"A Compleat System of Knavery": Folk Devils, Moral Panics and the Origins of Financial Regulation', *Current Legal Problems* 61, no. 1 (2008): 325–70, at 343.

23. 8 & 9 Will. III, c. 32.

24. Amy Froide, 'Navigating the Spaces and Places of England's First Stock Market: Women Investors and Brokers during the Financial Revolution, *c.*1690–1730', in *The Cultural Life of Risk and Innovation: Imaging New Markets from the Seventeenth Century to the Present*, edited by Chia Yin Hsu, Thomas M. Luckett, and Erika Vause (New York and London, 2021), 63–79, at 67.

25. P. G. M. Dickson, *The Financial Revolution in England: A Study in the Development of Public Credit, 1688–1756* (London, 1967), 501–3; S. R. Cope, 'The Stock Exchange Revisited: A New Look at the Market in Securities in London in the Eighteenth Century', *Economica* 45 (1978): 1–21, at 2–3.

26. Carlos and Neal, 'Women Investors', 205.

27. Froide, 'Navigating', 67–73.

28. Froide, *Silent Partners*, 190–1.

29. Froide, *Silent Partners*, 133.

30. Froide, *Silent Partners*, 81.

31. Froide, 'Navigating', 67.

32. Froide, *Silent Partners*, 182; Froide, 'Navigating', 64–5.

33. William Quinn and John D. Turner, *Boom and Bust: A Global History of Financial Bubbles* (Cambridge, 2020), 23–7; Richard Dale, *The First Crash: Lessons from the South Sea Bubble* (Princeton, 2004), ch. 6.

34. Huw Bowen, '"The Pests of Human Society": Stockbrokers, Jobbers and Speculators in Mid-eighteenth-century Britain', *History* 78, no. 252 (1993): 38–53, at 39–40.

35. [Edward Ward], *The London-Spy Compleat, In Eighteen-Parts* (London, 1703), 391.

36. *Weekly Journal or British Gazetteer*, 26 March 1720, 1561.

37. *Whitehall Evening Post*, 7 April 1720, 2; *Weekly Packet*, 9 April 1720, 2.

38. *Original Weekly Journal*, 4 June 1720, 3.

39. *Weekly Packet*, 26 March 1720, 2.

40. *Original Weekly Journal*, 23 April 1720, 1722–3.

41. Marieke de Goede, *Virtue, Fortune, and Faith: A Genealogy of Finance* (Minneapolis, 2005), 28–30.

42. Anne L. Murphy, '"We Have Been Ruined by Whores": Perceptions of Female Involvement in the South Sea Scheme', in *Boom, Bust, and Beyond: New Perspectives on the 1720 Stock Market Bubble*, edited by Stefano Condorelli and Daniel Menning (Berlin, 2019), 261–83, at 280.

43. James Milner, *Three Letters Relating to the South-Sea Company and the Bank* (London, 1720), 5: discussed in Catherine Ingrassia, 'The Pleasure of Business and the Business of Pleasure: Gender, Credit, and the South Sea Bubble', *Studies in Eighteenth-Century Culture* 24 (1995): 191–210, at 196.

44. Ingrassia, 'The Pleasure of Business', 195.

45. [Thomas Gordon], *A Learned Dissertation upon Old Women, Male and Female, Spiritual and Temporal, in All Ages; Whether in Church, State, or Exchange-Alley* (London, 1720), 26.

46. Clare Walcot, 'Figuring Finance: London's New Financial World and the Iconography of Speculation, circa 1689–1763' (PhD thesis, University of Warwick, 2003), 80–1.

47. *The South-Sea Scheme Detected; and the Management thereof Enquired Into* (1720) and *The Battle of the Bubbles. Shewing their several Constitutions, Alliances, Policies, and Wars* (1720), both quoted in Sandra Sherman, *Finance and Fictionality in the Early Eighteenth Century: Accounting for Defoe* (Cambridge, 1996), 53.

48. Murphy, 'We Have Been Ruined', 263.

49. De Goede, *Virtue, Fortune, and Faith*, 31.

50. De Goede, *Virtue, Fortune, and Faith*, 35. See also E. J. Clery, *The Feminization Debate in Eighteenth-Century England: Literature, Commerce and Luxury* (Houndmills, 2004), 56–60.

51. Urs Stäheli, *Spectacular Speculation: Thrills, the Economy, and Popular Discourse* (Stanford, CA, 2013), 176.

52. Laura Favero Carraro, 'The Language of the Emerging Financial Market and Early Eighteenth-Century English Plays', *Essays in Economic and Business History* 37 (2019): 206–41.

53. Christine Wiskin, 'Businesswomen and Financial Management: Three Eighteenth-Century Case Studies', *Accounting, Business and Financial History* 16, no. 2 (2006): 143–61, at 144.

54. Amy Louise Erickson, 'Wealthy Businesswomen, Marriage and Succession in Eighteenth-Century London', *Business History* 66, no. 1 (2024): 29–58, at 32.

NOTES TO PAGES 19–22   221

55. Judith M. Spicksley, '"Fly with a Duck in Thy Mouth": Single Women as Sources of Credit in Seventeenth-Century England', *Social History* 32, no. 2 (2007): 187–207.
56. Alexandra Shepard, 'Minding Their Own Business: Married Women and Credit in Early Eighteenth-Century London', *Transactions of the Royal Historical Society*, 25 (2015): 53–74, at 66.
57. Nicola Phillips, *Women in Business, 1700–1850* (Woodbridge, 2006), 130.
58. Amy Louise Erickson, review of Amy M. Froide, *Silent Partners*, *English Historical Review* 135, no. 573 (2020): 488–91, at 490.
59. *Daily Advertiser*, 4 November 1743, 1.
60. Jon Stobart, 'Selling (Through) Politeness: Advertising Provincial Shops in Eighteenth-Century England', *Cultural and Social History* 5, no. 3 (2008): 309–28; Sharlene S. Sayegh, '"For the Continuance of their Favours": Women, the Public Sphere and the Print Culture in England, 1750–1760' (Masters dissertation, University of Nevada, 1994), ch. 4.
61. *Whitehall Evening Post*, 5–8 January 1754, 3.
62. *Public Advertiser*, 16 January 1754, 2.
63. *Public Advertiser*, 21 November 1769, 1. The trade in lottery tickets was the mainstay of many stockbrokers' businesses: Harris, *Gambling in Britain*, 146.
64. *London Evening Post*, 3–5 November 1772, 4; *St James's Chronicle*, 16–19 January 1773, 1.
65. *Morning Chronicle*, 18 January 1773, 3; *Daily Advertiser*, 22 January 1773, 1; *Daily Advertiser*, 29 January 1773, 2.
66. *Daily Advertiser*, 10 May 1774, 1.
67. See, for example, *Gazetteer and New Daily Advertiser*, 4 June 1774, 3; *Daily Advertiser*, 2 July 1774, 1.
68. Bowen, 'Pests of Human Society', 40–1.
69. Samuel Johnson, *A Dictionary of the English Language*, 2 vols. (London, 1755), ii.
70. Anon., *The Life and Real Adventures of Hamilton Murray. Written by Himself*, 3 vols. (London, 1759), ii, 95.
71. [Thomas Mortimer], *Every Man His Own Broker: Or, A Guide to Exchange-Alley* (London, 1761), xi.
72. Thomas Mortimer, *Every Man His Own Broker: Or, A Guide to Exchange-Alley*, 10th edn (London, 1785), xix–xx.
73. Mortimer, *Every Man His Own Broker*, 10th edn, xvii–xviii.
74. Paul Crosthwaite, Peter Knight, Nicky Marsh, Helen Paul, and James Taylor, *Invested: How Three Centuries of Stock Market Advice Reshaped Our Money, Markets, and Minds* (Chicago, 2022), ch. 1.
75. E. Victor Morgan and W. A. Thomas, *The Stock Exchange: Its History and Functions*, 2nd edn (London, 1969), 68; Ranald Michie, *The London Stock Exchange: A History* (Oxford, 2001), 31; *British Magazine*, 1 December 1760, 721.
76. *Leeds Intelligencer*, 23 December 1760, 1; *London Evening Post*, 27–9 November 1760, 3. See also *London Evening Post*, 23–5 October 1760, 3.
77. *Public Advertiser*, 9 June 1762, 2.
78. *St James's Chronicle*, 12–15 June 1762, 4.
79. *Craftsman or Say's Weekly Journal*, 27 April 1771, 4; *Gazetteer and New Daily Advertiser*, 16 July 1772, 4.
80. *Daily Advertiser*, 15 July 1773, 1.
81. Michie, *London Stock Exchange*, 31; Duguid, *Story of the Stock Exchange*, 62.
82. 'An Historical, Emblematical, Patriotical and Political Print, representing the English Balloon, or National Debt in the Year 1782, with a full view of the Stock Exchange, and its supporters the Financiers, Bulls, Bears, Brokers, Lame Ducks, and others': The British Museum, <https://www.britishmuseum.org/collection/object/P_1866-1114-620>.
83. The print is signed by Elizabeth, after a design by William Phelps.
84. *The Times*, 8 November 1793, 1, 4.
85. *The World*, 16 November 1793, 4.
86. *London Chronicle*, 19–21 November 1793, 2. Another report said that James 'persuaded her to go in men's clothes, telling her no person would do business with a woman': *Morning Post*, 16 November 1793, 3.
87. Elizabeth Hennessy, *Coffee House to Cyber Market: 200 Years of the London Stock Exchange* (London, 2001), 21–4.
88. Morgan and Thomas, *The Stock Exchange*, 68–71.
89. *Rules and Regulations Adopted by the Committee for General Purposes of the Stock-Exchange* (London, 1812), 18.
90. The measure was imposed to protect market participants against losses that might be made in other sectors of the economy: Michie, *London Stock Exchange*, 38–40.

222 NOTES TO PAGES 23-8

91. Anne L. Murphy, *Virtuous Bankers: A Day in the Life of the Eighteenth-Century Bank of England* (Princeton and Oxford, 2023), ch. 3.
92. Daniel Michael Abramson, 'Money's Architecture: The Building of the Bank of England, 1731–1833' (PhD thesis, Harvard University, 1993), 251–6.
93. *The Diary or Woodfall's Register*, 3 August 1791, 2.
94. Bank of England, Secretary's Department: Committee of Inspection for the Accountant's Offices, Minutes (1802–06), M5/221: 5 March 1806, f. 188, Bank of England Archive; Secretary's Department: Committee of Inspection for the Accountant's Offices, Minutes (1797–1802), M5/220: 23 October 1800, f. 14, Bank of England Archive.
95. Bank of England, Secretary's Department: Committee of Inspection for the Accountant's Offices, Minutes (1802–06), M5/221: 5 March 1806, f. 188, Bank of England Archive.
96. Morgan and Thomas, *The Stock Exchange*, 53.
97. Anne Murphy's samplings of Bank of England transfer books highlight women as investors but not seemingly acting as jobbers or brokers: Murphy, *Virtuous Bankers*, 91–101.
98. J. G. A. Pocock, 'Virtues, Rights, and Manners: A Model for Historians of Political Thought', *Political Theory* 9, no. 3 (1981): 353–68, at 366. For a discussion, see Paul Langford, 'The Uses of Eighteenth-Century Politeness', *Transactions of the Royal Historical Society* 12 (2002): 311–31.
99. Thomas Mortimer, *Every Man His Own Broker: Or, A Guide to Exchange-Alley*, 5th edn (London, 1762), xii.
100. Mortimer, *Every Man His Own Broker*, 5th edn, 69–70.
101. *St James's Chronicle*, 28–30 January 1762, 4. See also Mortimer, *Every Man His Own Broker*, 5th edn, 92–4.
102. Charles Hales, *The Bank Mirror; Or, A Guide to the Funds* (London, [1796]), 44–5.
103. Anne L. Murphy, 'Performing Public Credit at the Eighteenth-Century Bank of England', *Journal of British Studies* 58, no. 1 (2019): 58–78, at 74; *St James's Chronicle*, 31 August–September 1786, 2; *Bell's Weekly Messenger*, 21 June 1801, 5.
104. The term 'waiter' was a legacy from the coffee house days, which was still used long into the twentieth century.
105. James Grant, *The Great Metropolis*, 2 vols. (Philadelphia, 1838), ii, 32–4.
106. 'The National Debt and the Stock Exchange', *Blackwood's Edinburgh Magazine* 66, no. 410 (December 1849), 668.
107. Amy Thomas, ' "Mart of the World": An Architectural and Geographical History of the London Stock Exchange', *The Journal of Architecture* 17, no. 6 (2012): 1009–48, at 1041.
108. 'A Peep into the Stock Exchange', *Metropolitan* 2, no. 6 (October 1831), 169.
109. 'A Peep', 170.
110. Karel, 'A Second Peep into the Stock Exchange, *Metropolitan* 2, no. 7 (November 1831), 314. The second article was signed 'Karel', who was explicitly identified as the author of the first article the previous month.
111. Karel, 'A Second Peep', 315–16.
112. 'A Peep', 170–1.
113. Ben Griffin, *The Politics of Gender in Victorian Britain: Masculinity, Political Culture, and the Struggle for Women's Rights* (Cambridge, 2012), 173.
114. 'A Peep', 171.
115. 'A Peep', 173.
116. Joyce Goggin and Frans De Bruyn, *Comedy and Crisis: Pieter Langendijk, the Dutch, and the Speculative Bubbles of 1720* (Liverpool, 2020).
117. Eugene N. White, 'The Paris Bourse, 1724–1814: Experiments in Microstructure', in *Finance, Intermediaries, and Economic Development*, edited by Stanley L. Engerman, Philip T. Hoffman, Jean-Laurent Rosenthal, and Kenneth L. Sokoloff (Cambridge, 2009), 34–74, at 41; Alex Preda, 'In the Enchanted Grove: Financial Conversations and the Marketplace in England and France in the 18th Century', *Journal of Historical Sociology* 14, no. 3 (2001): 276–307, at 286.
118. Nathalie Sigot, 'Breaking the Rules: Mathilde Méliot, the First Woman Economist and Feminist, Member of the French Société d'économie politique', Oeconomia 12, no.3 (2022): 519–51.
119. *Morning Post*, 4 November 1833, 4; *The Standard*, 13 August 1834, 3; *The News*, 17 August 1834, 5; *Boston Courier*, 6 February 1840, 4; *The Standard*, 19 October 1844, 4; Victoria E. Thompson, *The Virtuous Marketplace: Women and Men, Money and Politics in Paris, 1830–1870* (Baltimore, MD, 2000), 150–1.
120. *Bradford Observer*, 4 September 1834, 3; Thompson, *Virtuous Marketplace*, 151–6.
121. 'T. Q.', *A Wall-Street Bear in Europe* (New York, 1855), 168–9.
122. For a particularly hostile account, see 'The Stock Exchange', *Fraser's Magazine* 4 (December 1831), 577–85.

NOTES TO PAGES 28–35   223

123. Gillian Russell, '"Faro's Daughters": Female Gamesters, Politics, and the Discourse of Finance in 1790s Britain', *Eighteenth-Century Studies* 33, no. 4 (2000): 481–504, at 497–8.
124. Anon., *Smash: A Sketch of the Times, Past, Present, and Again to Come* (London, 1860), 19.
125. George Robb, *Ladies of the Ticker: Women and Wall Street from the Gilded Age to the Great Depression* (Urbana, 2017), 30–1.
126. *Morning Post*, 9 June 1836, 4.
127. David Kynaston, *Till Time's Last Sand: A History of the Bank of England, 1694–2013* (London, 2020), 135.
128. For examples, see Michie, *London Stock Exchange*, 44–7, 61.
129. Janette Rutterford and Josephine Maltby, '"The Nesting Instinct": Women and Investment Risk in a Historical Context', *Accounting History* 12, no. 3 (2007): 305–27, at 317–18; Robb, *Ladies of the Ticker*, ch. 2.
130. 'Mexican Bonds', *Cobbett's Weekly Political Register*, 22 September 1827, 776–8.
131. These included, among others, *The Standard*, the *Morning Chronicle*, the *Devizes and Wiltshire Gazette*, and the *Leicester Chronicle*.
132. *Punch*, 1 November 1845, 191.
133. 'The Railway Queen', *Bentley's Miscellany* 18 (July 1845), 387–9.
134. W. A. Thomas, *The Provincial Stock Exchanges* (Abingdon, 2014), 50; R. C. Michie, *Money, Mania and Markets: Investment, Company Formation and the Stock Exchange in Nineteenth-Century Scotland* (Edinburgh, 1981), 103–4.
135. *Leeds Times*, 3 May 1845, 5; 'Loidis', letter to *The Times*, 18 November 1845, 7.
136. *Sheffield Times*, repr. in *Liverpool Albion*, 30 August 1847, 8.
137. *The Standard*, 26 August 1847, 2.
138. *The Pilot*, 1 September 1847, 4.
139. This idea is explored in relation to the novels of Anthony Trollope in Nancy Henry, '"Ladies Do It?": Victorian Women Investors in Fact and Fiction', in *Victorian Literature and Finance*, edited by Francis O'Gorman (Oxford, 2007), 111–31, at 125–6.
140. For a classic study along these lines, see Martha Vicinus, ed., *Suffer and Be Still: Women in the Victorian Age* (Bloomington, IN, 1972).
141. Amanda Vickery, 'Golden Age to Separate Spheres? A Review of the Categories and Chronology of English Women's History', *Historical Journal* 36, no. 2 (1993): 383–414.
142. Henry, 'Ladies Do It?', 112.
143. Hannah Barker, *The Business of Women: Female Enterprise and Urban Development in Northern England, 1760–1830* (Oxford, 2006), 172.
144. Barker, *Business of Women*, 170.
145. Patricia E. Johnson, 'Unlimited Liability: Women and Capital in Margaret Oliphant's *Hester*', *Nineteenth-Century Gender Studies* 6, no. 1 (2010): 1–14, at 3–4. Women's involvement in banking was recognized in Margaret Oliphant's 1883 novel *Hester: A Story of Contemporary Life.*
146. Margaret Dawes and Nesta Selwyn, *Women Who Made Money: Women Partners in British Private Banks, 1752–1906* (Bloomington, IN, 2010), xi.
147. 'A Banker's Daughter', *A Guide to the Unprotected in Every-day Matters Relating to Property and Income* (London and Cambridge, 1863), 14.
148. Janette Rutterford and Josephine Maltby, '"The Widow, the Clergyman and the Reckless": Women Investors in England, 1830–1914', *Feminist Economics* 12, nos. 1–2 (2006): 111–38, at 119–20.
149. David Kynaston, *The City of London*, vol. 1, *A World of Its Own, 1815–1890* (London, 1995), 235–43.
150. 'Justicia', letter to *The Times*, 11 December 1866, 4.
151. *Weekly Dispatch*, 4 November 1866, 8.
152. *Punch's Pocket Book* for 1867, repr. in *Daily News*, 6 December 1866, 2.
153. *Punch*, 1 December 1866, 220.
154. Cited in Heidi Egginton and Zoë Thomas, eds., *Precarious Professionals: Gender, Identities and Social Change in Modern Britain* (London, 2021), 27.
155. Griffin, *Politics of Gender*, 178, 172.
156. Griffin, *Politics of Gender*, 191, 189.

Chapter 2

1. *New York Herald*, 20 January 1870, 9.
2. *New York Herald*, 22 January 1870, 10.
3. *New York Herald*, 22 January 1870, 10; *The World*, 8 February 1870, repr. in Victoria Claflin Woodhull and Tennessee C. Claflin, *The Human Body the Temple of God; Or, the Philosophy of Sociology* (London, 1890), 292–3.

224   NOTES TO PAGES 35-9

4. *New York Herald*, 22 January 1870, 10.
5. *The Revolution*, 10 March 1870, 154.
6. *The Revolution*, 24 March 1870, 188.
7. *New York Herald*, 5 February 1870, 8.
8. *New York Times*, 6 February 1870, 8; *Sycamore True Republican*, 9 February 1870, 1; Myra Macpherson, *The Scarlet Sisters: Sex, Suffrage, and Scandal in the Gilded Age* (New York, 2014), 3–27.
9. George Robb, *Ladies of the Ticker: Women and Wall Street from the Gilded Age to the Great Depression* (Urbana, 2017), 115–16.
10. *Berkshire County Eagle*, 17 March 1870, 4.
11. Lois Beachy Underhill, *The Woman Who Ran for President: The Many Lives of Victoria Woodhull* (Bridgehampton, NY, 1995), 72–4; Robb, *Ladies of the Ticker*, 120.
12. Robb, *Ladies of the Ticker*, 210 n. 65.
13. Robb, *Ladies of the Ticker*, 120–1, 125–8.
14. William Worthington Fowler, *Inside Life in Wall Street; Or How Great Fortunes are Lost and Won* (Hartford, CT, 1873), 456. See also Henry Clews, *Twenty-Eight Years in Wall Street* (New York, 1887), 439.
15. *The Times*, 7 February 1870, 4; *The Standard*, 24 February 1870, 5; *Dundee Courier*, 11 March 1870, 2.
16. *Ladies' Treasury*, 1 May 1871, 162.
17. *New York Times*, 14 March 1880, 11; *New York Times*, 12 January 1882, 10; *New York Times*, 11 September 1882, 8; *Northwest Enterprise*, 28 April 1883, 1; *Indianapolis Journal*, 6 December 1883, 2; *New York Times*, 8 April 1884, 8. Several are discussed in Robb, *Ladies of the Ticker*, 92–5, 129–31.
18. *Edinburgh Evening News*, 17 February 1880, 3; *Pall Mall Gazette*, 27 March 1883, 11.
19. Anthony Trollope, *Is He Popenjoy?*, 3rd edn (London, 1879), 391.
20. *Aldershot Military Gazette*, 10 October 1885, 6. The column appeared in many other provincial papers.
21. *Englishwoman's Review*, 15 October 1885, 452; *Exeter and Plymouth Gazette*, 27 October 1885, 3.
22. *Englishwoman's Review*, 15 January 1886, 25; *Bristol Mercury and Daily Post*, 6 February 1886, 6.
23. *Bristol Mercury and Daily Post*, 23 January 1886, 6.
24. *Lady of the House*, 15 September 1899, 1.
25. Opportunities in London retail are explored in Jessica P. Clark, 'Pomeroy v. Pomeroy: Beauty, Modernity, and the Female Entrepreneur in *Fin-de-Siècle* London', *Women's History Review* 22, no. 6 (2013): 877–903. For a study emphasizing later nineteenth-century levels of female activity outside the capital, see Jennifer Aston, *Female Entrepreneurship in Nineteenth-Century England: Engagement in the Urban Economy* (Cham, 2016).
26. Ranald C. Michie, *Guilty Money: The City of London in Victorian and Edwardian Culture, 1815–1914* (London, 2009), 75.
27. Charles Hollis, *Polly Mountemple: A Fin de Siècle Story of the Stage* (London, 1891), 87.
28. Ranald Michie, *The London Stock Exchange: A History* (Oxford, 2001), 88.
29. Michie, *London Stock Exchange*, 77, 85–6.
30. Michie, *London Stock Exchange*, 77.
31. Michie, *London Stock Exchange*, 99.
32. Jessica Ziparo, *This Grand Experiment: When Women Entered the Federal Workforce in Civil War-Era Washington DC* (Chapel Hill, NC, 2017). A handful of London mercantile firms had already started employing women clerks before this: Susanne Dohrn, 'Pioneers in a Dead-End Profession: The First Women Clerks in Banks and Insurance Companies', in *The White-Blouse Revolution: Female Office Workers since 1870*, edited by Gregory Anderson (Manchester, 1988), 48–66, at 53.
33. *Belfast News-Letter*, 4 October 1873, 3; *Morning Post*, 7 March 1874, 3.
34. David Kynaston, *Till Time's Last Sand: A History of the Bank of England, 1694–2013* (London, 2020), 241–2.
35. Ellen Jordan, 'The Lady Clerks at the Prudential: The Beginning of Vertical Segregation by Sex in Clerical Work in Nineteenth-Century Britain', *Gender and History* 8, no. 1 (1996): 65–81, at 79.
36. *Daily Telegraph*, 22 January 1897, 4; Timothy Alborn, 'Quill-Driving: British Life-Insurance Clerks and Occupational Mobility, 1800–1914', *Business History Review* 82, no. 1 (2008): 31–58, at 41.
37. Jordan, 'Lady Clerks at the Prudential', 66; Dohrn, 'Pioneers in a Dead-End Profession', 57.
38. Michael Heller, *London Clerical Workers, 1880–1914* (Abingdon, 2016), 124. The first superintendent of women clerks at the Bank of England eventually left to become a librarian because she felt she was stuck in a 'backwater' with 'no prospect of rising': Janet E. Courtney, *Recollected in Tranquillity* (London, 1926), 167–8.

NOTES TO PAGES 39–42 225

39. A. T. Vanderbilt, *What To Do With Our Girls; Or, Employments for Women* (London, 1884), 118–20. Clerical jobs were becoming more available in the General Post Office and the civil service: Peter Wardley, 'Women, Mechanization and Cost Savings in Twentieth Century British Banks and Other Financial Institutions', in *A Business and Labour History of Britain: Case Studies of Britain in the Nineteenth and Twentieth Centuries*, edited by Mike Richardson and Peter Nicholls (Houndmills, 2011), 32–59, at 33. The 1871 census listed 1,446 female clerks; by 1911, this had risen to 124,843: Heller, *London Clerical Workers*, 111.
40. Michie, *London Stock Exchange*, 103–4, 109–10, 200–1, 205.
41. David Kynaston, *The City of London*, vol. 1, *A World of its Own, 1815–1890* (London, 1995), 289.
42. *Daily Telegraph*, 22 January 1897, 4; *Northern Daily Mail and South Durham Herald*, 26 February 1898, 6.
43. *Pitman's Shorthand Writers' Phrase Books and Guides: Stockbroking and Finance* (London, 1914), 6.
44. In the economy more generally, women were often forced into entrepreneurial behaviour through lack of access to waged labour: Carry van Lieshout, Harry Smith, Piero Montebruno, and Robert J. Bennett, 'Female Entrepreneurship: Business, Marriage, and Motherhood in England and Wales, 1851–1911', *Social History* 44, no. 4 (2019): 440–68, at 442.
45. See, for example, *The Times*, 5 April 1866, 5.
46. Charles Duguid, *The Story of the Stock Exchange: Its History and Position* (London, 1901), 296–301.
47. *London and China Telegraph*, 28 November 1859, 16.
48. 1861 Census, RG 9/1739, f. 134, 9; for Goodeve's obituary, see: *Bristol Mercury and Daily Post*, 18 June 1884, 8.
49. *The Queen*, 26 August 1893, 390.
50. *Women's Penny Paper*, 22 December 1888, 1.
51. *Woman's Leader*, 1 April 1920, 211; Peter D. Groenewegen, 'A Weird and Wonderful Partnership: Mary Paley and Alfred Marshall, 1877–1924', *History of Economic Ideas* 1, no. 1 (1993): 71–109.
52. *Women's Penny Paper*, 22 December 1888, 1.
53. *Whitstable Times and Herne Bay Herald*, 17 October 1885, 2. Amy was one of the executors of Henry's will: Henry Hurry Goodeve, 15 August 1884, National Probate Calendar.
54. *The Queen*, 26 August 1893, 390.
55. *Englishwoman's Review*, 15 January 1886, 25; *The Queen*, 26 August 1893, 390.
56. Broader studies have also found women resorting to entrepreneurship at different stages of the lifecycle: see, for example, Alison C. Kay, *The Foundations of Female Entrepreneurship: Enterprise, Home and Household in London, c.1800–1870* (London, 2009), 121–2.
57. Hannah Barker, *The Business of Women: Female Enterprise and Urban Development in Northern England, 1760–1830* (Oxford, 2006), 105–10.
58. Members saw no problem with the rule, arguing that if a member fell seriously ill, 'his staff should be able to carry on his business for him': *The Standard*, 30 May 1912, 12.
59. Abbott had been the victim of the muckraking journalism of Henry Labouchere: James Taylor, '"Distrust all Advice…and Make No Exception in Favour of our Advice": Financial Knowledge and Knowingness in Late Victorian Britain', *English Historical Review* 136, no. 580 (2021): 619–50, at 629–31.
60. London Stock Exchange (hereafter LSE), General Purposes Committee Minutes, MS 14600/55: 14 May 1888, 55–6, Guildhall Library.
61. *Manchester Courier*, 16 April 1888, 7; *South Wales Daily News*, 9 May 1888, 3.
62. *Birkenhead News*, 12 May 1888, 2; *Railway News*, 4 August 1888, 190. By the 1891 census, Frances was of 'no occupation' and living in a small village in Hertfordshire: RG 12/1052, f. 57, 11.
63. Find a Grave, memorial page for Emma Patience Swanton Robson (11 Jul 1862–4 Nov 1920), <https://www.findagrave.com/memorial/241467049/emma_patience-robson>; *Evening Irish Times*, 18 October 1907, 4.
64. *Cork Constitution*, 20 February 1886, 4; *York Herald*, 13 February 1890, 6.
65. *North-Eastern Daily Gazette*, 12 February 1890, 3.
66. *Woman's Life*, 5 March 1898, 527–8.
67. William Robert Robson, 9 July 1890, National Probate Calendar; Anglican Parish Registers, 44M86/PR1, Edith Margaret Robson, baptised 14 November 1888: Hampshire Archives and Local Studies, Winchester, accessed Ancestry.co.uk.
68. *Woman's Life*, 5 March 1898, 527–8.
69. Eleanor Gordon and Gwyneth Nair, 'The Economic Role of Middle-Class Women in Victorian Glasgow', *Women's History Review* 9, no. 4 (2000): 791–814, at 794–6.
70. Van Lieshout et al., 'Female Entrepreneurship', 462.

226 NOTES TO PAGES 42–5

71. Macpherson, *Scarlet Sisters*, 259–75.
72. Indeed, the press recycled 'facts' that she and Victoria had invented about themselves, such as the claim that they descended from 'an old American family': *Hull News*, 4 February 1899, 23.
73. For examples, see *Banffshire Advertiser*, 20 June 1895, 6; *Wiltshire Chronicle*, 17 August 1895, 2; *Bucks Herald*, 24 August 1895, 6.
74. *Westminster Gazette*, 20 December 1898, 8.
75. *Westminster Gazette*, 20 December 1898, 8.
76. 1871 Census, RG 10/790, f. 37, 14; marriage of Lionel Godolphin Brooke and Gertrude Isabella Goodeve, 30 April 1895, Pembrokeshire Anglican Baptisms, Marriages and Burials, Archives Wales, accessed Ancestry.co.uk.
77. In 1901 they were lodging at a boarding house in Paddington, with two daughters aged 5 and 1; a third was to follow shortly: 1901 Census, RG 13/14, f. 9, 9; 1911 Census, RG 14/398, sch. 226.
78. *Manchester Courier*, 30 November 1906, 6; *Belfast Telegraph*, 12 June 1931, 11.
79. *Daily Mail*, 7 November 1912, 5.
80. *Bassett's Directory*, 1875–6; *Bassett's Directory*, 1880–1 (both via Clare County Library: <https://www.clarelibrary.ie/eolas/coclare/genealogy/genealog.htm>); *Freeman's Journal*, 13 Feb. 1883, 8.
81. *Sport* (Dublin), 18 October 1884, 5.
82. *Strand Magazine*, January 1892, 530–1; *Freeman's Journal*, 5 April 1886, 6; *Freeman's Journal*, 3 May 1887, 4; *Freeman's Journal*, 8 February 1894, 5; *Freeman's Journal*, 26 December 1894, 8; *Freeman's Journal*, 11 November 1899, 4; *Daily Telegraph*, 17 June 1904, 10.
83. *Freeman's Journal*, 3 July 1894, 3; *Daily Mail*, 17 June 1904, 3; Census of Ireland, 1901, National Archives of Ireland: <https://www.census.nationalarchives.ie/reels/nai003743351/>. The Dublin Stock Exchange did not ban members' wives from being engaged in business: W. A. Thomas, *The Stock Exchanges of Ireland* (Liverpool, 1986), 78, 96 n. 7.
84. *Manchester Courier*, 15 February 1866, 4; *London Gazette*, 28 March 1876, 2179; 1881 Census, RG 11/4223, f. 4, 2.
85. *Preston Herald*, 16 November 1912, 5.
86. The 1901 census lists them both as 'stock and sharebroker assistant', while in a later interview, Marianne stated that she was her father's chief assistant: RG 13/3963, f. 40, 5; *Preston Herald*, 16 November 1912, 5.
87. For evidence of the partnership, see *Financial Times* (hereafter *FT*), 10 October 1907, 3; *Preston Herald*, 19 December 1908, 1. For Marianne taking over the firm, see *Preston Herald*, 4 December 1909, 1; *Preston Herald*, 16 November 1912, 5. For Frederic's obituary, see *Manchester Courier*, 22 January 1910, 9.
88. Michie, *London Stock Exchange*, 71–3.
89. David R. Green, Alastair Owens, Josephine Maltby, and Janette Rutterford, 'Men, Women, and Money: An Introduction', in *Men, Women, and Money: Perspectives on Gender, Wealth, and Investment, 1850–1930*, edited by David R. Green, Alastair Owens, Josephine Maltby, and Janette Rutterford (Oxford, 2011), 1–30, at 27–8.
90. Mary Beth Combs, '"A Measure of Legal Independence": The 1870 Married Women's Property Act and the Portfolio Allocations of British Wives', *Journal of Economic History* 64, no. 4 (2005): 1028–57.
91. Janette Rutterford, David R. Green, Josephine Maltby, and Alastair Owens, 'Who Comprised the Nation of Shareholders? Gender and Investment in Great Britain, *c.*1870–1935', *Economic History Review* 64, no. 1 (2011): 157–87, at 169–72.
92. James Martin, *The Broker's Correspondent: Being a Letter Writer for Stock Exchange Business* (London, 1893), iv.
93. *Sheffield Evening Telegraph and Star*, 9 December 1895, 2; see also *Yorkshire Herald*, 13 April 1894, 4.
94. Female clients 'generally wanted about 15 per cent with absolute security', complained one broker: David T. Smith, 'A Stockbroker's Memories', *Blackwood's Magazine*, October 1933, 466–75, at 471. See also George Robb, 'Women and White-Collar Crime: Debates on Gender, Fraud and the Corporate Economy in England and America, 1850–1930', *British Journal of Criminology* 46, no. 6 (2006): 1058–72, at 1062–4; Janette Rutterford and Josephine Maltby, '"The Widow, the Clergyman and the Reckless": Women Investors in England, 1830–1914', *Feminist Economics* 12, nos. 1–2 (2006): 111–38, at 119–21.
95. *Lady's Pictorial*, repr. in *Bulletin of the National Anti-Gambling League*, May 1894, 86.
96. There were over 200 members of the Society of Women Journalists by 1896: Barbara Onslow, *Women of the Press in Nineteenth-Century Britain* (Houndmills, 2000), 49.

NOTES TO PAGES 45–50   227

97. Drew was a vocal advocate for the interests of women in journalism. Her 'Ladies' Column', under the penname 'Aurora', ran for over a quarter of a century: Anna M. Sebba, 'Drew, Catharine (1825/6–1910)', *Oxford Dictionary of National Biography* (hereafter *ODNB*); Susan Hamilton, '"Her Usual Daring Style": Feminist New Journalism, Pioneering Women, and Traces of Frances Power Cobbe', in *Women in Journalism at the* Fin de Siècle: *Making a Name for Herself*, edited by F. Elizabeth Gray (Houndmills, 2012), 39–43; *Illustrated London News*, 1 October 1910, 516.

98. *Aldershot Military Gazette*, 10 October 1885, 6.

99. *Englishwoman's Review*, 15 October 1885, 452.

100. *Bristol Mercury and Daily Post*, 23 January 1886, 6.

101. *The Echo*, 17 April 1888, 1.

102. *Leicester Chronicle*, 2 March 1907, 2.

103. *The Queen*, 26 August 1893, 390.

104. For examples, see *Myra's Journal*, 1 July 1888, 433; *Wrexham Advertiser*, 29 March 1890, 2; *Women's Penny Paper*, 5 July 1890, 439.

105. *The Echo*, 17 April 1888, 1.

106. *Englishwoman's Review*, 15 October 1888, 457; *North-Eastern Daily Gazette*, 12 September 1890, 4.

107. Paul Crosthwaite, Peter Knight, Nicky Marsh, Helen Paul, & James Taylor, *Invested: How Three Centuries of Stock Market Advice Reshaped Our Money, Markets and Minds* (Chicago, 2022), 79–80.

108. These appeared in the April, July, and October editions.

109. These appeared in the January and December 1893 editions. Additionally, in her spare time, she gave talks to societies promoting thrift for women: *The Queen*, 26 August 1893, 390.

110. *Woman's Weekly*, 21 January 1899, 3.

111. *Woman's Life*, 5 March 1898, 527.

112. *Englishwoman's Review*, 15 April 1892, 85–7.

113. *Women's Penny Paper*, 22 December 1888, 1.

114. *South Wales Daily News*, 9 December 1898, 8.

115. *Woman's Life*, 5 March 1898, 527.

116. *Preston Herald*, 16 November 1912, 5.

117. LSE, General Purposes Committee Minutes, MS 14600/86: Amy E. Bell to the Committee of the Stock Exchange, 15 February 1910, 16, Guildhall Library.

118. Stephen P. Walker, 'Professions and Patriarchy Revisited: Accountancy in England and Wales, 1887–1914', *Accounting History Review* 21, no. 2 (2011): 185–225; Vanessa Heggie, 'Women Doctors and Lady Nurses: Class, Education, and the Professional Victorian Woman', *Bulletin of the History of Medicine* 89, no. 2 (2015): 267–92, at 271–2; Nicola Verdon, 'Business and Pleasure: Middle-Class Women's Work and the Professionalization of Farming in England, 1890–1939', *Journal of British Studies* 51, no. 2 (2012): 393–415, at 402–3.

119. *The Queen*, 26 August 1893, 390.

120. Margaret Walsh, 'Gendered Endeavours: Women and the Reshaping of Business Culture', *Women's History Review* 14, no. 2 (2005): 181–202, at 193.

121. *Woman's Leader*, 19 March 1920, 166.

122. *The Queen*, 26 August 1893, 390.

123. *Woman's Leader*, 1 April 1920, 211.

124. [Dinah Craik], 'About Money', *Contemporary Review* 50 (September 1886): 364–72, at 367.

125. *The Queen*, 26 August 1893, 390.

126. Bell to the Committee of the Stock Exchange, 15 February 1910.

127. *Woman's Life*, 5 March 1898, 527; *Westminster Gazette*, 20 December 1898, 8.

128. *Preston Herald*, 16 November 1912, 5.

129. *Daily Express*, 15 August 1913, 7.

130. Rutterford and Maltby, 'The Widow, the Clergyman and the Reckless', 120.

131. Sally Mitchell, *The Fallen Angel: Chastity, Class and Women's Reading, 1835–1880* (Bowling Green, OH, 1981), 112; Craik, 'About Money', 365.

132. Craik, 'About Money', 365. See also Anon., *Counsel to Ladies and Easy-Going Men on Their Business Investments* (London, 1892), xi–xii.

133. [David Morier Evans], *The City: Or, The Physiology of London Business* (London, 1845), 62.

134. *Sheffield Independent*, 4 November 1871, 1.

135. John Handel, 'The Material Politics of Finance: The Ticker Tape and the London Stock Exchange, 1860s–1890s', *Enterprise and Society* 23, no. 3 (2022): 857–87.

136. James Taylor, 'Inside and Outside the London Stock Exchange: Stockbrokers and Speculation in Late Victorian Britain', *Enterprise and Society* 22, no. 3 (2021): 842–77, at 856–7.

228   NOTES TO PAGES 50–3

137. Dilwyn Porter, '"Speciousness is the Bucketeer's Watchword and Outrageous Effrontery his Capital": Financial Bucket Shops in the City of London, c.1880–1939', in *Cultures of Selling: Perspectives on Consumption and Society since 1700*, edited by John Benson and Laura Ugolini (Aldershot, 2006), 103–25.

138. It has proven impossible to identify Jane's maiden name.

139. The 1881 census gives her age as 39: RG 11/95, f. 49, 2. The *Post Office London Street Directory* for 1877 is the first to list her as living at 8 Arlington Street (p. 161).

140. 1881 Census, RG 11/95, f. 49, 2.

141. *The Standard*, 9 February 1887, 6; *South Wales Echo*, 9 February 1887, 3.

142. 1871 Census, RG 10/1657, f. 55, 8.

143. 1881 Census, RG 11/139, f. 56, 43–4.

144. It was becoming more common for women to dine unchaperoned in London restaurants: Brenda Assael, *The London Restaurant, 1840–1914* (Oxford, 2018), 199.

145. Marriage of Sidney Herbert Cronmire and Alice Matilda Cressey, 8 October 1885: Sutton, Surrey, Church of England Marriages and Banns, P42/1/5, accessed Ancestry.co.uk.

146. *The Standard*, 27 March 1895, 2.

147. *Montgomery v. Harrison*, reported in *The Standard*, 12 November 1885, 6; *The Times*, 12 November 1885, 7; *Devon and Exeter Daily Gazette*, 14 November 1885, 4.

148. *Old Bailey Proceedings Online*, February 1886, trial of Sidney Herbert Cronmire alias Herbert Harrison (20) (t18860208-282); *The Times*, 8 April 1886, 12.

149. *The Times*, 9 March 1894, 10; *Morning Post*, 26 March 1895, 6.

150. For an example of such a device, see *The Times*, 18 October 1889, 3.

151. *Morning Post*, 26 March 1895, 6.

152. *Morning Post*, 9 April 1895, 7; *Morning Post*, 10 April 1895, 6. Press adverts for W. Freeman began appearing in November 1889: *Freeman's Journal*, 9 November 1889, 3; *Belfast News-Letter*, 29 November 1889, 3.

153. *The Standard*, 10 April 1895, 6.

154. *The Times*, 14 May 1895, 14.

155. *The Standard*, 10 April 1895, 6.

156. 1881 Census, RG 11/2377, f. 42, 6.

157. Marriage of Frederick Henry Bingham and Olivia Jane Masters, 26 March 1882, City of Westminster Archives Centre, Westminster Church of England Parish Registers, Reference: STG/PR/7/72, accessed Ancestry.co.uk; 1881 Census, RG 11/93, f. 120, 26.

158. *Oakland Tribune*, 17 January 1926, 85; *The Register* (Adelaide), 27 March 1923, 11; Osgood Hardy, 'British Nitrates and the Balmaceda Revolution', *Pacific Historical Review* 17, no. 2 (1948): 165–80, at 176; William Edmundson, *The Nitrate King: A Biography of 'Colonel' John Thomas North* (New York, 2011).

159. 'Cheiro' (Count Louis Hamon), *Confessions: Memoirs of a Modern Seer* (London, 1932), 237.

160. The firm had operated unsuccessfully from this address in 1890–1, but at this point it was run as a partnership by William Ward, first with Richard Simpson, then with Arthur Millar. Olive Bingham took it over at some point after this. For the relevant dissolutions of partnership, see *London Gazette*, 12 June 1891, 3130; *London Gazette*, 22 December 1891, 7094.

161. Olivia Mary Stevens, baptised 21 August 1891, London Church of England Parish Registers, P84/Luk/001, 103; Arthur Frederick William de Courcy, baptised 19 August 1894, London Church of England Parish Registers, P84/Phi/004, 146, accessed Ancestry.co.uk.

162. *Hull Daily Mail*, 18 December 1890, 3.

163. Exchange Telegraph Company, Correspondence, Reports etc., Relating to the London Stock Exchange, MS 23028: H. W. Mackusick to Exchange Telegraph Company, 29 June 1894, London Metropolitan Archives.

164. *Pall Mall Gazette*, 15 June 1888, 16.

165. *Morning Post*, 10 April 1895, 6.

166. Lizzy [*sic*] Matilda Beech, baptised 10 December 1865, London Church of England Parish Registers, P82/Geo1/010, accessed Ancestry.co.uk; 1881 Census, RG 11/323, f. 88, 3.

167. In the 1891 census, her occupation was 'Stock dealer's clerk': RG 12/469, f. 117, 44.

168. Paul Johnson, *Making the Market: Victorian Origins of Corporate Capitalism* (Cambridge: Cambridge, 2010), 157–8.

169. Companies Registration Office, Files of Dissolved Companies, BT 31/3451/20868: Company No. 20868, Universal Stock Exchange Company Ltd. Incorporated in 1885: List of Persons Holding Shares in the Universal Stock Exchange Company, 6 August 1888, The National Archives (hereafter TNA).

NOTES TO PAGES 53–60   229

170. *FT*, 12 June 1893, 2; *FT*, 14 June 1893, 2; *Western Morning News*, 24 May 1894, 8.
171. *Women's Penny Paper*, 22 December 1888, 2.
172. David C. Itzkowitz, 'Fair Enterprise or Extravagant Speculation: Investment, Speculation, and Gambling in Victorian England', *Victorian Studies* 45, no. 1 (2002): 121–47, at 139–43.
173. Jennifer Aston and Paolo di Martino, 'Risk, Success, and Failure: Female Entrepreneurship in Late Victorian and Edwardian England', *Economic History Review* 70, no. 3 (2017): 837–58.
174. See, for example, advert for John Shaw, *The Times*, 13 June 1888, 14.
175. *Daily News*, 15 January 1885, 1.
176. *FT*, 7 November 1893, 2; *FT*, 15 February 1894, 4.
177. Walker was advertising commission-free terms in January 1885 when leading outsider John Shaw only began advertising such terms in November of that year: *Daily News*, 15 January 1885, 1; *The Standard*, 4 November 1885, 1.
178. *Daily Telegraph*, 5 January 1895, 10; *Daily Telegraph*, 16 January 1895, 4.
179. *The Standard*, 27 March 1895, 2; *Daily News*, 9 April 1895, 3.
180. *Daily News*, 9 April 1895, 3.
181. *The Times*, 9 March 1894, 10.
182. *Morning Post*, 9 April 1895, 7.
183. *Daily News*, 9 April 1895, 3.
184. Companies Registration Office, Files of Dissolved Companies, BT 31/5713/39941: Company No. 39941, Central Stock Exchange Ltd. Incorporated in 1893: Memorandum of Association of the Central Stock Exchange, Limited, 16 November 1893, TNA.
185. *Morning Post*, 23 March 1893, 1; *FT*, 7 November 1893, 2. A firm of the same name had operated in the 1880s from a different address, but this was unconnected to Beech's business: *The Times*, 1 December 1892, 3.
186. *Daily Telegraph*, 1 March 1894, 1.
187. *Oxford Journal*, 26 January 1895, 8; *Essex Standard*, 16 March 1895, 4; *Kent and Sussex Courier*, 26 April 1885, 4. For more on this technique, see Taylor, 'Inside and Outside', 864.
188. *FT*, 24 September 1895, 2; *Truth*, 19 September 1895, 695.
189. A point stressed by Kay, *Foundations of Female Entrepreneurship*, 11–17.
190. *FT*, 14 September 1895, 4; *FT*, 24 September 1895, 2.
191. *The Standard*, 13 January 1890, 1.
192. *Daily News*, 9 April 1895, 3.
193. *Truth*, 24 January 1895, 223; *Truth*, 28 June 1894, 1508.
194. *Truth*, 28 June 1894, 1508. It advertised its manager as 'L. Robarts': *Truth*, 22 November 1894, 1204.
195. *FT*, 14 September 1895, 4.
196. *Northampton Mercury*, 27 September 1895, 5.
197. *FT*, 21 September 1894, 2. See also *FT*, 1 November 1894, 2.
198. *Women's Penny Paper*, 22 December 1888, 1.
199. *Daily Mail*, 7 November 1912, 5.
200. As argued in Aston, *Female Entrepreneurship*, 44–5.
201. See, for example, Aston, *Female Entrepreneurship*, 100; Kay, *Foundations of Female Entrepreneurship*, 124–5.
202. Van Lieshout et al., 'Female Entrepreneurship', 441.

Chapter 3

1. Julian Sturgis, *A Master of Fortune* (New York and London, [1896]), 95.
2. Sturgis, *Master of Fortune*, 97.
3. Nancy Henry notes that late nineteenth-century novels 'feature women investors as a matter of course', with a particular focus on the theme of financial independence: Nancy Henry, *Women, Literature and Finance in Victorian Britain: Cultures of Investment* (Cham, 2018), 267–8.
4. Sturgis, *Master of Fortune*, 96.
5. Sturgis, *Master of Fortune*, 93.
6. Sturgis, *Master of Fortune*, 114–15.
7. Sturgis, *Master of Fortune*, 118.
8. Elizabeth Lee, revised by Katharine Chubbuck, 'Sturgis, Julian Russell (1848–1904), *ODNB*.
9. Sturgis, *Master of Fortune*, 85, 175.
10. Sturgis, *Master of Fortune*, 85. For Thackeray, see Chapter 1.
11. Sturgis, *Master of Fortune*, 97.
12. Sturgis, *Master of Fortune*, 176.

230 NOTES TO PAGES 60-6

13. Sturgis, *Master of Fortune*, 175.
14. Sturgis, *Master of Fortune*, 170.
15. Sturgis, *Master of Fortune*, 185.
16. *The Sketch*, 15 January 1896, 8.
17. *Liverpool Mercury*, 22 January 1896, 7.
18. *Daily News*, 18 February 1896, 6; *The Bookman*, February 1896, 162.
19. *Morning Post*, 23 April 1896, 4; *The Athenaeum*, 22 February 1896, 248.
20. *Saturday Review*, 9 May 1896, 488; *The Times*, 4 April 1896, 12.
21. *The Academy*, 7 March 1896, 195.
22. *The Times*, 26 March 1896, 13.
23. *Yorkshire Evening Post*, 27 March 1896, 2; *Huddersfield Daily Examiner*, 28 March 1896, 3.
24. *St James's Gazette*, 26 March 1896, 3; *Social Review*, 25 April 1896, 782.
25. *The Echo*, 26 March 1896, 2.
26. Margaret Beetham, *A Magazine of Her Own? Domesticity and Desire in the Woman's Magazine, 1800–1914* (London and New York, 1996), 116.
27. Arlene Young, *From Spinster to Career Woman: Middle-Class Women and Work in Victorian England* (Montreal and Kingston, 2019), 18, 3.
28. Young, *From Spinster to Career Woman*, 162–3; Sally Mitchell, *The New Girl: Girls' Culture in England, 1880–1915* (New York, 1995).
29. Young, *From Spinster to Career Woman*, 158–69.
30. Though some counsel against exaggerating the extent of progress made: Gillian Sutherland, *In Search of the New Woman: Middle-Class Women and Work in Britain, 1870–1914* (Cambridge, 2015).
31. *Northampton Mercury*, 13 June 1890, 3. Robinson was a vice-president of the Liberal League, the party's answer to the Conservative Primrose League, which was committed to gender equality: *The Queen*, 9 July 1887, 62; *Northampton Mercury*, 17 December 1887, 7.
32. Reported in *Glasgow Herald*, 23 December 1893, 5.
33. *Western Mail*, 29 October 1885, 2.
34. *St Stephen's Review*, 17 April 1886, 36.
35. *The Globe*, 2 January 1891, 1.
36. *Dewsbury Chronicle and West Riding Advertiser*, 31 March 1894, 7.
37. *The Sketch*, 22 November 1893, 174.
38. *Daily News*, 10 April 1895, 6; *Penny Illustrated Paper*, 20 April 1895, 246.
39. Beetham, *Magazine of Her Own*, 132.
40. *Daily News*, 9 April 1895, 3.
41. Sally Ledger, 'The New Woman and the Crisis of Victorianism', in *Cultural Politics at the Fin de Siècle*, edited by Sally Ledger and Scott McCracken (Cambridge, 1995), 22–44, at 24–6.
42. *Westminster Gazette*, 13 May 1895, 6.
43. *Westminster Gazette*, 8 April 1895, 5; *Sussex Agricultural Express*, 26 April 1895, 6.
44. *Coventry Evening Telegraph*, 9 April 1895, 2.
45. *The Sketch*, 25 September 1895, 514; *The Sketch*, 2 October 1895, 570.
46. James Taylor, 'Inside and Outside the London Stock Exchange: Stockbrokers and Speculation in Late Victorian Britain', *Enterprise and Society* 22, no. 3 (2021): 842–77, at 850.
47. *Folkestone Express*, 15 February 1908, 8; *FT*, 29 October 1906, 6; *FT*, 14 October 1907, 5; *Graphic*, 4 July 1908, 28.
48. Ledger, 'New Woman', 26–7.
49. Katrina Rolley, 'Fashion, Femininity and the Fight for the Vote', *Art History* 13, no. 1 (1990): 47–71.
50. *Women's Penny Paper*, 22 December 1888, 1–2.
51. *The Star*, 3 May 1888, 1. See also *Torquay Times and South Devon Advertiser*, 7 May 1886, 3.
52. *Woman's Life*, 5 March 1898, 527–8.
53. *Woman's Weekly*, 21 January 1899, 3.
54. *Gloucester Journal*, 16 November 1912, 7.
55. Hats were frequently deployed as reassuring markers of middle-class femininity: Amy L. Montz, '"Now She's all Hat and Ideas": Fashioning the British Suffrage Movement', *Critical Studies in Fashion and Beauty* 3, nos. 1–2 (2012): 55–67, at 57–8.
56. Jennifer Aston, *Female Entrepreneurship in Nineteenth-Century England: Engagement in the Urban Economy* (Cham, 2016), 215; Hannah Barker, *The Business of Women: Female Enterprise and Urban Development in Northern England, 1760–1830* (Oxford, 2006), 89–90.
57. *Post Office London Directory for 1885*, 1239; *The United Kingdom Stock and Sharebrokers' Directory* [hereafter *UKSSD*] *for 1885–6*, 60.
58. *Post Office London Directory for 1893*, 1592; *Post Office London Directory for 1895*, 1676; *UKSSD for 1898–99*, 115.

NOTES TO PAGES 66–9   231

59. *Post Office London Directory* for *1894*, 1612. Bingham sometimes used the name Olive, and sometimes went by the name Bower, her lover's surname: *Commercial Gazette*, 21 March 1894, 270.
60. *UKSSD for 1900–1*, 127.
61. W. A. Thomas, *The Provincial Stock Exchanges* (Abingdon, 2014), 61.
62. *Huddersfield Daily Chronicle*, 29 July 1899, 5.
63. *UKSSD for 1904–5*, 148.
64. *UKSSD for 1911–12*, 164, 246.
65. LSE, General Purposes Committee Minutes, MS 14600/86: Amy E. Bell to the Committee of the Stock Exchange, 15 February 1910, 16, Guildhall Library. Whiteheads and Coles had West Country connections: *Devon and Exeter Daily Gazette*, 20 October 1919, 1. They also shared office space with Bell in Bucklersbury.
66. *Daily Express*, 15 August 1913, 7.
67. *Westminster Gazette*, 20 December 1898, 8.
68. *Hartlepool Mail*, 5 October 1894, 3.
69. Bingham managed to keep hold of her two machines for a little longer, seemingly through committing not to advertise, though she too was eventually culled, along with dozens of others, in 1894. Exchange Telegraph Company, Correspondence, reports etc., relating to the London Stock Exchange, MS 23028: 'List of Non-Members of Stock Ex. "Struck Off" after Agreement with Stock Ex. 1886 up to Date of Stock Ex. Letter April 1894'; 'List of Non-Members cut off in accordance with the Stk Ex Letter of April 1894', London Metropolitan Archives.
70. LSE, General Purposes Committee Minutes, MS 14600/51: 1 April 1885, 216–17, Guildhall Library.
71. Bell to the Committee of the Stock Exchange, 15 February 1910.
72. *Morning Post*, 9 April 1895, 7.
73. *The Standard*, 9 February 1887, 6.
74. LSE, General Purposes Committee Minutes, MS 14600/86: Millicent Fawcett to the Committee of the Stock Exchange, 28 February 1910, 49, Guildhall Library.
75. *Women's Union Journal: The Organ of the Women's Protective and Provident League*, 1 October 1886, 97; 1 November 1886, 104; 16 July 1888, 49; *Woman's Signal*, 15 March 1894, 172; *The Queen*, 19 May 1894, 813; *Woman's Leader*, 19 March 1920, 166. The presence of 'a lady stockbroker' was noted at a Votes for Women march in London in 1908 and this is likely to have been Bell: *Nottingham Journal*, 15 June 1908, 5.
76. *Daily Chronicle*, repr. in *South Wales Daily News*, 9 December 1898, 8.
77. *Westminster Gazette*, 20 December 1898, 8.
78. *Daily Mail*, 7 November 1912, 5.
79. *Women's Penny Paper*, 22 December 1888, 1.
80. Maurice Mortimer, 'Fashionable Feminine Financiers', *Grand Magazine*, July 1907, 875–81, at 881; *Preston Herald*, 16 November 1912, 5.
81. The figure was later put as 'more than 20 and probably 30': *Daily News*, 9 April 1895, 3; *Morning Post*, 10 April 1895, 6.
82. 1901 Census, RG 13/1043, f. 95, 23.
83. 1911 Census, RG 14/2451, Sch. 275; Companies Registration Office, Files of Dissolved Companies, BT 31/5713/39941: Company No. 39941, Central Stock Exchange Ltd. Incorporated in 1893, TNA.
84. Another broker, a Mrs Hughes, who traded with her husband, offered to take on female pupils, promising to 'instruct them in the mysteries of stockbroking', which she considered 'a very good opening for women': *Woman's Herald*, 21 March 1891, 348.
85. Miss Edith Minnie Charles was listed as a stockbroker, trading from 43 King William Street, the same street where the Central Stock Exchange had started business: *Post Office London Directory for 1902*, 1011. For more on Maskell, see Chapters 4 and 5.
86. E. Hay, *Double Your Income: Or, Resources of the Money Market* (London, 1869), 27; [J. Hollingshead], 'Phases of the Funds', *All the Year Round*, 6 July 1861, 342–6, at 342.
87. *London Stock Exchange Commission: Report of the Commissioners*, Parliamentary Papers 1878, XIX, 9, 25–7.
88. David Kynaston, *The City of London*, vol. 1, *A World of Its Own, 1815–1890* (London, 1995), 284–5.
89. Larry Neal, 'The London Stock Exchange in the 19th Century: Ownership Structures, Growth and Performance', Working Paper No. 115, Oesterreichische Nationalbank (OeNB), Vienna, 14; Ranald Michie, 'Different in Name Only? The London Stock Exchange and Foreign Bourses, *c*.1850–1914', *Business History* 30, no. 1 (1988): 46–68, at 59.
90. Ranald Michie, *The London Stock Exchange: A History* (Oxford, 2001), 83–4.

232 NOTES TO PAGES 69–74

91. M. J. Daunton, '"Gentlemanly Capitalism" and British Industry, 1820–1914', *Past and Present* 122 (1989): 119–58, at 146–7.
92. [Charles Branch], 'A Defence of the Stock Exchange', *Fraser's Magazine* 14, no. 82 (October 1876): 493–503, at 499–500. In 1891 the rules were tightened so that members needed to have been resident for seven years and naturalized for two: David Kynaston, 'The London Stock Exchange, 1870–1914: An Institutional History' (PhD thesis, University of London, 1983), 88–9.
93. T. H. S. Escott, *England: Its People, Polity, and Pursuits* (London, 1881), 290.
94. Cited in Ranald C. Michie, *Guilty Money: The City of London in Victorian and Edwardian Culture, 1815–1914* (London, 2009), 178.
95. Kynaston, 'London Stock Exchange', 86.
96. This is R. W. Connell's influential term, meaning a dominant gender identity concerned with subordinating other masculinities as well as femininities: Ben Griffin, 'Hegemonic Masculinity as a Historical Problem', *Gender and History* 30, no. 2 (2018): 377–400.
97. [David Morier Evans], *The City: Or, The Physiology of London Business* (London, 1845), 191.
98. David Kynaston, *The City of London*, vol. 2, *Golden Years, 1890–1914* (London, 1996), 244. The change in norms of dress is also noted in Anon., 'The Mechanism of the Stock Exchange', *Cornhill Magazine* 3, no. 16 (October 1897): 490–9, at 490–1.
99. Hartley Withers, cited in Kynaston, 'London Stock Exchange', 84.
100. 'Stock Exchange Speculation', *Chambers's Journal*, 30 July 1887, 481–3.
101. John Tosh, *Manliness and Masculinities in Nineteenth-Century Britain: Essays on Gender, Family and Empire* (Harlow, 2005), 111.
102. Tosh, *Manliness and Masculinities*, 112–14.
103. Murray Griffith, 'Forty Years in the Best Club in London', *The Stock Exchange Christmas Annual*, 1925–6, cited in Kynaston, *World of Its Own*, 365–7.
104. Roland Belfort, 'Stockbrokers at Play', *Grand Magazine*, August 1907, 103–9, at 103.
105. Belfort, 'Stockbrokers at Play', 107–8.
106. Fabrice Neddam, 'Constructing Masculinities under Thomas Arnold of Rugby (1828–1842): Gender, Educational Policy and School Life in an Early-Victorian Public School', *Gender and Education* 16, no. 3 (2004): 303–26, at 314–16, 321.
107. Belfort, 'Stockbrokers at Play', 109.
108. As such it was consistent with the broader shift around this time to a culture of 'muscular masculinity' that emphasized 'toughness, physical strength, aggressiveness, and risk taking': Ava Baron, 'Masculinity, the Embodied Male Worker, and the Historian's Gaze', *International Labor and Working-Class History* 69 (2006): 143–60, at 146.
109. Godefroi Drew Ingall, 'The London Stock Exchange', in *Living London*, edited by George R. Sims (London, 1901), 261–6, at 263–5.
110. David T. Smith, 'A Stockbroker's Memories', *Blackwood's Magazine*, October 1933, 466–75, at 467.
111. Cited in Kynaston, *World of Its Own*, 365–7.
112. *Daily News*, 9 April 1895, 3.
113. *The Sketch*, 8 November 1899, 43.
114. Ardern Holt, *Fancy Dresses Described: Or, What to Wear at Fancy Balls* (London, [1879]), 78–9.
115. Rebecca N. Mitchell, 'The Victorian Fancy Dress Ball, 1870–1900', *Fashion Theory* 21, no. 3 (2017): 291–315, at 302.
116. Catherine Ingrassia, 'The Pleasure of Business and the Business of Pleasure: Gender, Credit, and the South Sea Bubble', *Studies in Eighteenth-Century Culture* 24 (1995): 191–210, at 198.
117. *Daily News*, 3 December 1887, 6.
118. Mitchell, 'Victorian Fancy Dress Ball', 302–3.
119. Beth Jenkins, 'Gender, Embodiment and Professional Identity in Britain, c.1890–1930', *Cultural and Social History* 17, no. 4 (2020): 499–514.
120. Erika Diane Rappaport, *Shopping for Pleasure: Women in the Making of London's West End* (Princeton, 2000).
121. Christopher P. Hosgood, '"Doing the Shops" at Christmas: Women, Men and the Department Store in England, c.1880–1914', in *Cathedrals of Consumption: The European Department Store, 1850–1939*, edited by Geoffrey Crossick and Serge Jaumain (Aldershot, 1998), 97–115.
122. John Benson and Laura Ugolini, 'Introduction', in *Cultures of Selling: Perspectives on Consumption and Society since 1700*, edited by John Benson and Laura Ugolini (Aldershot, 2006), 1–28, at 15–16.
123. *City Leader*, 28 December 1889, 295.
124. The game is described in Antony Guest, 'The London Stock Exchange', *Tinsleys' Magazine* 11 (April 1890): 363–8, at 363–5; Anon., 'Mechanism of the Stock Exchange', 491–2. It also applied to provincial exchanges: Smith, 'Stockbroker's Memories', 468.

125. *Sheffield Independent*, 1 January 1896, 4.
126. *Northampton Mercury*, 6 November 1886, 11; *Yorkshire Evening Post*, 28 August 1893, 2; *Sheffield Evening Telegraph and Star*, 28 August 1893, 2.
127. *Lady's Pictorial*, 28 December 1895, 1047.
128. *Woman's Herald*, 21 March 1891, 348. A point also made in the US context by 'a New York lady financier': *New York Herald*, repr. in *Northants Evening Telegraph*, 2 July 1904, 8.
129. *Westminster Gazette*, 20 December 1898, 8.
130. *Woman's Leader*, 1 April 1920, 211.
131. *Bristol Mercury and Daily Post*, 23 January 1886, 6.
132. *Herts Advertiser*, 30 March 1907, 2.
133. *The Echo*, 17 April 1888, 1.
134. *Daily Mail*, 17 June 1904, 3; *Weekly Irish Times*, 25 June 1904, 23.
135. *Dublin Evening Telegraph*, 16 June 1904, 2.
136. *Cork Examiner*, 16 June 1904, 5; *Irish Times*, 16 June 1904, 9.
137. *Daily Telegraph*, 17 June 1904, 10.
138. *Daily Express*, 28 June 1904, 5.
139. *FT*, 17 June 1904, 4.
140. *Daily News*, 18 June 1904, 12.
141. George Robb, *Ladies of the Ticker: Women and Wall Street from the Gilded Age to the Great Depression* (Urbana, 2017), 129–33.
142. *Madison Daily Leader*, 29 August 1890, 4; *Cambria Freeman*, 31 October 1890, 4.
143. Robb, *Ladies of the Ticker*, 132.
144. Robb, *Ladies of the Ticker*, 128–9.
145. In 1856 it was reported that women were gaining entry by 'going there in male attire': *Newcastle Journal*, 15 March 1856, 6.
146. Nathalie Sigot, 'Breaking the Rules: Mathilde Méliot, the First Woman Economist and Feminist, Member of the French *Société d'économie politique*', *Oeconomia* 12, no. 3 (2022): 519–51.
147. *Sporting Life*, 22 June 1897, 2; *FT*, 29 April 1942, 1.
148. *FT*, 23 July 1928, 1.
149. *Courier and Argus*, 2 May 1908, 5.
150. *Liverpool Echo*, 29 January 1909, 8; *Manchester Guardian*, 30 January 1909, 11; *Manchester Courier*, 30 January 1909, 9.
151. *Manchester Courier*, 26 June 1908, 4.
152. Nancy Henry, '"Ladies Do It?": Victorian Women Investors in Fact and Fiction', in *Victorian Literature and Finance*, edited by Francis O'Gorman (Oxford, 2007), 129–30.
153. Judith R. Walkowitz, 'The Indian Woman, the Flower Girl, and the Jew: Photojournalism in Edwardian London', *Victorian Studies* 42, no. 1 (1998–99): 3–46, at 4–5.
154. Mark Pottle, 'Malvery [married name Mackirdy], Olive Christian (1876/7–1914)', *ODNB*.
155. Walkowitz, 'Indian Woman', 11.
156. Olive Christian Malvery, *The Speculator* (London, 1908), 3.
157. Malvery, *Speculator*, 10.
158. Malvery, *Speculator*, 8.
159. Malvery, *Speculator*, 7.
160. Malvery, *Speculator*, 40–1.
161. Malvery, *Speculator*, 34.
162. Malvery, *Speculator*, 64, 27, 34. Helen chooses to be a foreigner because any perceived strangeness would be attributed to nationality rather than gender.
163. Malvery, *Speculator*, 38. Helen's words here evoke Thomas Mortimer's classic eighteenth-century investment guide which urged every *man* to be his own broker: Paul Crosthwaite, Peter Knight, Nicky Marsh, Helen Paul, and James Taylor, *Invested: How Three Centuries of Stock Market Advice Reshaped Our Money, Markets, and Minds* (Chicago, 2022), 30–8.
164. Malvery, *Speculator*, 41.
165. Malvery, *Speculator*, 28.
166. Malvery, *Speculator*, 42.
167. Malvery, *Speculator*, 42.
168. Malvery, *Speculator*, 46.
169. Malvery, *Speculator*, 97.
170. Malvery, *Speculator*, 99.
171. Malvery, *Speculator*, 101.
172. Malvery, *Speculator*, 250.

234   NOTES TO PAGES 80–4

173. Silvana Colella, 'Cross-Dressing in the City: Olive Malvery's *The Speculator*', *Journal of Victorian Culture* 26, no. 3 (2021): 435–48, at 442. See also Ann Heilmann, '(Un)Masking Desire: Cross-dressing and the Crisis of Gender in New Woman Fiction', *Journal of Victorian Culture* 5, no. 1 (2000): 83–111.
174. Malvery, *Speculator*, 10.
175. Malvery, *Speculator*, 62.
176. Malvery, *Speculator*, 60.
177. Malvery, *Speculator*, 108.
178. Malvery, *Speculator*, 288.
179. Malvery, *Speculator*, 305. This ending is consistent with the views outlined in an earlier article by Malvery, in which she made the case for a business education for women not on the grounds that it would help them develop their own careers, but because it would 'make them most complete and perfect helpmates of the men they marry': Mrs Archibald Mackirdy, 'Women and the Money Market', *Lady's Realm*, November 1906, 41–5, at 44.
180. *Review of Reviews*, February 1908, 215; *Yorkshire Post*, 5 February 1908, 4; *The Observer*, 26 January 1908, 4.
181. Colella, 'Cross-Dressing in the City', 448.
182. Patricia Branca, *Silent Sisterhood: Middle-Class Women in the Victorian Home* (Abingdon, 2013), 25–30; S. P. Walker, 'How to Secure Your Husband's Esteem: Accounting and Private Patriarchy in the British Middle Class Household during the Nineteenth Century', *Accounting, Organizations and Society* 23, nos. 5–6 (1998): 485–514.
183. Walker, 'How to Secure', 509.
184. Stephen P. Walker, 'Identifying the Woman behind the "Railed-In Desk": The Proto-Feminisation of Bookkeeping in Britain', *Accounting, Auditing and Accountability Journal* 16, no. 4 (2003): 606–39, at 609.
185. Walker, 'Identifying the Woman', 627–8.
186. Ken Shackleton, 'Gender Segregation in Scottish Chartered Accountancy: The Deployment of Male Concerns about the Admission of Women, 1900–25', *Accounting, Business and Financial History* 9, no. 1 (1999): 135–56; Linda M. Kirkham and Anne Loft, 'Gender and the Construction of the Professional Accountant', *Accounting, Organizations and Society* 18, no. 6 (1993): 507–58; Claire Evans and Nick Rumens, 'Gender Inequality and the Professionalisation of Accountancy in the UK from 1870 to the Interwar Years', *Business History* 64, no. 7 (2022): 1244–59.
187. *The Queen*, 13 July 1889, 74; *The Queen*, 13 June 1891, 965; *Woman's Signal*, 1 August 1895, 65; *Daily News*, 8 February 1904, 12; Stephen P. Walker, 'Smith, Mary Harris (1844–1934)', *ODNB*; Stephen P. Walker, 'Professions and Patriarchy Revisited: Accountancy in England and Wales, 1887–1914', *Accounting History Review* 21, no. 2 (2011): 185–225, at 189–90.
188. Walker, 'Professions and Patriarchy', 191–8.
189. Walker, 'Professions and Patriarchy', 198–203.
190. Stephen P. Walker, 'Ethel Ayres Purdie: Critical Practitioner and Suffragist', *Critical Perspectives on Accounting* 22, no. 1 (2011): 79–101, at 82–3.
191. *The Standard*, 28 April 1892, 9.
192. *FT*, 29 April 1892, 2.
193. *The Standard*, 29 April 1892, 1. George Gregory, aka Ashley Cronmire, was the older brother of Sidney Cronmire/Beauclerk, the 'infant stockbroker' husband of Alice. The episode may have been a stunt initiated by the firm itself, which was always alive to opportunities for publicity.
194. Constance Smedley, 'The Business Woman', *World's Work*, June 1907, 97–103, at 103, 98.
195. Molly Youngkin, 'Henrietta Stannard (1856–1911), Marie Corelli (1855–1924), and Annesley Kenealy (1861–1934?)', in *Kindred Hands: Letters on Writing by British and American Women Authors, 1865–1935*, edited by Jennifer Cognard-Black and Elizabeth MacLeod Walls (Iowa City, 2006), 147–162, at 150; Mike Callan, Conor Heffernan, and Amanda Spenn, 'Women's Jūjutsu and Judo in the Early Twentieth-Century: The Cases of Phoebe Roberts, Edith Garrud, and Sarah Mayer', *International Journal of the History of Sport* 35, no. 6 (2018): 530–53, at 534.
196. *Womanhood*, January 1902, 129–30.
197. *The Queen*, 11 December 1909, 1082.
198. *Preston Herald*, 16 November 1912, 5. Bell had not been overly encouraging about the prospects of women either, recommending that they should not consider stockbroking as a career unless they possessed independent means: *The Queen*, 26 August 1893, 390.
199. *Belfast Weekly News*, 14 April 1904, 9.
200. *The Englishwoman's Year Book and Directory* (London, 1911), 79–85.
201. 1911 Census, RG 14/1174, Sch. 449.
202. Amy Elizabeth Bell, 26 May 1920, National Probate Calendar.

NOTES TO PAGES 84–6   235

203. *FT*, 15 December 1908, 5; *John Bull*, 26 December 1908, 22. This was a common ruse among less reputable firms: Dilwyn Porter, ' "Speciousness is the Bucketeer's Watchword and Outrageous Effrontery his Capital": Financial Bucket Shops in the City of London, *c.*1880–1939', in *Cultures of Selling: Perspectives on Consumption and Society since 1700*, edited by John Benson and Laura Ugolini (Aldershot, 2006), 103–25, at 111.
204. *Truth*, 6 January 1909, 33; *FT*, 13 January 1909, 2; *FT*, 19 January 1909, 2; *FT*, 11 May 1909, 2.
205. The 1911 census lists her as 'clerk' in 'investment business', while the 1921 census specifies that she worked as a clerk for the Investment Registry. It seems likely that she was working for the Registry at the time of the 1911 census. 1911 Census, RG 14/2451, Sch. 275; 1921 Census, RG 15/02535, ED 16, Sch. 77.
206. Marriage of William Ferdinand Hermann Berghoff and Lizzie Matilda Beech, 30 December 1911, London Church of England Parish Registers, P92/MRY/386, 141, London Metropolitan Archives, accessed Ancestry.com.
207. The 1939 Register lists her as 'Clerical dept Manager, retired': RG 101/0071B/016.
208. Lizzie Matilda Berghoff, 28 May 1945, National Probate Calendar.
209. For a late advertisement, see *Truth*, 7 March 1895, 619.
210. 1901 Census, RG 13/1608, f. 37, 20.
211. Alice Matilda Beauclerk, 21 February 1922, National Probate Calendar.
212. *Morning Post*, 5 April 1886; *Cheltenham Looker-On*, 29 January 1887, 85; *Standard*, 9 February 1887, 6.
213. *Commercial Gazette*, 21 March 1894, 270; *Commercial Gazette*, 28 March 1984, 294; *Morning Post*, 7 June 1894, 7.
214. *Maidenhead Advertiser*, 23 October 1895, 3; *Daily Mail*, 5 January 1926, 7.
215. 1911 Census, RG 14/128, Sch. 357. By the time of the 1939 Register, she was still running a boarding house, now in Kentish Town, living with an estate agent named Norman Nash: RG 101/0496F/18. For more on women's lodging house keeping, see Alison C. Kay, *The Foundations of Female Entrepreneurship: Enterprise, Home and Household in London, c.1800–1870* (London, 2009), 108–19. For Arthur's exploits, see *Oakland Tribune*, 17 January 1926, 85.
216. Marriage of Thomas Hilton Renwick and Emma Patience Robson, 31 May 1898, Surrey Church of England Parish Registers, 2217/1/8, 120, Surrey History Centre, Woking; Thomas Hilton Renwick, family tree: <https://www.ancestry.co.uk/family-tree/person/tree/165623809/person/272155480707/facts>.
217. 1901 Census, RG 13/659, f. 55, 13. Medical gymnastics was a form of physiotherapy originating in Sweden: Pia Lundquist Wanneberg, 'Gymnastics as Remedy: A Study of Nineteenth-Century Swedish Medical Gymnastics', *Athens Journal of Sports* 5, no. 1 (2018): 33–52.
218. *London Gazette*, 22 August 1902, 5484; *The Queen*, 9 April 1904, 620; *Morning Post*, 15 February 1907, 10; *Vernon News*, 18 January 1917, 6.
219. Sir Francis Cook, 9 March 1901, National Probate Calendar. Inheriting £25,000 and the income from a further £50,000 during her lifetime may also have made a business life less attractive: *The Standard*, 13 March 1901, 4.
220. Mortimer, 'Fashionable Feminine Financiers', 881; Myra MacPherson, *The Scarlet Sisters: Sex, Suffrage, and Scandal in the Gilded Age* (New York, 2014), 298–305.
221. *Irish Times*, 7 October 1904, 9; *Irish Times*, 11 November 1904, 4.
222. *Nenagh Guardian*, 16 August 1905, 3; *Dublin Daily Express*, 24 May 1906, 4; *Freeman's Journal*, 2 June 1906, 1.
223. An advert for the hotel weeks before her death indicated all applications to be made to Mrs Bulger: *Freeman's Journal*, 22 September 1923, 11.
224. *Dublin Daily Express*, 20 January 1913, 5; *Belfast Evening Telegraph*, 10 May 1913, 6; *Irish Independent*, 10 June 1913, 9.
225. The 1908–9 edition of the *Stock and Sharebrokers' Directory* list only Frederic and Marianne as partners; Henry's firm is first listed in the 1910–11 edition: *UKSSD for 1908–09*, 234; *UKSSD for 1910–11*, 246.
226. The 1921 census records her as 'Stock & Sharebroker, Retired': RG 15/20702, ED 15, Sch. 19.
227. In 1920, the firm was listed as 'H. Bazett-Jones, with whom is amalgamated H. Bazett-Jones & Sons, 110A Fishergate', *UKSSD for 1920*, 175.
228. Civil Registration Death Index, vol. 8e, Deaths Registered in April, May and June, 1922, 742, accessed Ancestry.com.
229. *Lancashire Evening Post*, 28 September 1933, 9.
230. *T. P.'s Weekly*, 25 November 1904, 714.
231. *Truth*, 25 October 1888, 726.
232. Mortimer, 'Fashionable Feminine Financiers', 880–1.

236 NOTES TO PAGES 86–90

233. *Shrewsbury Chronicle*, 18 March 1910, 10; *Yorkshire Factory Times*, 24 March 1910, 1; *John Bull*, 26 March 1910, 432; *Farrow's Bank Gazette*, March 1910, 1, 13.
234. *Daily Herald*, 2 May 1913, 4; *Daily Chronicle*, 27 March 1913, 6. Farrow's collapsed in scandalous circumstances in 1920: Matthew Hollow, 'The 1920 Farrow's Bank Failure: A Case of Managerial Hubris?', *Journal of Management History* 20, no. 2 (2014): 164–78.
235. See Chapter 4.
236. *Financial News*, 15 November 1910, 4.
237. *The Financier*, 21 November 1910, 6.
238. Adverts for the 'Marjorie' column mentioned that it was by the same author as *The Practical Affairs of Life*, a book penned by Powell: H. Simonis, *The Street of Ink: An Intimate History of Journalism* (London, 1917), 120.
239. *Daily Mail*, 5 November 1912, 7.

Chapter 4

1. By late 1916, there had been a net increase of 866,000 women in the workforce since July 1914: David Swift, 'Women of the Left, Patriotism, and National Identity, 1914–28', *Twentieth Century British History* 33, no. 3 (2022): 369–91, at 383.
2. John Black, 'War, Women and Accounting: Female Staff in the UK Army Pay Department Offices, 1914–1920', *Accounting, Business and Financial History* 16, no. 2 (2006): 195–218, at 213; Keith Vernon and Oliver Wilkinson, 'Education and Opportunity during the First World War: Post-Compulsory Study at the Harris Institute, Preston, 1914–18', *Twentieth-Century British History* 34, no. 2 (2023): 192–219, at 217. The turn to female clerical labour was strongly promoted by government: *Report of the Clerical and Commercial Employments Committee*, Parliamentary Papers 1914–16, XIII.
3. *Daily Mail*, 2 June 1916, 3.
4. *The Times*, 22 August 1916, 9; *Daily Mirror*, 24 August 1916, 2; *City Press*, repr. in *Daily Mail*, 11 March 1918, 4.
5. *Evening Standard*, 13 January 1916, 6; *Daily News*, 8 July 1919, 4.
6. *Daily Mail*, 29 January 1916, 3. For a critical view, see *Evening Standard*, 21 January 1916, 4.
7. *Evening Standard*, 19 April 1916, 3.
8. Edwin Green, *Debtors to Their Profession: A History of the Institute of Bankers, 1879–1979* (Abingdon, 2012), 99; Jerry White, 'London in the First World War', *Cahiers Bruxellois* 46 (2014): 139–57, at 152.
9. Andrew J. Seltzer, 'Female Salaries and Careers in British Banking, 1915–41', *Explorations in Economic History* 48, no. 4 (2011): 461–77.
10. *Daily Telegraph*, 11 October 1916, 5; *Manchester Evening News*, 13 October 1916, 5. The war also saw limited gains in terms of women being promoted to management or director-level roles in other sectors: Janette Rutterford, 'Votes for Women: The Role of Women Shareholders in the Campaign for Women's Suffrage in Edwardian Britain', *Entreprises et Histoire* 107, no. 2 (2022): 88–107, at 105–6.
11. In 1919, women were admitted to full membership: Green, *Debtors to Their Profession*, 102.
12. Nicole Robertson, 'Women at Work: Activism, Feminism and the Rise of the Female Office Worker during the First World War and Its Immediate Aftermath', in *Labour and Working-Class Lives: Essays to Celebrate the Life and Work of Chris Wrigley*, edited by Keith Laybourn and John Shepherd (Manchester, 2017), 172–93, at 186.
13. Seltzer, 'Female Salaries', 463; David Kynaston, *The City of London*, vol. 3, *Illusions of Gold, 1914–1945* (London, 1999), 285–6; Peter Wardley, 'Women, Mechanization and Cost Savings in Twentieth Century British Banks and Other Financial Institutions', in *A Business and Labour History of Britain: Case Studies of Britain in the Nineteenth and Twentieth Centuries*, edited by Mike Richardson and Peter Nicholls (Houndmills, 2011), 32–59, at 38–43.
14. *Lancashire Evening Post*, 23 February 1931, 5.
15. Susan Kingsley Kent, 'The Politics of Sexual Difference: World War I and the Demise of British Feminism', *Journal of British Studies* 27, no. 3 (1988): 232–53, at 245; Deirdre Beddoe, *Back to Home and Duty: Women between the Wars, 1918–1939* (London, 1989), 135–40.
16. Julie V. Gottlieb, 'Introduction: "Flour Power" and Feminism between the Waves', in *Feminism and Feminists after Suffrage*, edited by Julie V. Gottlieb (London, 2016), 1–5, at 5.
17. For examples, see Caitriona Beaumont, *Housewives and Citizens: Domesticity and the Women's Movement in England, 1928–64* (Manchester and New York, 2013); Jane Clarke, 'Feminism and the Legacy of the First World War in the Journals of the Old Comrades Associations, 1919–1935', *Women's History Review* 28, no. 7 (2019): 1177–99.

NOTES TO PAGES 90–5   237

18. J. B. Jefferys, 'Trends in Business Organisation in Great Britain since 1856' (PhD thesis, University of London, 1938), 330, 360.
19. F. Lavington, *The English Capital Market* (London, 1921), 221.
20. *UKSSD for 1923*, 181.
21. W. A. Thomas, *The Provincial Stock Exchanges* (Abingdon, 2014), 106.
22. Geoffrey Jones and Mary B. Rose, 'Family Capitalism', in *Family Capitalism*, edited by Geoffrey Jones and Mary B. Rose (Abingdon, 2012), 1–16, at 6.
23. Thomas, *Provincial Stock Exchanges*, 109–12.
24. Leeds Stock Exchange, Managing Committee Minute Book, WYL543/1/7: 24 May 1917, 229, West Yorkshire Archive Service, Leeds; *UKSSD for 1919*, 147.
25. Leeds Stock Exchange, Managing Committee Minute Book, WYL543/1/7: 29 December 1921, 265; *London Gazette*, 3 March 1922, 1877. Other examples include Mary Irving Merry in Northampton and Edith Dodd in Penrith: *UKSSD for 1937*, 171; *UKSSD for 1938*, 176.
26. *Exeter and Plymouth Gazette*, 19 November 1904, 5.
27. *The Vote*, 11 May 1923, 147.
28. Irish Stock Exchange, *Oonah Keogh: A Celebration* (Dublin, 2014), 9–10.
29. *The Times*, 17 September 1956, 11.
30. *The Times*, 17 September 1956, 11; Irish Stock Exchange, *Oonah Keogh*, 12–13.
31. *Manchester Courier*, 2 December 1893, 9; *Manchester Courier*, 9 September 1903, 2. Phyllis's mother, Mabel, was the daughter of a bank inspector: 1881 Census, RG 11/662, f. 142, 30.
32. 1921 Census, RG 15/18760, ED 7, Sch. 213.
33. *Rochdale Observer*, 26 November 1938, 13.
34. 1911 Census, RG 14/536, Sch. 1; Census of Ireland, 1911, National Archives of Ireland: <https://www.census.nationalarchives.ie/reels/nai000117671/>.
35. He sustained serious injuries in the Great War, which made it impossible for him to resume his training. He did become a clerk in his father's firm, but plagued by ill health, he died in 1927: 1921 Census, RG 15/10390, ED 28, Sch. 29; *Exeter and Plymouth Gazette*, 4 July 1927, 8.
36. 1911 Census, RG 14/24643, Sch. 153; 1921 Census, RG 15/19960, ED 3, Sch. 321.
37. Arlene Young, *From Spinster to Career Woman: Middle-Class Women and Work in Victorian England* (Montreal and Kingston, 2019), 115.
38. *Shafts*, quoted in Young, *From Spinster to Career Woman*, 118; Gladys Carnaffan, 'Commercial Education and the Female Office Worker', in *The White-Blouse Revolution: Female Office Workers since 1870*, edited by Gregory Anderson (Manchester, 1988), 67–87, at 82.
39. Serena Kelly, 'Hubbard, Louisa Maria (1836–1906)', *ODNB*.
40. The 1891 census lists her occupation as Daily Governess, Sub-Editor, and Organist: RG 12/141, f. 160, 11. For her other activities: *Pall Mall Gazette*, 5 August 1889, 7; *Hendon and Finchley Times*, 15 April 1892, 3; *The Queen*, 9 February 1895, 260.
41. In 1895, Maskell had to take over the editing of *The Englishwoman's Yearbook* from Hubbard, who was seriously ill. By 1901, she had begun work as a stockbroker's clerk: 1901 Census, RG 13/475, f. 72, 18.
42. 1911 Census, RG 14/3417, Sch. 50; 1921 Census, RG 15/03529, ED 13, Sch. 481. She had taken over the firm from Brooke by August 1914: *UKSSD for 1914–15*, 165. See also *Daily Graphic*, 9 April 1919, 11, though this article writes Brooke out of the picture.
43. Christopher Keep, 'The Cultural Work of the Type-Writer Girl', *Victorian Studies* 40, no. 3 (1997): 401–26, at 419.
44. *Girl's Own Paper*, 1901, cited in Jessica Vivien Gray, 'Office Girls in Turn-of-the-Century Fiction: Work, Technology and Everyday Modernity' (PhD thesis, University of Kent, 2019), 16.
45. Meta Zimmeck, 'Jobs for the Girls: The Expansion of Clerical Work for Women, 1850–1914', in *Unequal Opportunities: Women's Employment in England, 1900–1918*, edited by Angela V. John (Oxford, 1986), 153–77, at 158.
46. *Daily Telegraph*, 11 January 1900, 2.
47. *Lewisham Borough News*, 17 September 1909, 6.
48. Miss Gordon Holmes, *In Love with Life: A Pioneer Career Woman's Story* (London, 1944), 46–7.
49. Holmes, *In Love with Life*, 17, 46–7, 52.
50. Holmes, *In Love with Life*, 72–3; Gordon Holmes, 'Stockbroking and Finance', *Good Housekeeping*, November 1925, 145.
51. Holmes, *In Love with Life*, 77. For more on trusts, see Janette Rutterford, 'Learning from One Another's Mistakes: Investment Trusts in the UK and the US, 1868–1940', *Financial History Review* 16, no. 2 (2009): 157–81.
52. Carnaffan, 'Commercial Education', 73–4.

238   NOTES TO PAGES 95-8

53. 1881 Census, RG 11/4585, f. 76, 22; 1891 Census, RG 12/3623, f. 156, 13; *The Vote*, 31 March 1933, 98; *Nottingham Journal*, 8 April 1933, 5.
54. The 1911 census lists Midgley as a commercial clerk at a printing works, but she must have started at a stockbroker's office later that year: RG 14/26754, Sch. 38. An advertisement she placed in 1936 boasts of twenty-five years' experience: *Yorkshire Observer*, 23 January 1936, 4. When she first attempted to apply to join the Bradford Stock Exchange in 1930, she had been working in stockbroking for nineteen years.
55. Robertson, 'Women at Work', 176–7.
56. The figure was 20 per cent for London's banks: *Report of the Board of Trade on the State of Employment in the United Kingdom in October 1914*, Parliamentary Papers 1914–16, XXI, 13. For the closure, see Ranald Michie, *The London Stock Exchange: A History* (Oxford, 2001), 145.
57. *Report to the Board of Trade on the State of Employment in the United Kingdom in February 1915*, Parliamentary Papers 1915, XXI, 15.
58. *Western Daily Press*, 19 November 1915, 8. The London Stock Exchange was less keen to employ women itself, reducing from 17 to 15 the age for male unauthorized and Settling-Room clerks: *Birmingham Daily Post*, 9 October 1915, 8.
59. *Leeds Mercury*, 2 May 1918, 2. See also *Financial News*, 27 June 1917, 2.
60. Michie, *London Stock Exchange*, 155.
61. Thomas, *Provincial Stock Exchanges*, 235.
62. 1911 Census, RG 14/18465, Sch. 144; *Midland Counties Tribune*, 31 December 1937, 9.
63. David Thackeray, *Conservatism for the Democratic Age: Conservative Cultures and the Challenge of Mass Politics in Early Twentieth-Century England* (Manchester, 2016), 26, 39.
64. *The Vote*, 18 April 1924, 121; *Leicester Evening Mail*, 4 February 1931, 17.
65. 1891 Census, RG 12/1934, f. 111, 24; 1901 Census, RG 13/2339, f. 119, 21; 1911 Census, RG 14/14694, Sch. 78.
66. *Bath Chronicle and Herald*, 29 April 1916, 1. The advert expressed a preference for a school-leaver, though White was by this point 25.
67. 1921 Census, RG 15/11479, ED 10, Sch. 66.
68. *The Vote*, 11 May 1923, 147.
69. Holmes, 'Stockbroking and Finance', 146; Holmes, *In Love with Life*, 88; *Daily Express*, 11 October 1924, 9.
70. Holmes, *In Love with Life*, 80.
71. Robertson, 'Women at Work', 183–91.
72. They were still outnumbered by male clerks, however: Rosalie Silverstone, 'Office Work for Women: An Historical Review', *Business History* 18, no. 1 (1976): 98–110, at 109.
73. 1901 Census, RG 13/1244, f. 23, 37; 1881 Census, RG 11/1685, f. 50, 19.
74. 1921 Census, RG 15/20173, ED 34, Sch. 203.
75. *Yorkshire Evening Post*, 9 April 1931, 9.
76. Michie, *London Stock Exchange*, 109–10.
77. Montagu Williams QC, *Round London: Down East and Up West* (London, 1892), 138–42; *Womanhood*, May 1901, xi.
78. Maurice Mortimer, 'Fashionable Feminine Financiers', *Grand Magazine*, July 1907, 875–81, at 876.
79. *Modern Man*, 24 May 1913, 56. For a more sober account making the same point, see *Daily Mail*, 8 November 1912, 7.
80. Mortimer, 'Fashionable Feminine Financiers', 875–6; *Answers*, 23 March 1912, 511. Their numbers were large and growing, one journalist estimating in 1907 that there were no fewer than 20,000 half-commission men and women operating across the country: Roland Belfort, 'How Stockbrokers "Beat up" Business', *Grand Magazine*, June 1907, 665–71, at 666.
81. *The Sphere*, 14 November 1925, 214.
82. *Manchester Guardian*, 4 July 1941, 8. This led to the oft-repeated and inflated claim that she had been a stockbroker: *Daily Mirror*, 10 July 1930, 11; *Derby Daily Telegraph*, 31 December 1930, 1.
83. *Daily Telegraph*, 28 June 1937, 29. See also *Jus Suffragii: The International Woman Suffrage News*, February 1928, 80.
84. Maurice Powell, 'Fox, Charles Jr. (1871–1939)', Manx Music Dot Com: <https://www.manxmusic.com/mobile/bio_page_560035.html>.
85. Court for Divorce and Matrimonial Causes, J 77/1917/9962: Divorce Court File 9962. Appellant: Charles Wilfred Tatham; Respondent: Mabel Tatham; Co-Respondent: Harry Theodore Gosnell, 1922, TNA; Civil Registration Marriage Index, vol. 8b, Marriages Registered in July, August and September, 1922, 274, accessed Ancestry.com.

NOTES TO PAGES 98–102   239

86. Stephen Wagg, '"Who D'You Think You Are? Stirling Moss?" British Racing Drivers and the Politics of Celebrity: 1896 to 1992', in *The History and Politics of Motor Racing: Lives in the Fast Lane*, edited by Damion Sturm, Stephen Wagg, and David L. Andrews (Cham, 2023), 477–518, at 483; Gosnell Family Tree: <http://gosnell.org.uk/genealogy/gosnell/ppl/x/q/XQ8LYVKOB498T54WRC.html>.

87. The series in the *Yorkshire Post* ran from February to August 1922. For more on other racing women from this era, see Wagg, 'British Racing Drivers', 485–8.

88. *Daily Mirror*, 25 June 1936, 2; *Daily Express*, 25 June 1936, 1.

89. Hilda McKean was another half-commission woman working for a member firm who, like Gosnell, started by managing investments for friends: *Daily News*, 31 January 1928, 2; *Daily Express*, 10 May 1928, 9. It was impossible to identify McKean reliably in the census.

90. *John Bull*, 25 May 1935, 19.

91. *Daily Herald*, 9 July 1937, 3.

92. See, for example, *Truth*, 24 June 1925, 1182; *Truth*, 13 January 1926, 57; *John Bull*, 30 October 1926, 14. For an account of female share-pushing: *John Bull*, 12 September 1931, 11.

93. Prevention of Fraud (Investments) Acts 1939–1958, BT 298/69: Sharepushers Prosecutions 1910–1916, Schedule—B, TNA. Dorothy Brander faced prosecution in 1937 as a director of a share-pushing concern, but was acquitted when it was found that she was a typist who had been exploited by her employer: *Daily Mail*, 14 September 1937, 7.

94. Friends Elizabeth Jane Bedingfield and Edith Marjorie Russell established the Lincoln Trust, the Sterling Trust, and the Sentinal Trust, to push shares in limited companies. The trusts were not real entities, merely aliases registered under the Business Names Act, while the firms they were promoting had very poor prospects: *Truth*, 14 February 1923, 295; *Truth*, 22 August 1923, 322; *Truth*, 23 January 1924, 168; *Truth*, 8 October 1924, 638; *Truth*, 4 February 1925, 207; *John Bull*, 4 July 1925, 11; *John Bull*, 7 November 1925, 14.

95. *UKSSD for 1925*, 117.

96. *The Vote*, 28 January 1927, 27.

97. *UKSSD for 1926*, 201.

98. *The Vote*, 18 April 1924, 121.

99. *Rochdale Observer*, 11 December 1937, 11; *Rochdale Observer*, 26 November 1938, 13.

100. 1921 Census, RG 15/19960, ED 3, Sch. 321; RG 15/19999, ED 2, Sch. 49.

101. *Bath Chronicle and Herald*, 30 May 1931, 12; William Ernest Jefferis, 10 June 1931, National Probate Calendar.

102. Departmental Committee on Share-Pushing: Evidence and Correspondence, Third Part, BT 55/109: Evidence of Herbert Goodes, 12 March 1937, 9, TNA.

103. Holmes, *In Love with Life*, 88.

104. Holmes, *In Love with Life*, 88–9, 75.

105. Holmes, *In Love with Life*, 89.

106. Holmes, *In Love with Life*, 97.

107. Holmes, *In Love with Life*, 100.

108. Holmes, *In Love with Life*, 100–1.

109. Holmes, *In Love with Life*, 103. It is a coincidence that they used the same name that Alice Beauclerk had used for one of her bucket shops in the 1890s.

110. Holmes, *In Love with Life*, 101.

111. 1921 Census, RG 15/14466, ED 21, Sch. 118; *UKSSD for 1922*, 174; *The Vote*, 18 April 1924, 121.

112. 1921 Census, RG 15/20173, ED 34, Sch. 203; *UKSSD for 1936*, 116; *Daily Express*, 19 October 1936, 17.

113. *UKSSD for 1934*, 114. Details of Midgley's working history can be found in Women's Freedom League (hereafter WFL), Annual Conference Reports, 2WFL/2/23: Twenty-Sixth Annual Conference, 29 April 1933, 77–9, The Women's Library, London School of Economics.

114. Marie Corelli, *The Love of Long Ago, and Other Stories* (London, 1920).

115. Marie Corelli, 'Claudia's Business', *Nash's and Pall Mall Magazine*, December 1916, 218–30.

116. See Chapter 3.

117. Janet Galligani Casey, 'Mary Mackay', in *British Short-Fiction Writers, 1880–1914: The Romantic Tradition*, Gale Dictionary of Literary Biography, vol. 156 (Detroit, 1995). Casey comments that Corelli's work 'seems to offer a feminist surface without really challenging the Victorian status quo for women'.

118. *Westminster Gazette*, 12 June 1924, 5; *The Era*, 18 June 1924, 1; *The Stage*, 19 June 1924, 14; *Birmingham Daily Gazette*, 5 May 1925, 4.

119. *Daily Express*, 3 July 1919, 3.

240 NOTES TO PAGES 102–7

120. *Westminster Gazette*, 9 January 1923, 9. Gordon Holmes was often described as London's 'first' or 'only' female stockbroker: see, for example, *Daily Express*, 24 March 1928, 11; *Staffordshire Sentinel*, 7 February 1929, 6; *Yorkshire Evening Post*, 7 December 1940, 5.
121. *FT*, 16 February 1926, 11.
122. Helena Normanton, 'Stockbroking as a Profession for Women', *Good Housekeeping*, May 1928, 138; *Westminster Gazette*, 9 January 1923, 9.
123. Adrian Bingham, *Gender, Modernity, and the Popular Press in Inter-War Britain* (Oxford, 2004), 23.
124. Holmes, *In Love with Life*, 117.
125. In fact, it was reported that her salary 'ran well into four figures': *Daily Mirror*, 10 October 1924, 2.
126. Laura Beers, 'A Model MP? Ellen Wilkinson, Gender, Politics and Celebrity Culture in Interwar Britain', *Cultural and Social History* 10, no. 2 (2013): 231–50.
127. The same was true of press coverage of female barristers: Ren Pepitone, 'Gender, Space, and Ritual: Women Barristers, the Inns of Court, and the Interwar Press', *Journal of Women's History* 28, no. 1 (2016): 60–83.
128. *Daily Mirror*, 18 April 1927, 12; *Irish Times*, 17 August 1927, 11; *Manchester Guardian*, 14 May 1928, 11; *Staffordshire Sentinel*, 7 February 1929, 6. Moreton was also occasionally consulted on such matters by the Midlands press: *Midland Counties Tribune*, 19 August 1927, 7.
129. For more on the blurring of roles between different types of financial firm, see Brian O'Sullivan, *From Crisis to Crisis: The Transformation of Merchant Banking, 1914–1939* (Basingstoke, 2018), 4–6.
130. *Daily Express*, 19 October 1936, 17.
131. Evidence of Herbert Goodes, 49–50.
132. *Telegraph and Argus*, 20 February 1939, 6.
133. *Daily Mirror*, 30 September 1916, 5; *Daily Express*, 3 July 1919, 3; *Answers*, 28 January 1922, 227.
134. *Nottingham Evening Post*, 16 June 1928, 3. For more on share-pushers, see Matthew Hollow, 'A Nation of Investors or a Procession of Fools? Reevaluating the Behaviour of Britain's Shareholding Population through the Prism of the Interwar Sharepushing Crime Wave', *Enterprise and Society* 20, no. 1 (2019): 132–58.
135. *The Vote*, 18 April 1924, 121. See also *The Vote*, 5 June 1925, 177; *Daily Mirror*, 17 May 1933, 5.
136. Normanton, 'Stockbroking as a Profession', 138.
137. *The Graphic*, 13 December 1919, 893; *The Graphic*, 24 January 1920, 119.
138. *Radio Times*, 23 January 1925, 205.
139. *Radio Times*, 22 October 1926, 241.
140. *Radio Times*, 4 March 1927, 400; 18 March 1927, 604; 1 April 1927, 22; 8 April 1927, 71.
141. *Daily Express*, 14 January 1920, 4; *Daily Mirror*, 4 October 1927, 9.
142. *Daily News*, 31 January 1928, 2.
143. *Daily Mirror*, 17 April 1928, 6. For similar views, see *Daily Mail*, 7 March 1928, 9; *Daily Mail*, 8 March 1928, 11; *Nottingham Evening Post*, 30 October 1929, 3.
144. Janette Rutterford, David R. Green, Josephine Maltby, and Alastair Owens, 'Who Comprised the Nation of Shareholders? Gender and Investment in Great Britain, c.1870–1935', *Economic History Review* 64, no. 1 (2011): 157–87, at 169.
145. *Truth*, 9 July 1930, 63.
146. *Daily Mirror*, 22 April 1930, 18.
147. Similarly progressive views were also becoming more common in the interwar American press: George Robb, *Ladies of the Ticker: Women and Wall Street from the Gilded Age to the Great Depression* (Urbana, 2017), 76–7.
148. Rutterford, 'Votes for Women'.
149. *New York Times*, 23 January 1927, 13; *New York Times*, 1 May 1928, 43; Robb, *Ladies of the Ticker*, 74–5.
150. Normanton, 'Stockbroking as a Profession', 138.
151. Holmes, *In Love with Life*, 83.
152. *Daily Mail*, 25 November 1938, 5.
153. *Rochdale Observer*, 26 November 1938, 13.
154. *Daily Express*, 19 October 1936, 17.
155. *FT*, 16 February 1939, 4; *Daily Graphic*, 9 April 1919, 11. Even those women who were employed by inside firms specifically to deal with female investors also developed male client lists: *Daily News*, 31 January 1928, 2.
156. Holmes, *In Love with Life*, 77–9.

157. *FT*, 20 February 1915, 3; *The Times*, 20 February 1915, 3.
158. *Truth*, 24 February 1915, 289–90.
159. *The Times*, 7 October 1918, 12; *FT*, 19 September 1918, 2.
160. *Truth*, 3 August 1921, 208.
161. For examples, see *Truth*, 21 May 1924, 976; *Truth*, 15 April 1925, 687; *FT*, 5 June 1925, 4; *FT*, 24 September 1928, 1.
162. Hansard, 5th series, vol. 343, 1652 (14 February 1939).
163. For an exception, see *Truth*, 15 February 1922, 269.
164. Edith Russell and Elizabeth Bedingfield also used alluring circulars to attract capital and, as with Holmes, criticisms in the press rarely mentioned their gender, as they too traded under their initials rather than their full names: *The Times*, 25 September 1922, 17; *Daily Mail*, 30 October 1923, 3; *John Bull*, 24 November 1923, 11. For an exception, see *Truth*, 13 September 1922, 441.
165. *Daily Graphic*, 9 April 1919, 11.
166. *FT*, 17 July 1934, 5. It was common practice to commit to sell shares one did not own to buy them back—hopefully at a lower price—before the settlement day: a bear transaction. By indicating that he held the shares, Lesser was signalling to White that this was a safe transaction for her to facilitate.
167. *Bath Chronicle and Herald*, 7 July 1934, 16; 21 July 1934, 16.
168. *Belfast Telegraph*, 25 November 1932, 11; *Western Daily Press*, 16 August 1933, 5.
169. *Rochdale Observer*, 11 December 1937, 11; *Rochdale Observer*, 26 November 1938, 13; *Daily Mail*, 25 November 1938, 5; *Manchester Guardian*, 25 November 1938, 5.
170. *Manchester Evening News*, 24 November 1938, 9; *Rochdale Observer*, 26 November 1938, 10.
171. The *UKSSD* marked with an asterisk those firms which were registered, indicating that, of the brokers discussed in this chapter, Holmes, Moreton, Mortimer, Robinson, and White were, at various points, on the list.
172. LSE, General Purposes Committee Minutes, MS 14600/114: 26 November 1923, 31, Guildhall Library.
173. *FT*, 21 December 1927, 6.
174. Indeed, by 1919 she had switched from Bucklersbury to premises on Throgmorton Street occupied by Whiteheads, likely for the convenience of being close to the firm: *UKSSD for 1919*, 85.
175. *UKSSD for 1923*, 131; 1921 Census, RG 15/10315, ED 3, Sch. 38.
176. *Exeter Express and Echo*, 27 January 1940, 7.
177. Dear's name appears as a partner in the 1937 edition of the *UKSSD*, but disappears again by 1939; *London Gazette*, 13 October 1953, 5466.
178. *FT*, 5 June 1925, 4; *FT*, 29 January 1927, 7; *Truth*, 1 February 1928, 206–7.
179. *Western Mail*, 10 August 1927, 7.
180. Holmes, *In Love with Life*, 7.
181. Holmes, *In Love with Life*, 64.
182. Holmes joined the club in June: *Daily Herald*, 13 June 1924, 5.
183. Helen McCarthy, 'Service Clubs, Citizenship and Equality: Gender Relations and Middle-Class Associations in Britain between the Wars', *Historical Research* 81, no. 213 (2008): 531–52, at 533–6; David Doughan and Peter Gordon, *Women, Clubs and Associations in Britain* (London, 2006), ch. 8.
184. For the formation of the London Club, see *Belfast Telegraph*, 13 September 1923, 6; *Hull Daily Mail*, 29 November 1923, 7; *The Bystander*, 23 January 1924, 216.
185. McCarthy, 'Service Clubs', 533.
186. Not to be confused with the British Federation of Business and Professional Women, established in 1935: Linda Perriton, 'Forgotten Feminists: The Federation of British Professional and Business Women, 1933–1969', *Women's History Review* 16, no. 1 (2007): 79–97.
187. Dorothy V. Hall, *Making Things Happen: History of the National Federation of Business and Professional Women's Clubs of Great Britain and Northern Ireland* (London, 1963), 256.
188. *Manchester Evening News*, 3 April 1954, 4; *Bradford Observer*, 1 March 1941, 4.
189. *Yorkshire Observer*, 27 April 1940, 6; *Yorkshire Observer*, 1 March 1941, 4.
190. Holmes, *In Love with Life*, 116.
191. McCarthy, 'Service Clubs', 545.
192. Holmes, *In Love with Life*, 184.
193. M. F. Adams, cited in McCarthy, 'Service Clubs', 545.
194. *Daily Mail*, 29 July 1936, 5. She repeated the dictum in her autobiography: Holmes, *In Love with Life*, 85.
195. *Daily Mirror*, 10 October 1924, 2.

242   NOTES TO PAGES 111–14

196. *Staffordshire Sentinel*, 22 July 1930, 7.
197. Holmes, *In Love with Life*, 167.
198. *Westminster Gazette*, 9 January 1923, 9. Maskell was speaking anonymously, but her identity can be gleaned from information given in the article.
199. *Daily Mirror*, 28 December 1936, 19. Edith Midgley spoke along similar lines: *Bradford Observer*, 1 April 1940, 2.
200. Articles before this had already measured Holmes's success in terms of technology, one impressed visitor to her offices being particularly taken with the 'dozens of typewriters and dictaphones; stamp machines, addressing machines and multigraph machines': *Staffordshire Sentinel*, 22 July 1930, 7.
201. *Falkirk Herald*, 22 May 1937, 3.
202. Holmes, 'Stockbroking and Finance', 146. She also supported equal pay: *Daily News*, 10 August 1927, 3.
203. *Daily Herald*, 26 February 1932, 8.
204. *Manchester Guardian*, 10 October 1924, 9.
205. *Daily Telegraph*, 1 May 1929, 9; *Lincolnshire Echo*, 5 February 1931, 4.
206. *Daily News*, 31 January 1928, 2.
207. Ray Strachey, *Careers and Openings for Women: A Survey of Women's Employment and a Guide for Those Seeking Work* (London, 1935), 240.
208. Nevertheless, studies of American business culture have shown that women faced very similar obstacles to their British counterparts: Angel Kwolek-Folland, *Incorporating Women: A History of Women and Business in the United States* (New York, 2002); Edith Sparks, *Boss Lady: How Three Women Entrepreneurs Built Successful Big Businesses in the Mid-Twentieth Century* (Chapel Hill, NC, 2017).
209. *Daily Mail Atlantic Edition*, 10 January 1925, 6. For an American opinion, see *Dundee Evening Telegraph*, 25 July 1930, 6.
210. *Nottingham Journal*, 10 March 1938, 5. For other comments and comparisons, see *Daily Telegraph*, 27 October 1923, 13; *Vote*, 28 December 1923, 2; *Daily Mail*, 11 May 1928, 5; *Daily Mail Atlantic Edition*, 18 October 1928, 3.
211. *Sixteenth Census of the United States: 1940. Population: Comparative Occupation Statistics for the United States, 1870 to 1940* (Washington, 1943), 69.
212. *Census of England & Wales 1921: Occupation Tables* (London, 1924), 16–17.
213. *Census of England & Wales 1931: Occupation Tables* (London, 1934), 11, 29.
214. In the 1931 census, a further eighty-six women were listed under 'Other Finance and Insurance Occupations'. In Scotland, Margaret Dow and Marion Dinwoodie were partners in brokerages in Stirling and Perth respectively, while Jeanette Lamb was a partner in Wilkie & Dundas, a Kirriemuir law firm that also offered stockbroking services. They were listed in editions of the *UKSSD* between 1932 and 1940.
215. *Daily Mail*, 29 July 1930, 5.
216. Normanton, 'Stockbroking as a Profession', 140–1.
217. *Daily Mail*, 8 January 1937, 8.
218. *Staffordshire Sentinel*, 22 July 1930, 7.
219. *Daily Mirror*, 10 October 1924, 2.
220. *Daily Express*, 11 October 1924, 9; *Staffordshire Sentinel*, 22 July 1930, 7.
221. Holmes, 'Stockbroking and Finance', 146. For marriage bars, see Helen Glew, 'Embracing the Language of Human Rights: International Women's Organisations, Feminism and Campaigns Against the Marriage Bar, *c.*1919–1960', *Gender and History* 35, no. 3 (2023): 780–94, at 782–3.
222. Normanton, 'Stockbroking as a Profession', 35. Holmes had similar advice, recommending that girls start at a bank as a typist straight after school, study for the Institute of Bankers examination, before progressing to a brokerage: Holmes, 'Stockbroking and Finance', 67.
223. Teresa Davy, ' "A Cissy Job for Men; a Nice Job for Girls": Women Shorthand Typists in London, 1900–1939', in *Our Work, Our Lives, Our Words: Women's History and Women's Work*, edited by Leonore Davidoff and Belinda Westover (Houndmills, 1986), 124–44, at 136; D. W. Hughes, *Careers for our Daughters* (London, 1936), 81.
224. *The Times*, 11 July 1928, 3.
225. *FT*, 12 July 1937, 12.
226. *Hampshire Telegraph*, 24 November 1933, 4; Irish Stock Exchange, *Oonah Keogh*, 16–17.
227. At Barclays, the policy was dismissal on marriage, though a few married women were rehired as 'temporary' clerks: Margaret Ackrill and Leslie Hannah, *Barclays: The Business of Banking, 1690–1996* (Cambridge, 2001), 77.

NOTES TO PAGES 115–20 **243**

228. *Daily Mirror*, 25 June 1936, 2.
229. *Leicester Evening Mail*, 4 February 1931, 17. Her own firm was last listed in the 1932 edition of the *UKSSD*.
230. *Hinckley Echo*, 2 May 1941, 5; *Leicester Evening Mail*, 4 February 1931, 17; *Evening Dispatch*, 4 March 1935, 5.
231. *Midland Counties Tribune*, 27 September 1935, 10; *Midland Counties Tribune*, 31 December 1937, 9; *Coventry Evening Telegraph*, 18 November 1938, 5.
232. *Irish Independent*, 22 April 1943, 2; *Irish Independent*, 23 April 1943, 4.
233. Both described themselves as 'Stockbroker and Incorporated Insurance Broker': 1939 Register, RG 101/4316B/18; *Manchester Evening News*, 20 August 1943, 5.
234. *Manchester Evening News*, 15 April 1952, 5.
235. *Manchester Evening News*, 13 February 1954, 1; *Manchester Evening News*, 3 April 1954, 4; Civil Registration Marriage Index, vol. 10b, Marriages Registered in July, August, and September 1954, 140, accessed Ancestry.com.
236. Holmes, *In Love with Life*, 193, 69–70.
237. *Daily News*, 22 November 1951, 5.
238. Patricia Lewis, 'The Quest for Invisibility: Female Entrepreneurs and the Masculine Norm of Entrepreneurship', *Gender, Work and Organization* 13, no. 5 (2006): 453–69.

Chapter 5

1. *Westminster Gazette*, 1 July 1919, 5.
2. *Devon and Exeter Daily Gazette*, 1 July 1919, 6.
3. *Daily Express*, 3 July 1919, 3. See also *Westminster Gazette*, 1 July 1919, 5.
4. Nicoletta F. Gullace, *'The Blood of Our Sons': Men, Women, and the Renegotiation of British Citizenship during the Great War* (New York, 2002), 9; Adrian Bingham, 'The British Press and the 1918 Reform Act', *Parliamentary History* 37, no. 1 (2018): 150–67.
5. Mari Takayanagi, 'Women and the Vote: The Parliamentary Path to Equal Franchise, 1918–28', *Parliamentary History* 37, no. 1 (2018): 168–85, at 171.
6. Mari Takayanagi, 'Sacred Year or Broken Reed? The Sex Disqualification (Removal) Act 1919', *Women's History Review* 29, no. 4 (2020): 563–82, at 565–6.
7. Sex Disqualification (Removal) Act, 1919, 9 & 10 Geo. 5, c. 71, s. 1.
8. The quotes are from Martin Pugh and Meta Zimmeck: cited in Takayanagi, 'Sacred Year', 564.
9. Caroline Morris, 'Dr Ivy Williams: Inside yet Outside', *Women's History Review* 29, no. 4 (2020): 583–614, at 585–6.
10. Takayanagi, 'Sacred Year', 576; Anne Logan, 'In Search of Equal Citizenship: The Campaign for Women's Magistrates in England and Wales, 1910–1939', *Women's History Review* 16, no. 4 (2007): 501–18, at 503.
11. Takayanagi, 'Sacred Year', 570.
12. Takayanagi, 'Sacred Year', 576.
13. *Daily Express*, 14 January 1920, 4.
14. Leeds Stock Exchange, Managing Committee Minute Book, WYL543/1/7: 24 May 1917, 229, West Yorkshire Archive Service, Leeds.
15. Leeds Stock Exchange, Association Minute Book, WYL543/2/3: Special General Meeting, 25 June 1917, 39.
16. Leeds Stock Exchange, Secretary's Letter Book, WYL543/4/20: William Holmes to Annie Lawson, 25 June 1917.
17. *Financial News*, 27 June 1917, 2.
18. *The Accountant*, 14 July 1917, 26. See also *The Globe*, 9 August 1917, 4.
19. Leeds Stock Exchange, Association Minute Book, WYL543/2/3: Special General Meeting, 4 January 1922, 54.
20. *Daily Graphic*, 9 April 1919, 11.
21. *Sheffield Daily Telegraph*, 15 November 1929, 6.
22. Hargreaves Parkinson, *The ABC of Stocks and Shares: A Handbook for the Investor* (London, 1925), 9.
23. David Kynaston, *The Financial Times: A Centenary History* (London, 1988), 87.
24. *FT*, 5 September 1933, 1. See also *FT*, 11 September 1933, 1; *FT*, 30 September 1941, 1; *FT*, 29 April 1942, 1.
25. R. C. Michie, 'Friend or Foe? Information Technology and the London Stock Exchange since 1700', *Journal of Historical Geography* 23, no. 3 (1997): 304–26, at 309–10.
26. W. A. Thomas, *The Provincial Stock Exchanges* (Abingdon, 2014), 194–6.

244 NOTES TO PAGES 120–4

27. *The Economist*, 31 August 1912, 403; Thomas, *Provincial Stock Exchanges*, 212.
28. *Citizen*, 11 May 1923, 3. For the formation and early activities of the association, see *FT*, 29 April 1914, 7; *FT*, 29 June 1914, 7; *FT*, 22 October 1915, 2.
29. *FT*, 8 May 1916, 3; Thomas, *Provincial Stock Exchanges*, 212–13. See also Council of the Associated Stock Exchanges, AGMs, GB124.B18/2/1/1: Proceedings at the Annual Meeting, 8 October 1915, 4–12, Manchester Archives and Local Studies.
30. *Western Morning News*, 3 May 1923, 5; *Devon and Exeter Daily Gazette*, 4 May 1923, 10; *The Vote*, 18 April 1924, 121.
31. *Citizen*, 11 May 1923, 3.
32. *Daily Mail*, 11 April 1919, 2; *FT*, 3 April 1925, 4.
33. Thomas, *Provincial Stock Exchanges*, 212.
34. *FT*, 14 March 1924, 4.
35. *Woman's Leader*, 15 June 1923, 154.
36. *The Vote*, 28 January 1927, 27; *FT*, 17 December 1927, 6; *Daily Telegraph*, 25 August 1956, 7. Reasons for the abandonment of the charter are discussed in *FT*, 12 September 1938, 4.
37. *Manchester Guardian*, 27 May 1925, 13.
38. Thomas Mohr, 'The Rights of Women under the Constitution of the Irish Free State', *Irish Jurist* 41 (2006): 20–59, at 37.
39. *Irish Independent*, 27 May 1925, 7.
40. W. A. Thomas, *The Stock Exchanges of Ireland* (Liverpool, 1986), 86; *Weekly Irish Times*, 6 June 1925, 8.
41. *Cork Examiner*, 29 May 1925, 7.
42. *Irish Independent*, 29 May 1925, 6.
43. Irish Stock Exchange, *Oonah Keogh: A Celebration* (Dublin, 2014), 4.
44. *The Vote*, 5 June 1925, 177. When Holmes set up her firm in 1921, she did not consider applying for membership: Miss Gordon Holmes, *In Love with Life: A Pioneer Career Woman's Story* (London, 1944), 103.
45. *Daily Express*, 11 March 1924, 7; *Nottingham Evening Post*, 13 March 1924, 4; *Daily Mirror*, 18 March 1924, 9. For Mortimer's denial of the rumour, see *FT*, 14 March 1924, 4.
46. *FT*, 12 March 1924, 5.
47. The step was taken 'In view of the election of a lady as a member of the Dublin Stock Exchange': LSE, General Purposes Committee Minutes, MS 14600/116: 2 June 1925, 128.
48. Twenty-five members were present on this occasion, with twenty-four voting to exclude women and one abstaining: MS 14600/116: 15 June 1925, 145.
49. LSE, Selected Appendices to the Minutes of the General Purposes Committee, MS 19515/5: Travers Smith, Braithwaite, & Co. to Edward Satterthwaite, 19 June 1925, item 364.
50. LSE, General Purposes Committee Minutes, MS 14600/116: 6 July 1925, 186.
51. *Sheffield Daily Telegraph*, 21 May 1928, 6.
52. WFL, Annual Conference Reports, 2WFL/2/23: Twenty-Sixth Annual Conference, 29 April 1933, 77–8, The Women's Library, London School of Economics; *The Vote*, 13 March 1931, 84; *Manchester Guardian*, 9 April 1931, 16; *Yorkshire Evening Post*, 9 April 1931, 9; *The Vote*, 2 September 1932, 284; *Daily Mirror*, 17 May 1933, 5.
53. *FT*, 18 February 1939, 4.
54. LSE, Selected Appendices to the Minutes of the General Purposes Committee, MS 19515/6: Mab. Gosnell to Secretary of the Committee for General Purposes, 18 June 1936, item 397.
55. LSE, Selected Appendices to the Minutes of the General Purposes Committee, MS 19515/6: Fred H. E. Branson to A. L. F. Green, 16 June 1936, item 397.
56. LSE, General Purposes Committee Minutes, MS 14600/133: 22 June 1936, 97–8.
57. *FT*, 18 February 1939, 4.
58. *Sunday Times*, 3 September 1933, 17.
59. *Yorkshire Evening Post*, 9 April 1931, 9.
60. *The Vote*, 2 September 1932, 284.
61. *The Vote*, 2 September 1932, 284.
62. Council of the Associated Stock Exchanges, AGMs, GB124.B18/2/1/1: *Résumé of the Work of the Administration during the Year 1935–36*, 11.
63. Council of the Associated Stock Exchanges, AGMs, GB124.B18/2/1/1: Minutes of the Proceedings at the Forty-Sixth Annual Meeting of the Council, 16 October 1936, 8.
64. Departmental Committee on Share-Pushing: Evidence and Correspondence, Third Part, BT 55/109: Evidence of Richard Sefton Turner, 26 February 1937, 22, TNA.
65. Adrian Bingham, '"An Era of Domesticity?" Histories of Women and Gender in Interwar Britain', *Cultural and Social History* 1, no. 2 (2004): 225–33.

NOTES TO PAGES 125–9   245

66. *Manchester Guardian*, 9 April 1931, 16.
67. *Daily Telegraph*, 27 June 1930, 11.
68. *Manchester Guardian*, 9 April 1931, 16; *Manchester Guardian*, 25 April 1931, 22.
69. *Nottingham Evening Post*, 18 April 1931, 5. For more on the context, see Harold L. Smith, 'British Feminism and the Equal Pay Issue in the 1930s', *Women's History Review* 5, no. 1 (1996): 97–110.
70. *The Vote*, 17 April 1931, 124.
71. WFL, Annual Conference Reports, 2WFL/2/21: Twenty-Fourth Annual Conference, 18 April 1931, 35–8; *The Times*, 20 April 1931, 11.
72. WFL, Annual Conference Reports, 2WFL/2/22: Twenty-Fifth Annual Conference, 16 April 1932, 33–5; *The Observer*, 17 April 1932, 20.
73. In 1933 Midgley stood for election to the WFL's executive committee but failed to secure sufficient votes: WFL, Annual Conference Reports, 2WFL/2/23: Twenty-Sixth Annual Conference, 29 April 1933, 92–3.
74. They are discussed in LSE, General Purposes Committee Minutes, MS 14600/114: 17 December 1923, 64–6.
75. *The Times*, 17 December 1932, 9.
76. *The Vote*, 23 December 1932, 412.
77. *Daily Telegraph*, 31 December 1932, 10; *Daily Herald*, 31 December 1932, 3.
78. *Dundee Evening Telegraph*, 3 January 1933, 4.
79. *Daily Mirror*, 17 May 1933, 5.
80. Catriona Beaumont, 'Citizens not Feminists: The Boundary Negotiated between Citizenship and Feminism by Mainstream Women's Organizations in England, 1928–39', *Women's History Review* 9, no. 2 (2000): 411–29, at 412.
81. The 1935 conference in Bradford reportedly attracted this number: *Yorkshire Post*, 18 May 1935, 11.
82. WFL, Annual Conference Reports, 2WFL/2/21: Twenty-Fourth Annual Conference, 18 April 1931, 37.
83. WFL, Annual Conference Reports, 2WFL/2/23: Twenty-Sixth Annual Conference, 29 April 1933, 78.
84. William Leach, Hansard, 5th series, vol. 343, 1628 (14 February 1939).
85. *Yorkshire Observer*, 3 July 1936, 7.
86. This is documented by Florence Underwood: WFL, Annual Conference Reports, 2WFL/2/21: Twenty-Fourth Annual Conference, 18 April 1931, 36.
87. Adrian Bingham, 'Enfranchisement, Feminism and the Modern Woman: Debates in the British Popular Press, 1918–1939', in *The Aftermath of Suffrage: Women, Gender, and Politics in Britain, 1918–1945*, edited by Julie V. Gottlieb and Richard Toye (Houndmills, 2013), 87–104.
88. Ren Pepitone, 'Gender, Space, and Ritual: Women Barristers, the Inns of Court, and the Interwar Press', *Journal of Women's History* 28, no. 1 (2016): 60–83, at 62. Bingham also stresses the duality of press coverage: Bingham, 'Enfranchisement, Feminism and the Modern Woman', 88.
89. For more on this idea, see Linda McDowell, *Capital Culture: Gender at Work in the City* (Oxford, 1997), 145.
90. *Daily Mirror*, 23 May 1933, 11; *Daily Mirror*, 25 May 1933, 11.
91. *Daily Herald*, 16 February 1939, 9.
92. *Daily Mirror*, 17 May 1933, 5. Another broker 'laughed heartily': *Daily Express*, 3 July 1919, 3.
93. *Daily Mail*, 4 September 1933, 9.
94. *Daily Mail*, 26 June 1936, 10; *Daily Telegraph*, 7 September 1935, 10.
95. Beth Jenkins, 'Gender, Embodiment and Professional Identity in Britain, *c.*1890–1930', *Cultural and Social History* 17, no. 4 (2020): 499–514, at 504.
96. *Dundee Courier*, 2 May 1903, 5.
97. *Hull Daily Mail*, 2 May 1912, 6; *FT*, 2 May 1912, 9.
98. For a typical report, see *FT*, 23 January 1922, 6.
99. *FT*, 23 May 1914, 6.
100. Ian F. W. Beckett, *The Great War, 1914–1918*, 2nd edn (Abingdon, 2013), 291.
101. Ava Baron, 'Masculinity, the Embodied Male Worker, and the Historian's Gaze', *International Labor and Working-Class History*, 69 (2006): 143–60, at 151.
102. The phrase is Michael Kimmel's: cited in Fiona O'Rourke and Craig Haslop, '"We're Respectful Boys...We're Not Misogynistic!": Analysing Defensive, Contradictory and Changing Performances of Masculinity within Young Men's In-Person and Digitally Mediated Homosocial Spaces', *Journal of Gender Studies*, online (2024): 1–18, at 3.
103. *Yorkshire Evening Post*, 9 April 1931, 9.
104. *Daily Express*, 10 May 1928, 9.

246 NOTES TO PAGES 129–34

105. *Yorkshire Post*, 25 June 1936, 10. A related argument was that women brokers would be unpopular with members, which would make their position untenable, 'popularity being as valuable an asset as brains to a stockbroker': *Daily Express*, 3 July 1919, 3.
106. Jenkins, 'Gender, Embodiment and Professional Identity', 310.
107. Virginia Woolf, *A Room of One's Own and Three Guineas* (Oxford, 2015), 212.
108. *The Vote*, 17 April 1931, 124.
109. *Daily Telegraph*, 27 June 1930, 11.
110. *Manchester Guardian*, 9 April 1931, 16.
111. *Daily Express*, 25 June 1936, 1; *Daily Mirror*, 25 June 1936, 2.
112. *Daily Mail*, 26 June 1936, 10.
113. *Daily Mail*, 4 September 1933, 10.
114. *Somerset County Gazette*, cited in *The Vote*, 29 September 1933, 307.
115. *Thanet Advertiser*, 18 September 1936, 6.
116. *Daily Mirror*, 28 June 1932, 9. Ivar Kreuger and Clarence Hatry were financiers who went bust in 1932 and 1929 respectively.
117. Hansard, 5th series, vol. 343, 1631 (14 February 1939). Tate was one of several interwar female MPs who attempted to push the Conservative Party into more progressive stances on women's issues: Julie V. Gottlieb, 'Modes and Models of Conservative Women's Leadership in the 1930s', in *Rethinking Right-Wing Women: Gender and the Conservative Party, 1880s to the Present*, edited by Clarisse Berthezène and Julie V. Gottlieb (Manchester, 2017), 89–103, at 94, 98.
118. *Daily Express*, 15 February 1939, 8.
119. Kynaston, *Financial Times*, 88, 524.
120. *FT*, 15 March 1924, 4; *FT*, 17 December 1927, 6.
121. *Daily Express*, 10 May 1928, 9.
122. *The Vote*, 23 December 1932, 412; Florence Underwood in *Dundee Evening Telegraph*, 3 January 1933, 4.
123. *The Accountant*, 14 July 1917, 26.
124. *New York Herald* (European edn), 11 January 1914, 7; *New York Times*, 23 January 1927, 13; *New York Herald* (European edn), 29 June 1936, 4.
125. *New York Times*, 4 October 1928, 43.
126. *Daily Telegraph*, 27 October 1923, 13; *Woman's Leader*, 23 November 1923, 337; *The Vote*, 28 December 1923, 410; *The Vote*, 8 May 1931, 147.
127. *New York Herald* (European edn), 21 March 1928, 1; *Daily Mail*, 21 March 1928, 12; *Brownsville Herald*, 9 June 1929, 14. Edna Manovill was another unsuccessful applicant in 1929: *New York Herald* (European edn), 8 August 1931, 2. See also George Robb, *Ladies of the Ticker: Women and Wall Street from the Gilded Age to the Great Depression* (Urbana, 2017), 76.
128. *The Vote*, 9 May 1919, 183; *Jus Suffragii: The International Woman Suffrage News*, July 1919, 136; *The Vote*, 26 December 1919, 442.
129. For Amsterdam: *Algemeen Handelsblad*, 17 April 1923, 3; *Dublin Evening Telegraph*, 19 April 1923, 4; *The Vote*, 11 May 1923, 147. For Berlin: Owen Lyons, 'An Inverted Reflection: Representations of Finance and Speculation in Weimar Cinema' (PhD thesis, Carleton University, Ottawa, 2015), 163, 170. Else Goldsmit was reported as joining the Berlin Stock Exchange in 1928: *Aberdeen Press and Journal*, 4 April 1928, 6.
130. *The Vote*, 2 September 1932, 284.
131. *Birmingham Post*, 14 September 1956, 24; *The Times*, 17 September 1956, 11.
132. *Dublin Evening Press*, 15 May 1971, 8.
133. Catriona Beaumont, 'Women, Citizenship and Catholicism in the Irish Free State, 1922–1948', *Women's History Review* 6, no. 4 (1997): 563–85.
134. *Irish Times*, 26 June 1942, 3; *Irish Independent*, 27 June 1942, 2.
135. Departmental Committee on Share-Pushing: Evidence and Correspondence, Second Part, BT 55/108: Sir Thomas Inskip, 'Bucket Shops', 11 April 1935.
136. Hansard, 5th series, vol. 314, 2116 (15 July 1936).
137. Chris Swinson, *Regulation of the London Stock Exchange: Share Trading, Fraud and Reform, 1914–1945* (Abingdon, 2018), 195.
138. Kieran Heinemann, *Playing the Market: Retail Investment and Speculation in Twentieth-Century Britain* (Oxford, 2021), 37.
139. Finance: Stock Exchange, Measures to Curb Activities of Outside Brokers, 'Bucket Shops', and Share Pushers, T 160/1195/3: 'Share Pushing: Warning to the Public'.
140. *Daily News*, 20 March 1937, 1.
141. *Yorkshire Observer*, 3 July 1936, 7.

NOTES TO PAGES 134–8   247

142. Departmental Committee on Share-Pushing: Evidence and Correspondence, Third Part, BT 55/109: Evidence of R. B. Pearson, 11 March 1937, 36.
143. Departmental Committee on Share-Pushing: Miscellaneous Notes and Reports, BT 55/104: 'Memorandum by the Secretary on the Question of Evidence and Certain Points of Procedure', 4 December 1936, 3; Departmental Committee on Share-Pushing: Share-Pushing Legislation, 1937–38, BT 55/106: J. G. Henderson to Florence A. Underwood, 17 December 1936.
144. WFL, National Executive Committee Minutes, 2WFL/1/12: 30 January 1937, 67–8; Departmental Committee on Share-Pushing: Share-Pushing Legislation, 1937–38, BT 55/106: Florence A. Underwood to J. G. Henderson, 2 February 1937.
145. WFL minutes record that Holmes had been 'persuaded by us' to give evidence: WFL, National Executive Committee Minutes, 2WFL/1/12: 13 March 1937, 83.
146. Council of the Associated Stock Exchanges, AGMs, GB124.B18/2/1/1: Minutes of the Proceedings at the Forty-Seventh Annual Meeting of the Council, 15 October 1937, 3. Turner had in fact written to the committee secretary informing him that Holmes 'will be coming with me, in view of the very great interest we have in the matter, in order that she may hear all that transpires': Departmental Committee on Share-Pushing: Evidence and Correspondence, Third Part, BT 55/109: Richard Sefton Turner to J. G. Henderson, 15 February 1937.
147. Departmental Committee on Share-Pushing: Evidence and Correspondence, Third Part, BT 55/109: Evidence of Richard Sefton Turner, 26 February 1937, 22.
148. Holmes recounted the exchange in her autobiography: Holmes, *In Love with Life*, 127–8.
149. Council of the Associated Stock Exchanges, AGMs, GB124.B18/2/1/1: Minutes of the Proceedings at the Forty-Seventh Annual Meeting of the Council, 15 October 1937, 3–4.
150. *Yorkshire Observer*, 3 July 1936, 7.
151. Hansard, 5th series, vol. 325, 380W (16 June 1937); vol. 326, 345–6 (7 July 1937); vol. 326, 1507–8W (15 July 1937); vol. 342, 999–1000 (6 December 1938).
152. Swinson, *Regulation of the London Stock Exchange*, 198–202.
153. Hansard, 5th series, vol. 343, 1627–9 (14 February 1939).
154. WFL, National Executive Committee Minutes, 2WFL/1/12: 4 February 1939, 291.
155. Hansard, 5th series, vol. 343, 1629–34 (14 February 1939).
156. Hansard, 5th series, vol. 343, 1631–7 (14 February 1939).
157. *Daily Mail*, 15 February 1939, 3; *Sunderland Echo and Shipping Gazette*, 15 February 1939, 7; *Nottingham Journal*, 15 February 1939, 7; *Yorkshire Post*, 15 February 1939, 8.
158. Prevention of Fraud (Investments) Act, 1939: 2 & 3 Geo. 6, c. 16.
159. *Share-Pushing: Report of the Departmental Committee Appointed by the Board of Trade*, Parliamentary Papers 1936–7, XV, 44–7.
160. *FT*, 9 February 1938, 5.
161. *FT*, 9 February 1938, 5; *FT*, 9 July 1938, 5; *FT*, 24 August 1938, 7; *The Times*, 12 November 1938, 18.
162. By 1940, Jeanette Lamb in Kirriemuir had become a member, as had Merry & Sons, in which Mary Merry was a partner: *UKSSD for 1940*, 89–90.
163. They were Marion Dinwoodie, Edith Dodd, Margaret Dow, Doris Mortimer, Phyllis Robinson, Helen Tyrrell, and Ellen White: *UKSSD for 1940*, 98–101.
164. The registration provisions of the Act were due to come into force in September 1939, but war delayed this until 1944: Swinson, *Regulating the London Stock Exchange*, 219–20.
165. Council of the Associated Stock Exchanges, AGMs, GB124.B18/2/1/1: *Résumé of the Work of the Administration from March 1941 to October 1942*, 9.
166. Ranald Michie, *The London Stock Exchange: A History* (Oxford, 2001), 298.
167. In contrast to the experience of 1914–15, it closed for just a week at the start of September 1939: Michie, *London Stock Exchange*, 288.
168. *FT*, 1 September 1941, 2. See also *The Scotsman*, 27 August 1941, 2; *Liverpool Daily Post*, 27 August 1941, 2.
169. The London Stock Exchange had a system of 'dual control', the Committee for General Purposes representing the members, and the Trustees' and Managers' Committee representing the proprietors, a system which sometimes generated conflict: Michie, *London Stock Exchange*, 48–50.
170. *Daily Mirror*, 23 September 1941, 3.
171. *Daily News*, 23 September 1941, 4. The NYSE permitted thirty-six 'quote girls' onto the floor of its exchange in 1943: *FT*, 18 August 1943, 3.
172. *The Times*, 23 September 1941, 8.
173. *Illustrated London News*, 4 October 1941, 24.
174. LSE, General Purposes Committee Minutes, MS 14600/139: 29 September 1941, 50.

248 NOTES TO PAGES 138–42

175. *Daily News*, 23 September 1941, 4; *The Times*, 23 September 1941, 8; *The Economist*, 27 September 1941, 389.
176. LSE, General Purposes Committee Minutes, MS 14600/138: 5 August 1941, 394.
177. *The Scotsman*, 7 October 1941, 2; *FT*, 28 April 1942, 3.
178. *FT*, 6 October 1941, 1.
179. LSE, General Purposes Committee Minutes, MS 14600/138: 5 August 1941, 394.
180. LSE, General Purposes Committee Minutes, MS 14600/139: 29 September 1941, 50.
181. LSE, General Purposes Committee Minutes, MS 14600/139: 6 October 1941, 62; 1 December 1941, 134.
182. LSE, General Purposes Committee Minutes, MS 14600/139: 16 March 1942, 268.
183. LSE, General Purposes Committee Minutes, MS 14600/139: 20 April 1942, 321.
184. LSE, General Purposes Committee Minutes, MS 14600/139: 27 April 1942, 329–30. For commentary, see *FT*, 5 May 1942, 3; *The Times*, 5 May 1942, 7; *FT*, 18 May 1942, 1.
185. LSE, General Purposes Committee Minutes, MS 14600/139: 4 May 1942, 343.
186. *FT*, 28 April 1942, 3.
187. *FT*, 20 May 1942, 3. By this point, there were five women on the marking boards: *FT*, 29 April 1942, 1.
188. In a six-month period in 1944 (May–October), nine women clerks were approved, and five were withdrawn: LSE, General Purposes Committee Minutes, MS 14600/142: 59–239.
189. *FT*, 10 September 1943, 3.
190. *FT*, 8 May 1942, 1, 9; *The Economist*, 16 May 1942, 686–7; *FT*, 26 May 1942, 2; *FT*, 23 October 1942, 4.
191. The firm believed it was the first member of any UK stock exchange to make such a request: *FT*, 9 March 1942, 2; *FT*, 16 March 1942, 2; *Liverpool Daily Post*, 1 June 1968, 5.
192. 1939 Register, RG 101/3583G/002.
193. 1939 Register, RG 101/3509D/015; *London Gazette*, 16 December 1941, 7139.
194. *Sunday Mirror*, 20 October 1968, 35.
195. Sheffield Stock Exchange, Minutes of Members' and Annual Meetings, LD 2007/1/4(a): 26 May 1941, 56; 12 August 1942, 78; 14 August 1942, 78, Sheffield City Archives.
196. *Manchester Guardian*, 10 December 1943, 4.
197. Clementine Churchill to Winston Churchill, 10 December 1943, cited in Sonia Purnell, *First Lady: The Life and Wars of Clementine Churchill* (London, 2015), 279.
198. *FT*, 16 March 1944, 3. See also *Daily Telegraph*, 15 March 1944, 5; *The Observer*, 19 March 1944, 2.
199. Lucy Noakes, *Women in the British Army: War and the Gentle Sex, 1907–1948* (London, 2006), 131.
200. Penny Summerfield and Corinna Peniston-Bird, 'Women in the Firing Line: The Home Guard and the Defence of Gender Boundaries in Britain in the Second World War', *Women's History Review* 9, no. 2 (2000): 231–55, at 231–2.
201. LSE, General Purposes Committee Minutes, MS 14600/133: Mabel Gosnell to Secretary, 14 July 1936, 141.
202. LSE, General Purposes Committee Minutes, MS 14600/133: 27 July 1936, 141.
203. For an example of the former, see *Yorkshire Observer*, 23 January 1936, 4.
204. LSE, General Purposes Committee Minutes, MS 14600/133: 25 May 1936, 63–4; 2 June 1936, 73; 8 June 1936, 74.
205. *Daily Telegraph*, 4 September 1956, 6.
206. Mabel Gosnell, 24 November 1972, National Probate Calendar.
207. *London Gazette*, 13 October 1953, 5466.
208. Edith Midgley, 20 September 1960, National Probate Calendar.
209. *Daily News*, 22 November 1951, 5; *Yorkshire Evening Post*, 22 November 1951, 6; *Belfast Telegraph*, 22 November 1951, 4; *Daily Mail*, 23 November 1951, 7.
210. *Coventry Evening Telegraph*, 28 March 1952, 22.
211. By 1930 she had moved from her Throgmorton Street premises to basement offices in Copthall Court, an environment thick with stockbrokers: *Post Office London Directory for 1930*, 233.
212. Edith Mary Maskell, 4 July 1933, National Probate Calendar.
213. *Exeter Express and Echo*, 27 January 1940, 7.
214. 1939 Register, RG 101/6754H/013.
215. Doris Ellen Mortimer, 7 July 1947, National Probate Calendar.
216. 1939 Register, RG 101/5681F/018.
217. *Coventry Evening Telegraph*, 22 February 1951, 15; *Coventry Evening Telegraph*, 1 January 1954, 24.

NOTES TO PAGES 142–7   249

218. *Coventry Evening Telegraph*, 31 January 1972, 1; Amy Hargraves Moreton, 12 April 1972, National Probate Calendar.
219. *London Gazette*, 22 January 1960, 647. The business continued to thrive, and was still trading early this century: *Lancashire Telegraph*, 10 January 2003: <https://www.lancashiretelegraph.co.uk/news/5924665.firm-joins-broker-network/>.
220. Phyllis Moscrop Eastwood, 19 February 1975, National Probate Calendar.
221. 1939 Register RG 101/7004J/009; *London Gazette*, 3 June 1932, 3633; *Bath Chronicle and Herald*, 4 November 1933, 3; *Bath Chronicle and Herald*, 2 September 1950, 4; *London Gazette*, 12 November 1954, 6439.
222. *FT*, 31 March 1964, 8.
223. Ellen Rose White, 23 April 1968, National Probate Calendar.
224. *FT*, 31 March 1964, 8; *The Times*, 12 August 1969, 21.
225. Helen Gladys Tyrrell, 8 August 1976, National Probate Calendar.

Chapter 6

1. Other banks had proven more progressive: the Birmingham Municipal Bank had employed female branch managers during the Second World War, three of whom continued to work in this capacity from 1946. For details, see The History of the Birmingham Municipal Bank website, 'Lady Branch Managers': <https://www.bmbstaff.org.uk/bmb-staff_162.htm>.
2. *Daily Telegraph*, 17 May 1958, 13; *The Times*, 17 May 1958, 4.
3. Helen McCarthy, 'Social Science and Married Women's Employment in Post-War Britain', *Past and Present* 233 (2016): 269–305, at 277.
4. Cited in McCarthy, 'Social Science', 285.
5. Arthur McIvor, *Working Lives: Work in Britain since 1945* (London, 2013), 93.
6. Patricia M. Thane, 'What Difference Did the Vote Make? Women in Public and Private Life in Britain since 1918', *Historical Research* 76, no. 192 (2003): 268–85, at 278.
7. Harold L. Smith, 'The Politics of Conservative Reform: The Equal Pay for Equal Work Issue, 1945–1955', *Historical Journal* 35, no. 2 (1992): 401–15.
8. Kate Murphy, '"Careers for Women": BBC Women's Radio Programmes and the "Professional", 1923–1955', *Women's History Review* 32, no. 6 (2023): 809–27, at 810, 818; Peter Scott, 'From "Pin Money" to Careers: Britain's Late Move to Equal Pay, Its Consequences, and Broader Implications', *Enterprise and Society* 25, no. 2 (2024): 376–401, at 395–6.
9. For a sociological study with a more pronounced historical dimension, see Rosemary Crompton, 'Women in Banking: Continuity and Change since the Second World War', *Work, Employment and Society* 3, no. 2 (1989): 141–56.
10. Kieran Heinemann, 'Investment, Speculation and Popular Stock Market Engagement in 20th-Century Britain', *Archiv für Sozialgeschichte* 56 (2016): 249–72, at 267–8.
11. Orsi Husz identifies a 'feminization of finance' in Sweden around the same time: Orsi Husz, 'The Birth of the Finance Consumer: Feminists, Bankers and the Re-Gendering of Finance in Mid-Twentieth-Century Sweden', *Contemporary European History*, online (2023): 1–20, at 1.
12. *FT*, 16 January 1962, 9.
13. *Sunday Telegraph*, 12 December 1971, 26.
14. Ruth Dudley Edwards, *The Pursuit of Reason: The Economist, 1843–1993* (London 1993), 469.
15. *The Times*, 30 September 1972, 20.
16. David Kynaston, *The Financial Times: A Centenary History* (London, 1988), 280.
17. *Punch*, 21 April 1971, 24.
18. *Sunday Times*, 9 April 1967, 107.
19. *Daily Telegraph*, 30 October 1971, 23; *The Times*, 24 June 1972, 20. The pieces were by Stella Shamoon and Sally White respectively.
20. *Daily Mail*, 30 August 1963, 11; *Daily Telegraph*, 31 October 1963, 15.
21. *Daily Mail*, 3 April 1964, 3; *FT*, 3 April 1964, 26; *Daily Mail*, 8 June 1964, 9; *FT*, 8 June 1964, 2.
22. *The Times*, 9 July 1962, 13.
23. *Sunday Telegraph*, 25 April 1965, 9.
24. *Daily Telegraph*, 20 July 1968, 4.
25. *The Guardian*, 30 April 1970, 11.
26. *Daily Telegraph*, 26 June 1958, 7.
27. *Census 1951, England and Wales: Occupation Tables* (London, 1956), 16. It is possible that some of the 370 women listed under 'Other finance occupations' were involved in broking. Subsequent censuses did not report occupational data to this level of detail.
28. Kieran Heinemann, *Playing the Market: Retail Investment and Speculation in Twentieth-Century Britain* (Oxford, 2021), 54–8.

250   NOTES TO PAGES 147–51

29. Cited in F. A. A. Menzler, *The Sunday Times Career Books: The Stock Exchange* (London, 1961), 39.
30. Ranald Michie, *The London Stock Exchange: A History* (Oxford, 2001), 378.
31. For an example, see Cathy Courtney and Paul Thompson, *City Lives: The Changing Voices of British Finance* (London, 1996), 38.
32. David Kynaston, *The City of London*, vol. 4, *A Club No More, 1945–2000* (London, 2002), 170.
33. Heinemann, *Playing the Market*, 172.
34. *FT*, 15 February 1941, 3; *FT*, 4 February 1946, 2; *FT*, 16 December 1947, 4.
35. Michie, *London Stock Exchange*, 380.
36. *Daily Express*, 8 December 1965, 3.
37. This was her second marriage, having been previously married briefly to Conservative MP John Langford-Holt: *Daily Telegraph*, 10 June 1944, 2. Details of her early life are reported in her obituaries: *FT*, 4 January 2007, 20; *Daily Telegraph*, 16 January 2007, 25; *The Times*, 12 February 2007, 48.
38. For examples, see *The Tatler and Bystander*, 10 April 1957, 78; 29 April 1959, 242; 4 November 1959, 266.
39. This business was in fact only formed in 1966 as the result of a merger of two firms, Hedderwick Hunt Cox & Co. and Borthwick & Co. It is unclear which of these firms Rivers-Bulkeley originally worked for: *FT*, 17 February 1966, 16.
40. Records of Careers for Women, Conference Papers, 6CFW/E/25, Box 6: National Advisory Centre on Careers for Women (NACCW) Careers Course 1972, 'The Stock Exchange', Mrs E. Rivers-Bulkeley, 1, The Women's Library, London School of Economics.
41. Rosemary Crompton, 'The Feminisation of the Clerical Labour Force since the Second World War', in *The White-Blouse Revolution: Female Office Workers since 1870*, edited by Gregory Anderson (Manchester, 1988), 121–43.
42. Menzler, *The Stock Exchange*, 58; Crompton, 'Women in Banking', 145. The turn to women in post-war banking was driven by recruitment problems rather than any principled shift: Margaret Ackrill and Leslie Hannah, *Barclays: The Business of Banking, 1690–1996* (Cambridge, 2001), 344.
43. Amy Thomas, *The City in the City: Architecture and Change in London's Financial District* (Cambridge, MA, 2023), 269–78.
44. Thomas, *City in the City*, 284.
45. The career path is described in Stephen Raven, interview with Bernard Attard, 16 May 1990, London Stock Exchange Oral History: <https://sas-space.sas.ac.uk/2766/>.
46. 1921 Census, RG 15/06345, ED 19, Sch. 26; *Illustrated London News*, 11 March 1967, 29; Kynaston, *A Club No More*, 159.
47. *Daily Telegraph*, 22 June 1968, 5.
48. Cited in Kynaston, *A Club No More*, 159; *Reading Evening Post*, 31 January 1967, 4.
49. *Daily Telegraph*, 22 June 1968, 5.
50. Kynaston, *A Club No More*, 159.
51. Michie, *London Stock Exchange*, 384.
52. Michie, *London Stock Exchange*, 441; Heinemann, *Playing the Market*, 13–14, 61–2.
53. Kynaston, *A Club No More*, 163.
54. Michie, *London Stock Exchange*, 432; *FT*, 19 October 1966, 15; *FT*, 5 August 1967, 9.
55. Kynaston, *A Club No More*, 331–2.
56. Aled Davies, *The City of London and Social Democracy: The Political Economy of Finance in Britain, 1959–1979* (Oxford, 2017), 39.
57. Though long a feature of the American market, investment analysis had taken longer to gain a foothold in Britain.
58. *FT*, 2 May 1955, 1.
59. Michie, *London Stock Exchange*, 384; W. J. Reader and David Kynaston, *Phillips & Drew: Professionals in the City* (London, 1998), 67.
60. *Daily Telegraph*, 14 July 1973, 25.
61. *Daily Telegraph*, 23 January 1971, 15.
62. *FT*, 18 May 1961, 13.
63. *Sunday Telegraph*, 15 March 1970, 32; Menzler, *The Stock Exchange*, 40, 43; Kynaston, *A Club No More*, 172.
64. Michie, *London Stock Exchange*, 379.
65. *Daily Telegraph*, 2 May 1968, 19.
66. *FT*, 25 February 1966, 8.
67. Claire G. Jones, 'Women, Science and Professional Identity, *c.*1860–1914', in *Precarious Professionals: Gender, Identities and Social Change in Modern Britain*, edited by Heidi Egginton and Zoë Thomas (London, 2021), 63–85; Leslie Howsam, 'Legal Paperwork and Public Policy: Eliza Orme's Professional Expertise in Late-Victorian Britain', in *Precarious Professionals*, 107–24.

NOTES TO PAGES 151–7   251

68. Robert M. Blackburn and Jennifer Jarman, 'Changing Inequalities in Access to British Universities', *Oxford Review of Education* 19, no. 2 (1993): 197–215, at 200.
69. *The Times*, 27 October 1969, 6. See also *Daily Telegraph*, 14 July 1973, 25.
70. *Aberdeen Press and Journal*, 5 December 1944, 4; 29 June 1964, 3; *Aberdeen Evening Express*, 15 August 1961, 5.
71. *Aberdeen Press and Journal*, 1 February 1973, 7; 2 February 1973, 2; *FT*, 2 February 1973, 11; *Daily Mirror*, 2 February 1973, 20.
72. *Sunday Telegraph*, 15 March 1970, 32.
73. Hilary Pearson, interview with author, 20 January 2023.
74. Anthea Gaukroger, interview with author, 20 January 2023.
75. *The Guardian*, 13 December 1965, 10.
76. *Sunday Telegraph*, 21 September 1986, 63.
77. Gillian Murray, 'Taking Work Home: The Private Secretary and Domestic Identities in the Long 1950s', *Women's History Review* 26, no. 1 (2017): 62–76, at 64.
78. E. Rivers-Bulkeley, 'The Stock Exchange', NACCW Careers Course 1972, 2.
79. *Daily Telegraph*, 6 May 1972, 23; *FT*, 27 April 2002, 16.
80. *Cosmopolitan*, July 1975, 100; *Aberdeen Press and Journal*, 24 May 1971, 2; *Daily Telegraph*, 3 May 1972, 19.
81. *Newcastle Journal*, 21 May 1971, 8; *Aberdeen Press and Journal*, 24 May 1971, 2.
82. The visitors' gallery and its guides are discussed at more length in Chapter 7.
83. This firm was unconnected to Doris Mortimer's firm of the same name based in Exeter discussed in earlier chapters.
84. The information in this paragraph is from Susan Shaw, interview with author, 11 July 2024. See also Malvern Alumnae 100 Profiles, Susan Shaw: <https://www.malvernstjames.co.uk/ma100/susan-shaw>.
85. *FT*, 31 March 1964, 8.
86. 1939 Register RG 101/6426C/013; *FT*, 31 March 1964, 8; *Lincolnshire Echo*, 8 April 1974, 9; *Lincolnshire Echo*, 6 November 1979, 9.
87. 1921 Census, RG 15/20871, ED 23, Sch. 30; 1939 Register RG 101/4804A/012; *Manchester Evening News*, 13 April 1964, 10. Her name was Mary Constance, but she was known as Connie.
88. *FT*, 31 March 1964, 8; *The Scotsman*, 11 January 1969, 3; *Daily Telegraph*, 4 October 1974, 23.
89. *The Times*, 29 March 1962, 18.
90. *Airdrie and Coatbridge Advertiser*, 26 June 1926, 5; 9 October 1926, 5; *Coatbridge Express*, 7 September 1927, 2.
91. The earliest reference I have to her working at the firm is 1955, but in 1969 she was described as having 'given a lifetime of service' to the firm: *Edinburgh Gazette*, 29 April 1955, 265; *FT*, 10 January 1969, 19.
92. *The Scotsman*, 10 January 1969, 10.
93. 1881 Census, RG 11/3775, f. 12, 18; 1911 Census, RG 14/17972, Sch. 265; 1921 Census, RG 15/13990, ED 33, Sch. 404; William Henry Jones, 22 September 1924, National Probate Calendar.
94. Civil Registration Marriage Index, vol. 6d, Marriages Registered in July, August, and September 1931, 236, accessed Ancestry.com; 1939 Register, RG 101/5569H/020.
95. *Birmingham Daily Gazette*, 24 August 1956, 1; *Daily Mirror*, 24 August 1956, 5.
96. For the Wards, see *Sunday Mirror*, 20 October 1968, 35; for Melvin, see *Aberdeen Press and Journal*, 31 August 1977, 7.
97. Margaret Holt obituary, 4 January 2021, *The Guardian*: <https://www.theguardian.com/business/2021/jan/04/margaret-holt-obituary>.
98. *Daily Telegraph*, 3 May 1972, 19.
99. *Liverpool Echo*, 6 April 1972, 1; *FT*, 7 April 1972, 23.
100. *The Times*, 7 April 1972, 21. She may have responded to this advert: *Liverpool Echo*, 21 June 1967, 13.
101. McIvor, *Working Lives*, 21.
102. *Sunday Telegraph*, 15 November 1970, 28; Courtney and Thompson, *City Lives*, 121–2.
103. *Sunday Telegraph*, 3 August 1969, 19; *Daily Mail*, 23 June 1971, 16; *Daily Telegraph*, 4 March 1972, 21; *The Times*, 23 September 1972, 20; *FT*, 26 March 1973, 12.
104. Paul Thompson, 'The Pyrrhic Victory of Gentlemanly Capitalism: The Financial Elite of the City of London, 1945–90, Part 2', *Journal of Contemporary History* 32, no. 4 (1997): 427–40, at 430–1.
105. Cited in Davies, *City of London*, 40–1.

252 NOTES TO PAGES 157–9

106. Janette Rutterford and Dimitris P. Sotiropoulos, 'The Rise of the Small Investor in the United States and United Kingdom, 1895 to 1970', *Enterprise and Society* 18, no. 3 (2017): 485–535, at 522.
107. Amy Edwards, '"Manufacturing Capitalists": The Wider Share Ownership Council and the Problem of "Popular Capitalism", 1958–92', *Twentieth Century British History* 27, no. 1 (2016): 100–23, at 105.
108. *The Times*, 14 December 1959, 11; *Liverpool Daily Post*, 19 February 1959, 2. The latter article already identified the 'cloth cap investor' as a 'financial cliché'.
109. *How Does Britain Save? A Summary of the Results of a Survey Conducted for the London Stock Exchange by the British Market Research Bureau Limited* (London, 1966), 28–9. The survey was based on over 3,200 interviews.
110. John Treasure, 'The British Shareholder', *Stock Exchange Journal*, October 1966, 9.
111. *Daily Mail*, 15 November 1972, 18. The survey was a small one, based on under 4,000 respondents: *FT*, 26 November 1971, 19. City brokerages were allowed to establish branches from the mid-1960s, but few opted to do so: Michie, *London Stock Exchange*, 458–9.
112. Treasure, 'British Shareholder', 10.
113. Dilwyn Porter, '"Hoping You'll Give Me Some Guidance about This Thing Called Money": The *Daily Mirror* and Personal Finance, *c.*1960–81', in *People, Places, and Identities: Themes in British Social and Cultural History, 1700s–1980s*, edited by Alan Kidd and Melanie Tebbutt (Manchester, 2017), 202–20.
114. Heinemann, *Playing the Market*, 65–81. For the post-war shift away from investigations of poverty towards studies of 'ordinary' or 'affluent' Britain, see Jon Lawrence, 'Class, "Affluence" and the Study of Everyday Life in Britain, *c.*1930–64', *Cultural and Social History* 10, no. 2 (2013): 273–99.
115. *FT*, 2 March 1949, 4; Rutterford and Sotiropoulos, 'Rise of the Small Investor'.
116. *Daily Express*, 28 November 1956, 12; *Evening Standard*, 17 May 1962, 3; *The Guardian*, 16 January 1967, 6.
117. *Evening Standard*, 13 February 1962, 3.
118. *Daily Mail*, 28 January 1964, 10.
119. Edwards, *Are We Rich Yet?*, 212.
120. Heinemann, *Playing the Market*, 76; *The Times*, 6 November 1961, 6; *Sunday Mirror*, 21 October 1962, 24; *Daily Mail*, 7 November 1961, 8; *FT*, 14 December 1962, 19.
121. Second prize was shared by a woman, and four of the ten runners-up spots were taken by women: *Daily Mail*, 7 January 1960, 2.
122. *Daily Mail*, 30 April 1958, 8.
123. *Birmingham Post*, 2 February 1973, 8; *Daily Mail*, 3 July 1982, 27.
124. *Sunday Mirror*, 5 March 1967, 28.
125. *Sunday Mirror*, 12 March 1967, 33.
126. *Daily Telegraph*, 6 May 1972, 23.
127. *Birmingham Post*, 21 January 1969, 10.
128. *The Guardian*, 16 January 1967, 6; *Daily Telegraph*, 6 May 1972, 23. Another report gave the figure as 750: *Daily Mail*, 18 January 1967, 9.
129. An exception was attaché Dorothy Griffin, born in 1899, who began work before the Second World War, and 'specialises in advising women clients who have no financial knowledge': *Investors Chronicle*, 24 May 1968, 793.
130. Fraser built up a diverse client list of around 500, while Root's list was equally divided between men and women: *Daily Telegraph*, 6 May 1972, 23; *Aberdeen Press and Journal*, 17 May 1972, 10; *FT*, 27 April 2002, 16; Pearson, interview with author.
131. *FT*, 31 March 1964, 8.
132. *The Guardian*, 7 April 1972, 7.
133. *Aberdeen Evening News*, 1 February 1973, 7.
134. *The Times*, 6 May 1972, 18. For similar sentiments from Peachey, see *Daily Telegraph*, 3 May 1972, 19.
135. *Stock Exchange Gazette*, 27 January 1967, 237; *Illustrated London News*, 11 March 1967, 32. Another example was Edna Stokes: *Evening Standard*, 21 March 1973, 51; *Daily Telegraph*, 27 March 1973, 21.
136. Her clients 'were mostly friends and family, and friends of friends': Gaukroger, interview with author; *The Times*, 1 February 1973, 23.
137. E. Rivers-Bulkeley, 'The Stock Exchange', NACCW Careers Course 1972. Another attaché, Dorothy Griffin, who worked for Southard Gilbey McNish, had 'visited overseas Exchanges and studied them in detail': *Investors Chronicle*, 24 May 1968, 793.

NOTES TO PAGES 160–4   253

138. *Women's Report*, July–August 1973, 4.
139. For the example of Hermione Bridges, see *Sunday Telegraph*, 26 November 1972, 32.
140. *Daily Mail*, 18 March 1970, 19.
141. *FT*, 10 January 1969, 19.
142. *The Guardian*, 4 January 2021: <https://www.theguardian.com/business/2021/jan/04/margaret-holt-obituary>.
143. LSE, General Purposes Committee Minutes, MS 14600/114: 17 December 1923, 64–6; *FT*, 16 September 1929, 1; H. H. West, 'What Sort of Examination for Stock Exchange Members and Whom Would It Benefit?', *Stock Exchange Journal*, June 1963, 4–6.
144. For the pro-case, see F. C. Simon to the *FT*, 27 January 1950, 4; F. E. Armstrong to the *FT*, 1 February 1950, 4.
145. Donald Cobbett, 'Professional Status for Members?', *Stock Exchange Journal*, Spring 1959, 105.
146. *The Times*, 30 April 1951, 9; *FT*, 21 January 1952, 1.
147. *FT*, 6 November 1962, 2. Federation is discussed at more length in Chapter 7.
148. *FT*, 12 February 1964, 1.
149. *FT*, 3 May 1968, 17; *Stock Exchange Journal*, June 1968, 2.
150. *Daily Mail*, 12 February 1964, 8.
151. *Evening Standard*, 11 February 1964, 3. See also *Daily Mail*, 12 February 1964, 8; *The Times*, 14 June 1968, 13.
152. *FT*, 19 January 1959, 2; *Stock Exchange Journal*, Winter 1958–9, 78.
153. *Newcastle Journal*, 21 May 1971, 8.
154. *FT*, 30 September 1970, 18.
155. Gaukroger and Pearson, interview with author; *Sunday Times*, 23 May 1971, 45.
156. *Daily Mail*, 19 July 1971, 16. See also *Investors Chronicle*, 3 May 1968, 438.
157. *FT*, 26 August 1971, 15.
158. *FT*, 7 April 1972, 23. See also *Sunday Telegraph*, 27 August 1972, 26.
159. *Sunday Mirror*, 14 February 1965, 33. See also *Sunday Telegraph*, 24 May 1964, 16.
160. *Evening Standard*, 13 February 1962, 3.
161. *Evening Standard*, 13 September 1960, 2.
162. Stuart Aveyard, Paul Corthorn, and Sean O'Connell, *The Politics of Consumer Credit in the UK, 1938–1992* (Oxford, 2018), 181–4; Libby Assassi, *The Gendering of Global Finance* (Houndmills, 2009), 91–2.
163. *Investors Chronicle*, 23 September 1960, 1113; *Investors Chronicle*, 30 September 1960, 1199.
164. *Investors Chronicle*, 7 October 1960, 11. This is also discussed in Heinemann, 'Investment, Speculation and Popular Stock Market Engagement', 267–8 n. 131.
165. See, for example, *Daily Telegraph*, 20 January 1965, 15; *Daily Telegraph*, 10 February 1965, 15.
166. *Sunday Telegraph*, 20 September 1970, 25.
167. Jessica Prestidge, 'Housewives Having a Go: Margaret Thatcher, Mary Whitehouse and the Appeal of the Right Wing Woman in Late Twentieth-Century Britain', *Women's History Review* 28, no. 2 (2019): 277–96.
168. *Aberdeen Press and Journal*, 9 June 1971, 6.
169. *Daily Telegraph*, 20 July 1968, 4.
170. *Aberdeen Press and Journal*, 9 June 1971, 6.
171. *FT*, 23 April 1970, 18.
172. *Aberdeen Press and Journal*, 1 February 1973, 7.
173. *FT*, 3 February 1961, 10.
174. *Newcastle Journal*, 21 May 1971, 8.
175. *Daily Mail*, 23 November 1964, 14.
176. *Daily Mail*, 23 November 1964, 14.
177. Shaw, interview with author. Anthea Gaukroger makes the same point: Gaukroger, interview with author.
178. *Daily Mail*, 18 March 1970, 19.
179. As well as chairing the Calthorpe Women's Luncheon Club, originally an offshoot of the local Conservative association, she was 'a member of the ladies' committee of the Royal Commonwealth Society for the Blind, of the ladies' committee of Birmingham and Midland Eye Hospital and is a member of the local rating and valuation panel': *Birmingham Post*, 5 November 1962, 3.
180. *Birmingham Post*, 12 January 1961, 4; *Birmingham Post*, 5 April 1968, 1.
181. Gaukroger and Root were not members of any such clubs, and press reports rarely highlighted memberships among other women working for City brokerages: Gaukroger and Pearson, interview with author.

254 NOTES TO PAGES 164–9

182. *Daily Telegraph*, 8 May 1967, 13.
183. This was in the context of a wider City culture which was by this point overwhelmingly hostile to the Labour Party: Kynaston, *A Club No More*, 8–9.
184. *The Guardian*, 2 February 1973, 13; *Daily Telegraph*, 2 February 1973, 3; *Stock Exchange Gazette*, 27 January 1967, 237.
185. *Daily Mail*, 7 April 1972, 15.
186. David Swift, 'From "I'm Not a Feminist, But..." to "Call Me an Old-Fashioned Feminist...": Conservative Women in Parliament and Feminism, 1979–2017', *Women's History Review* 28, no. 2 (2019): 317–36.
187. Valerie Bryson and Timothy Heppell, 'Conservatism and Feminism: The Case of the British Conservative Party', *Journal of Political Ideologies* 15, no. 1 (2010): 31–50, at 40–1.
188. Swift, 'I'm Not a Feminist', 330.
189. Patricia Lewis, 'The Quest for Invisibility: Female Entrepreneurs and the Masculine Norm of Entrepreneurship', *Gender, Work and Organization* 13, no. 5 (2006): 453–69.
190. Linda McDowell, *Capital Culture: Gender at Work in the City* (Oxford, 1997), 137.
191. McDowell, *Capital Culture*, 139.
192. Margaret Allen, 'Women in a Man's World', *Stock Exchange Journal*, March 1963, 25.
193. *Sunday Mirror*, 24 March 1963, 19.
194. *Daily Mail*, 23 November 1964, 14.
195. *Investors Review*, 5 October 1973, 9.
196. *Sydney Morning Herald*, 23 February 1975, 106.
197. *The Observer*, 5 March 1967, 9.
198. *Evening Standard*, 16 May 1958, 4; *Daily Mirror*, 17 May 1958, 7; ITN broadcast, 1 December 1958:<https://www.gettyimages.co.uk/detail/video/interview-with-miss-hilda-harding-britains-first-woman-news-footage/1313872778>.
199. *Daily Mail*, 30 April 1958, 8.
200. *Daily Mail*, 23 November 1964, 14.
201. *Cosmopolitan*, July 1975, 100
202. *Sunday Telegraph*, 22 January 1967, 5.
203. *FT*, 31 March 1964, 8; *Lincolnshire Echo*, 8 April 1971, 10.
204. *Lincolnshire Echo*, 8 April 1971, 10; 8 April 1974, 9.
205. *London Gazette*, 3 December 1971, 13320.
206. Information from William Richmond, 29 January 2023, Facebook.
207. *Sunday Times*, 26 March 1967, 33.
208. Michie, *London Stock Exchange*, 433.
209. *The Times*, 11 February 1971, 24; *Sunday Times*, 4 February 1973, 55.
210. *Sunday Telegraph*, 26 November 1972, 32.
211. *Daily Telegraph*, 2 August 1978, 13.
212. Margaret Ellen Fraser, The Peerage, Person Page 58457: <https://www.thepeerage.com/p58457.htm#i584570>.
213. *Daily Telegraph*, 6 May 1972, 23.
214. *FT*, 30 September 1970, 18; *Daily Telegraph*, 6 May 1972, 23.
215. Cited in Courtney and Thompson, *City Lives*, 177.
216. *The Observer*, 5 March 1967, 9.
217. *Daily Telegraph*, 6 May 1972, 23.
218. More generally, growing levels of women's employment were largely driven by the fourfold increase in numbers of part-time workers in the 1950s and 1960s: Dolly Smith Wilson, 'A New Look at the Affluent Worker: The Good Working Mother in Post-War Britain', *Twentieth Century British History* 17, no. 2 (2006): 206–29, at 208.
219. *The Observer*, 1 April 1973, 19.
220. Shaw, interview with author; email correspondence with author, 19 July 2024.
221. *Daily Telegraph*, 5 September 1970, 16.
222. *Daily Telegraph*, 21 December 1973, 9.
223. *Daily Telegraph*, 16 January 2007, 25.
224. *FT*, 30 September 1970, 18; *Evening Standard*, 21 May 1971, 3. Spending longer in the United States was former model, Manchester-born Vivien Ellis, who worked for New York brokerage Shields & Co. *The Times*, 20 June 1967, 23.
225. *Daily Mail*, 9 June 1971, 18; Reader and Kynaston, *Phillips & Drew*, 131–2.
226. For the 'qualifications lever', see Crompton, 'Women in Banking', 142–3; for a sceptical view of the 'lever', see Fiona Devine, 'Gender Segregation in the Engineering and Science Professions: A Case of Continuity and Change', *Work, Employment and Society* 6, no. 4 (1992): 557–75.

NOTES TO PAGES 170–6   255

227. *Birmingham Post*, 30 August 1956, 4.
228. *Newcastle Journal*, 21 May 1971, 8.
229. *Daily Telegraph*, 6 May 1972, 23; *Daily Mail*, 18 March 1970, 19.
230. *Daily Telegraph*, 6 May 1972, 23.
231. West, 'What Sort of Examination', 6; Minutes of the Stock Exchange Council, 17 October 1955, cited in Kynaston, *A Club No More*, 161–2.
232. Cited in Reader and Kynaston, *Phillips & Drew*, 101.
233. Hugh Vanderfelt, senior partner of Vanderfelt & Co., cited in Kynaston, *A Club No More*, 162.
234. When appointing staff, one of the key qualities Swan looked for was 'flair', and his golden rule was 'no egg heads': Reader and Kynaston, *Phillips & Drew*, 96.
235. Courtney and Thompson, *City Lives*, 122.

Chapter 7

1. Kieran Heinemann, *Playing the Market: Retail Investment and Speculation in Twentieth-Century Britain* (Oxford, 2021), 60–1.
2. LSE, General Purposes Committee Minutes, MS 14600/143: 14 May 1945, 87; 2 July 1945, 147.
3. LSE, General Purposes Committee Minutes, MS 14600/143: 12 Nov. 1945, 336–7.
4. *Liverpool Daily Post*, 1 June 1968, 5.
5. Council of the Associated Stock Exchanges, Committee Minute Book, GB124.B18/2/2/3: 28 January 1949, 86–7.
6. The records of the Halifax Stock Exchange are no longer available, and the episode does not seem to have been reported in the local press.
7. *The Times*, 1 February 1973, 23.
8. *The Guardian*, 3 May 1972, 16.
9. *Daily Telegraph*, 6 May 1972, 23.
10. *FT*, 2 February 1973, 11. See also *Investors' Guardian*, 14 May 1971, 1134.
11. *Daily Telegraph*, 22 June 1968, 5.
12. Cited in Duncan Sutherland, 'Peeresses, Parliament and Prejudice: The Admission of Women to the House of Lords, 1918–1963', *Parliaments, Estates and Representation* 20, no. 1 (2000): 215–31, at 226.
13. Sutherland, 'Peeresses, Parliament and Prejudice', 226.
14. Birmingham Stock Exchange (hereafter BSE), Minutes of Committee of Management, MS 1598/1/4/29: Jack Sabin to Percy Rudge, 8 December 1955, no. 20089, Wolfson Centre for Archival Research, Birmingham.
15. As one commentator put it, they 'were in a tizzwazz as to what to do', *Stock Exchange Gazette*, 15 September 1956, 817.
16. BSE, Minutes of Committee of Management, MS 1598/1/4/29: 3 January 1956, no. 20102; 6 March 1956, no. 20140.
17. Council of the Associated Stock Exchanges, AGMs, GB124.B18/2/1/1: *Résumé of the Work of the Administration during the Year 1955–56*, 3, Manchester Archives and Local Studies.
18. BSE, Minutes of Committee of Management, MS 1598/1/4/29: Council of Associated Stock Exchanges to the Secretary of the BSE, 15 May 1956, no. 20189.
19. *The Times*, 7 September 1956, 5.
20. BSE, Minutes of Committee of Management, MS 1598/1/4/29: 5 June 1956, no. 20189.
21. BSE, Minutes of Committee of Management, MS 1598/1/4/29: 3 July 1956, no. 20207; MS 1598/1/4/30: 14 September 1956, no. 20249.
22. BSE, Minutes of Committee of Management, MS 1598/1/4/29: 31 July 1956, no. 20226.
23. BSE, Minutes of Committee of Management, MS 1598/1/4/30: 14 September 1956, no. 20249.
24. *Birmingham Post*, 23 August 1956, 1, 8.
25. *Evening Standard*, 24 August 1956, 4.
26. *Daily Telegraph*, 24 August 1956, 6.
27. *Birmingham Post*, 27 August 1956, 4; 28 August 1956, 4; 29 August 1956, 4; 30 August 1956, 4; 31 August 1956, 4; *Daily Telegraph*, 29 August 1956, 6; 31 August 1956, 6.
28. Reported in *Birmingham Post*, 8 September 1956, 1.
29. BSE, Minutes of Committee of Management, MS 1598/1/4/30: 22 October 1956, no. 20279.
30. BSE, Minutes of Committee of Management, MS 1598/1/4/30: 6 May 1958, no. 20694; 9 May 1958, no. 20696.
31. *Birmingham Daily Gazette*, 13 October 1956, 5; *Birmingham Post*, 13 October 1956, 7; *Birmingham Post*, 29 October 1956, 7; *FT*, 29 October 1956, 7; *Belfast News-Letter*, 25 October 1956, 4.
32. Council of the Associated Stock Exchanges, AGMs, GB124.B18/2/1/1: *Résumé of the Work of the Administration during the Year 1956–57*, 4.

256 NOTES TO PAGES 176–80

33. The National Council of Women wrote to the Birmingham Stock Exchange in similar terms in November 1957: BSE, Minutes of Committee of Management, MS 1598/1/4/30: 26 November 1957, no. 20519.
34. *Birmingham Post*, 20 May 1958, 7; *Birmingham Post*, 21 May 1958, 6; *Birmingham Post*, 22 May 1958, 7; *Birmingham Post*, 29 May 1958, 6.
35. *Birmingham Post*, 17 May 1958, 7.
36. *Birmingham Post*, 20 May 1958, 7.
37. BSE, Minutes of Committee of Management, MS 1598/1/4/30: N. Neale to the Secretary of the BSE, 22 July 1958, no. 20741.
38. BSE, Minutes of Committee of Management, MS 1598/1/4/30: 29 July 1958, no. 20741; Percy Rudge to Mrs Neale, 13 August 1958, no. 20753.
39. BSE, Minutes of Committee of Management, MS 1598/1/4/31: J. H. Sabin to William Pritchett, 22 January 1960, no. 21255; A. C. Griffiths, Frederick W. Brooks, and Harold W. Oakley to Percy Rudge, 22 February 1960, no. 21284.
40. BSE, Minutes of Committee of Management, MS 1598/1/4/31: 15 March 1960, no. 21303.
41. BSE, Minutes of Committee of Management, MS 1598/1/4/31: 3 May 1960, no. 21347.
42. BSE, Minutes of Annual Meetings of Members, MS 1598/1/1/4: 23 November 1960.
43. Heineman, *Playing the Market*, 13–14.
44. Ranald Michie, *The London Stock Exchange: A History* (Oxford, 2001), 368; J. Walter Thompson Company, Client Account Files, Stock Exchange, A710 Data: Planning, 1951–54, HAT 50/1/172/3/1/2: 'What Can Be Done to Expand Stock Exchange Business and Protect it for the Future?', May 1950, History of Advertising Trust Archive, Raveningham.
45. The *Stock Exchange Journal* was launched in 1955; *My Word Is My Bond* started showing in 1959.
46. David Kynaston, *The City of London*, vol. 4, *A Club No More, 1945–2000* (London, 2002), 31.
47. Lynn Zekanis, 'The New York Stock Exchange: Marketing the Marketplace', *Journal of American Culture* 10, no. 2 (1987): 91–8, at 91–2.
48. *FT*, 8 January 1951, 1; *Daily Telegraph*, 11 May 1951, 1; *FT*, 12 May 1951, 5.
49. *Daily Telegraph*, 27 August 1951, 7; *FT*, 20 June 1952, 8; *The Times*, 21 November 1952, 11.
50. *Daily Telegraph*, 27 August 1951, 7.
51. *The Times*, 28 January 1953, 10.
52. *Daily Telegraph*, 29 January 1953, 6; *The Times*, 25 February 1953, 12.
53. LSE, Council Minutes, MS 14600A/011: Francis, How & Lowndes to Secretary of the Council, 30 January 1953, 174.
54. LSE, Council Minutes, MS 14600A/011: 23 February 1953, 204–6; *FT*, 25 February 1953, 1; *The Times*, 24 March 1953, 11; *FT*, 16 November 1953, 1.
55. *FT*, 11 November 1953, 1; *Illustrated London News*, 21 November 1953, 827.
56. *Daily Telegraph*, 19 July 1957, 2.
57. *Stock Exchange Journal*, July 1957, 4.
58. *FT*, 16 September 1958, 1.
59. Their photograph appeared in *Daily Mirror*, 12 November 1958, 2.
60. *The Times*, 12 November 1958, 17; *Western Mail*, 11 November 1958, 4; *Stock Exchange Journal*, Autumn 1958, 36.
61. *The Economist*, 27 September 1958, 1059.
62. *Daily Herald*, 16 September 1958, 7.
63. *Daily Telegraph*, 12 November 1958, 15.
64. *Daily Mirror*, 12 November 1958, 2; *The Times*, 12 November 1958, 17.
65. *Halifax Daily Courier and Guardian*, 15 November 1958, 4; *Daily Telegraph*, 7 November 1958, 10.
66. *Daily Telegraph*, 12 November 1958, 15.
67. *Daily Mirror*, 12 November 1958, 2.
68. *The Times*, 12 November 1958, 17. For a contrasting view, see S. P., 'Women in the House', *Stock Exchange Journal*, Winter 1958–9, 78–9.
69. *Sunday Mirror*, 27 October 1963, 7; *FT*, 8 May 1959, 3.
70. J. Walter Thompson Company, Client Account Files, Stock Exchange, Call Reports: 1965, HAT 50/1/172/1/4: Report of Meeting, 1 September 1965, 1; Correspondence, 1966, HAT 50/1/172/2/2: John Spencer to W. Sanders, 8 August 1966.
71. For examples, see *Stock Exchange Journal*, Spring 1961, 4; July 1962, 3; December 1963, 6; March 1965, 2; December 1970, 26; *Daily Mail*, 20 May 1961, 2; *The Times*, 20 May 1964, 18; *Daily Express*, 10 March 1966, 10; *Daily Telegraph*, 19 May 1969, 21.
72. *Daily Mail*, 30 April 1958, 8.

NOTES TO PAGES 180–4   257

73. Anthony Sampson, *Anatomy of Britain* (London, 1962), 351; *Sunday Times*, 4 September 1960, 37.
74. *FT*, 13 September 1960, 9.
75. *Daily Express*, 15 September 1960, 3.
76. *The Economist*, 21 January 1967, 261.
77. As she later recollected, 'my application never reached the appropriate authorities': Records of Careers for Women, Conference Papers, 6CFW/E/25, Box 6: National Advisory Centre on Careers for Women (NACCW) Careers Course 1972, 'The Stock Exchange', Mrs E. Rivers-Bulkeley, 1, The Women's Library, London School of Economics.
78. *The Guardian*, 16 January 1967, 6.
79. *FT*, 18 January 1967, 14; *The Times*, 18 January 1967, 18.
80. *FT*, 3 February 1961, 10. The article was picked up elsewhere: *Daily Express*, 4 February 1961, 3; *Arbroath Herald*, 24 February 1961, 14.
81. *Evening Standard*, 3 March 1961, 3; *The Guardian*, 16 January 1967, 6.
82. Referred to in *Daily Mail*, 11 November 1966, 5; *The Times*, 18 January 1967, 18.
83. *FT*, 1 March 1962, 11; 2 March 1962, 10; *The Times*, 7 August 1962, 14.
84. *Report of the Company Law Committee*, Parliamentary Papers 1961–2, XII, 94–5; W. A. Thomas, *The Provincial Stock Exchanges* (Abingdon, 2014), 271–2.
85. Michie, *London Stock Exchange*, 459; *Daily Telegraph*, 12 February 1964, 1; *The Times*, 2 July 1965, 18.
86. *FT*, 3 January 1964, 11.
87. Northern Stock Exchange, General Correspondence, 332 LSE 3/3/2: 'Report by the Joint Committee Appointed to Supervise Detailed Planning of the Formation of a "Scottish Stock Exchange"', 11 April 1963, 3, Liverpool Record Office.
88. *FT*, 26 March 1964, 1; *The Times*, 30 June 1964, 15.
89. *The Times*, 31 July 1965, 11; *FT*, 31 July 1965, 4; *The Times*, 3 August 1965, 12.
90. The first chairman of the Northern Stock Exchange admitted that its draft constitution was 'based almost entirely on the Scottish Stock Exchange': Northern Stock Exchange, General Correspondence, 332 LSE 3/3/1: C. T. Ockleston to N. Kemp, 21 January 1965.
91. Sheffield Stock Exchange, Minutes of Members' and Annual Meetings, LD 2007/1/4(a): 2 June 1965, 261–2, Sheffield City Archives.
92. Northern Stock Exchange, Records re. the Formation of the Northern Stock Exchange, Application Letters, 332 LSE 3/1/16.
93. Northern Stock Exchange, Membership Book, 332 LSE 3/4/1: inside front cover; *FT*, 7 January 1961, 7; *The Economist*, 6 November 1965, xviii.
94. For exceptions, see *Daily Express*, 28 March 1964, 8; *Birmingham Post*, 29 June 1965, 10. Ward's election was missed by the *FT*.
95. J. Walter Thompson Company, Client Account Files, Stock Exchange, Call Reports, 1964, HAT 50/1/172/1/3: Report of a Meeting, 11 September 1964, 1.
96. See, for example, J. Walter Thompson Company, Client Account Files, Stock Exchange, Correspondence, 1965, HAT 50/1/172/2/1: A. E. Yuill to C. D. T. Fitch, 20 October 1965.
97. There are practically no references to the matter in the collection of materials from J. Walter Thompson's Stock Exchange account housed at the History of Advertising Trust collection.
98. *The Times*, 29 June 1965, 5.
99. *Daily Express*, 29 June 1965, 10; *FT*, 29 June 1965, 9; *The Guardian*, 29 June 1965, 12.
100. *The Economist*, 3 July 1965, 70.
101. *FT*, 29 April 1966, 25; *The Times*, 29 April 1966, 14; *FT*, 20 May 1966, 20; Michie, London Stock Exchange, 435–6.
102. *The Guardian*, 29 April 1966, 18; *Daily Mail*, 20 May 1966, 12.
103. *Daily Express*, 11 November 1966, 17; *The Times*, 18 January 1967, 18.
104. This was reported in the press as her third attempt: *Evening Post*, 31 January 1967, 4.
105. *Daily Express*, 11 November 1966, 17; *Daily Mail*, 11 November 1966, 5; *Daily Mail*, 12 November 1966, 6.
106. *Sunday Times*, 13 February 1966, 21.
107. *Florence Nagle v. Feilden and Others* [1966] EWCA Civ J0222-1, 22 February 1966, 4–5, 14, 16, 19; *Daily Mirror*, 23 February 1966, 20; *Daily Telegraph*, 23 February 1966, 21; *Sunday Telegraph*, 27 February 1966, 25.
108. *Daily Mail*, 21 July 1966, 14; *Daily Mirror*, 29 July 1966, 5.
109. *Nagle v. Feilden*, 16.
110. *Daily Telegraph*, 18 January 1967, 2; *FT*, 18 January 1967, 15; *The Times*, 18 January 1967, 18.

258   NOTES TO PAGES 184–9

111. *Daily Express*, 20 February 1967, 9; *The Guardian*, 24 February 1967, 12; *FT*, 24 February 1967, 6; *The Times*, 24 February 1967, 19; *Birmingham Post*, 24 February 1967, 10.
112. *The Times*, 25 February 1967, 13.
113. David LeRoy-Lewis, interview with Bernard Attard, 20 December 1989, London Stock Exchange Oral History: <https://sas-space.sas.ac.uk/2596/>; *FT*, 25 February 1967, 14.
114. *The Times*, 25 February 1967, 13; *Daily Express*, 27 February 1967, 9; *Newcastle Journal*, 25 February 1967, 5.
115. *Birmingham Post*, 1 March 1967, 6; *Stock Exchange Gazette*, 3 March 1967, 597.
116. Turnout was relatively high at 62 per cent.
117. *Daily Mirror*, 1 March 1967, 3; *Birmingham Post*, 1 March 1967, 6; *The Guardian*, 1 March 1967, 11.
118. *Daily Telegraph*, 1 March 1967, 13; *Illustrated London News*, 11 March 1967, 32.
119. *Sunday Telegraph*, 5 March 1967, 7.
120. E. Mautner to *FT*, 6 March 1967, 4; *The Times*, 1 March 1967, 15.
121. *The Times*, 15 April 1967, 15; *New York Times*, 15 April 1967, 38.
122. *New York Times*, 11 November 1965, 69; *FT*, 22 November 1965, 11.
123. Sheri J. Caplan, *Petticoats and Pinstripes: Portraits of Women in Wall Street's History* (Santa Barbara, CA, 2013), ch. 11.
124. *The Times*, 12 January 1968, 7; *The Observer*, 14 January 1968, 33; *FT*, 8 February 1968, 14; *Daily Mail*, 28 February 1968, 15.
125. *Birmingham Post*, 6 April 1968, 10.
126. *FT*, 5 May 1970, 20.
127. *FT*, 11 May 1968, 13; *Daily Telegraph*, 11 May 1968, 3; 11; *The Times*, 11 May 1968, 13; *Daily Mail*, 11 May 1968.
128. *FT*, 23 May 1968, 34; *FT*, 29 May 1968, 1.
129. *Daily Telegraph*, 29 May 1968, 3.
130. Margaret Rix to *Daily Telegraph*, 29 August 1956, 6.
131. *Investors Chronicle*, 17 May 1968, 676.
132. *Newcastle Journal*, 21 May 1971, 8.
133. *Daily Express*, 28 November 1956, 12.
134. *The Guardian*, 22 May 1971, 10. See also *Sunday Mirror*, 20 October 1968, 35; *Investors Review*, 5 June 1971, 306.
135. *The Times*, 22 May 1971, 5; *Irish Times*, 22 May 1971, 14.
136. Helen McCarthy, 'Women, Marriage and Paid Work in Post-War Britain', *Women's History Review* 26, no. 1 (2017): 46–61, at 53.
137. Michael Roper, *Masculinity and the British Organization Man since 1945* (Oxford, 1994), 191–2, 209–11. Women were regarded as 'too emotional to perform higher status work', but as 'talented emotional workers able to perform unremunerated emotional labour' at work: Claire Langhamer, 'Feelings, Women and Work in the Long 1950s', *Women's History Review* 26, no. 1 (2017): 77–92.
138. *Stock Exchange Journal*, October 1956, 52.
139. Anthea Gaukroger, interview with author, 20 January 2023.
140. R. J. Wharton to *FT*, 19 February 1970, 2.
141. *Birmingham Post*, 2 February 1973, 8.
142. *Newcastle Evening Chronicle*, 12 May 1972, 18.
143. Leslie Cristall to *FT*, 5 June 1968, 4.
144. Martin Francis, 'The Domestication of the Male? Recent Research on Nineteenth- and Twentieth-Century British Masculinity', *Historical Journal* 45, no. 3 (2002): 637–52, at 645–6.
145. Richard Hall, 'Being a Man, Being a Member: Masculinity and Community in Britain's Working Men's Clubs, 1945–1960', *Cultural and Social History* 14, no. 1 (2017): 73–88, at 75.
146. Roper, *Masculinity and the British Organization Man*, 112–13.
147. The last national serviceman was demobbed in 1963.
148. Richard Vinen, *National Service: Conscription in Britain, 1945–1963* (London, 2014).
149. Stephen Raven, interview with Bernard Attard, 16 May 1990, London Stock Exchange Oral History: <https://sas-space.sas.ac.uk/2766/>.
150. Christopher Landon, *Stone Cold Dead in the Market* (London, 1955), 69–70, 100, 156–7, 188–9, 253.
151. Kaitlynn Mendes, 'Framing Feminism: News Coverage of the Women's Movement in British and American Newspapers, 1968–1982', *Social Movement Studies* 10, no. 1 (2011): 81–98, at 90.

NOTES TO PAGES 189–94   259

152. For examples of this kind of language, see *The Guardian*, 21 February 1969, 1; *The Times*, 19 May 1969, 25; *The Times*, 7 April 1972, 21; *Birmingham Post*, 3 May 1972, 4.
153. Daniella McCahey, ' "The Last Refuge of Male Chauvinism": Print Culture, Masculinity, and the British Antarctic Survey (1960–1996)', *Gender, Place and Culture* 29, no. 6 (2022): 751–71.
154. *The Guardian*, 16 January 1967, 6.
155. *Daily Express*, 25 August 1956, 6.
156. *Birmingham Post*, 2 February 1973, 8.
157. *Daily Telegraph*, 6 May 1972, 23.
158. Nicky Marsh, *Money, Speculation and Finance in Contemporary British Fiction* (London, 2007), 3–4, 41.
159. Sampson, *Anatomy of Britain*, 352–3.
160. Adrian Bingham, 'The "K-Bomb": Social Surveys, the Popular Press, and British Sexual Culture in the 1940s and 1950s', *Journal of British Studies* 50, no. 1 (2011): 156–79.
161. *Daily Herald*, 17 May 1958, 2.
162. *Stock Exchange Gazette*, 15 September 1956, 818.
163. The series ran from July 1969 to August 1975.
164. *Sunday Telegraph*, 1 February 1970, 30.
165. *Sunday Telegraph*, 2 April 1970, 30.
166. *Daily Telegraph*, 11 May 1968, 3.
167. *The Times*, 5 June 1970, 29.
168. *Birmingham Post*, 8 September 1956, 8.
169. *Sunday Telegraph*, 5 March 1967, 7.
170. One paper noted that 'the sanctity of the trading floor has become a fetish, a kind of symbol of the Old Order, when everyone knew what was what': *Investors' Guardian*, 14 May 1971, 1134.
171. ITN Report, 20 May 1971: <https://www.gettyimages.ae/detail/video/stock-exchange-reluctant-to-take-women-england-london-news-footage/1214954565>.
172. *Daily Mirror*, 8 May 1971, 2.
173. *Daily Telegraph*, 22 June 1968, 5.
174. *Birmingham Post*, 29 May 1968, 4.
175. 'Another Member' to *Birmingham Post*, 28 August 1956, 4.
176. Graham H. Greenwell to *The Times*, 25 June 1971, 15.
177. *The Times*, 26 June 1971, 13.
178. *Aberdeen Press and Journal*, 17 May 1972, 10.
179. BSE, Minutes of Committee of Management, MS 1598/1/4/33: 22 May 1964, no. 23082; 4 June 1964, no. 23102; 18 June 1964, no. 23126.
180. *FT*, 18 August 1966, 9; 5 October 1966, 19.
181. BSE, Minutes of Committee of Management, MS 1598/1/4/35: 19 January 1967, no. 24512; 2 February 1967, no. 24535.
182. BSE, Minutes of Committee of Management, MS 1598/1/4/35: Hatwell Pritchett & Co. to Rudge, 11 October 1967, 535–6.
183. BSE, Minutes of Committee of Management, MS 1598/1/4/35: 4 January 1968, 548; 1 February 1968, 554–5.
184. BSE, Minutes of Committee of Management, MS 1598/1/4/35: 27 February 1968, 559; 7 March 1968, 561; 4 April 1968, 568.
185. *Birmingham Post*, 5 April 1968, 1.
186. BSE, Minutes of Committee of Management, MS 1598/1/4/35, 4 April 1968, 567.
187. *Birmingham Post*, 5 April 1968, 4.
188. *FT*, 2 May 1968, 23; *The Guardian*, 2 May 1968, 11.
189. *FT*, 10 January 1969, 19.
190. *FT*, 18 November 1971, 16.
191. *FT*, 7 April 1972, 23; 3 May 1972, 38.
192. *Birmingham Post*, 19 November 1971, 4.
193. *The Times*, 11 May 1968, 13. See also *The Guardian*, 2 May 1968, 11.
194. *The Guardian*, 7 February 1970, 12; *Newcastle Journal*, 7 February 1970, 4.
195. *Daily Mirror*, 7 February 1970, 2; *Daily Mail*, 7 February 1970, 1; *The Times*, 7 February 1970, 13; *Daily Mail*, 18 March 1970, 19.
196. Heather McConnell to *FT*, 13 February 1970, 2.
197. H. R. E. Bradshaw to *FT*, 17 February 1970, 2.
198. *FT*, 23 May 1969, 15.

260 NOTES TO PAGES 194–99

199. *The Times*, 19 June 1970, 27; *FT*, 23 June 1970, 33.
200. *Daily Telegraph*, 31 January 1967, 2; *FT*, 31 January 1967, 13.
201. Cynthia Cockburn, *In the Way of Women: Men's Resistance to Sex Equality in Organizations* (Ithaca, NY, 1991), 30.
202. Carol Dyhouse, *Students: A Gendered History* (London, 2006), 108; Jane Lewis, 'From Equality to Liberation: Contextualizing the Emergence of the Women's Liberation Movement', in *Cultural Revolution? The Challenge of the Arts in the 1960s*, edited by Bart Moore-Gilbert and John Seed (London, 1992), 96–117.
203. *FT*, 29 October 1970, 13; *Sunday Times*, 1 November 1970, 47; *The Observer*, 1 November 1970, 12.
204. *The Monopolies Commission: A Report on the General Effect on the Public Interest of Certain Restrictive Practices so far as they Prevail in Relation to the Supply of Professional Services*, Parliamentary Papers 1970–1, XXXII, 16, 77, 86–7.
205. Hansard, 5th series, vol. 805, 132–4 (28 October 1970). The Department of Trade and Industry replaced the Board of Trade following Heath's victory in 1970.
206. *FT*, 2 November 1970, 2. See also *Sunday Telegraph*, 1 November 1970, 23.
207. *FT*, 22 January 1971, 28; *Daily Telegraph*, 3 February 1971, 15.
208. *FT*, 8 May 1971, 26; *The Guardian*, 8 May 1971, 14.
209. *Daily Telegraph*, 20 May 1971, 19; *Daily Telegraph*, 8 May 1971, 15.
210. *FT*, 22 May 1971, 1. Another resolution to permit members to advertise was also defeated, by an even heavier margin.
211. *Daily Mail*, 22 May 1971, 20; *Daily Express*, 22 May 1971, 13.
212. *The Guardian*, 22 May 1971, 20. See also *Investors Review*, 5 June 1971, 306.
213. *Daily Telegraph*, 22 May 1971, 15.
214. *FT*, 22 May 1971, 1.
215. Wilkinson asked Winser to wait a year, referencing the forthcoming mergers, discussed below: *FT*, 27 April 2002, 16.
216. *The Guardian*, 31 May 1971, 16. See also *The Times*, 22 June 1971, 13.
217. Hansard, 5th series, vol. 819, 370 (25 June 1971).
218. Hansard, 5th series, vol. 820, 553–4 (1 July 1971). Fookes herself did not raise the issue again in parliament, seemingly reassured following an invitation to the Stock Exchange as Wilkinson's guest in August: *Daily Mirror*, 24 August 1971, 4.
219. Michie, *London Stock Exchange*, 459–60.
220. *The Times*, 8 August 1969, 23.
221. *Birmingham Post*, 3 May 1972, 1.
222. *The Times*, 12 August 1969, 21.
223. *FT*, 19 November 1971, 16; *Daily Telegraph*, 19 November 1971, 19.
224. One Scottish opponent of the deal predicted 'the smashing of the provincial Stock Exchanges and the channeling of nearly all business to London': J. R. Gibb to *FT*, 10 December 1971, 2.
225. *Birmingham Post*, 25 October 1971, 4; *Birmingham Post*, 19 November 1971, 4; *Birmingham Post*, 9 February 1972, 4.
226. *FT*, 4 March 1972, 1.
227. *Daily Telegraph*, 6 May 1972, 23.
228. *Evening Standard*, 3 March 1972, 36; *Daily Mirror*, 4 March 1972, 11.
229. *Daily Telegraph*, 6 May 1972, 23.
230. Kynaston, *A Club No More*, 420; Michie, *London Stock Exchange*, 483–4.
231. *Evening Standard*, 3 March 1972, 36.
232. *The Times*, 3 May 1972, 1; *FT*, 3 May 1972, 38.
233. *Evening Standard*, 31 January 1973, 5.
234. *Evening Standard*, 20 March 1973, 51.
235. *The Times*, 27 March 1973, 21.
236. *The Observer*, 1 April 1973, 19.
237. *Daily Express*, 27 March 1973, 7.
238. *Daily Mail*, 27 March 1973, 11; *Newcastle Journal*, 27 March 1973, 14.
239. *Evening Standard*, 11 June 1973, 51; *Newcastle Journal*, 11 June 1973, 4; *The Times*, 16 June 1973, 18.
240. Michie, *London Stock Exchange*, 484; *Evening Standard*, 27 June 1971, 51.
241. *Evening Standard*, 29 June 1973, 51.
242. *Daily Mirror*, 14 April 1973, 1.
243. *Waterloo Region Record*, 7 May 1973, 36.

NOTES TO PAGES 199–205 261

244. *Evening Standard*, 4 July 1973, 7; *Daily Mail*, 5 July 1973, 10.
245. *Evening Standard*, 5 July 1973, 5. For more on the sexualization of the office in these years, see Amy Thomas, *The City in the City: Architecture and Change in London's Financial District* (Cambridge, MA, 2023), 280–1.
246. *Midland Counties Tribune*, 19 August 1927, 7; *Irish Times*, 17 August 1927, 11.
247. *Daily Express*, 18 May 1973, 16.
248. For Holt's guide, see Chapter 3.
249. *Daily Telegraph*, 26 March 2013, 22.
250. Gaukroger and Pearson, interview with author.
251. *Daily Telegraph*, 7 April 1973, 28.
252. 'Hilary Pearson: One of the first women to trade at the London Stock Exchange', Bremhill Parish History Group: <https://www.bremhillparishhistory.com/article/hilary-pearson/>.
253. *Aberdeen Evening Express*, 1 September 1972, 3; *The Scotsman*, 10 January 1969, 10; *Birmingham Post*, 2 January 1976, 6; Yorkshire Live, 4 June 2013: <https://www.examinerlive.co.uk/news/west-yorkshire-news/obituarymary-ward-4883470>.
254. *Aberdeen Press and Journal*, 31 August 1977, 7; 26 May 1978, 3.
255. *FT*, 23 December 1981, 20. She died in 1997.
256. She died in 2006: *FT*, 4 January 2007, 20; *The Times*, 12 February 2007, 48.
257. Susan Shaw, interview with author, 11 July 2024.

Epilogue

1. Kieran Heinemann, *Playing the Market: Retail Investment and Speculation in Twentieth-Century Britain* (Oxford, 2021), 165.
2. *Sunday Telegraph*, 9 April 1978, 25; *Liverpool Daily Post*, 4 September 1974, 17.
3. After taking a correspondence course, Holt left her firm to work as the borough solicitor for Knowsley Council, eventually becoming a barrister in property law: *Daily Telegraph*, 13 January 1977, 20; *The Guardian*, 4 January 2021: <https://www.theguardian.com/business/2021/jan/04/margaret-holt-obituary>.
4. Susan Shaw, interview with author, 11 July 2024.
5. *FT*, 10 August 1973, 4; *FT*, 4. April 1975, 7; *Daily Telegraph*, 2 August 1978, 13.
6. *The Observer*, 8 January 1984, 28.
7. *Manchester Evening News*, 11 September 1980, 19.
8. *The Observer*, 21 September 1986, 7.
9. *Liverpool Daily Post*, 5 September 1979, 16; *Liverpool Daily Post*, 6 March 1985, 21.
10. Jane Partington, cited in Cathy Courtney and Paul Thompson, *City Lives: The Changing Voices of British Finance* (London, 1996), 175.
11. *FT*, 21 March 2023: <https://www.ft.com/content/aff6433f-5231-465a-a96c-a2219c2d1dc1>.
12. Jane Partington, cited in *City Lives*, 175.
13. *Punch*, 20 September 1978, 435.
14. *Daily Mail*, 20 August 1986, 12.
15. *Manchester Evening News*, 11 September 1980, 19.
16. *FT*, 21 March 2023.
17. Sarah E. Stoller, *Inventing the Working Parent: Work, Gender, and Feminism in Neoliberal Britain* (Cambridge, MA, 2023), 121–2.
18. *Liverpool Daily Post*, 6 March 1985, 21.
19. *Nottingham Evening Post*, 13 January 1976, 8.
20. *Punch*, 20 September 1978, 435.
21. *Liverpool Daily Post*, 25 March 1983, 7.
22. *The Observer*, 8 January 1984, 28.
23. *The Observer*, 8 January 1984, 28.
24. *Daily Mail*, 20 August 1986, 12.
25. *Sunday Times*, 5 October 1986, 43.
26. Ranald Michie, *The London Stock Exchange: A History* (Oxford, 2001), 580.
27. Michie, *London Stock Exchange*, 585, 602.
28. Michie, *London Stock Exchange*, 603.
29. David Kynaston, *The City of London*, vol. 4, *A Club No More, 1945–2000* (London, 2002), 724.
30. *Sunday Times*, 26 October 1986, 68.
31. *The Times*, 27 October 1986, 38. For more on their design and American origins, see Amy Thomas, *The City in the City: Architecture and Change in London's Financial District* (Cambridge, MA, 2023), 227–35.

262 NOTES TO PAGES 205-10

32. *Daily Telegraph*, 7 July 1986, 21.
33. *Daily Telegraph*, 28 October 1986, 17. See also *The Times*, 27 October 1986, 38.
34. *Sunday Times*, 26 October 1986, 69.
35. *Daily Mail*, 28 October 1986, 32.
36. *The Times*, 27 October 1986, 38.
37. Cited in Thomas, *City in the City*, 235.
38. Thomas, *City in the City*, 234.
39. Linda McDowell, 'The Men and the Boys: Bankers, Burger Makers and Barmen', in *Spaces of Masculinities*, edited by Bettina van Hoven and Kathrin Hörschelmann (London and New York, 2005), 17–27, at 22.
40. *Daily Mail*, 27 October 1986, 28.
41. *Sunday Times*, 5 October 1986, 40.
42. *FT*, 27 October 1986, xviii.
43. *FT*, 27 October 1986, xviii.
44. *Daily Mail*, 8 December 1987, 24.
45. *Sunday Telegraph*, 21 September 1986, 63.
46. Stoller, *Inventing the Working Parent*, 159.
47. *FT*, 22 February 1995, 38.
48. *Birmingham Post*, 12 November 1993, 9.
49. Linda McDowell, *Capital Culture: Gender at Work in the City* (Oxford, 1997), 176.
50. McDowell, *Capital Culture*, 201.
51. Adrienne Roberts, 'Gender, Financial Deepening and the Production of Embodied Finance: Towards a Critical Feminist Analysis', *Global Society* 29, no. 1 (2015): 107–27.
52. Nicky Marsh, *Money, Speculation and Finance in Contemporary British Fiction* (London, 2007), 134.
53. Marsh, *Money, Speculation and Finance*, 135.
54. Marsh, *Money, Speculation and Finance*, 137.
55. Marsh, *Money, Speculation and Finance*, 142.
56. *The Associate* (1996), dir. Donald Petrie.
57. Micky Lee and Monika Raesch, 'Women, Gender, and the Financial Markets in Hollywood Films', in *Feminist Erasures: Challenging Backlash Culture*, edited by Kumarini Silva and Kaitlynn Mendes (Houndmills, 2015), 129–49.
58. The film drew on a 1928 novel by Jenaro Prieto, *El Socio*, in which a man invents a business partner.
59. *FT*, 18 January 2000, 3; *Daily Telegraph*, 10 March 2000, 8.
60. *Daily Telegraph*, 13 March 2001, 9; *Sunday Times*, 8 April 2001, 4.
61. *Daily Mail*, 20 November 2002, 23.
62. *The Times*, 11 April 2001, 9.
63. *FT*, 24 January 2001, 1.
64. *Daily Telegraph*, 10 November 2001, 32.
65. *The Independent*, 18 February 2003, 6; *Daily Telegraph*, 17 February 2003, 3.
66. Michael Roper, *Masculinity and the British Organization Man since 1945* (Oxford, 1994), 210, 206.
67. Cited in Sarah Hall and Lindsey Appleyard, 'Financial Business Education: The Remaking of Gendered Investment Banking Subjects in the (Post-Crisis) City of London', *Journal of Cultural Economy* 5, no. 4 (2012): 457–72, at 457.
68. Elisabeth Prügl, '"If Lehman Brothers Had Been Lehman Sisters…": Gender and Myth in the Aftermath of the Financial Crisis', *International Political Sociology* 6, no. 1 (2012): 21–35, at 21; Christine Lagarde, 'Women, Power and the Challenge of the Financial Crisis', 10 May 2010, *New York Times*: <https://www.nytimes.com/2010/05/11/opinion/11iht-edlagarde.html>.
69. House of Commons Treasury Committee, *Women in the City: Tenth Report of Session 2009–10*, HC 482, 22 March 2010, 3: <https://publications.parliament.uk/pa/cm200910/cmselect/cmtreasy/482/482.pdf>.
70. *Women in the City*, 36.
71. Joris Luyendijk, 'Voices of Finance: The Institutional Stockbroker', *The Guardian*, 28 October 2011:<https://www.theguardian.com/commentisfree/2011/oct/28/voices-of-finance-institutional-stockbroker>.
72. Joris Luyendijk, 'Women in Finance', *The Guardian*, 3 November 2011: <https://www.theguardian.com/commentisfree/2011/nov/03/voices-of-finance-women>.

73. Joris Luyendijk, 'Voices of Finance: Investment Management Adviser', *The Guardian*, 23 October 2011: <https://www.theguardian.com/commentisfree/joris-luyendijk-banking-blog/2011/oct/23/voices-of-finance-investment-management-adviser>.
74. Luyendijk, 'Women in Finance', *The Guardian*, 3 November 2011.
75. In the United States, a disproportionate number of women were laid off in the wake of the crash and were seriously underrepresented in regulatory reform plans: Prügl, 'Lehman Brothers', 31.
76. James Brassett and Frederic Heine, '"Men Behaving Badly"? Representations of Masculinity in Post-Global Financial Crisis Cinema', *International Feminist Journal of Politics* 23, no. 5 (2021): 763–84, at 775.
77. Brassett and Heine, 'Men Behaving Badly?', 776.
78. Cited in Brassett and Heine, 'Men Behaving Badly', 776.
79. Philip Roscoe, *How to Build a Stock Exchange: The Past, Present and Future of Finance* (Bristol, 2023), 83.
80. Stoller, *Inventing the Working Parent*, 113.
81. Davies Report, *Women on Boards*, February 2011, 3: <https://assets.publishing.service.gov.uk/media/5a78c710e5274a277e68f637/11-745-women-on-boards.pdf>; Jane Martinson, 'Companies Must Promote Women to Change "Terrible State" of UK Boards', *The Guardian*, 14 October 2011: <https://www.theguardian.com/business/2011/oct/14/companies-missing-boardroom-targets-women>.
82. HM Treasury and Virgin Money, 'Empowering Productivity: Harnessing the Talents of Women in Financial Services', 5, 8, 36: <https://uk.virginmoney.com/virgin/assets/pdf/Virgin-Money-Empowering-Productivity-Report.pdf>.
83. HM Treasury and Virgin Money, 'Empowering Productivity', 9; HM Treasury, *Women in Finance Charter*: <https://assets.publishing.service.gov.uk/media/5a7f44e9ed915d74e62296df/women_in_finance_charter.pdf>.
84. House of Commons Treasury Committee, *Women in Finance: Fifteenth Report of Session 2017–19*, HC 477, 13 June 2018, 11, 38–40: <https://publications.parliament.uk/pa/cm201719/cmselect/cmtreasy/477/477.pdf>.
85. Robin J. Ely and David A. Thomas, 'Getting Serious about Diversity: Enough Already with the Business Case', *Harvard Business Review* 98, no. 6 (2020): 114–22.
86. Kalyeena Makortoff, 'Aviva chair warns shareholders against repeat of sexism at AGM', *The Guardian*, 19 April 2023: <https://www.theguardian.com/business/2023/apr/19/george-culmer-aviva-chair-warns-shareholders-against-repeat-sexism-agm>.
87. Kalyeena Makortoff, '"Unacceptable": Aviva CEO hits back at shareholder sexism', *The Guardian*, 12 May 2022: <https://www.theguardian.com/inequality/2022/may/11/used-to-it-aviva-ceo-responds-after-sexist-comments-at-agm>.
88. Leigh Gilmore, *The #MeToo Effect: What Happens When We Believe Women* (New York, 2023).
89. Kalyeena Makortoff, 'Parliament Launches New Inquiry into Sexism and Misogyny in the City', *The Guardian*, 14 July 2023: <https://www.theguardian.com/business/2023/jul/14/parliament-launches-new-inquiry-into-city-sexism-after-scandals>.
90. Kalyeena Makortoff, 'Sexism in the City', *The Guardian*, 4 March 2024: <https://www.theguardian.com/business/2024/mar/04/sexism-in-the-city-no-matter-how-hard-i-work-they-will-never-ever-recognise-me#:~:text=The%20committee%27s%202018%20review%2C%20published,and%20disadvantaged%20women%20in%20finance>.
91. House of Commons Treasury Committee, *Sexism in the City, Sixth Report of Session 2023–24*, HC 240, 5 March 2024, 3, 8, 29, 35, 38, 39: <https://committees.parliament.uk/publications/43731/documents/217019/default/>.
92. Julia Hoggett, 'Importance of Diversity and Inclusion as Indisputable as Climate Change', 26 September 2022, *The Banker*: <https://www.thebanker.com/Julia-Hoggett-Importance-of-diversity-and-inclusion-as-indisputable-as-climate-change-1664178493>.
93. *Financial News*, 9 August 2022: <https://www.fnlondon.com/articles/lse-chief-julia-hoggett-profile-diversity-capital-markets-20220809>.
94. Hoggett, 'Importance of Diversity'.
95. London Stock Exchange, *Charting 50 Years of Change for Women in the UK's Finance Sector* (2023), 1: <https://docs.londonstockexchange.com/sites/default/files/documents/charting-50-years-change-women-UKs-%20finance-sector-final.pdf>.
96. George Robb, *Ladies of the Ticker: Women and Wall Street from the Gilded Age to the Great Depression* (Urbana, 2017), 182.
97. Melissa S. Fisher, *Wall Street Women* (Durham, NC, and London, 2012), 3.

Bibliography

Primary Works

Unpublished

Archives

Bank of England Archive

Bank of England, Secretary's Department: Committee of Inspection for the Accountant's Offices, Minutes, M5/220, 221.

Guildhall Library

London Stock Exchange:
General Purposes Committee Minutes, MS 14600/51, 55, 86, 114, 116, 133, 138, 139, 142, 143.
Council Minutes, MS 14600A/011.
Selected Appendices to the Minutes of the General Purposes Committee, MS 19515/5, 6.

History of Advertising Archive, Raveningham

J. Walter Thompson Company, Client Account Files, Stock Exchange:
Call Reports, 1964, HAT 50/1/172/1/3.
Call Reports: 1965, HAT 50/1/172/1/4.
Correspondence, 1965, HAT 50/1/172/2/1.
Correspondence, 1966, HAT 50/1/172/2/2.
A710 Data: Planning, 1951–54, HAT 50/1/172/3/1/2.

Liverpool Record Office

Northern Stock Exchange:
Records re. the Formation of the Northern Stock Exchange, Application Letters, 332 LSE 3/1/16.
General Correspondence, 332 LSE 3/3/1, 2.
Membership Book, 332 LSE 3/4/1.

London Metropolitan Archives

Exchange Telegraph Company, Correspondence, Reports etc., Relating to the London Stock Exchange, MS 23028.

Manchester Archives and Local Studies

Council of the Associated Stock Exchanges:
AGMs, GB124.B18/2/1/1.
Committee Minute Book, GB124.B18/2/2/3.

The National Archives

Companies Registration Office:
Files of Dissolved Companies, BT 31/3451/20868.
Files of Dissolved Companies, BT 31/5713/39941.
Departmental Committee on Share-Pushing:
Miscellaneous Notes and Reports, BT 55/104.
Share-Pushing Legislation, 1937–38, BT 55/106.
Evidence and Correspondence, Second Part, BT 55/108.
Evidence and Correspondence, Third Part, BT 55/109.
Prevention of Fraud (Investments) Acts 1939–1958, BT 298/69.
Court for Divorce and Matrimonial Causes, J 77/1917/9962.

266   BIBLIOGRAPHY

Finance: Stock Exchange, Measures to Curb Activities of Outside Brokers, 'Bucket Shops', and Share Pushers, T 160/1195/3.

Sheffield City Archives

Sheffield Stock Exchange, Minutes of Members' and Annual Meetings, LD 2007/1/4(a).

West Yorkshire Archive Service, Leeds

Leeds Stock Exchange:
 Managing Committee Minute Book, WYL543/1/7.
 Association Minute Book, WYL543/2/3.
 Secretary's Letter Book, WYL543/4/20.

Wolfson Centre for Archival Research, Birmingham

Birmingham Stock Exchange:
 Minutes of Annual Meetings of Members, MS 1598/1/1/4.
 Minutes of Committee of Management, MS 1598/1/4/29, 30, 31, 33, 34, 35.

The Women's Library, London School of Economics

Women's Freedom League:
 National Executive Committee Minutes, 2WFL/1/12.
 Annual Conference Reports, 2WFL/2/21, 22, 23.
Records of Careers for Women, Conference Papers, 6CFW/E/25, Box 6.

Genealogical Sources

1841–1921 Census of England and Wales (accessed Ancestry.co.uk and Findmypast.co.uk).
1939 Register of England and Wales (accessed Ancestry.co.uk and Findmypast.co.uk).
National Probate Calendar (accessed <https://probatesearch.service.gov.uk>).
Various registers of Births, Baptisms, Marriages, and Deaths (accessed Ancestry.co.uk and Findmypast.co.uk).

Published

Parliamentary Papers

London Stock Exchange Commission: Report of the Commissioners, 1878.
Report of the Board of Trade on the State of Employment in the United Kingdom in October 1914.
Report of the Clerical and Commercial Employments Committee, 1914–16.
Report to the Board of Trade on the State of Employment in the United Kingdom in February 1915.
Share-Pushing: Report of the Departmental Committee Appointed by the Board of Trade, 1936–7.
Report of the Company Law Committee, 1961–2.
The Monopolies Commission: A Report on the General Effect on the Public Interest of Certain Restrictive Practices so far as they Prevail in Relation to the Supply of Professional Services, 1970–1.
House of Commons Treasury Committee, *Women in the City: Tenth Report of Session 2009–10*.
House of Commons Treasury Committee, *Women in Finance: Fifteenth Report of Session 2017–19*.
House of Commons Treasury Committee, *Sexism in the City: Sixth Report of Session 2023–24*.
Hansard's Parliamentary Debates, 5th series

Legal Proceedings

Old Bailey Proceedings Online, February 1886, trial of Sidney Herbert Cronmire alias Hebert Harrison (20) (t18860208-282).
Florence Nagle v. Feilden and Others [1966] EWCA Civ J0222-1, 22 February 1966.

Legislation

Act to Restrain the Number and Ill Practice of Brokers and Stock Jobbers, 1697: 8 & 9 Will. III, c. 32.

BIBLIOGRAPHY 267

Sex Disqualification (Removal) Act, 1919: 9 & 10 Geo. 5, c. 71.
Prevention of Fraud (Investments) Act, 1939: 2 & 3 Geo. 6, c. 16.

Newspapers and Periodicals

Aberdeen Evening News
Aberdeen Press and Journal
The Academy
The Accountant
Airdrie and Coatbridge Advertiser
Aldershot Military Gazette
Algemeen Handelsblad
Answers
The Athenaeum
Banbury Advertiser
Banffshire Advertiser
Bath Chronicle and Herald
Belfast (Evening) Telegraph
Belfast News-Letter
Belfast Weekly News
Bell's Weekly Messenger
Bentley's Miscellany
Berkshire County Eagle
Berrows Worcester Journal
Birkenhead News
Birmingham Daily Gazette
Birmingham (Daily) Post
The Bookman
Boston Courier
Bradford Observer
Bristol Mercury and Daily Post
Brownsville Herald
Bucks Herald
Bury and Norwich Post
The Bystander
Caledonian Mercury
Cambria Freeman
Cheltenham Looker-On
Citizen
City Leader
Coatbridge Express
Cobbett's Weekly Political Register
Commercial Gazette
Cork Examiner
Cosmopolitan
Courier and Argus
Coventry Evening Telegraph
Craftsman or Say's Weekly Journal
Daily Advertiser
Daily Chronicle
Daily Express
Daily Graphic
Daily Herald
Daily Mail
Daily Mail (Atlantic Edition)

268 BIBLIOGRAPHY

Daily Mirror
Daily News
Daily Telegraph
Derby Daily Telegraph
Devizes and Wiltshire Gazette
Devon and Exeter Daily Gazette
Dewsbury Chronicle and West Riding Advertiser
The Diary or Woodfall's Register Gazetteer and New Daily Advertiser
Dublin Daily Express
Dublin Evening Press
Dublin Evening Telegraph
Dundee Courier
Dundee Evening Telegraph
The Echo
The Economist
Edinburgh Evening News
Edinburgh Gazette
Englishwoman's Review
The Englishwoman's Yearbook
The Era
Essex Standard
Evening Dispatch
Evening Irish Times
Evening Standard
Exeter and Plymouth Gazette
Exeter Express and Echo
Falkirk Herald
Farrow's Bank Gazette
Finance
Financial News
Financial Times
The Financier
Folkestone Express
Freeman's Journal
General Evening Post
Glasgow Herald
The Globe
Gloucester Journal
Halifax Daily Courier and Guardian
Hampshire Chronicle
Hampshire Telegraph
Hartlepool Mail
Hendon and Finchley Times
Herts Advertiser
Hinckley Echo
Huddersfield Daily Chronicle
Huddersfield Daily Examiner
Hull Daily Mail
Hull News
Illustrated London News
Indianapolis Journal
Investors Chronicle
Investors' Guardian
Investors Review

BIBLIOGRAPHY 269

Irish Independent
Irish Times
John Bull
Jus Suffragii: The International Woman Suffrage News
Kent and Sussex Courier
Ladies' Treasury
Lady of the House
Lady's Pictorial
Lancashire Evening Post
Lancashire Telegraph
Leeds Intelligencer
Leeds Mercury
Leeds Times
Leicester Chronicle
Leicester Evening Mail
Lewisham Borough News
Lincolnshire Echo
Liverpool Albion
Liverpool Daily Post
Liverpool Echo
Liverpool Mercury
London and China Telegraph
London Chronicle
London Evening Post
London Gazette
Madison Daily Leader
Maidenhead Advertiser
Manchester Courier
Manchester Evening News
(Manchester) Guardian
Metropolitan
Midland Counties Tribune
Modern Man
Morning Chronicle
Morning Post
Myra's Journal
Nenagh Guardian
New York Herald
New York Herald (European edition)
New York Times
Newcastle Journal
The News
North-Eastern Daily Gazette
Northampton Mercury
Northern Daily Mail and South Durham Herald
Northwest Enterprise
Nottingham Evening Post
Nottingham Guardian
Nottingham Journal
Oakland Tribune
The Observer
Original Weekly Journal
Oxford Journal
Pall Mall Gazette

270 BIBLIOGRAPHY

Penny Illustrated Paper
The Pilot
Preston Herald
Public Advertiser
Punch
The Queen
Radio Times
Railway News
Reading Evening Post
The Register (Adelaide)
Review of Reviews
The Revolution
Reynolds's Illustrated News
Rochdale Observer
St James's Chronicle
St James's Gazette
St Stephen's Review
Saturday Review
The Scotsman
Sheffield Daily Telegraph
Sheffield Evening Telegraph and Star
Sheffield Independent
Shrewsbury Chronicle
The Sketch
Social Review
South Wales Daily News
South Wales Echo
The Sphere
Sport (Dublin)
Sporting Life
Staffordshire Sentinel
The Stage
The Standard
The Star
Stock Exchange Gazette
Stock Exchange Journal
Strand Magazine
Sunday Mirror
Sunday Telegraph
Sunday Times
Sunderland Echo and Shipping Gazette
Sussex Agricultural Express
Sycamore True Republican
Sydney Morning Herald
The Tatler and Bystander
Telegraph and Argus
Thanet Advertiser
The Times
Torquay Times and South Devon Advertiser
T. P.'s Weekly
Truth
Vernon News
The Vote
Waterloo Region Record

BIBLIOGRAPHY 271

Weekly Dispatch
Weekly Irish Times
Weekly Journal or British Gazetteer
Weekly Packet
Western Daily Press
Western Mail
Western Morning News
Westminster Gazette
Wexford People
Whitehall Evening Post
Whitstable Times and Herne Bay Herald
Wiltshire Chronicle
Womanhood
Woman's Herald
Woman's Leader
Woman's Life
Woman's Signal
Woman's Weekly
Women's Gazette
Women's Penny Paper
Women's Report
Women's Union Journal: The Organ of the Women's Protective and Provident League
Wrexham Advertiser
Yorkshire Evening Post
Yorkshire Factory Times
Yorkshire Herald
Yorkshire Observer
Yorkshire Post

Directories

Bassett's Directory
Post Office London Directory
United Kingdom Stock and Sharebrokers Directory

Interviews

Gaukroger, Anthea, interview with author, 20 January 2023.
LeRoy-Lewis, David, interview with Bernard Attard, 20 December 1989, London Stock
    Exchange Oral History: <https://sas-space.sas.ac.uk/2596/>.
Pearson, Hilary, interview with author, 20 January 2023.
Raven, Stephen, interview with Bernard Attard, 16 May 1990, London Stock Exchange Oral
    History: <https://sas-space.sas.ac.uk/2766/>.
Shaw, Susan, interview with author, 11 July 2024; email correspondence with author, 19 July 2024.

Contemporary Books and Articles

'A Banker's Daughter', *A Guide to the Unprotected in Every-day Matters Relating to Property and
    Income* (London and Cambridge, 1863).
A Gentleman, *A Tour Thro' the Whole Island of Great Britain, Divided into Circuits or Journeys*
    (London, 1724).
Anon., *The Life and Real Adventures of Hamilton Murray. Written by Himself*, 3 vols. (London,
    1759).
Anon., *Counsel to Ladies and Easy-Going Men on their Business Investments* (London, 1892).
Anon., 'The Mechanism of the Stock Exchange', *Cornhill Magazine* 3, no. 16 (October 1897):
    490–9.
Bateson, Margaret, *Professional Women upon their Professions* (London, 1895).

272 BIBLIOGRAPHY

Belfort, Roland, 'How Stockbrokers "Beat up" Business', *Grand Magazine*, June 1907, 665–71.
Belfort, Roland, 'Stockbrokers at Play', *Grand Magazine*, August 1907, 103–9.
[Branch, Charles], 'A Defence of the Stock Exchange', *Fraser's Magazine* 14, no. 82 (October 1876): 493–503.
Census of England & Wales 1921: Occupation Tables (London, 1924).
Census of England & Wales 1931: Occupation Tables (London, 1934).
Census 1951, England and Wales: Occupation Tables (London, 1956).
'Cheiro' (Count Louis Hamon), *Confessions: Memoirs of a Modern Seer* (London, 1932).
Clews, Henry, *Twenty-Eight Years in Wall Street* (New York, 1887).
Corelli, Marie, 'Claudia's Business', *Nash's and Pall Mall Magazine*, December 1916, 218–30.
Corelli, Marie, *The Love of Long Ago, and Other Stories* (London, 1920).
Coulson, Margaret, 'The Politics of Women's Liberation', *Socialist Woman*, March–April 1971.
Courtney, Janet E., *Recollected in Tranquillity* (London, 1926).
[Craik, Dinah], 'About Money', *Contemporary Review* 50 (September 1886): 364–72.
[Defoe, Daniel], *The Anatomy of Exchange Alley: Or, A System of Stock-Jobbing* (London, 1719).
The Englishwoman's Year Book and Directory (London, 1911).
Escott, T. H. S., *England: Its People, Polity, and Pursuits* (London, 1881).
Fowler, William Worthington, *Inside Life in Wall Street; Or How Great Fortunes are Lost and Won* (Hartford, CT, 1873).
[Gordon, Thomas], *A Learned Dissertation upon Old Women, Male and Female, Spiritual and Temporal, in All Ages; Whether in Church, State, or Exchange-Alley* (London, 1720).
Grant, James, *The Great Metropolis*, 2 vols. (Philadelphia, 1838).
Guest, Antony, 'The London Stock Exchange', *Tinsleys' Magazine* 11 (April 1890): 363–8.
Hales, Charles, *The Bank Mirror; Or, A Guide to the Funds* (London, [1796]).
Hay, E., *Double Your Income: Or, Resources of the Money Market* (London, 1869).
[Hollingshead, J.], 'Phases of the Funds', *All the Year Round*, 6 July 1861, 342–6.
Hollis, Charles, *Polly Mountemple: A Fin de Siècle Story of the Stage* (London, 1891).
Holmes, Gordon, 'Stockbroking and Finance', *Good Housekeeping*, November 1925.
Holmes, Miss Gordon, *In Love with Life: A Pioneer Career Woman's Story* (London, 1944).
Holt, Ardern, *Fancy Dresses Described: Or, What to Wear at Fancy Balls* (London, [1879]).
How Does Britain Save? A Summary of the Results of a Survey Conducted for the London Stock Exchange by the British Market Research Bureau Limited (London, 1966).
Hughes, D. W., *Careers for our Daughters* (London, 1936).
Ingall, Godefroi Drew, 'The London Stock Exchange', in *Living London*, edited by George R. Sims (London, 1901), 261–6.
Johnson, Samuel, *A Dictionary of the English Language*, 2 vols. (London, 1755).
Landon, Christopher, *Stone Cold Dead in the Market* (London, 1955).
Lavington, F., *The English Capital Market* (London, 1921).
Mackirdy, Mrs Archibald, 'Women and the Money Market', *Lady's Realm*, November 1906, 41–5.
Malvery, Olive Christian, *The Speculator* (London, 1908).
Martin, James, *The Broker's Correspondent: Being a Letter Writer for Stock Exchange Business* (London, 1893).
Menzler, F. A. A., *The Sunday Times Career Books: The Stock Exchange* (London, 1961).
Milner, James, *Three Letters Relating to the South-Sea Company and the Bank* (London, 1720).
[Morier Evans, David], *The City: Or, The Physiology of London Business* (London, 1845).
Mortimer, Maurice, 'Fashionable Feminine Financiers', *Grand Magazine*, July 1907, 875–81.
[Mortimer, Thomas], *Every Man His Own Broker: Or, A Guide to Exchange-Alley* (London, 1761).
Mortimer, Thomas, *Every Man His Own Broker: Or, A Guide to Exchange-Alley*, 5th edn (London, 1762).
Mortimer, Thomas, *Every Man His Own Broker: Or, A Guide to Exchange-Alley*, 10th edn (London, 1785).
Normanton, Helena, 'Stockbroking as a Profession for Women', *Good Housekeeping*, May 1928.
Parkinson, Hargreaves, *The ABC of Stocks and Shares: A Handbook for the Investor* (London, 1925).

BIBLIOGRAPHY 273

Pitman's Shorthand Writers' Phrase Books and Guides: Stockbroking and Finance (London, 1914).
Rules and Regulations Adopted by the Committee for General Purposes of the Stock-Exchange (London, 1812).
Sampson, Anthony, *Anatomy of Britain* (London, 1962).
Simonis, H., *The Street of Ink: An Intimate History of Journalism* (London, 1917).
Sixteenth Census of the United States: 1940. Population: Comparative Occupation Statistics for the United States, 1870 to 1940 (Washington, 1943).
Sloley, Iris, 'Feminism and the Women's Liberation Movement', *Women's Struggle* 2, no. 3 (1972): 111–34.
Smash: A Sketch of the Times, Past, Present, and Again to Come (London, 1860).
Smedley, Constance, 'The Business Woman', *World's Work*, June 1907, 97–103.
Smith, David T., 'A Stockbroker's Memories', *Blackwood's Magazine*, October 1933, 466–75.
'Stock Exchange Speculation', *Chambers's Journal*, 30 July 1887, 481–3.
Strachey, Ray, *Careers and Openings for Women: A Survey of Women's Employment and a Guide for Those Seeking Work* (London, 1935).
Sturgis, Julian, *A Master of Fortune* (New York and London, [1896]).
'T. Q.', *A Wall-Street Bear in Europe* (New York, 1855).
Trollope, Anthony, *Is He Popenjoy?*, 3rd edn (London, 1879).
Vanderbilt, A. T., *What To Do With Our Girls; Or, Employments for Women* (London, 1884).
[Ward, Edward], *The Picture of a Coffee-House: Or, The Humour of the Stock-Jobbers* (London, 1700).
[Ward, Edward], *The London-Spy Compleat, In Eighteen-Parts* (London, 1703).
Williams, Montagu, QC, *Round London: Down East and Up West* (London, 1892).
Woodhull, Victoria Claflin, and Tennessee C. Claflin, *The Human Body the Temple of God; Or, the Philosophy of Sociology* (London, 1890).

Film and Television

ITN broadcast, 1 December 1958: <https://www.gettyimages.co.uk/detail/video/interview-with-miss-hilda-harding-britains-first-woman-news-footage/1313872778>.
ITN Report, 20 May 1971: <https://www.gettyimages.ae/detail/video/stock-exchange-reluctant-to-take-women-england-london-news-footage/1214954565>.
The Associate (1996), dir. Donald Petrie.

Other Online Sources

Davies Report, *Women on Boards*, February 2011: <https://assets.publishing.service.gov.uk/media/5a78c710e5274a277e68f637/11-745-women-on-boards.pdf>.
HM Treasury, *Women in Finance Charter*: <https://assets.publishing.service.gov.uk/media/5a7f44e9ed915d74e62296df/women_in_finance_charter.pdf>.
HM Treasury and Virgin Money, 'Empowering Productivity: Harnessing the Talents of Women in Financial Services', 5, 8, 36: <https://uk.virginmoney.com/virgin/assets/pdf/Virgin-Money-Empowering-Productivity-Report.pdf>.
London Stock Exchange, *Charting 50 Years of Change for Women in the UK's Finance Sector* (2023): <https://docs.londonstockexchange.com/sites/default/files/documents/charting-50-years-change-women-UKs-%20finance-sector-final.pdf>.

Secondary Works

Abramson, Daniel Michael, 'Money's Architecture: The Building of the Bank of England, 1731–1833' (PhD thesis, Harvard University, 1993).
Acheson, Graeme G., Gareth Campbell, Aine Gallagher, and John D. Turner, 'Independent Women: Investing in British Railways, 1870–1922', *Economic History Review* 74, no. 2 (2021): 471–95.
Acheson, Graeme G., Gareth Campbell, and John D. Turner, 'Who Financed the Expansion of the Equity Market? Shareholder Clienteles in Victorian Britain', *Business History* 59, no. 4 (2017): 607–37.

274 BIBLIOGRAPHY

Ackrill, Margaret, and Leslie Hannah, *Barclays: The Business of Banking, 1690–1996* (Cambridge, 2001).

Alborn, Timothy, 'Quill-Driving: British Life-Insurance Clerks and Occupational Mobility, 1800–1914', *Business History Review* 82, no. 1 (2008): 31–58.

Alexander, Sally, and Anna Davin, 'Feminist History', *History Workshop* 1 (1976): 4–6.

Assael, Brenda, *The London Restaurant, 1840–1914* (Oxford, 2018).

Assassi, Libby, *The Gendering of Global Finance* (Houndmills, 2009).

Aston, Jennifer, *Female Entrepreneurship in Nineteenth-Century England: Engagement in the Urban Economy* (Cham, 2016).

Aston, Jennifer, and Catherine Bishop, eds., *Female Entrepreneurs in the Long Nineteenth Century: A Global Perspective* (London, 2020).

Aston, Jennifer, and Paolo Di Martino, 'Risk, Success, and Failure: Female Entrepreneurship in Late Victorian and Edwardian England', *Economic History Review* 70, no. 3 (2017): 837–58.

Attard, Bernard, 'The Jobbers of the London Stock Exchange: An Oral History', *Oral History* 22, no. 1 (1994): 43–8.

Attard, Bernard, 'Making a Market: The Jobbers of the London Stock Exchange, 1800–1986', *Financial History Review* 7, no. 1 (2000): 5–24.

Aveyard, Stuart, Paul Corthorn, and Sean O'Connell, *The Politics of Consumer Credit in the UK, 1938–1992* (Oxford, 2018).

Banner, Stuart, *Anglo-American Securities Regulation: Cultural and Political Roots, 1690–1860* (Cambridge, 1998).

Barker, Hannah, *The Business of Women: Female Enterprise and Urban Development in Northern England, 1760–1830* (Oxford, 2006).

Barker, Hannah, *Family and Business during the Industrial Revolution* (Oxford, 2017).

Baron, Ava, 'Masculinity, the Embodied Male Worker, and the Historian's Gaze', *International Labor and Working-Class History*, 69 (2006): 143–60.

Beaumont, Catriona, 'Women, Citizenship and Catholicism in the Irish Free State, 1922–1948', *Women's History Review* 6, no. 4 (1997): 563–85.

Beaumont, Catriona, 'Citizens not Feminists: The Boundary Negotiated between Citizenship and Feminism by Mainstream Women's Organizations in England, 1928–39', *Women's History Review* 9, no. 2 (2000): 411–29.

Beaumont, Caitriona, *Housewives and Citizens: Domesticity and the Women's Movement in England, 1928–64* (Manchester and New York, 2013).

Beckett, Ian F. W., *The Great War, 1914–1918*, 2nd edn (Abingdon, 2013).

Beddoe, Deirdre, *Back to Home and Duty: Women between the Wars, 1918–1939* (London, 1989).

Beers, Laura, 'A Model MP? Ellen Wilkinson, Gender, Politics and Celebrity Culture in Interwar Britain', *Cultural and Social History* 10, no. 2 (2013): 231–50.

Beetham, Margaret, *A Magazine of Her Own? Domesticity and Desire in the Woman's Magazine, 1800–1914* (London and New York, 1996).

Benson, John, and Laura Ugolini, eds., *Cultures of Selling: Perspectives on Consumption and Society since 1700* (Aldershot, 2006).

Berg, Maxine, 'What Difference Did Women's Work Make to the Industrial Revolution?', *History Workshop Journal* 35, no. 1 (1993): 22–44.

Bingham, Adrian, '"An Era of Domesticity?" Histories of Women and Gender in Interwar Britain', *Cultural and Social History* 1, no. 2 (2004): 225–33.

Bingham, Adrian, *Gender, Modernity, and the Popular Press in Inter-War Britain* (Oxford, 2004).

Bingham, Adrian, 'The "K-Bomb": Social Surveys, the Popular Press, and British Sexual Culture in the 1940s and 1950s', *Journal of British Studies* 50, no. 1 (2011): 156–79.

Bingham, Adrian, 'Enfranchisement, Feminism and the Modern Woman: Debates in the British Popular Press, 1918–1939', in *The Aftermath of Suffrage: Women, Gender, and Politics in Britain, 1918–1945*, edited by Julie V. Gottlieb and Richard Toye (Houndmills, 2013), 87–104.

Bingham, Adrian, 'The British Press and the 1918 Reform Act', *Parliamentary History* 37, no. 1 (2018): 150–67.

Bishop, Catherine, *Minding Her Own Business: Colonial Businesswomen in Sydney* (Sydney, 2015).

BIBLIOGRAPHY 275

Black, John, 'War, Women and Accounting: Female Staff in the UK Army Pay Department Offices, 1914–1920', *Accounting, Business and Financial History* 16, no. 2 (2006): 195–218.

Blackburn, Robert M., and Jennifer Jarman, 'Changing Inequalities in Access to British Universities', *Oxford Review of Education* 19, no. 2 (1993): 197–215.

Bowen, Huw V., '"The Pests of Human Society": Stockbrokers, Jobbers and Speculators in Mid-Eighteenth-Century Britain', *History* 78, no. 252 (1993): 38–53.

Branca, Patricia, *Silent Sisterhood: Middle-Class Women in the Victorian Home* (Abingdon, 2013).

Brassett, James, and Frederic Heine, '"Men Behaving Badly"? Representations of Masculinity in Post-Global Financial Crisis Cinema', *International Feminist Journal of Politics* 23, no. 5 (2021): 763–84.

Bryson, Valerie, and Timothy Heppell, 'Conservatism and Feminism: The Case of the British Conservative Party', *Journal of Political Ideologies* 15, no. 1 (2010): 31–50.

Buddle, Melanie, *The Business of Women: Marriage, Family, and Entrepreneurship in British Columbia, 1901–51* (Vancouver, 2010).

Buddle, Melanie, 'Gender and Business: Recent Literature on Women and Entrepreneurship', *Histoire Sociale/Social History* 51, no. 104 (2018): 401–7.

Cain, P. J., and A. G. Hopkins, 'Gentlemanly Capitalism and British Expansion Overseas I: The Old Colonial System, 1688–1850', *Economic History Review* 39, no. 4 (1986): 501–25.

Callan, Mike, Conor Heffernan, and Amanda Spenn, 'Women's Jūjutsu and Judo in the Early Twentieth-Century: The Cases of Phoebe Roberts, Edith Garrud, and Sarah Mayer', *International Journal of the History of Sport* 35, no. 6 (2018): 530–53.

Caplan, Sheri J., *Petticoats and Pinstripes: Portraits of Women in Wall Street's History* (Santa Barbara, CA, 2013).

Carlos, Ann M., Karen Maguire, and Larry Neal, 'Financial Acumen, Women Speculators, and the Royal African Company during the South Sea Bubble', *Accounting, Business and Financial History* 16, no. 2 (2006): 219–43.

Carlos, Ann M., and Larry Neal, 'Women Investors in Early Capital Markets, 1720–1725', *Financial History Review* 11, no. 2 (2004): 197–224.

Carlos, Ann M., and Jill L. van Stone, 'Stock Transfer Patterns in the Hudson's Bay Company: A Study of the English Capital Market in Operation, 1670–1730', *Business History* 38, no. 2 (1995): 15–39.

Carnaffan, Gladys, 'Commercial Education and the Female Office Worker', in *The White-Blouse Revolution: Female Office Workers since 1870*, edited by Gregory Anderson (Manchester, 1988), 67–87.

Carraro, Laura Favero, 'The Language of the Emerging Financial Market and Early Eighteenth-Century English Plays', *Essays in Economic and Business History* 37 (2019): 206–41.

Carruthers, Bruce G., *City of Capital: Politics and Markets in the English Financial Revolution* (Princeton, 1999).

Chua, Wai-Fong, and Stewart Clegg, 'Professional Closure: The Case of British Nursing', *Theory and Society* 19, no. 2 (1990): 135–72.

Clark, Jessica P., '*Pomeroy* v. *Pomeroy*: Beauty, Modernity, and the Female Entrepreneur in Fin-de-Siècle London', *Women's History Review* 22, no. 6 (2013): 877–903.

Clark, Jessica P., *The Business of Beauty: Gender and the Body in Modern London* (London, 2020).

Clarke, Jane, 'Feminism and the Legacy of the First World War in the Journals of the Old Comrades Associations, 1919–1935', *Women's History Review* 28, no. 7 (2019): 1177–99.

Clery, E. J., *The Feminization Debate in Eighteenth-Century England: Literature, Commerce and Luxury* (Houndmills, 2004).

Cockburn, Cynthia, *In the Way of Women: Men's Resistance to Sex Equality in Organizations* (Ithaca, NY, 1991).

Colella, Silvana, 'Cross-Dressing in the City: Olive Malvery's *The Speculator*', *Journal of Victorian Culture* 26, no. 3 (2021): 435–48.

Combs, Mary Beth, '"A Measure of Legal Independence": The 1870 Married Women's Property Act and the Portfolio Allocations of British Wives', *Journal of Economic History* 64, no. 4 (2005): 1028–57.

276 BIBLIOGRAPHY

Cope, S. R., 'The Stock Exchange Revisited: A New Look at the Market in Securities in London in the Eighteenth Century', *Economica* 45 (1978): 1–21.

Copelman, Dina, *London's Women Teachers: Gender, Class and Feminism, 1870–1930* (London, 1996).

Courtney, Cathy, and Paul Thompson, *City Lives: The Changing Voices of British Finance* (London, 1996).

Cowman, Krista, and Louise A. Jackson, 'Introduction: Middle-Class Women and Professional Identity', *Women's History Review* 14, no. 2 (2005): 165–80.

Craig, Béatrice, *Women and Business since 1500: Invisible Presences in Europe and North America?* (London, 2016).

Crompton, Rosemary, 'The Feminisation of the Clerical Labour Force since the Second World War', in *The White-Blouse Revolution: Female Office Workers since 1870*, edited by Gregory Anderson (Manchester, 1988), 121–43.

Crompton, Rosemary, 'Women in Banking: Continuity and Change since the Second World War', *Work, Employment and Society* 3, no. 2 (1989): 141–56.

Crosthwaite, Paul, Peter Knight, Nicky Marsh, Helen Paul, and James Taylor, *Invested: How Three Centuries of Stock Market Advice Reshaped Our Money, Markets and Minds* (Chicago, 2022).

Dale, Richard, *The First Crash: Lessons from the South Sea Bubble* (Princeton, 2004).

Daunton, M. J., '"Gentlemanly Capitalism" and British Industry, 1820–1914', *Past and Present* 122 (1989): 119–58.

Davidoff, Leonore, and Catherine Hall, *Family Fortunes: Men and Women of the English Middle Class, 1780–1850* (London, 1997).

Davies, Aled, *The City of London and Social Democracy: The Political Economy of Finance in Britain, 1959–1979* (Oxford, 2017).

Davies, Celia, 'The Sociology of Professions and the Profession of Gender', *Sociology* 30, no. 4 (1996): 661–78.

Davin, Anna, 'Feminism and Labour History', in *People's History and Socialist Theory*, edited by Raphael Samuel (Abingdon, 2016), 176–81.

Davy, Teresa, '"A Cissy Job for Men; a Nice Job for Girls": Women Shorthand Typists in London, 1900–1939', in *Our Work, Our Lives, Our Words: Women's History and Women's Work*, edited by Leonore Davidoff and Belinda Westover (Houndmills, 1986), 124–44.

Dawes, Margaret, and Nesta Selwyn, *Women Who Made Money: Women Partners in British Private Banks, 1752–1906* (Bloomington, 2010).

Dean, Hannah, Linda Perriton, Scott Taylor, and Mary Yeager, 'Margins and Centres: Gender and Feminism in Business History', *Business History* 66, no. 1 (2024): 1–13.

Devine, Fiona, 'Gender Segregation in the Engineering and Science Professions: A Case of Continuity and Change', *Work, Employment and Society* 6, no. 4 (1992): 557–75.

Dickson, P. G. M., *The Financial Revolution in England: A Study in the Development of Public Credit, 1688–1756* (London, 1967).

Doe, Helen, 'Waiting for Her Ship to Come In? The Female Investor in Nineteenth-Century Sailing Vessels', *Economic History Review* 63, no. 1 (2010): 85–106.

Dohrn, Susanne, 'Pioneers in a Dead-End Profession: The First Women Clerks in Banks and Insurance Companies', in *The White-Blouse Revolution: Female Office Workers since 1870*, edited by Gregory Anderson (Manchester, 1988), 48–66.

Doughan, David, and Peter Gordon, *Women, Clubs and Associations in Britain* (London, 2006).

Duguid, Charles, *The Story of the Stock Exchange: Its History and Position* (London, 1901).

Durepos, Gabrielle, Alan McKinlay, and Scott Taylor, 'Narrating Histories of Women at Work: Archives, Stories, and the Promise of Feminism', *Business History* 58, no. 8 (2017): 1261–79.

Dyhouse, Carol, *Students: A Gendered History* (London, 2006).

Edmundson, William, *The Nitrate King: A Biography of 'Colonel' John Thomas North* (New York, 2011).

Edwards, Amy, '"Manufacturing Capitalists": The Wider Share Ownership Council and the Problem of "Popular Capitalism", 1958–92', *Twentieth Century British History* 27, no. 1 (2016): 100–23.

Edwards, Amy, *Are We Rich Yet? The Rise of Mass Investment Culture in Contemporary Britain* (Oakland, CA, 2022).

Edwards, Ruth Dudley, *The Pursuit of Reason:* The Economist, *1843–1993* (London 1993).

Egginton, Heidi, and Zoë Thomas, eds., *Precarious Professionals: Gender, Identities and Social Change in Modern Britain* (London, 2021).

Ely, Robin J., and David A. Thomas, 'Getting Serious about Diversity: Enough Already with the Business Case', *Harvard Business Review* 98, no. 6 (2020): 114–22.

Erickson, Amy Louise, 'Coverture and Capitalism', *History Workshop Journal* 59, no. 1 (2005): 1–16.

Erickson, Amy Louise, review of Amy M. Froide, *Silent Partners*, *English Historical Review* 135, no. 573 (2020): 488–91.

Erickson, Amy Louise, 'Wealthy Businesswomen, Marriage and Succession in Eighteenth-Century London', *Business History* 66, no. 1 (2024): 29–58.

Evans, Claire, and Nick Rumens, 'Gender Inequality and the Professionalisation of Accountancy in the UK from 1870 to the Interwar Years', *Business History* 64, no. 7 (2022): 1244–59.

Ewen, Misha, 'Women Investors and the Virginia Company in the Early Seventeenth Century', *Historical Journal* 62, no. 4 (2019): 853–74.

Fara, Patricia, *A Lab of One's Own: Science and Suffrage in the First World War* (Oxford, 2018).

Fisher, Melissa S., *Wall Street Women* (Durham, NC, and London, 2012).

Francis, Martin, 'The Domestication of the Male? Recent Research on Nineteenth- and Twentieth-Century British Masculinity', *Historical Journal* 45, no. 3 (2002): 637–52.

Freeman, Mark, Robin Pearson, and James Taylor, '"A Doe in the City": Women Shareholders in Eighteenth- and Early Nineteenth-Century Britain', *Accounting, Business and Financial History* 16, no. 2 (2006): 265–91.

Freeman, Mark, Robin Pearson, and James Taylor, 'Between Madam Bubble and Kitty Lorimer: Women Investors in British and Irish Stock Companies', in *Women and Their Money, 1700–1950: Essays on Women and Finance*, edited by Anne Laurence, Josephine Maltby, and Janette Rutterford (Abingdon, 2009), 95–114.

Froide, Amy M., *Silent Partners: Women as Public Investors during Britain's Financial Revolution, 1690–1750* (Oxford, 2017).

Froide, Amy, 'Navigating the Spaces and Places of England's First Stock Market: Women Investors and Brokers during the Financial Revolution, c.1690–1730', in *The Cultural Life of Risk and Innovation: Imaging New Markets from the Seventeenth Century to the Present*, edited by Chia Yin Hsu, Thomas M. Luckett, and Erika Vause (New York and London, 2021), 63–79.

Gabriel, Mary, *Notorious Victoria: The Uncensored Life of Victoria Woodhull—Visionary, Suffragist, and First Woman to Run for President* (Chapel Hill, NC, 1998).

Galligani Casey, Janet, 'Mary Mackay', in *British Short-Fiction Writers, 1880–1914: The Romantic Tradition*, Gale Dictionary of Literary Biography, vol. 156 (Detroit, 1995).

Gamber, Wendy, 'Gendered Concerns: Thoughts on the History of Business and the History of Women', *Business and Economic History* 23, no. 1 (1994): 129–40.

Gamber, Wendy, *The Female Economy: The Millinery and Dressmaking Trades, 1860–1930* (Urbana and Chicago, 1997).

Gamber, Wendy, 'A Gendered Enterprise: Placing Nineteenth-Century Businesswomen in History', *Business History Review* 72, no. 2 (1998): 188–217.

Garrett-Scott, Shennette, *Banking on Freedom: Black Women in US Finance before the New Deal* (Columbia, 2019).

Gilmore, Leigh, *The #MeToo Effect: What Happens When We Believe Women* (New York, 2023).

Gleadle, Kathryn, 'Revisiting *Family Fortunes*: Reflections on the Twentieth Anniversary of the Publication of L. Davidoff & C. Hall (1987) *Family Fortunes*', *Women's History Review* 16, no. 5 (2007): 773–82.

Glew, Helen, 'Embracing the Language of Human Rights: International Women's Organisations, Feminism and Campaigns Against the Marriage Bar, c.1919–1960', *Gender and History* 35, no. 3 (2023): 780–94.

Goede, Marieke de, *Virtue, Fortune, and Faith: A Genealogy of Finance* (Minneapolis, 2005).

278 BIBLIOGRAPHY

Goggin, Joyce, and Frans de Bruyn, *Comedy and Crisis: Pieter Langendijk, the Dutch, and the Speculative Bubbles of 1720* (Liverpool, 2020).

Gordon, Eleanor, and Gwyneth Nair, 'The Economic Role of Middle-Class Women in Victorian Glasgow', *Women's History Review* 9, no. 4 (2000): 791–814.

Gottlieb, Julie V., ed., *Feminism and Feminists after Suffrage* (London, 2016).

Gottlieb, Julie V., 'Modes and Models of Conservative Women's Leadership in the 1930s', in *Rethinking Right-Wing Women: Gender and the Conservative Party, 1880s to the Present*, edited by Clarisse Berthezène and Julie V. Gottlieb (Manchester, 2017), 89–103.

Gray, Jessica Vivien, 'Office Girls in Turn-of-the-Century Fiction: Work, Technology and Everyday Modernity' (PhD thesis, University of Kent, 2019).

Green, David R., and Alastair Owens, 'Gentlewomanly Capitalism? Spinsters, Widows, and Wealth Holding in England and Wales, *c*.1800–1860', *Economic History Review* 56, no. 3 (2003): 510–36.

Green, David R., Alastair Owens, Josephine Maltby, and Janette Rutterford, eds., *Men, Women, and Money: Perspectives on Gender, Wealth, and Investment, 1850–1930* (Oxford, 2011).

Green, Edwin, *Debtors to Their Profession: A History of the Institute of Bankers, 1879–1979* (Abingdon, 2012).

Griffin, Ben, *The Politics of Gender in Victorian Britain: Masculinity, Political Culture, and the Struggle for Women's Rights* (Cambridge, 2012).

Griffin, Ben, 'Hegemonic Masculinity as a Historical Problem', *Gender and History* 30, no. 2 (2018): 377–400.

Griffin, Penny, 'Gendering Global Finance: Crisis, Masculinity, and Responsibility', *Men and Masculinities* 16, no. 1 (2013): 9–34.

Groenewegen, Peter D., 'A Weird and Wonderful Partnership: Mary Paley and Alfred Marshall, 1877–1924', *History of Economic Ideas* 1, no. 1 (1993): 71–109.

Gullace, Nicoletta F., *'The Blood of Our Sons': Men, Women, and the Renegotiation of British Citizenship during the Great War* (New York, 2002).

Haan, Sarah C., 'Corporate Governance and the Feminization of Capital', *Stanford Law Review* 74, no. 3 (2022): 515–602.

Hall, Dorothy V., *Making Things Happen: History of the National Federation of Business and Professional Women's Clubs of Great Britain and Northern Ireland* (London, 1963).

Hall, Richard, 'Being a Man, Being a Member: Masculinity and Community in Britain's Working Men's Clubs, 1945–1960', *Cultural and Social History* 14, no. 1 (2017): 73–88.

Hall, Sarah, and Lindsey Appleyard, 'Financial Business Education: The Remaking of Gendered Investment Banking Subjects in the (Post-Crisis) City of London', *Journal of Cultural Economy* 5, no. 4 (2012): 457–72.

Hamilton, Susan, '"Her Usual Daring Style": Feminist New Journalism, Pioneering Women, and Traces of Frances Power Cobbe', in *Women in Journalism at the Fin de Siècle: Making a Name for Herself*, edited by F. Elizabeth Gray (Houndmills, 2012), 39–43.

Handel, John, 'The Material Politics of Finance: The Ticker Tape and the London Stock Exchange, 1860s–1890s', *Enterprise and Society* 23, no. 3 (2022): 857–87.

Hardy, Osgood, 'British Nitrates and the Balmaceda Revolution', *Pacific Historical Review* 17, no. 2 (1948): 165–80.

Harris, Bob, 'Fantasy, Speculation, and the British State Lottery in the Eighteenth Century', in *Revisiting the Polite and Commercial People: Essays in Georgian Politics, Society, and Culture in Honour of Professor Paul Langford*, edited by Elaine Chalus and Perry Gauci (Oxford, 2019), 119–35.

Harris, Bob, *Gambling in Britain in the Long Eighteenth Century* (Cambridge, 2022).

Heggie, Vanessa, 'Women Doctors and Lady Nurses: Class, Education, and the Professional Victorian Woman', *Bulletin of the History of Medicine* 89, no. 2 (2015): 267–92.

Heilmann, Ann, '(Un)Masking Desire: Cross-dressing and the Crisis of Gender in New Woman Fiction', *Journal of Victorian Culture* 5, no. 1 (2000): 83–111.

Heinemann, Kieran, 'Investment, Speculation and Popular Stock Market Engagement in 20th-Century Britain', *Archiv für Sozialgeschichte* 56 (2016): 249–72.

BIBLIOGRAPHY   279

Heinemann, Kieran, *Playing the Market: Retail Investment and Speculation in Twentieth-Century Britain* (Oxford, 2021).

Heller, Michael, *London Clerical Workers, 1880–1914* (Abingdon, 2016).

Hennessy, Elizabeth, *Coffee House to Cyber Market: 200 Years of the London Stock Exchange* (London, 2001).

Henry, Nancy, "'Ladies Do It?'": Victorian Women Investors in Fact and Fiction', in *Victorian Literature and Finance*, edited by Francis O'Gorman (Oxford, 2007), 111–31.

Henry, Nancy, *Women, Literature and Finance in Victorian Britain: Cultures of Investment* (Cham, 2018).

Hinds, Hilary, and Jackie Stacey, 'Imagining Feminism, Imagining Femininity: The Bra-Burner, Diana, and the Woman Who Kills', *Feminist Media Studies* 1, no. 2 (2001): 153–77.

Hollow, Matthew, 'The 1920 Farrow's Bank Failure: A Case of Managerial Hubris?', *Journal of Management History* 20, no. 2 (2014): 164–78.

Hollow, Matthew, 'A Nation of Investors or a Procession of Fools? Reevaluating the Behaviour of Britain's Shareholding Population through the Prism of the Interwar Sharepushing Crime Wave', *Enterprise and Society* 20, no. 1 (2019): 132–58.

Honeyman, Katrina, 'Engendering Enterprise', *Business History* 43, no. 1 (2001): 119–26.

Horrell, Sara, and Jane Humphries, 'Women's Labour Force Participation and the Transition to the Male-Breadwinner Family, 1790–1865', *Economic History Review* 48, no. 1 (1995): 89–117.

Hosgood, Christopher P., "'Doing the Shops" at Christmas: Women, Men and the Department Store in England, c.1880–1914', in *Cathedrals of Consumption: The European Department Store, 1850–1939*, edited by Geoffrey Crossick and Serge Jaumain (Aldershot, 1998), 97–115.

Howsam, Leslie, 'Legal Paperwork and Public Policy: Eliza Orme's Professional Expertise in Late-Victorian Britain', in *Precarious Professionals: Gender, Identities and Social Change in Modern Britain*, edited by Heidi Egginton and Zoë Thomas (London, 2021), 107–24.

Humphries, Jane, "'Lurking in the Wings…'": Women in the Historiography of the Industrial Revolution', *Business and Economic History* 20 (1991): 32–44.

Husz, Orsi, 'The Birth of the Finance Consumer: Feminists, Bankers and the Re-Gendering of Finance in Mid-Twentieth-Century Sweden', *Contemporary European History*, online (2023), 1–20.

Ingrassia, Catherine, 'The Pleasures of Business and the Business of Pleasure: Gender, Credit, and the South Sea Bubble', *Studies in Eighteenth-Century Culture* 24 (1995): 191–210.

Irish Stock Exchange, *Oonah Keogh: A Celebration* (Dublin, 2014).

Itzkowitz, David C., 'Fair Enterprise or Extravagant Speculation: Investment, Speculation, and Gambling in Victorian England', *Victorian Studies* 45, no. 1 (2002): 121–47.

Jefferys, J. B., 'Trends in Business Organisation in Great Britain since 1856' (PhD thesis, University of London, 1938).

Jenkins, Beth, 'Gender, Embodiment and Professional Identity in Britain, c.1890–1930', *Cultural and Social History* 17, no. 4 (2020): 499–514.

Johnson, Patricia E., 'Unlimited Liability: Women and Capital in Margaret Oliphant's *Hester*', *Nineteenth-Century Gender Studies* 6, no. 1 (2010): 1–14.

Johnson, Paul, *Making the Market: Victorian Origins of Corporate Capitalism* (Cambridge, 2010).

Jones, Claire G., 'Women, Science and Professional Identity, c.1860–1914', in *Precarious Professionals: Gender, Identities and Social Change in Modern Britain*, edited by Heidi Egginton and Zoë Thomas (London, 2021), 63–85.

Jones, Geoffrey, and Mary B. Rose, eds., *Family Capitalism* (Abingdon, 2012), 1–16.

Jordan, Ellen, 'The Exclusion of Women from Industry in Nineteenth-Century Britain', *Comparative Studies in Society and History* 31, no. 2 (1989): 273–96.

Jordan, Ellen, 'The Lady Clerks at the Prudential: The Beginning of Vertical Segregation by Sex in Clerical Work in Nineteenth-Century Britain', *Gender and History* 8, no. 1 (1996): 65–81.

Kay, Alison C., 'A Little Enterprise of Her Own: Lodging-House Keeping and the Accommodation Business in Nineteenth-Century London' *London Journal* 28, no. 2 (2003): 41–53.

Kay, Alison C., *The Foundations of Female Entrepreneurship: Enterprise, Home and Household in London, c.1800–1870* (London, 2009).

280 BIBLIOGRAPHY

Keep, Christopher, 'The Cultural Work of the Type-Writer Girl', *Victorian Studies* 40, no. 3 (1997): 401–26.

Kent, Susan Kingsley, 'The Politics of Sexual Difference: World War I and the Demise of British Feminism', *Journal of British Studies* 27, no. 3 (1988): 232–53.

Kirkham, Linda M., and Anne Loft, 'Gender and the Construction of the Professional Accountant', *Accounting, Organizations and Society* 18, no. 6 (1993): 507–58.

Kwolek-Folland, Angel, *Incorporating Women: A History of Women and Business in the United States* (New York, 2002).

Kynaston, David, 'The London Stock Exchange, 1870–1914: An Institutional History' (PhD thesis, University of London, 1983).

Kynaston, David, *The Financial Times: A Centenary History* (London, 1988).

Kynaston, David, *The City of London*, vol. 1, *A World of Its Own, 1815–1890* (London, 1995).

Kynaston, David, *The City of London*, vol. 2, *Golden Years, 1890–1914* (London, 1996).

Kynaston, David, *The City of London*, vol. 3, *Illusions of Gold, 1914–1945* (London, 1999).

Kynaston, David, *The City of London*, vol. 4, *A Club No More, 1945–2000* (London, 2002).

Kynaston, David, *Till Time's Last Sand: A History of the Bank of England, 1694–2013* (London, 2020).

Langford, Paul, 'The Uses of Eighteenth-Century Politeness', *Transactions of the Royal Historical Society* 12 (2002): 311–31.

Langhamer, Claire, 'Feelings, Women and Work in the Long 1950s', *Women's History Review* 26, no. 1 (2017): 77–92.

Laurence, Anne, 'Lady Betty Hastings, Her Half-Sisters, and the South Sea Bubble: Family Fortunes and Strategies', *Women's History Review* 15, no. 4 (2006): 533–40.

Laurence, Anne, 'Women Investors, "That Nasty South Sea Affair" and the Rage to Speculate in Early Eighteenth-Century England', *Accounting, Business and Financial History* 16, no. 2 (2006): 245–64.

Laurence, Anne, 'The Emergence of a Private Clientele for Banks in the Early Eighteenth Century: Hoare's Bank and Some Women Customers', *Economic History Review* 61, no. 3 (2008): 565–86.

Laurence, Anne, Josephine Maltby, and Janette Rutterford, eds., *Women and Their Money, 1700–1950: Essays on Women and Finance* (Abingdon, 2009).

Lawrence, Jon, 'Class, "Affluence" and the Study of Everyday Life in Britain, *c*.1930–64', *Cultural and Social History* 10, no. 2 (2013): 273–99.

Ledger, Sally, 'The New Woman and the Crisis of Victorianism', in *Cultural Politics at the Fin de Siècle*, edited by Sally Ledger and Scott McCracken (Cambridge, 1995), 22–44.

Lee, Micky, and Monika Raesch, 'Women, Gender, and the Financial Markets in Hollywood Films', in *Feminist Erasures: Challenging Backlash Culture*, edited by Kumarini Silva and Kaitlynn Mendes (Houndmills, 2015), 129–49.

Lerner, Gerda, 'Placing Women in History: Definitions and Challenges', *Feminist Studies* 3, nos. 1–2 (1975): 5–14.

Lewis, Jane, 'From Equality to Liberation: Contextualizing the Emergence of the Women's Liberation Movement', in *Cultural Revolution? The Challenge of the Arts in the 1960s*, edited by Bart Moore-Gilbert and John Seed (London, 1992), 96–117.

Lewis, Patricia, 'The Quest for Invisibility: Female Entrepreneurs and the Masculine Norm of Entrepreneurship', *Gender, Work and Organization* 13, no. 5 (2006): 453–69.

Lieshout, Carry van, Harry Smith, Piero Montebruno, and Robert J. Bennett, 'Female Entrepreneurship: Business, Marriage and Motherhood in England and Wales, 1851–1911', *Social History* 44, no. 4 (2019): 440–68.

Logan, Anne, 'In Search of Equal Citizenship: The Campaign for Women Magistrates in England and Wales, 1910–1939', *Women's History Review* 16, no. 4 (2007): 501–18.

Longlands, Helen, *Gender, Space and City Bankers* (Abingdon, 2020).

Lundquist Wanneberg, Pia, 'Gymnastics as Remedy: A Study of Nineteenth-Century Swedish Medical Gymnastics', *Athens Journal of Sports* 5, no. 1 (2018): 33–52.

Lyons, Owen, 'An Inverted Reflection: Representations of Finance and Speculation in Weimar Cinema' (PhD thesis, Carleton University, Ottawa, 2015).

BIBLIOGRAPHY   281

McCahey, Daniella, '"The Last Refuge of Male Chauvinism": Print Culture, Masculinity, and the British Antarctic Survey (1960–1996)', *Gender, Place and Culture* 29, no. 6 (2022): 751–71.

McCarthy, Helen, 'Service Clubs, Citizenship and Equality: Gender Relations and Middle-Class Associations in Britain between the Wars', *Historical Research* 81, no. 213 (2008): 531–52.

McCarthy, Helen, *Women of the World: The Rise of the Female Diplomat* (London, 2014).

McCarthy, Helen, 'Social Science and Married Women's Employment in Post-War Britain', *Past and Present* 233 (2016): 269–305.

McCarthy, Helen, 'Women, Marriage and Paid Work in Post-War Britain', *Women's History Review* 26, no. 1 (2017): 46–61.

McDowell, Linda, *Capital Culture: Gender at Work in the City* (Oxford, 1997).

McDowell, Linda, 'The Men and the Boys: Bankers, Burger Makers and Barmen', in *Spaces of Masculinities*, edited by Bettina van Hoven and Kathrin Hörschelmann (London and New York, 2005), 17–27.

McIvor, Arthur, *Working Lives: Work in Britain since 1945* (London, 2013).

Maclean, Kate, 'Gender, Risk and the Wall Street Alpha Male', *Journal of Gender Studies* 25, no. 4 (2016): 427–44.

Macpherson, Myra, *The Scarlet Sisters: Sex, Suffrage, and Scandal in the Gilded Age* (New York, 2014).

Maltby, Josephine, and Janette Rutterford, '"She Possessed Her Own Fortune": Women Investors from the Late Nineteenth Century to the Early Twentieth Century', *Business History* 48, no. 2 (2006): 220–53.

Marsh, Nicky, *Money, Speculation and Finance in Contemporary British Fiction* (London, 2007).

Matthews, Jill, 'Feminist History', *Labour History* 50 (1986): 147–53.

Mendes, Kaitlynn, 'Framing Feminism: News Coverage of the Women's Movement in British and American Newspapers, 1968–1982', *Social Movement Studies* 10, no. 1 (2011): 81–98.

Michie, R. C., *Money, Mania and Markets: Investment, Company Formation and the Stock Exchange in Nineteenth-Century Scotland* (Edinburgh, 1981).

Michie, Ranald, 'Different in Name Only? The London Stock Exchange and Foreign Bourses, c.1850–1914', *Business History* 30, no. 1 (1988): 46–68.

Michie, R. C., 'Friend or Foe? Information Technology and the London Stock Exchange since 1700', *Journal of Historical Geography* 23, no. 3 (1997): 304–26.

Michie, Ranald, *The London Stock Exchange: A History* (Oxford, 2001).

Michie, Ranald C., *Guilty Money: The City of London in Victorian and Edwardian Culture, 1815–1914* (London, 2009).

Mills, Albert J., and Kristin S. Williams, 'Feminist Frustrations: The Enduring Neglect of a Women's Business History and the Opportunity for Radical Change', *Business History* 66, no. 1 (2024): 14–28.

Mitchell, Matthew David, '"The Extravagant Humour of Stock-Jobbing" and the Members of the English Body Politic, 1690–1720', *Essays in Economic and Business History* 30 (2012): 49–62.

Mitchell, Rebecca N., 'The Victorian Fancy Dress Ball, 1870–1900', *Fashion Theory* 21, no. 3 (2017): 291–315.

Mitchell, Sally, *The Fallen Angel: Chastity, Class and Women's Reading, 1835–1880* (Bowling Green, OH, 1981).

Mitchell, Sally, *The New Girl: Girls' Culture in England, 1880–1915* (New York, 1995).

Mohr, Thomas, 'The Rights of Women under the Constitution of the Irish Free State', *Irish Jurist* 41 (2006): 20–59.

Montz, Amy L., '"Now She's all Hat and Ideas": Fashioning the British Suffrage Movement', *Critical Studies in Fashion and Beauty* 3, nos. 1–2 (2012): 55–67.

Morgan, E. Victor, and W. A. Thomas, *The Stock Exchange: Its History and Functions*, 2nd edn (London, 1969).

Morris, Caroline, 'Dr Ivy Williams: Inside yet Outside', *Women's History Review* 29, no. 4 (2020): 583–614.

Murphy, Anne L., 'Lotteries in the 1690s: Investment or Gamble?', *Financial History Review* 12, no. 2 (2005): 227–46.

282 BIBLIOGRAPHY

Murphy, Anne L., *The Origins of English Financial Markets: Investment and Speculation before the South Sea Bubble* (Cambridge, 2012).

Murphy, Anne L., 'Performing Public Credit at the Eighteenth-Century Bank of England', *Journal of British Studies* 58, no. 1 (2019): 58–78.

Murphy, Anne L., '"We Have Been Ruined by Whores": Perceptions of Female Involvement in the South Sea Scheme', in *Boom, Bust, and Beyond: New Perspectives on the 1720 Stock Market Bubble*, edited by Stefano Condorelli and Daniel Menning (Berlin, 2019), 261–83.

Murphy, Anne L., *Virtuous Bankers: A Day in the Life of the Eighteenth-Century Bank of England* (Princeton and Oxford, 2023).

Murphy, Kate, '"Careers for Women": BBC Women's Radio Programmes and the "Professional", 1923–1955', *Women's History Review* 32, no. 6 (2023): 809–27.

Murray, Gillian, 'Taking Work Home: The Private Secretary and Domestic Identities in the Long 1950s', *Women's History Review* 26, no. 1 (2017): 62–76.

Neal, Larry, 'The London Stock Exchange in the 19th Century: Ownership Structures, Growth and Performance', Working Paper No. 115, Oesterreichische Nationalbank (OeNB), Vienna.

Neddam, Fabrice, 'Constructing Masculinities under Thomas Arnold of Rugby (1828–1842): Gender, Educational Policy and School Life in an Early-Victorian Public School', *Gender and Education* 16, no. 3 (2004): 303–26.

Newton, Lucy, and Philip L. Cottrell, 'Female Investors in the First English and Welsh Commercial Joint-Stock Banks', *Accounting, Business and Financial History* 16, no. 2 (2006): 315–40.

Noakes, Lucy, *Women in the British Army: War and the Gentle Sex, 1907–1948* (London, 2006).

O'Day, Rosemary, 'Matchmaking and Moneymaking in a Patronage Society: The First Duke and Duchess of Chandos, c.1712–35', *Economic History Review* 66, no. 1 (2013): 273–96.

O'Rourke, Fiona, and Craig Haslop, '"We're Respectful Boys...We're Not Misogynistic!": Analysing Defensive, Contradictory and Changing Performances of Masculinity within Young Men's In-Person and Digitally Mediated Homosocial Spaces', *Journal of Gender Studies*, online (2024): 1–18.

Onslow, Barbara, *Women of the Press in Nineteenth-Century Britain* (Houndmills, 2000).

O'Sullivan, Brian, *From Crisis to Crisis: The Transformation of Merchant Banking, 1914–1939* (Basingstoke, 2018).

Peiss, Kathy, '"Vital Industry" and Women's Ventures: Conceptualizing Gender in Twentieth Century Business History', *Business History Review* 72, no. 2 (1998): 218–41.

Pepitone, Ren, 'Gender, Space, and Ritual: Women Barristers, the Inns of Court, and the Interwar Press', *Journal of Women's History* 28, no. 1 (2016): 60–83.

Perriton, Linda, 'Forgotten Feminists: The Federation of British Professional and Business Women, 1933–1969', *Women's History Review* 16, no. 1 (2007): 79–97.

Phillips, Nicola, *Women in Business, 1700–1850* (Woodbridge, 2006).

Pocock, J. G. A., 'Virtues, Rights, and Manners: A Model for Historians of Political Thought', *Political Theory* 9, no. 3 (1981): 353–68.

Porter, Dilwyn, '"Speciousness is the Bucketeer's Watchword and Outrageous Effrontery his Capital": Financial Bucket Shops in the City of London, c.1880–1939', in *Cultures of Selling: Perspectives on Consumption and Society since 1700*, edited by John Benson and Laura Ugolini (Aldershot, 2006), 103–25.

Porter, Dilwyn, '"Hoping You'll Give Me Some Guidance about This Thing Called Money": The *Daily Mirror* and Personal Finance, c.1960–81', in *People, Places, and Identities: Themes in British Social and Cultural History, 1700s–1980s*, edited by Alan Kidd and Melanie Tebbutt (Manchester, 2017), 202–20.

Preda, Alex, 'In the Enchanted Grove: Financial Conversations and the Marketplace in England and France in the 18th Century', *Journal of Historical Sociology* 14, no. 3 (2001): 276–307.

Preda, Alex, *Framing Finance: The Boundaries of Markets and Modern Capitalism* (Chicago, 2009).

Prestidge, Jessica, 'Housewives Having a Go: Margaret Thatcher, Mary Whitehouse and the Appeal of the Right Wing Woman in Late Twentieth-Century Britain', *Women's History Review* 28, no. 2 (2019): 277–96.

Prügl, Elisabeth, "'If Lehman Brothers Had Been Lehman Sisters...': Gender and Myth in the Aftermath of the Financial Crisis', *International Political Sociology* 6, no. 1 (2012): 21–35.

Purnell, Sonia, *First Lady: The Life and Wars of Clementine Churchill* (London, 2015).

Purvis, June, 'Women's History in Britain: An Overview', *European Journal of Women's Studies* 2, no. 1 (1995): 7–19.

Quinn, William, and John D. Turner, *Boom and Bust: A Global History of Financial Bubbles* (Cambridge, 2020).

Ramsay, G. D., *The City of London in International Politics at the Accession of Elizabeth Tudor* (Manchester, 1975).

Rappaport, Erika Diane, *Shopping for Pleasure: Women in the Making of London's West End* (Princeton, 2000).

Rawlings, Philip, "'A Compleat System of Knavery": Folk Devils, Moral Panics and the Origins of Financial Regulation', *Current Legal Problems* 61, no. 1 (2008): 325–70.

Reader, W. J., and David Kynaston, *Phillips & Drew: Professionals in the City* (London, 1998).

Robb, George, 'Women and White-Collar Crime: Debates on Gender, Fraud and the Corporate Economy in England and America, 1850–1930', *British Journal of Criminology* 46, no. 6 (2006): 1058–72.

Robb, George, *Ladies of the Ticker: Women and Wall Street from the Gilded Age to the Great Depression* (Urbana, 2017).

Roberts, Adrienne, 'Gender, Financial Deepening and the Production of Embodied Finance: Towards a Critical Feminist Analysis', *Global Society* 29, no. 1 (2015): 107–27.

Robertson, Nicole, 'Women at Work: Activism, Feminism and the Rise of the Female Office Worker during the First World War and Its Immediate Aftermath', in *Labour and Working-Class Lives: Essays to Celebrate the Life and Work of Chris Wrigley*, edited by Keith Laybourn and John Shepherd (Manchester, 2017), 172–93.

Rolley, Katrina, 'Fashion, Femininity and the Fight for the Vote', *Art History* 13, no. 1 (1990): 47–71.

Roper, Michael, *Masculinity and the British Organization Man since 1945* (Oxford, 1994).

Roscoe, Philip, *How to Build a Stock Exchange: The Past, Present and Future of Finance* (Bristol, 2023).

Roth, Louise Marie, *Selling Women Short: Gender and Money on Wall Street* (Princeton, 2006).

Russell, Gillian, "'Faro's Daughters": Female Gamesters, Politics, and the Discourse of Finance in 1790s Britain', *Eighteenth-Century Studies* 33, no. 4 (2000): 481–504.

Rutterford, Janette, 'Learning from One Another's Mistakes: Investment Trusts in the UK and the US, 1868–1940', *Financial History Review* 16, no. 2 (2009): 157–81.

Rutterford, Janette, 'Votes for Women: The Role of Women Shareholders in the Campaign for Women's Suffrage in Edwardian Britain', *Entreprises et Histoire* 107, no. 2 (2022): 88–107.

Rutterford, Janette, David R. Green, Josephine Maltby, and Alastair Owens, 'Who Comprised the Nation of Shareholders? Gender and Investment in Great Britain, c.1870–1935', *Economic History Review* 64, no. 1 (2011): 157–87.

Rutterford, Janette, and Josephine Maltby, "'The Widow, the Clergyman and the Reckless": Women Investors in England, 1830–1914', *Feminist Economics* 12, nos. 1–2 (2006): 111–38.

Rutterford, Janette, and Josephine Maltby, "'The Nesting Instinct": Women and Investment Risk in a Historical Context', *Accounting History* 12, no. 3 (2007): 305–27.

Rutterford, Janette, and Dimitris P. Sotiropoulos, 'The Rise of the Small Investor in the United States and United Kingdom, 1895 to 1970', *Enterprise and Society* 18, no. 3 (2017): 485–535.

Sayegh, Sharlene S., "'For the Continuance of Their Favours": Women, the Public Sphere and the Print Culture in England, 1750–1760' (Masters dissertation, University of Nevada, 1994).

Schneider, Daniel, 'Gendering Profession: Experiences of Nursing in the United States' (PhD thesis, University of California, 2016).

Scott, Joan W., 'Conceptualizing Gender in American Business History', *Business History Review* 72, no. 2 (1998): 242–9.

Scott, Peter, 'From "Pin Money" to Careers: Britain's Late Move to Equal Pay, Its Consequences, and Broader Implications', *Enterprise and Society* 25, no. 2 (2024): 376–401.

284 BIBLIOGRAPHY

Scranton, Philip, 'Introduction: Gender and Business History', *Business History Review* 72, no. 2 (1998): 185–7.

Seltzer, Andrew J., 'Female Salaries and Careers in British Banking, 1915–41', *Explorations in Economic History* 48, no. 4 (2011): 461–77.

Shackleton, Ken, 'Gender Segregation in Scottish Chartered Accountancy: The Deployment of Male Concerns about the Admission of Women, 1900–25', *Accounting, Business and Financial History* 9, no. 1 (1999): 135–56.

Shepard, Alexandra, 'Minding Their Own Business: Married Women and Credit in Early Eighteenth-Century London', *Transactions of the Royal Historical Society* 25 (2015): 53–74.

Sherman, Sandra, *Finance and Fictionality in the Early Eighteenth Century: Accounting for Defoe* (Cambridge, 1996).

Sigot, Nathalie, 'Breaking the Rules: Mathilde Méliot, the First Woman Economist and Feminist, Member of the French *Société d'économie politique*', *Oeconomia* 12, no. 3 (2022): 519–51.

Silverstone, Rosalie, 'Office Work for Women: An Historical Review', *Business History* 18, no. 1 (1976): 98–110.

Smith, Harold L., 'The Politics of Conservative Reform: The Equal Pay for Equal Work Issue, 1945–1955', *Historical Journal* 35, no. 2 (1992): 401–15.

Smith, Harold L., 'British Feminism and the Equal Pay Issue in the 1930s', *Women's History Review* 5, no. 1 (1996): 97–110.

Sparks, Edith, *Boss Lady: How Three Women Entrepreneurs Built Successful Big Businesses in the Mid-Twentieth Century* (Chapel Hill, NC, 2017).

Spicksley, Judith M., '"Fly with a Duck in Thy Mouth": Single Women as Sources of Credit in Seventeenth-Century England', *Social History* 32, no. 2 (2007): 187–207.

Stäheli, Urs, *Spectacular Speculation: Thrills, the Economy, and Popular Discourse* (Stanford, CA, 2013).

Staves, Susan, 'Investments, Votes, and "Bribes": Women as Shareholders in the Chartered National Companies', in *Women Writers and the Early Modern British Political Tradition*, edited by Hilda L. Smith (Cambridge, 1998), 259–78.

Stobart, Jon, 'Selling (Through) Politeness: Advertising Provincial Shops in Eighteenth-Century England', *Cultural and Social History* 5, no. 3 (2008): 309–28.

Stoller, Sarah E., *Inventing the Working Parent: Work, Gender, and Feminism in Neoliberal Britain* (Cambridge, MA, 2023).

Stringham, Edward, 'The Emergence of the London Stock Exchange as a Self-Policing Club', *Journal of Private Enterprise* 17, no. 2 (2002): 1–19.

Summerfield, Penny, and Corinna Peniston-Bird, 'Women in the Firing Line: The Home Guard and the Defence of Gender Boundaries in Britain in the Second World War', *Women's History Review* 9, no. 2 (2000): 231–55.

Sussman, Nathan, 'Financial Developments in London in the Seventeenth Century: The Financial Revolution Revisited', *Journal of Economic History* 82, no. 2 (2022): 480–515.

Sutherland, Duncan, 'Peeresses, Parliament and Prejudice: The Admission of Women to the House of Lords, 1918–1963', *Parliaments, Estates and Representation* 20, no. 1 (2000): 215–31.

Sutherland, Gillian, *In Search of the New Woman: Middle-Class Women and Work in Britain, 1870–1914* (Cambridge, 2015).

Swift, David, 'From "I'm Not a Feminist, But…" to "Call Me an Old-Fashioned Feminist…": Conservative Women in Parliament and Feminism, 1979–2017', *Women's History Review* 28, no. 2 (2019): 317–36.

Swift, David, 'Women of the Left, Patriotism, and National Identity, 1914–28', *Twentieth Century British History* 33, no. 3 (2022): 369–91.

Swinson, Chris, *Regulation of the London Stock Exchange: Share Trading, Fraud and Reform, 1914–1945* (Abingdon, 2018).

Takayanagi, Mari, 'Women and the Vote: The Parliamentary Path to Equal Franchise, 1918–28', *Parliamentary History* 37, no. 1 (2018): 168–85.

Takayanagi, Mari, 'Sacred Year or Broken Reed? The Sex Disqualification (Removal) Act 1919', *Women's History Review* 29, no. 4 (2020): 563–82.

Taylor, James, '"Distrust all Advice...and Make No Exception in Favour of our Advice": Financial Knowledge and Knowingness in Late Victorian Britain', *English Historical Review* 136, no. 580 (2021): 619–50.

Taylor, James, 'Inside and Outside the London Stock Exchange: Stockbrokers and Speculation in Late Victorian Britain', *Enterprise and Society* 22, no. 3 (2021): 842–77.

Thackeray, David, *Conservatism for the Democratic Age: Conservative Cultures and the Challenge of Mass Politics in Early Twentieth-Century England* (Manchester, 2016).

Thane, Patricia M., 'What Difference Did the Vote Make? Women in Public and Private Life in Britain since 1918', *Historical Research* 76, no. 192 (2003): 268–85.

Thomas, Amy, '"Mart of the World": An Architectural and Geographical History of the London Stock Exchange', *The Journal of Architecture* 17, no. 6 (2012): 1009–48.

Thomas, Amy, *The City in the City: Architecture and Change in London's Financial District* (Cambridge, MA, 2023).

Thomas, W. A., *The Stock Exchanges of Ireland* (Liverpool, 1986).

Thomas, W. A., *The Provincial Stock Exchanges* (Abingdon, 2014).

Thompson, Paul, 'The Pyrrhic Victory of Gentlemanly Capitalism: The Financial Elite of the City of London, 1945–90, Part 2', *Journal of Contemporary History* 32, no. 4 (1997): 427–40.

Thompson, Victoria E., *The Virtuous Marketplace: Women and Men, Money and Politics in Paris, 1830–1870* (Baltimore, MD, 2000).

Todd, Barbara J., 'Property and a Woman's Place in Restoration London', *Women's History Review* 19, no. 2 (2010): 181–200.

Todd, Barbara J., 'Fiscal Citizens: Female Investors in Public Finance before the South Sea Bubble', in *Challenging Orthodoxies: The Social and Cultural Worlds of Early Modern Women*, edited by Sigrun Haude and Melinda S. Zook (Farnham, 2014), 53–74.

Tosh, John, *Manliness and Masculinities in Nineteenth-Century Britain: Essays on Gender, Family and Empire* (Harlow, 2005).

Tusan, Michelle Elizabeth, *Women Making News: Gender and Journalism in Modern Britain* (Illinois, 2005).

Underhill, Lois Beachy, *The Woman Who Ran for President: The Many Lives of Victoria Woodhull* (Bridgehampton, NY, 1995).

Verdon, Nicola, 'Business and Pleasure: Middle-Class Women's Work and the Professionalization of Farming in England, 1890–1939', *Journal of British Studies* 51, no. 2 (2012): 393–415.

Vernon, Keith, and Oliver Wilkinson, 'Education and Opportunity during the First World War: Post-Compulsory Study at the Harris Institute, Preston, 1914–18', *Twentieth-Century British History* 34, no. 2 (2023): 192–219.

Vicinus, Martha, ed., *Suffer and Be Still: Women in the Victorian Age* (Bloomington, IN, 1972).

Vickery, Amanda, 'Golden Age to Separate Spheres? A Review of the Categories and Chronology of English Women's History', *Historical Journal* 36, no. 2 (1993): 383–414.

Vinen, Richard, *National Service: Conscription in Britain, 1945–1963* (London, 2014).

Wagg, Stephen, '"Who D'You Think You Are? Stirling Moss?" British Racing Drivers and the Politics of Celebrity: 1896 to 1992', in *The History and Politics of Motor Racing: Lives in the Fast Lane*, edited by Damion Sturm, Stephen Wagg, and David L. Andrews (Cham, 2023), 477–518.

Walcot, Clare, 'Figuring Finance: London's New Financial World and the Iconography of Speculation, circa 1689–1763' (PhD thesis, University of Warwick, 2003).

Walker, S. P., 'How to Secure Your Husband's Esteem: Accounting and Private Patriarchy in the British Middle Class Household during the Nineteenth Century', *Accounting, Organizations and Society* 23, nos. 5–6 (1998): 485–514.

Walker, Stephen P., 'Identifying the Woman behind the "Railed-In Desk": The Proto-Feminisation of Bookkeeping in Britain', *Accounting, Auditing and Accountability Journal* 16, no. 4 (2003): 606–39.

Walker, Stephen P., 'Ethel Ayres Purdie: Critical Practitioner and Suffragist', *Critical Perspectives on Accounting* 22, no. 1 (2011): 79–101.

Walker, Stephen P., 'Professions and Patriarchy Revisited: Accountancy in England and Wales, 1887–1914', *Accounting History Review* 21, no. 2 (2011): 185–225.

BIBLIOGRAPHY

Walkowitz, Judith R., 'The Indian Woman, the Flower Girl, and the Jew: Photojournalism in Edwardian London', *Victorian Studies* 42, no. 1 (1998–9): 3–46.

Walsh, Margaret, 'Gendered Endeavours: Women and the Reshaping of Business Culture', *Women's History Review* 14, no. 2 (2005): 181–202.

Walsh, Patrick, *The South Sea Bubble and Ireland: Money, Banking and Investment, 1690–1721* (Woodbridge, 2014).

Wardley, Peter, 'Women, Mechanization and Cost Savings in Twentieth Century British Banks and Other Financial Institutions', in *A Business and Labour History of Britain: Case Studies of Britain in the Nineteenth and Twentieth Centuries*, edited by Mike Richardson and Peter Nicholls (Houndmills, 2011), 32–59.

White, Eugene N., 'The Paris Bourse, 1724–1814: Experiments in Microstructure', in *Finance, Intermediaries, and Economic Development*, edited by Stanley L. Engerman, Philip T. Hoffman, Jean-Laurent Rosenthal, and Kenneth L. Sokoloff (Cambridge, 2009), 34–74.

White, Jerry, 'London in the First World War', *Cahiers Bruxellois* 46 (2014): 139–57.

Wilson, Dolly Smith, 'A New Look at the Affluent Worker: The Good Working Mother in Post-War Britain', *Twentieth Century British History* 17, no. 2 (2006): 206–29.

Wiskin, Christine, 'Businesswomen and Financial Management: Three Eighteenth-Century Case Studies', *Accounting, Business and Financial History* 16, no. 2 (2006): 143–61.

Witz, Anne, 'Patriarchy and Professions: The Gendered Politics of Occupational Closure', *Sociology* 24, no. 4 (1990): 675–90.

Witz, Anne, *Professions and Patriarchy* (London and New York, 2004).

Young, Arlene, *From Spinster to Career Woman: Middle-Class Women and Work in Victorian England* (Montreal and Kingston, 2019).

Youngkin, Molly, 'Henrietta Stannard (1856–1911), Marie Corelli (1855–1924), and Annesley Kenealy (1861–1934?)', in *Kindred Hands: Letters on Writing by British and American Women Authors, 1865–1935*, edited by Jennifer Cognard-Black and Elizabeth MacLeod Walls (Iowa City, 2006), 147–62.

Zekanis, Lynn, 'The New York Stock Exchange: Marketing the Marketplace', *Journal of American Culture* 10, no. 2 (1987): 91–8.

Zimmeck, Meta, 'Jobs for the Girls: The Expansion of Clerical Work for Women, 1850–1914', in *Unequal Opportunities: Women's Employment in England, 1900–1918*, edited by Angela V. John (Oxford, 1986), 153–77.

Ziparo, Jessica, *This Grand Experiment: When Women Entered the Federal Workforce in Civil War-Era Washington DC* (Chapel Hill, NC, 2017).

Websites

<https://www.bmbhistory.org.uk/bmb-history_002.htm>
<https://www.bremhillparishhistory.com>
<https://www.examinerlive.co.uk/news/>
<https://www.fnlondon.com>
<https://www.malvernstjames.co.uk>
<https://www.manxmusic.com>
<https://www.oxforddnb.com>
<https://www.thebanker.com>
<https://www.thepeerage.com>
<https://www.womenmoneymarkets.co.uk>
<https://womenwhomeantbusiness.com/the-ft-she-100/>

Index

Note: Figures are indicated by an italic '*f*'.

Since the index has been created to work across multiple formats, indexed terms for which a page range is given (e.g., 52–53, 66–70, etc.) may occasionally appear only on some, but not all of the pages within the range.

Abbott, Frances 41–2
Aberdeen Stock Exchange 181–2
accountancy, for women 1, 6, 48, 81–3, 118, 131, 142–3
Adams, Jane 19
advertising 4–5, 49–50, 102, 120, 147–8, 182
by women stockbrokers 19–20, 53–6, 64–5, 67–8, 106–7, 141, 241 n.164
advice for women 31–2, 45–9, 52–3, 86–7, 104–5, 130–1, 141, 157–8, 162–3
Allen, Margaret 145–6, 151–2, 165
American Stock Exchange 185. *See also* New York Stock Exchange
Amsterdam Stock Exchange 132
Andrews, Suzan 159–60, 163–4, 169–70, 194
antisemitism 17, 69–70
Archer, Hazel 166
Associate, The 207–8
Association of Stock and Share Dealers 137
Association of Women Clerks and Secretaries 110
Association of Women Shareholders 146, 163
Aston, Jennifer 4–5
attachés *see* half-commission agents
'Aurora' *see* Drew, Catherine

Bailey, Lorraine 204
Bailey, Mary 15–16
Bailey, Muriel 149*f*, 197*f*, 198*f*
applies to join London Stock Exchange 180, 183–4, 197–8, 257 n.104
attaché 169–70
clients of 149–50, 158–9
early life 149–50
elected to London Stock Exchange 197–8
on examinations 161
favourite lunch bar 166–7
later career 200
on London Stock Exchange votes 185–6, 189–92, 196
marries 168
progression during Second World War 149–50

publicity given to 158–9, 183, 185
uninterested in working on trading floor 173
on Women's Liberation 164–5
writes to London Stock Exchange 196
Baldwin, Harriett 212–13
Bank of England 15–16, 21–2, 28, 133–4
female employees 39, 62–3, 88–9, 224 n.38
formation of 13
nationalization of 172
Rotunda 22–5, 23*f*, 28
stock 14–16, 22–3
banking
employment policies in 206–7
women as clerks in 39, 62–3, 88–9, 95–6, 148–9, 238 n.56, 250 n.42
women as managers in 86–9, 144–5, 249 n.1,
women as partners in 5–6, 31–3, 35
Baradon, Tamara 194
Barings Bank 39, 60
Barker, Hannah 4, 30–1
Barrie, Jane 166, 197–9, 197*f*
barristers, female 1, 103–4, 118, 126–7, 131
Bateman, May 86
Bateson, Margaret 48
Bazett Jones, Marianne
anti-suffragist 83
employs female 'office boy' 68–9
death 85–6
early life 43–4
lives in family home 57
registers with Somerset House 66–7
remains single 57
retirement from stockbroking 85–6
rift with brother 85–6
sceptical about stockbroking for women 83
takes control of family firm 43–4
views on women clients 47, 49
Beauclerk, Alice 63*f*, 71–2
advertising by 56
as adviser 52–3
appoints male manager 67–8

288   INDEX

Beauclerk, Alice (*cont.*)
   client of Exchange Telegraph Company 67–8
   death 84
   early life 51, 56–7
   establishes bucket shops 51–2
   hires female clerks 68–9
   management of bucket shops 54–5
   marriage 51, 62–4
   retirement from business 84
   trades incognito 56
Beauclerk, Sidney 51–5, 62–4, 63*f*, 84
Bedingfield, Elizabeth Jane 239 n.94, 241 n.164
Beech, Lizzie
   advertising by 54–6, 64–5, 67–8
   clerk at Universal Stock Exchange 53
   client of Exchange Telegraph Company 67–8
   clients of 67
   death 83–4
   early life 53, 56–7
   establishes Central Stock Exchange 53, 55–6
   establishes Union Stock Exchange 53, 55–6
   failure of Central Stock Exchange 83–4
   hires female clerks 68–9
   lists in trade directory 66
   lives with parents 57
   marries 83–4
   relocation of business 64–5
   trades incognito 56, 64–5
Belfort, Roland 70–1
Bell, Amy 46*f*, 53–4, 62, 82–3
   advice for female investors 45–9, 104
   appearance of 65
   appoints female clerk 68–9
   clients of 45–9
   content to remain outside London Stock
      Exchange 74–5, 81–2
   death 83–4
   early life 40–1, 56–7
   establishes brokerage 36–8, 41, 45, 62
   health 74–5
   lists in trade directory 66
   perceived uniqueness of 38
   on prospects of women in
      stockbroking 234 n.198
   publicity given to 46
   registers with Somerset House 66–7
   relations with male brokers 67
   relocation to Bucklersbury 46
   remains single 57
   retirement 43, 83–4
   writes to London Stock Exchange 47–8
Berlin Stock Exchange 132
Bevin, Ernest 139–40
'Big Bang' 204–7

Bingham, Olive
   becomes proprietor of Holborn Stock
      Exchange 52, 228 n.160
   business of the Holborn Stock Exchange 54–6
   children 52, 57
   client of Exchange Telegraph Company
      67–8, 231 n.69
   early life 52, 56–7
   failure of Holborn Stock Exchange 84–5
   lists in trade directory 66
   as lodging house keeper 84–5
   relationship with Arthur Bower 52
Birmingham Stock Exchange 174–7, 187, 192–3
Black, Sheila 145–6
Blanc, Amanda 212
Board of Trade 68–9, 81–2, 120, 133–4, 136–7,
      169–70, 180–1, 194–5
Bodkin Committee 133–7, 142, 182–3
bonds, government 2–3, 13, 16, 22–3
Bonnell, Jane 14
bookkeeping *see* accountancy, for women
Bower, Arthur de Courcy 52, 84–5.
      See also Bingham, Olive
Bradford Stock Exchange 122–9, 181–2
Bradshaw, Richard 153–4, 158–9, 185, 194–5, 200
Braithwaite, John 177–80
Brander, Dorothy 239 n.93
breadwinner model 62–3, 186–7, 202
Bridges, Hermione 167–8, 253 n.139
Brooke, Gertrude 66*f*
   appearance of 65–6
   has children 43, 57
   clients of 49
   daily routine 57
   early life 43, 56–7
   marries 43
   relations with male brokers 67
   retires from stockbroking 93–4
   takes on business from Amy Bell 43,
      66–7, 83–4
   on women in finance 68
Brown, Hazel 197–8, 197*f*
bucket shops 49–56, 64–5, 68–9, 99, 107, 133–4
Buckmaster & Moore 151–2, 159, 166
Bulger, Anne
   applies to join Dublin Stock Exchange 75, 121–2
   death 85
   early life 43
   marries 43
   quits stockbroking 85
   takes over family firm 43
bulls and bears 18, 21, 24, 62, 75, 126–7, 127*f*, 175
business case for diversity 211–12
Butler, Joyce 194–5

INDEX 289

Campbell, Sir Archibald 125–6
Canadian and General Trust 94, 96–7, 100, 106–7, 109–10
Cazenove's 147, 204–5
Central Stock Exchange (Limited) *see* Beech, Lizzie
Chambers, Kathleen 124–5
Charles, Edith 68–9, 231 n.85
children and stockbroking 19–20, 42–3, 52, 57, 114–15, 168–9, 204, 207
Churchill, Clementine 140–1
Churchill, Sarah 14
Churchill, Winston 76–7, 140
City of London Corporation 12–13, 15, 28, 40, 50–1
Claflin, Tennessee 37*f*
  appoints female clerks 68–9
  clients of 49
  establishes brokerage in London 42–3
  interview with 65
  London brokerage fails 84–5
  marriage to Francis Cook 42–3, 56–7, 65
  publicity 47
  rejects speculative business 47
  relations with male brokers 67
  as stockbroker in New York 35–6, 73, 131
  wants to join London Stock Exchange 74–5
  widowhood 84–5
  on women's rights 68
Claudia's Business see Corelli, Marie
Cleary, Peggy 132
clerks, female 39–40, 81–3, 88–9, 97, 148–9, 224 n.32
  employed by stockbrokers 39–40, 52–3, 68–9, 82–3, 89, 91–7, 100–1, 110, 113–14, 122–3, 137–40, 148–9, 172–3, 198–9, 202
clothing, women stockbrokers and 1, 60, 65–6, 72–3, 101–2, 129–30, 189–90, 194, 199–200, 203
Cobbett, William 28–9
Cock, Johanna 14–15
coffee shops 3, 12–13, 16, 21–4
Cole, Jean 154
Colella, Silvana 80
commission charged by brokers 15–16, 21, 47–8, 53–4, 67–8, 120, 154–5, 204–6. *See also* half-commission agents
computerization 148–9, 204–6
Condon, Violet 133
Cook, Lady *see* Claflin, Tennessee
Corelli, Marie 101–2
Cornah, Primrose 172–3
Council of Associated Stock Exchanges 120, 124, 135, 172–4, 176–7

coverture 2–3, 14
Craggs, Anne 19–22
Craig, Diana Laird 198–200
Craik, Dinah 48–9
Cressall, Joan 178–9
Cronmire, Sidney *see* Beauclerk, Sidney
Crook, Mary 178–9
Cross, Ronald 136–7
cross-dressing 21–2, 56, 76, 78–80, 207–8, 233 n.145
Cruikshank, Don 208–9

Danes, Sarah 203
Davidoff, Leonore 2–5, 31
Davis, William 162, 203
Dawson, Enoch 91–2, 99–100, 106, 108–9
Defoe, Daniel 13–15, 17–18
Deterding, Henriette 132
Dimbleby, Richard 177–8
Dinwoodie, Marion 242 n.214, 247 n.163
directories, trade 66–7, 105
Dodd, Edith 237 n.25, 247 n.163
domestic roles *see* separate spheres
Dow, Margaret 242 n.214, 247 n.163
Drew, Catherine 36–8, 45, 227 n.97
Drummond, Isabel 166, 197–8, 197*f*
du Cann, Edward 156–8
Dublin Stock Exchange 10, 43, 75, 85, 121–2, 124, 132–3
Dundee Stock Exchange 76–7, 120, 181
Dunne, Helen 207

East India Company 12–16, 40–1
Ellis, Frederick 183, 186
Ellis, Vivien 254 n.224
emasculation 17–18, 26–7, 60, 62–4, 188, 209
emotions 186–7, 191–2
  control of 6–7, 18, 26–7, 70, 80
employment, women's 39–40, 62, 68, 81–3, 88–9, 93–6, 125, 144–5, 186–7, 194–5, 204, 206–7
enfranchisement, women's 48–9, 90, 102–3, 110–11, 117–18
entrepreneurship, women's 4–6, 30–1, 40–3, 48, 56–8, 84–5, 100, 116, 154–5, 225 n.44, 225 n.56
Equal Opportunities Commission 204
equal pay 1–2, 144–5, 194–5, 204, 242 n.202
Erickson, Amy 2–3, 18–19
Evans, Gillian 178–9
examinations *see* professionalization of stockbroking
Exchange Alley 12–13, 16–17, 19–23, 33
Exchange Telegraph Company 50, 64–5, 67–8

290 INDEX

family
  and investment 2–3, 14, 18–19, 31
  stockbroking 4, 16, 43–4, 83, 91–2, 99–100, 113–14, 147, 151, 154, 200
Farrow's Bank 86–7
Federation of Stock Exchanges 160–1, 180–1, 195–6. *See also* United Stock Exchange
feminism
  and historiography 1–2, 7–8
  and female stockbrokers 68, 164–5, 204, 208–9
  interwar 90, 110–11, 124–5
  second-wave 144–5, 189–90
femininity 6, 17–18, 31–2, 62, 70–1, 170
  incompatible with finance 80, 101–2, 207–8, 210
  loss of 17, 28–30, 59, 102, 209–10
  performance of 60, 65–6, 165, 207
  and risk-aversion 7, 209, 214
Fielding Newson Smith 152–3, 166
financial advice *see* advice for women
financial journalists, female 86–7, 145–6, 151–2, 163–5, 185–6, 208
Financial Times 56, 76, 82, 114, 122, 128, 139, 157–9, 180–1, 195
  critical of women stockbrokers 75, 119, 138–9
  hires female journalist 145–6
  supportive of women stockbrokers 131
Fookes, Janet 195, 260 n.218
First World War 88–9, 91–2, 95–7, 106–7, 128
France *see* Paris Bourse
Franklin, Olga 158, 166–7, 176, 179–80
Fraser, Ellen *see* Winser, Ellen
fraud 31–2, 44, 69, 85, 99, 103–4, 107–9, 130–1, 133–7, 147, 169–70
friends and investment 3, 14, 49, 59–60, 82–3, 98–9, 141–2, 157–8, 252 n.136
Froide, Amy 2–3, 14–16
Fukuda, Haruko 156, 170–1
Furse, Clara 208–9

Galton, Emma 31–2, 47
Gamber, Wendy 2, 4, 8
Gaukroger, Anthea 197f
  develops private client list 159–60, 252 n.136
  election to London Stock Exchange 197–8
  on examinations 161
  first job in finance 152
  on importance of membership 173
  on London Stock Exchange votes 187–8
  trains as secretary 152
  visits trading floor 200
Gawthorpe, Mary 76–7
Geddes, Audrey 197f
  clients of 159
  death 200

early life 151–2
election to London Stock Exchange 197–8
first job in finance 151–2
on prejudice 163–4
gender-blindness in business 116, 163–5, 204, 208–9, 213
gentlemanly capitalism 2–3, 147, 150–1, 206
George Gregory & Co. 64–5, 82, 234 n.193
Glasgow Stock Exchange 30, 120, 123–4, 181
Global Financial Crisis of 2008 7, 209–11, 214, 263 n.75
Goldberg, Whoopi 207–8
Goodison, Nicholas 205
Gordon, Thomas 17–18
Gosnell, Mabel 130f
  advises friends on investments 98–9, 141
  attempts to join London Stock Exchange 123, 128–30
  becomes half-commission agent 98–9
  on careers for women in finance 111–12
  on daily commute 114–15
  early life 98–9
  involvement in motorsports 98–9
  marries 98–9
  press attention 129–30
  prevented from writing advice columns 141
  retirement and death 141–2
  travel 98–9
Graham, Sue 206
Green, Ann 202, 204
Green, Hetty 5–6, 86, 131
Greenwell, Graham 191–2
Greenwood, Mary 82–3
Griffin, Ben 26–7
Griffin, Dorothy 252 n.129, 252 n.137
Griffith, Murray 70–2

half-commission agents 97–9, 104–5, 107–8, 147–8, 156, 169–70, 173, 180, 238 n.80, 252 n.129
Halifax Stock Exchange 172–4, 181–2
Hall, Catherine 2–5, 31
Harding, Hilda 144–5, 166, 176, 190
Haselden, W. K. 126–8
Hedderwick Borthwick & Co. 147–8, 180
Henry, Nancy 3, 30–1, 77, 229 n.3
higher education 40–1, 114, 151–4, 156, 210
Hill, Elizabeth 154, 167
Hoggett, Julia 213
Holborn Stock Exchange *see* Bingham, Olive
Holmes, Beatrice Gordon 112f
  advertising by 106–7
  advice for women investors 104
  advocacy of financial careers for women 111–14

and Association of Stock and Share Dealers 137
and Bodkin Committee 135–6, 247 n.146
and business partner 100, 109, 135, 137
clients of 106
conflict with boss 100
death 142
does not consider applying to join London
  Stock Exchange 244 n.44
early life 94
employs women 113–14
establishes National Securities Corporation
  (Limited) 100
establishes other companies 109
and feminism 164–5
goes by the name Gordon Holmes 105
and National Federation of Business and
  Professional Women's Clubs 110–11
and the press 102–3, 175, 199–200
radio lecture 104
lives with mother 115–16
salary 100, 109
and Soroptimists 110–11
starts at Canadian and General Trust 94
on stockbrokers in the United States 113
visits the United States 115–16
works as typist 94
writes autobiography 102–3, 105
runs Canadian and General Trust during war
  96–7, 149–50
Holt, Ardern 72–3, 199–200
Holt, Margaret
  changes firm 160
  clients of 159
  early life 156
  elected to Manchester Stock Exchange 193
  joins brokerage 156
  opposes women's organizations 164–5
  passes stock exchange examination 161
  retrains as lawyer 202, 261 n.3
Hornsby-Smith, Patricia 146
Horsbrugh, Florence 136–7
House of Commons 33–4, 76–7, 129–31,
  136–7, 195–6
House of Lords 125–6, 173–4
Hubbard, Louisa 93–4
Huddersfield Stock Exchange 181–2, 193
Hughes, Mrs 231 n.84
hysteria 6–7, 18, 27, 191

identities, women stockbrokers' professional
  8–9, 68–9, 106–16, 163–6, 169–71, 207
industrialization 2, 4–5
Ingrassia, Catherine 6–7, 17–18
Institute of Bankers 88–9, 236 n.11, 242 n.222

intuition, feminine 59, 68, 106, 130–1, 162, 170
investment
  advice *see* advice for women
  analysis 150–2, 156, 159–61, 166–7, 170, 210
  clubs 157–8, 162
Investors Chronicle 131, 145–6, 162–3, 186
investors, institutional 150–1, 156–7, 159, 210
investors, women 2–3, 12–13
  attitude to women stockbrokers 86,
    103–4, 158–9
  criticism of 2–3, 16–18, 21, 44, 103–5
  growth of 44, 105, 157
  participation in general meetings 13, 105,
    146, 163
  positive attitudes to 49, 104–5, 157–8
  reject gendered advice 162–3
  supposed vulnerability of 28, 31–2, 44–5,
    97–8, 103–4

J. H. Sabin & Co. 155–6, 174–7, 192
J. Walter Thompson Company 177–80, 182,
  257 n.97
James Capel & Co. 152–3, 168, 200
Jefferis, Ernest 96, 100
Jeffs, Alfred 175
Jockey Club 183–4
Jonathan's *see* coffee shops
Jospeh Sebag & Co. 147, 153, 161, 163–4
Judge, Tania 169

Kay, Alison 4–5
Kenealy, Annesley 82
Keogh, Joseph 91–2, 99–100, 114–15, 121–2, 132–3
Keogh, Oonah 93*f*
  early life 91–2
  enters partnership with father 99–100
  experiences on the Dublin Stock
    Exchange 132–3
  joins Dublin Stock Exchange 121–2
  joins family firm 91–2
  marries 114–15
  quits stockbroking 114–15, 133
  relationship with father 115
Kither, Joyce 154
Kotchie, James 51–3, 55

Labour governments 156–7, 172, 182, 194–5,
  254 n.183
Lady Credit 17–18
Lagarde, Christine 209
Lamb, Jeanette 242 n.214, 247 n.162
Landells, Walter 119, 138–9
Landon, Christopher 189
Langley, Carole 202

292 INDEX

Lankester, Phebe 36–8, 45, 74–5
law, as profession for women 6, 62, 68, 103–4,
  118, 126–9
Lawson, Annie 91, 118–19, 123–4
Leach, William 136–7
Lee, Auriol 98
Leeds Stock Exchange 30, 118–19, 123–4, 181–2
Liverpool Stock Exchange
  advises Birmingham Stock Exchange 174
  allows female clerks on trading floor
    139–40, 172–3
  establishment of 30
  first female manager 202
  and formation of Council of Associated Stock
    Exchanges 120
  loses staff during First World War 95–6
  member of Northern Stock Exchange 181–2
  rowdy 74–5
  visited by Muriel Matters 76–7
Lloyd's of London 167, 180
London County Council 125–6, 160–1
London Stock Exchange 9–10, 28
  admission of women in 1973 1–2, 4, 7, 196–8,
    200–2, 214
  applications and approaches by women to 4,
    122–3, 129–30, 138, 180, 183
  athleticism and 70–1, 128–9
  attitudes to 28, 69, 74, 177–8, 184, 193, 195
  ban on advertising by members 49–50, 102,
    147–8, 214, 260 n.210
  and Bodkin Committee 134–5
  careers work 147, 151
  as club 70–1, 119, 135–7, 172–4, 183–5, 191–2
  deregulation 204–5
  dress code of 70–2, 72f
  employment of women by 138–40, 199,
    208–9, 213
  establishment in 1773 3, 21–3
  examinations for members 160–1, 169–70, 182
  and Exchange Telegraph Company 50,
    64–5, 67–8
  incursions by women into 76–80, 117, 194
  masculinity and 7, 25–8, 33–4, 70–2, 74–5, 79,
    128–9, 188–90, 194, 205–6, 210–11
  membership of 38–9, 69–70, 95–6, 202, 204–5
  meritocracy of 71–2, 172, 179–80
  opposition to a royal charter 69, 134–5
  PR efforts of 172, 177–80, 182–3
  restriction of entry to in 1801 3, 22
  rules of 22, 39–42, 120, 122–4, 150, 183–4,
    195–6, 204–6, 232 n.92, 252 n.111
  and the Settling Room 138–40, 148–9, 172–3
  violence of 24–7, 71, 79, 128–9, 188
  visitors' gallery 153–4, 169, 177–80, 190–1, 202–5

votes on women's membership 184–92, 194–5
waiters 25, 117, 178–9, 188–9, 194, 222 n.104
and war 95–6, 137–41
writes to female stockbrokers 141
Long, Elizabeth 169
lotteries 13–14, 19, 21
Lowenfeld, Henry 53, 83–4
Luyendijk, Joris 210

Mackusick, Howard Montague 52–3
McCarthy, Helen 110–11, 186–7
McConnell, Heather 194
McDowell, Linda 165, 205–7
McEwan, John 135–6
McKean, Hilda 104–5, 239 n.89
Malvery, Olive 77–80, 101–2, 207–8, 234 n.179
Manchester Stock Exchange 30, 120, 174, 181–2,
  193, 202
Manovill, Edna 246 n.127
marriage and stockbroking 14, 42–3, 51, 62–4,
  167–9, 204
marriage bar 39, 113–15, 144–5, 148–9, 167–8,
  242 n.227
Married Women's Property Acts 44, 61
masculinity 6, 18, 26–7, 33–4, 60, 62–4, 80, 165,
  170, 207
  and business history 4, 7–9
  and stock exchanges 7, 25–8, 33–4, 70–2,
    74–6, 79, 128–9, 188–90, 194, 205–6, 210–11
Maskell, Edith
  on careers for women in finance 111–12
  clients of 106–8
  death 142
  early life 93–4, 237 nn.40–41
  employed as clerk by Amy Bell 68–9, 93–4
  moves office 241 n.174, 248 n.211
  on prospects for women's admission to
    London Stock Exchange 119
  relations with male brokers 109
  takes over firm from Gertrude Brooke
    93–4, 100
A Master of Fortune see Sturgis, Julian
Matters, Muriel 76–7
#MeToo 212–13
medicine, as profession for women 6, 45, 48,
  62, 68, 128
Méliot, Mathilde 76, 78
Melvin, Muriel
  and Federation of Stock Exchanges 195–6
  joins Scottish Stock Exchange 181–2, 192
  achieves partnership 200
  later career and death 200
  starts at secretarial level 155–6
Merry, Mary Irving 237 n.25, 247 n.162

INDEX 293

Midgley, Edith 95f
  advertising 141
  applies to join Bradford Stock Exchange 122–9
  and Bodkin Committee 134–6
  on financial careers for women 242 n.199
  clients of 106
  early life 95
  establishes own brokerage 100–1, 126
  joins women's associations 110
  partnerships with male brokers 109, 126, 141–2
  press interest in 103, 175
  and regulation 136–7
  retirement and death 141–2
  starts as stockbroker's clerk 95
  trades under initial 105
  and WFL 125–7, 135–7
Midlands and Western Stock Exchange 192–3
misogyny 7, 189–90, 200–1, 207–9, 212–13
Monopolies Commission 194–5
Moreton, Amy
  clients of 109
  early life 96
  earns OBE 142
  establishes own brokerage 100–1
  involved in Conservative politics 114–15, 142
  literary interests 96, 114–15
  and the press 199–200, 240 n.128
  radio lectures 104
  retirement and death 142
  returns to Nuneaton after war 100–1
  trades under initials 105
  travels 114–15
  works at London stockbrokers 96
Mortimer, Doris 92f
  early life 91–2
  illness and death 142
  joins family firm 91–2, 96–7
  joins Provincial Stock and Share Brokers' Association 120–1
  partnership with male broker 109, 142
  rumours regarding 122
  runs family firm 96–7, 99–100
Mortimer, Thomas 21, 24, 233 n.163

Nagle, Florence 183–4, 192–3
National Federation of Business and Professional Women's Clubs 110, 164, 176
National Securities Corporation see Holmes, Beatrice Gordon
national service 188–9
Naylor, Margot 145–6, 151–2, 161–3, 166, 168–9
Neale, Nellie
  attempts to join Birmingham Stock Exchange 174–7, 186–7, 192–3

  clients of 174, 176–7
  early life 156
  involved in women's clubs 164, 176
  marries 156, 167
  starts working in finance 156
  sudden death 193
  threatens legal action 192–3
'New Woman', the 59, 62, 64–5
New York Stock Exchange
  admits Muriel Siebert 5–6, 185
  allows 'quote girls' on trading floor 247 n.171
  appoints first woman to executive role 132
  examinations 160–1, 169
  female partners in member firms 132
  masculine culture of 76
  public gallery 178
Newport Stock Exchange 124
Nomura 204–5, 208
Normanton, Helena 103–6, 113–14, 118
Northern Stock Exchange 181–2, 193, 202, 257 n.90

occupational closure 6–7
Okura, Kazuko 156
Oldham Stock Exchange 99–100, 181–2
Open Door Council 124–6
outside stockbrokers 4, 15, 34, 40, 49–55, 66–7, 99, 102, 109, 120, 133–7, 142, 147, 169–70
Overend and Gurney crash 31–3

Panmure Gordon 159–60, 169–70, 194
Paris Bourse 27–8, 76, 185
Parkinson, Hargreaves 119
parliamentary investigations 69, 180–1, 209–13
Partington, Jane 202–3
partnerships, women stockbrokers and 19–20, 43–4, 91, 99–100, 109, 122–3, 132, 141–2, 167, 173, 200
Patmore, Coventry 119
pawnbroking 18–19
Peachey, Louise 197f
  on difficulties at work 166–7
  election to London Stock Exchange 197–8
  on gender at work 163–4
  on male fears 186
  professional identity 169–70
  on rationale for excluding women 191–2
  secretarial work 153
  starts working in finance 153
  studies for the Stock Exchange Certificate 161, 169–70
  visits trading floor 198
Pearson, Allison 207
Pearson, Hilary see Root, Hilary

294   INDEX

Pearson, Robert 134–5, 140
'Penelope' *see* Lankester, Phebe
Pethwick-Lawrence, Emmeline 125
Phillips & Drew 148–51, 169–70
Pitt, Edith 176
Pollard, Marie 76
Powell, Ellis 86–7
Pretty, Susan *see* Shaw, Susan
Prevention of Fraud (Investments) Act, 1939
    136–7, 147, 169–70, 247 n.164
Priestman, Neville 197–8, 197*f*
professionalization of stockbroking 150–1,
    160–1, 169–71, 186
professions, women and 6–7, 83, 106, 117–18,
    128–9, 131, 134–5
Provincial Brokers' Stock Exchange
    admits women 120–1, 133, 137, 142–3, 154, 193
    anticipated by Provincial Stock and Share
        Brokers' Association 120
    establishment of 121
    examinations for members 154–5, 160–1
    membership of 154–5
    supports women 9–10, 137, 142, 172–3
provincial stock exchanges
    amalgamation 195–6
    attitudes to women 119, 123–4, 174, 193, 195–6,
        200–1, 260 n.224
    closure of 202
    establishment of 30, 120
    federation 180–2
    rowdiness of 71
    rules of 31
    staffing during wartime 137–8
Prudential 39, 81, 156
public schools 70–1, 163, 194, 204
Punch 29, 32–3
Purdie, Ethel Ayres 81–2

railways, investment in 3, 29–30
Raven, Stephen 188–9
regionalization of stock exchanges 181–2,
    192, 195–6
registration with Somerset House 66–7, 109,
    241 n.171
Reilly, Kate 86
Richardson, Ian 193
risk, and women 4–5, 7, 12–13, 28–9, 31–2, 54,
    59–60, 68, 111, 209, 214
Ritchie, Lord 162–3, 179–80, 182–3
Rivers-Bulkeley, Elisabeth 149*f*, 197*f*
    applies to London Stock Exchange 180, 183
    clients of 148, 159, 167
    election to London Stock Exchange 197–8
    on financial careers for women 153

early life 147–8, 250 n.37
later life 200
on London Stock Exchange votes 186, 195
marriage 147–8, 167, 180
professional identity 163–4
publicity given to 180, 183, 190–1
recruited as attaché 147–8
relocates to the United States 169
travels to the United States 159–60
writes for the *Daily Telegraph* 162–3
Rix, Margaret 145–6, 151–2, 186
Robb, George 5–6, 214
Robinson, Hugh Moscrop 91–2, 99–100, 115, 120–1
Robinson, Phyllis Moscrop
    early life 91–2
    enters partnership with father 99–100
    joins family firm 91–2
    joins Provincial Brokers' Stock Exchange 121
    marries 115
    qualifies as insurance broker 99–100
    relationship with father 115
    retirement and death 142–3
    and Soroptimists 110
    takes on male partner 142–3
Robson, Emma
    clients of 47, 49
    has daughter 42
    early life 42
    eschews speculative business 47
    interviewed 47, 65
    lists in trade directory 66
    marries 42, 84–5
    quits stockbroking 84–5
    travels to Africa 42
    widowed 42, 56–7
Rogers, Patricia 197–8, 197*f*
Root, Hilary 197*f*
    attends anniversary celebration 213
    clients of 159, 252 n.130
    election to London Stock Exchange 197–8
    on examinations 161
    first job in finance 152
    secures partnership 200
    visits trading floor 200
Roper, Michael 186–8, 209
Rotary Club 110, 124–5
Rothschilds 39, 156
Rotunda *see* Bank of England Rotunda
Royal Exchange 12–13
Russell, Edith Marjorie 239 n.94, 241 n.164

St James's Stock Exchange *see* Walker, Jane
Schultz, Jean 163–4, 183
Scottish Stock Exchange 181, 192–3, 257 n.90

INDEX   295

Second World War 137–41, 188–9
secretaries *see* clerks, female
separate spheres 3–5, 7–8, 30–1, 57, 62, 81–2, 90,
   119, 186–8
Sex Discrimination Act 1975 204
Sex Disqualification (Removal) Act,1919 117–18,
   120–3, 125–6
sexual harassment 199, 203, 208, 212–13
sexualization of women in the market 17–18, 28–9,
   97–9, 126–7, 189–91, 199–200, 207–8, 214
share-pushing 99, 103–5, 107, 133–7. *See also*
   outside stockbrokers
shareholders *see* investors, women
Shaw, Susan
   attends anniversary celebration 213
   becomes guide at London Stock Exchange
      visitors' gallery 153–4
   benefits of working on trading floor 173
   has children 168–9
   does not meet other female brokers 163–4
   early life 153–4
   election to London Stock Exchange 197–8
   family life 168–9
   first appearance on the stock exchange floor
      1, 197–8, 200
   later career 200
   on women in 1980s City 204
   marries 167–8
   secretarial work 153–4
   starts work with Richard Bradshaw 153–4, 158
   on unemployment in later 1970s 202
Sheffield Stock Exchange 140, 181–2
Sheppards & Chase 150, 152, 159–60, 200
Siebert, Muriel 5–6, 185
Sieghart, Mary Ann 208
Smedley, Constance 82
Smellie, Helen 155f
   becomes member of Scottish Stock Exchange
      193, 195–6
   becomes partner 200
   secretarial training 155–6
   specializes in company research 160
   starts work at brokerage 155–6, 251 n.91
Smith, Mary Harris 81–2, 118
Society of Investment Analysts 150–1, 161
Society for Promoting the Employment of
   Women 81–2, 93–4
Soroptimist Clubs
   foundation of 110
   Gordon Holmes's speech for 111–12
   and Nellie Neale 164, 176
   relationship with feminism 110–11
   membership of 110
   survey of stock exchanges 124, 135

South Sea Bubble 6–7, 16–18, 105
speculation, women and 6–7, 12, 16–18, 28–30,
   47, 54–6, 59–61, 64–5, 73, 77–8, 80, 86, 101,
   105, 108–9, 132
The Speculator see Malvery, Olive
Spurgeon, Freda 146, 163–4
Stäheli, Urs 6–7, 18
Standing Conference of Women's
   Organizations 176
Stanfield, Lilian 138–9
Status of Women Committee 194
Stone Cold Dead in the Market see Landon,
   Christopher
Sternberg Flower 168–70
stockbroking
   criticisms of 20–1, 24, 69–70, 157
   early development of 15, 20–1
stockjobbing 16–17, 20, 28–9
Stokes, Edna 197–8, 197f
Strachey, Ray 113
Sturgis, Julian 59–61, 65, 77
suffrage *see* enfranchisement, women's
Sullivan, Elizabeth 203
Swinburne, Kay 208
sworn brokers 15, 40
Synge, Richard 172–4

tape machines 50, 53–5, 59, 64–5, 67–8
Tate, Mavis 130–1, 136–7, 246 n.117
Taylor, Adela
   clients of 106
   early life 91–2
   found guilty of fraud 108–9
   joins family firm 91–2
   plays market 108–9
   takes over management of family firm 99–100
telephones and women stockbrokers 65–6,
   101–2, 111–12, 242 n.200
Terrillon, Isabelle 208
Terry, Ellen 76
Thackeray, William 29, 60, 62
Thorold, William James 94, 96–7, 100,
   106–7, 109
ticker *see* tape machines
training, commercial 93–5, 125–6
Treacy, Linda 203
Turner, Richard 100, 109, 113–14, 135, 137
typewriting 39, 82, 93–4
typists *see* clerks, female
Tyrrell, Helen
   clients of 106
   death 142–3
   early life 97
   establishes own brokerage 100–1

296 INDEX

Tyrrell, Helen (*cont.*)
  later career 154
  member of Provincial Brokers' Stock
    Exchange 247 n.163
  press interest in 103
  trades under initials 105
  works as stockbroker's clerk 97

Underwood, Florence 125–6
Union Stock Exchange (Limited) *see* Beech, Lizzie
unit trusts 146, 157–9, 163
United States, women stockbrokers in 5–6,
  35–6, 76, 86, 101–2, 105, 113, 132, 185
United Stock Exchange 195–8, 202. *See also*
  Federation of Stock Exchanges
Universal Stock Exchange (Limited) 52–3,
  68–9, 83–4

Vaughan Williams, Justice 51–2, 64, 71–2
Vickers da Costa 156, 170
Vote see Women's Freedom League

Wagle, Asha 156
Walker, Jane 55–6
  adopts commission-free dealing 54
  advertising 54
  appoints male manager 67–8, 84
  early life 51, 56–7
  establishes St James's Stock Exchange 51
  failure and bankruptcy 84
  lists in trade directory 66
  press criticism of 62
  writes to London Stock Exchange 67–8
Wall Street 7, 35–6, 76, 101–2, 207–8
Wall Street 205–6, 210–11
Ward, Constance
  clerk in father's firm 140, 155–6
  elected member of Sheffield Stock Exchange
    181–2, 193
  on prospect of United Stock Exchange 195–6
  tries to join Sheffield Stock Exchange as
    authorized clerk 140, 181–2
Ward, Mary 156, 193, 195–6, 200
Ward, Ned 12–13, 16
Warner, Jane 193, 200, 204
Watson, Elizabeth 19
Wedd Durlacher 202–3
West End 38–9, 73–4, 97–8, 144
Wheeler, Jane 68–9
White, Ellen
  accountancy work 142–3
  defrauded by client 107–8

  early life 96
  later career 154
  member of Provincial Brokers' Stock
    Exchange 247 n.163
  retirement and death 142–3
  takes over firm from boss 100
  works as stockbroker's clerk 96
Whittaker, Connie 154, 167
Wider Share Ownership Council 156–7
widows
  as businesswomen 3–5, 18–19, 41–2
  and credit 162
  as investors 31–2, 49
  as stockbrokers 14–15, 19, 42, 51, 57, 83,
    91, 118–19
Wilkinson, Ellen 124–5, 129
Wilkinson, Martin 182–6, 191–2, 195, 197*f*
Wilkinson, Robert 134–5, 182–3
Willoughby, Cassandra 14
Winser, Ellen 197*f*
  clients of 153, 159, 169–70, 252 n.130
  elected to London Stock Exchange 197–8
  marries 168–9
  achieves partnership 200
  starts work in finance 152–3
  on London Stock Exchange votes 191–2
  studies at secretarial college 152–3
  threatens legal action 195
Wolf of Wall Street 210–11
women, as shoppers 35, 38–9, 73–4, 162–3
Women in Finance Charter 211–13
Women's Freedom League (WFL) 9
  and Bodkin Committee 135
  and Edith Midgley 110, 124–7, 135–7
  and Liverpool Stock Exchange 76–7
  and *Vote* 103–4, 125–6, 129, 131–2
women's rights movements
  interwar 90
  postwar 1–2, 164–5, 194–5
  in the United States 35–6
  Victorian and Edwardian 68, 76–9, 81–2,
    84–5, 87, 93–4
Women's Social and Political Union
  76–7, 110
Wood, Kingsley Sir 139–40
Wood, Muriel *see* Bailey, Muriel
Woodhull, Victoria 5–6, 35–6, 37*f*,
  42–3, 73
Woolf, Virginia 128–9

Yates, Lucy Helen 86
Yoicks! 102